T0229869

Online News
and the Public

Online News
and the Public

Edited by

MICHAEL B. SALWEN
BRUCE GARRISON
PAUL D. DRISCOLL

Routledge
Taylor & Francis Group

NEW YORK AND LONDON

First Published by

Lawrence Erlbaum Associates, Inc., Publishers
10 Industrial Avenue
Mahwah, New Jersey 07430
www.erlbaum.com

This edition published 2011 by Routledge
711 Third Avenue, New York, NY 10017
2 Park Square, Milton Park, Abingdon, Oxon, OX14 4RN

Cover concept and graphic by Alex Ohannessian
Cover design by Sean Sciarrone

Library of Congress Cataloging-in-Publication Data

Online news and the public / edited by Michael B. Salwen, Bruce Garrison,
    Paul D. Driscoll.
        p.   cm. — (LEA's communication series)
    Includes bibliographical references and index.
    ISBN 0-8058-4822-3 (cloth : alk. paper)
    ISBN 0-8058-4823-1 (pbk. : alk. paper)
    1. Electronic newspapers. I. Salwen, Michael Brian. II. Garrison, Bruce,
        1950- III. Driscoll, Paul D. IV. Series.
    PN4833.O55   2004
    070.4—dc22   2003064152
                                                                CIP

Publisher's Note
The publisher has gone to great lengths to ensure the quality of this reprint
but points out that some imperfections in the original may be apparent.

Contents

Preface   ix

Acknowledgments   xv

About the Authors   xvii

Part I: Overview

1 Online Newspapers   3
       Bruce Garrison

2 Online News Trends   47
       Michael B. Salwen

3 Legal Issues in Online Journalism   81
       Paul D. Driscoll

Part II: Studies of Online News Audiences and Content

4 The Baseline Survey Projects: Exploring Questions   121
       Michael B. Salwen, Bruce Garrison, and Paul D. Driscoll

5 Online News Credibility   147
Rasha A. Abdulla, Bruce Garrison, Michael B. Salwen,
Paul D. Driscoll, and Denise Casey

6 Public Fear of Terrorism and the News Media   165
Paul D. Driscoll, Michael B. Salwen, and Bruce Garrison

7 Third-Person Perceptions of Fear During the War
on Terrorism: Perceptions of Online News Users   185
Michael B. Salwen, Paul D. Driscoll, and Bruce Garrison

8 Under Construction: Measures of Community
Building at Newspaper Web Sites   205
Cassandra Imfeld and Glenn W. Scott

9 Uses and Gratifications of Online and Offline News:
New Wine in an Old Bottle?   221
Carolyn Lin, Michael B. Salwen, and Rasha A. Abdulla

10 Online News as a Functional Substitute for Offline News   237
Carolyn Lin, Michael B. Salwen, Bruce Garrison,
and Paul D. Driscoll

11 Online Newspaper Market Size and the Use
of World Wide Web Technologies   257
Wendy Dibean and Bruce Garrison

Part III: Online News Posters

12 What They Post: Arabic-Language Message Boards
After the September 11 Attacks   279
Rasha A. Abdulla

13 Why They Chat: Predicting Adoption and Use
of Chat Rooms   303
David J. Atkin, Leo Jeffres, Kimberly Neuendorf,
Ryan Lange, and Paul Skalski

Appendix: National Telephone Survey Questionnaires,
2001–2002   323

Author Index   363

Subject Index   371

Preface

Online news, as we know it today, did not exist a decade ago. It did not exist at all just two decades ago. Today, there are thousands of newspapers, television and radio stations, magazines, and other publications that have a presence on the World Wide Web. Every day, millions of Web users read the news, view it, or listen to it on demand.

In recent years, communication researchers have conducted a number of studies about computer-mediated communication. Interest in the Internet and World Wide Web suggests we can expect an explosion of more research in coming years. Ironically, the early history of the computer gave no hint that this technology would evolve into a mass communication medium. "Computers were not originally perceived as communication tools," Rogers and Malhotra (2000) noted. "The early use of computers was limited to number-crunching and other repetitive data-handling tasks. The potential of computers for human communication, and thus for digital democracy, however, has been realized most fully only in the 1990s with the rapid diffusion of the Internet" (p. 10).

Perhaps the most pertinent application of the Internet and World Wide Web to "digital democracy" is as a news medium. Society extols the "informed citizen" conversant in public issues. It also prizes a vibrant news media, furnishing citizens with information about public issues. Admittedly, the informed citizen and the vibrant news media are ideals. Nonetheless, both concepts underscore the role of citizens and the news media in sustaining democracy (Bertelsen, 1992; Bogart, 1995; Carpini, 2000; Poindexter & McCombs, 2001; Wilkins, 2000). New media, or new forms of delivery of media messages, raise hopes and concerns about whether they will contribute to an informed public.

This book examines issues related to the public and online news. The heart of the book involves empirical studies—mostly social surveys—grounded in the media effects and uses traditions. Most of these chapters are grounded in theoretical frameworks and bring much-needed theory to the study of online news. Some of the frameworks guiding these studies include media credibility, the third-person effect, media displacement, and uses and gratifications. The majority of these studies were conducted by the editors. Prior to these empirical studies, Part I of the book includes extended essays examining online newspapers, original online news, and legal issues related to online news. The book ends with Part III, devoted to research on online chat rooms.

The editors have conducted five national surveys from the University of Miami, each designed to yield multiple studies. During the course of planning our studies, the September 11, 2001, terrorist attacks on the World Trade Center and the Pentagon occurred. We could not ignore these events. Where applicable, we included these events to examine how people use the Web for news in the context of these events.

The book is organized into three parts. In Part I, the overview, discussions of online newspapers, online news use, and legal issues of online news are offered. In Chapter 1, co-editor Bruce Garrison provides an overview of online newspapers and includes a discussion of current issues and problems. The chapter contains a section describing the leading online newspapers in the United States, including *The New York Times, Washington Post,* and *USA Today*. The chapter also offers discussions of the leading economic and content models of online newspapers. The chapter contains original information gathered from in-depth interviews with newspaper online news managers.

Chapter 2, authored by co-editor Michael B. Salwen, describes recent trends in online journalism, especially those related to original content in online news. It devotes considerable attention to the online "independents," especially *Salon* and *Slate*.

Legal issues and online journalism are the focus of Chapter 3, written by co-editor Paul D. Driscoll. The explosive growth of news on the Internet raises a host of legal questions ranging from the application of traditional press law in an online environment to the changing definition of a journalist. This chapter examines some of the perplexing legal issues surrounding online news, including application of the First Amendment to the Internet, jurisdiction, and statutory immunity for information providers.

In Part II, a series of studies of online news audiences and content are presented. In Chapter 4, baseline survey projects and basic issues are discussed by editors Michael B. Salwen, Bruce Garrison, and Paul D. Driscoll. This chapter, largely based on data from two national surveys, is a compilation of descriptive findings about the audience for online news. Unlike the other chapters in this section, it is largely atheoretical. Nonetheless, it answers many provocative questions that scholars have posed about the public and online news.

Chapter 5, which looks at online news credibility, is authored by Rasha A. Abdulla, Bruce Garrison, Michael B. Salwen, Paul D. Driscoll, and Denise Casey. The chapter centers on a national survey that examined public views of credibility of online news as well as newspapers and television news. The chapter reviews previous literature and factors shown to be involved in the credibility of news media and looks at recent studies of online news credibility.

Chapter 6 evaluates public fear during the war on terrorism. Editors Paul D. Driscoll, Michael B. Salwen, and Bruce Garrison examine the possible relationships between self-reports of fear about terrorism and attitudes toward restrictions on civil liberties, support for government restrictions on the news media, media use levels, and third-person effects. It also presents descriptive data about online news readers and their uses and perceptions of online news media coverage of the war on terrorism.

In Chapter 7, editors Michael B. Salwen, Paul D. Driscoll, and Bruce Garrison evaluate third-person perception of fear during the war on terrorism. This study, a follow-up on the previous chapter, examines public fear and public perceptions of fear in the aftermath of the U.S.-led war on terrorism. It draws on the third-person effect, which asserts that individuals believe that other people are more susceptible than themselves to harmful media influence. The study extended third-person perception from the traditional cognitive realm of persuasive influence to the affective realm of fear. Because online news is becoming an increasingly popular news source, this study also examined people's perceptions of media-induced fear effects on generalized others of "the public" and on specified others who used the World Wide Web for news about the war on terrorism.

In Chapter 8, authors Cassandra Imfeld and Glenn W. Scott examine measures of community building at online newspaper Web sites. Working from the conceptualizations of Rheingold (2000), Outing (2000), Preece (2000), and Kim (2000), this study examines the structure of interactive discussion forums embedded in U.S. newspapers' online news sites. Researchers carried out a content analysis of 47 news sites, coding for 19 variables. Online sites of newspapers in four circulation strata were sampled. The study found no difference in structure based on newspaper circulation size but found suggestions that production choices can have implications for local discourse associated with the news.

Chapter 9, written by Carolyn Lin, Michael B. Salwen, and Rasha A. Abdulla, focuses on the uses and gratifications of offline newspapers and online news. This study explored audience motives and uses of online news and printed newspapers. A representative U.S. sample of 387 respondents who read both printed newspapers and online news answered questions used in past uses and gratifications studies. The sets of gratification dimensions for each news medium were the same, lending construct validity to the measures. Findings indicated no differences between offline and online evaluations in the entertainment and interpersonal communication gratification dimensions. However, respondents exhibited greater scanning for online news use and greater skimming for newspaper

use. The study conceptualized the information learning and surveillance gratifications to reflect a behavior-centric approach to offline and online news use.

Chapter 10, written by Carolyn Lin, Michael B. Salwen, Bruce Garrison, and
Paul D. Driscoll, focuses on online news and displacement effects on traditional
news media consumption habits. This study examines how and whether online
news use displaces or supplements traditional news media consumption. It particularly focuses on how self-described "news junkies" use online news media.

In Chapter 11, authors Wendy Dibean and Bruce Garrison analyze how six
online daily newspapers use Web technologies. This study examined use of available technologies, including multimedia and interactivity, for development of
online newspaper sites. It looks at local, regional, and national market use of features commonly found in Web design. Content analysis of online newspapers
was conducted during two different 11-day time periods. Most online newspapers have adopted Web technology innovations (e.g., links to related information) and consumer services (e.g., searchable classified advertising). The empha-
sis seems to be on electronic commerce, perhaps at the expense of news content
delivery itself. National online editions show growth in most areas, including forums, links to related information, video, audio, electronic mail, search engines,
consumer services, sign-up for personal delivery, and instantaneous updates. Regional online newspapers showed a decline in use of search engines and growth in
use of forums, video, other language use, and consumer services. Local online
newspapers showed a decline in use of Java applets and growth in audio, electronic mail, search engines, and consumer services.

In Part III, we examine online news posters and news chat rooms. Chapter 12,
written by Rasha A. Abdulla, studied Arabic-language news posts after the September 11 attacks. This chapter involves a combination quantitative–qualitative
content analysis of leading Arabic-language message boards during the weeks after the attacks. The purpose was to intercept the major themes of discourse
among elites in the Arab world during this period. The major themes are described and quantified, and examples are given.

In our concluding Chapter 13, researchers David J. Atkin, Leo Jeffres,
Kimberly Neuendorf, Ryan Lange, and Paul Skalski study online news posters'
motivations. This study involves a representative survey of online news posters. It
attempts to measure the reasons and motivations people have for expressing their
political opinions in online message boards.

The book also includes study questionnaires from five of the studies in the Appendix.

—*Michael B. Salwen, Bruce Garrison, and Paul D. Driscoll*
Editors
Coral Gables, Florida

REFERENCES

Bertelsen, D. A. (1992). Media form and government: Democracy as an archetypal image in the electronic age. *Communication Quarterly, 40*, 325–337.

Bogart, L. (1995). Media and democracy. *Media Studies Journal, 9*(3), 1–10.

Carpini, M. X. D. (2000). In search of the informed citizen: What Americans know about politics and why it matters. *The Communication Review, 4*(1), 129–164.

Kim, A. J. (2000). *Community building on the Web*. Berkeley, CA: Peachpit Press.

Outing, S. (2000, September 6, 2000). *What's wrong with newspaper discussion boards?* Retrieved October 13, 2002, from http://www.mediainfo.com/editorandpublisher/index.jsp.

Poindexter, P. M., & McCombs, M. E. (2001). Revisiting the civic duty to keep informed in the new media environment. *Journalism & Mass Communication Quarterly, 78*, 113–126.

Preece, J. (2000). *Online communities: Designing usability, supporting sociability*. Chichester, England: Wiley.

Rheingold, H. (2000). *The virtual community: Homesteading on the electronic frontier* (Rev. ed.). Cambridge, MA: MIT Press.

Rogers, E. M., & Malhotra, S. (2000). Computers as communication: The rise of digital democracy. In K. L. Hacker & J. van Dijk (Eds.), *Digital democracy: Issues of theory and practice* (pp. 10–29). London: Sage.

Wilkins, K. G. (2000). The role of media in public disengagement from political life. *Journal of Broadcasting & Electronic Media, 44*, 569–580.

Acknowledgments

The editors and authors have many individuals to thank for the success of this project. At the top of the list is Edward Pfister, Dean of the School of Communication at the University of Miami, who provided the resources for the research that is the foundation for much of the work presented on these pages.

We also wish to thank our graduate assistants, graduate students, and undergraduates who have contributed in various ways to the original research. These individuals include Rasha A. Abdulla, Denise Casey, Kristin Campbell, Jesus Arroyave, Yu He, Juliet Gill, Paula Nino, and Margarita Martin-Hidalgo.

We also wish to express appreciation to Janet McCabe, public relations representative for comScore Networks, Inc. and comScore Media Metrix XPC in Chicago for providing the 2003 Internet use data presented in Chapter 1.

Finally, we thank our families for their encouragement and support during the time required to complete this work.

About the Authors

Michael B. Salwen is a professor in the School of Communication at the University of Miami. His research interests include the social effects of mass communication, the media and public opinion, and international communication. He is associate editor of *Journalism & Mass Communication Quarterly*, former book review editor of *Journalism Studies*, and former book review editor of *World Communication*. Salwen is the former head of the Association for Education in Journalism and Mass Communication's International Communication division. He serves or has served on the advisory board of many journals, including *Journalism & Mass Communication*, *Journal of Communication*, *World Communication*, and *Communication Research*. He is the author or editor of several books, including *An Integrated Approach to Communication Theory and Research* (Lawrence Erlbaum Associates, 1996, with Don Stacks) and *Evelyn Waugh in Ethiopia: The Story Behind Scoop* (Edward Mellen Press, 2001). Salwen has published in many leading journals, including *Journalism & Mass Communication Quarterly*, *Newspaper Research Journal*, *Mass Communication and Society*, *Journal of Communication*, *Media Psychology*, the *Howard Journal of Communications*, *Critical Studies in Mass Communication*, *Journal of Broadcasting & Electronic Media*, and *Communication Research*.

Bruce Garrison is a professor in the School of Communication at the University of Miami. Garrison is author of several books, including *Computer-Assisted Reporting* (Lawrence Erlbaum Associates, 2nd edition, 1998) and *Successful Strategies for Computer-Assisted Reporting* (Lawrence Erlbaum Associates, 1996). He is also author of *Professional Feature Writing* (Lawrence Erlbaum Associates, 4th edition, 2004).

Garrison specializes in computer applications in news reporting and information gathering. In addition, he has written numerous articles and reviews in academic journals and industry publications about computer hardware and software in news reporting. Garrison has also authored other books about news
reporting, news writing, feature writing, sports reporting, and journalism in
Latin America. He has also written articles for a wide range of academic journals
in mass communication, journalism, and other disciplines. Garrison serves on
the editorial board of several academic journals and other educational publications, including *Journalism & Mass Communication Quarterly* and the *Newspaper
Research Journal.*

He has been a University of Miami faculty member since 1981. He is a member of numerous national and international professional associations, including
the Society of Professional Journalists, the Online News Association, Investigative Reporters and Editors, the National Institute for Computer-Assisted Reporting, and the Special Libraries Association. He is also an active member of the
Association for Education in Journalism and Mass Communication as well as the
American Association for Public Opinion Research.

Paul D. Driscoll is an associate professor in the School of Communication at the
University of Miami. His research interests include media regulation and the social effects of mass media. He is the director of the broadcasting, broadcast journalism, and media management programs at the University of Miami. His work
has been published as book chapters and in numerous academic journals.

Other chapter authors and contributors include the following:

Rasha A. Abdulla recently completed her doctoral work in the School of Communication at the University of Miami, Coral Gables. She is assistant professor of
Journalism and Mass Communication at the American University in Cairo,
Egypt. Her research interests include the uses and effects of new media, development communication and entertainment education, and music as a medium.

David J. Atkin is a visiting professor in the Department of Communication Sciences at the University of Connecticut.

Denise Casey recently completed her doctoral work in the School of Communication at the University of Miami, Coral Gables, and is a faculty member at
Gonzaga University in Spokane, WA.

Wendy Dibean is Webmaster of the University of Miami.

Cassandra Imfeld recently completed her doctoral work in the School of Journalism at the University of North Carolina at Chapel Hill. She works in public relations in Atlanta, GA.

Leo Jeffres is a professor in the Department of Communication at Cleveland State University.

Ryan Lange is a doctoral student in communication at Michigan State University.

Carolyn Lin is a professor in the Department of Communication Sciences at the University of Connecticut.

Kimberly Neuendorf is a professor in the Department of Communication at Cleveland State University.

Glenn W. Scott is a doctoral student in the School of Journalism at the University of North Carolina at Chapel Hill. He is an assistant professor at Elon University in Elon, NC.

Paul Skalski is a doctoral student at Michigan State University.

PART ONE

OVERVIEW

CHAPTER ONE

Online Newspapers

Bruce Garrison

Electronic versions of newspapers evolved in the 1980s in videotext and other various forms on proprietary services such as America Online, Prodigy, and CompuServe before finding their way to the new World Wide Web in 1994 and 1995. There had been newspapers and other news media on the Internet before the Web emerged, such as editions that were found on Gopher networks. The *Palo Alto Weekly* in California is credited as the first Web newspaper. The twice-a-week Bay-area newspaper debuted in January 1994 (Carlson, 2003), and was soon followed by other Silicon Valley area publications and others across the United States in the next 2 years. *The Chicago Tribune* debuted on the Web in 1995 and *The New York Times* came online on the Web in 1996.

The *San Jose Mercury News* (http://www.bayarea.com) created a stir in 1996 with its controversial series about the Central Intelligence Agency's links to the sale of crack cocaine in Southern California. The federal government denied the story and much debate ensued over some of the allegations in the series. Regardless, the newspaper was praised for coordinating its print and online news coverage of the episode when online newspapers were still in their infancy and most were unsure how to use the new medium (Weise, 1997). As part of the *Mercury News'* creative coverage, readers could interact with each other and discuss the credibility of the series. Editors also provided extensive links to many of the original sources used in reporting the series (Weise, 1997). Today, such practices have become common in online journalism.

Similarly, the *Dallas Morning News* (http://www.dallasnews.com) created a sensation in the newspaper industry when, in 1997, it carried an exclusive story in its online version reporting that then-alleged Oklahoma City bomber Timothy J. McVeigh had claimed responsibility for the Oklahoma City bombing. The story did something that rarely occurred among online newspapers: The online edition scooped its print edition with a major national news story. The story had ethical ramifications regarding whether it jeopardized McVeigh's chance to get a fair trial, but ethical concerns were overshadowed by the newspaper's extraordinary decision to run an online exclusive. The *Morning News'* editors may have released the story online as a legal ruse to avoid a possible court injunction had the newspaper waited to run the story in its print version. The *Morning News'* editors claimed they put the story online because they feared CNN would scoop them had they waited to run the story the next day.

Media observers hailed the *Morning News'* decision as a new day in online journalism—that major news organizations would compete with television and radio on breaking news stories and investigations (Kenworthy, 1997; Weise, 1997). They predicted a day when editorial staff on online newspapers would operate independent of and in competition with their print counterparts. For the most part, we are still waiting for that new day to come. Online newspapers may publish breaking news in their online editions when they believe television or radio may get the story first, but otherwise, most newspapers fear competing against their print versions and losing readers. Most also see little practical economic value in having separate online and print staff in competition with each other. Considerable financial investments in investigations by online newspapers are virtually unknown.

These examples underscore that newspapers can use their online versions creatively. However, whether they will make full use of the online medium remains a question. Certain constraints, such as reluctance to compete against the money-making print version or pour considerable resources into unprofitable online sites may cause newspaper editors and managers to be cautious and hold back news that they believe may cause readers to skip reading the print versions.

This chapter discusses online newspapers in the United States at the beginning of the new century. It takes readers through the origins of online newspapers, describes economic models that have succeeded and failed, presents the most common service models, discusses content and connectivity models, and describes the varying approaches to online newspaper markets. The chapter ends by describing the operations of leading online newspapers and by offering a short discussion of the form and coloration hypothesis in a case study of the Arab and Israeli online newspapers during the 2002 Middle East crisis.

ORIGINS OF ONLINE NEWSPAPERS

Online news sites took off in the mid-1990s, with the popularity of the World Wide Web, but the origins of online news can be traced to the early 1980s. In 1983, the Knight-Ridder newspaper group and AT&T launched a revolutionary experiment to bring people news on demand through their computers or television sets.[1] The videotext service, called Viewtron,[2] was a forerunner of online news media. Knight-Ridder suspended Viewtron operations on April 1, 1986, with fewer than 20,000 subscribers and having lost a staggering $50 million. A similar venture at the *Los Angeles Times* called Gateway also closed operations in 1986, with only 3,000 users. The failed ventures left journalists wondering whether there would ever be a market for news on demand via computers (Burgess, 1993; Keefe, 1996).

Had Viewtron's managers adopted rapidly developing PCs into their service, things may have been quite different and Viewtron may have become an America Online or a CompuServe, distinguishing itself with a strong component of news and information. Had the service existed only 5 years later, it would have been at the edge of the then-new Internet resource called the World Wide Web.

In 1990, Tim Berners-Lee invented the server and client software that would become the Web, which he envisioned as a net or web of interconnected files of information operating on different computer systems but still able to share information. The technology created by Berners-Lee and others at that time makes it easier to organize, search, and retrieve information. The Web, based on hypermedia and hypertext technology, rapidly evolved to encompass sound and graphics, which for online news media meant the capacity to offer live and archived audio and video content. The Web caught on among a close-knit Internet community, but it still was not popular among the public because it was not easy to use.

In 1993, a University of Illinois graduate student named Marc Andreessen wrote a browser program called Mosaic that made the Web point-and-click friendly. A year later, Andreessen and Jim Clark founded Mosaic Communications, Inc., which was later renamed Netscape. At about the same time, a fledgling company called America Online (AOL) was gaining popularity, reaching 1 million subscribers in the summer of 1994. The "digerati" derided AOL, claiming it was for the simple-minded computer user. However, they missed the point: Average people with home and office computers wanted a simple way to access the Web to bring them into the online world of shopping, banking, researching, communicating, and keeping up with the news.

The *Chicago Tribune* (http://www.chicagotribune.com) was the first newspaper to go online when it provided same-day editorial content to AOL in May 1992 (Carlson, 2003; Palser, 2002). Soon afterward, in May 1993, the *San Jose Mercury News* (http://www.bayarea.com/mld/mercurynews) was the first newspaper to put virtually its entire contents online on AOL.[3] At the time, when only 3

---

[1]AT&T dropped out of the project in 1984.

[2]Viewtron was founded in 1978. It took almost 6 years before the service was launched.

[3]Most observers regard the *Mercury News* as the first online newspaper. It was not surprising that a San Jose newspaper would lead the way in online journalism. Given its location, it considers itself the paper of record in the Silicon Valley.

million Americans were online, the *Mercury News'* decision to put the newspaper's Mercury Center online was simply an experiment. The newspaper's editor, Robert D. Ingle, was not concerned that the online newspaper would compete against the *Mercury News.* "I don't think anyone in their right mind would use this as a substitute for the newspaper," he said. "That's not the goal. We are attempting to extend the reach of the newspaper. It's the information-store concept: Whenever you need information, you think of us first" (Kurtz, 1993, p. A1). The Mercury Center was one of AOL's most heavily promoted content providers and no doubt contributed to AOL's rapid growth (Palser, 2002).

Of course, modems were slower when Ingle made his comments. Few users would put up with waiting 20 seconds or more for a page to appear. Today, with faster computers, sharper screen images, and portable computers that can be used while traveling, it is no longer far-fetched to imagine a time when people will read online news as casually as they read printed newspapers. The transition will be slow, of course, but it is underway already. The proportion of homes in the United States with Internet access exceeded the percentage of homes subscribing to a daily newspaper in 2000 (Samoriski, 2002).

Worldwide, online newspapers and other online news media grew rapidly during the last half of the 1990s. Because most newspapers did not have an online presence prior to the popularization of the World Wide Web, they took advantage of the ease of use and common availability. The result was fast expansion of news online. Newspapers were among the early news organizations to move to the Web. This rapid growth has stabilized, of course, in recent years. The World Association of Newspapers (WAN) said only about 50 new online editions appeared in 2002, estimating the number of online newspapers at 2,959 in 2002 compared to 2,909 a year earlier. During the expansion period, the number grew 120% from 1997 to 2001, WAN reported about countries providing the information (Balding, 2002). Although the number of online newspapers has just about flattened, the use of these sites continues to expand. Online advertising is growing in some nations, also, but other nations experienced declines in 2001, WAN data show (Balding, 2002).

The number of online newspapers in the United States has grown steadily in the past decade. Whereas there were only a handful of Web-based newspapers before 1996, there were more than 800 in the United States and 1,600 worldwide by the end of 1996 (Levins, 1997). They are found among the top 10 leading online news sources and the top 10 online parent companies and brands (see Tables 1.1–1.6 and Figs. 1.1 and 1.2) in the United States and worldwide. Primarily, the leading online newspapers are from the metropolitan areas of the country and are as popular as their print editions tend to be, NewsLink rankings in Table 1.7 indicate. However, smaller newspapers remain popular with their audiences, also, by providing unique content of interest to local readers. Newspapers, more than any other medium, raced to go online during the mid-1990s. Their owners and managers had expected to be part of a digital gold rush (Dibean & Garrison, 2001; Quint, 1994).

TABLE 1.1
World News on the Internet

	February 2003	March 2003	April 2003	May 2003	June 2003
Total Internet	**350,355,966**	**356,545,541**	**371,166,691**	**371,989,727**	**378,881,763**
News/Information	**198,138,770**	**204,689,955**	**207,685,485**	**219,350,358**	**217,133,857**
1. msnbc.com	28,581,118	33,933,087	30,795,727	25,618,916	25,640,601
2. cnn.com	34,052,582	42,579,101	33,561,320	27,257,931	23,852,131
3. cnet.com	13,230,352	15,670,248	13,808,564	16,050,156	14,856,871
4. time.com	18,480,773	19,594,120	18,036,453	15,605,006	13,177,252
5. nytimes.com	10,831,740	11,768,942	10,998,505	10,226,940	9,957,306
6. indiatimes.com	5,923,413	6,355,146	7,282,323	7,544,783	8,154,859
7. marketwatch.com	8,096,677	7,622,953	7,164,939	7,456,732	7,173,399
8. gmx.de	6,164,461	6,034,383	6,332,121	6,368,473	6,387,883
9. washingtonpost.com	5,165,435	6,657,058	5,898,335	4,844,443	6,294,240
10. wanadoo.nl	7,047,879	6,826,698	6,320,525	6,270,927	6,254,351

Note. Unique visitors by month, 2003. From comScore Media Metrix XPC, Chicago, July 2003.

7

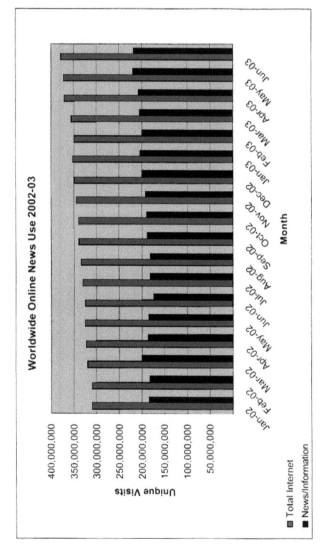

FIG. 1.1. World news on the Internet. Unique visitors by month, 2003. From comScore Media Metrix XPC, Chicago, July 2003.

TABLE 1.2
United States News on the Internet

	February 2003	March 2003	April 2003	May 2003	June 2003
Total Internet	**141,231,063**	**143,396,330**	**144,665,142**	**145,306,393**	**145,383,949**
News/information	**87,800,886**	**87,232,214**	**85,123,351**	**91,881,677**	**89,184,403**
1. msnbc.com	20,874,110	24,067,460	21,464,355	18,102,503	18,368,896
2. cnn.com	23,621,990	26,648,122	21,336,577	18,944,603	16,019,305
3. time.com	14,494,704	15,112,355	13,708,333	11,337,358	9,472,868
4. nytimes.com	8,523,685	8,992,521	8,347,355	7,896,227	7,899,307
5. cnet.com	6,237,307	7,134,169	6,141,030	6,853,661	6,471,847
6. marketwatch.com	7,107,316	6,608,979	6,239,089	6,484,369	6,235,870
7. washingtonpost.com	3,914,530	4,776,867	4,355,669	3,648,871	4,688,676
8. Ew.com	5,645,124	3,224,755	2,096,533	4,045,081	4,479,502
9. abcnews.com	6,093,139	6,415,434	5,237,748	4,658,457	4,214,148
10. usatoday.com	4,433,503	4,362,090	3,885,165	3,558,005	3,464,197

Note. Unique visitors by month, 2003. From comScore Media Metrix XPC, Chicago, July 2003.

9

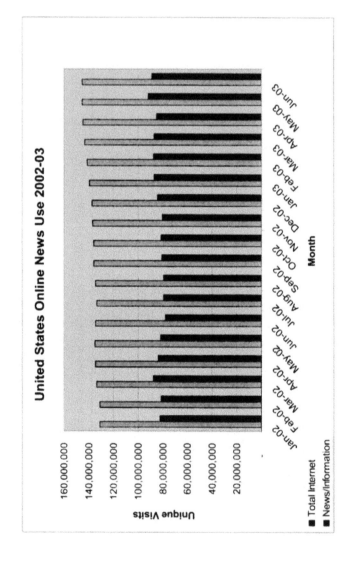

FIG. 1.2.   United States news on the Internet. Unique visitors by month, 2003. From comScore Media Metrix XPC, Chicago, July 2003.

TABLE 1.3
Newspapers in the Top 10 Online News Sites

Source	Site	Average Monthly Visitors (Millions)
1. MSNBC	MSNBC.com	10.7
2. CNN	CNN.com	9.5
3. **New York Times**	**NYTimes.com**	**4.8**
4. ABC News	ABCnews.com	3.9
5. **USA Today**	**USAToday.com**	**3.3**
6. **Washington Post**	**WashingtonPost.com**	**3.1**
7. *Time* magazine	Time.com	2.0
8. **Los Angeles Times**	**LATimes.com**	**1.9**
9. Fox News	FoxNews.com	1.4
10. **Wall Street Journal**	**WSJ.com**	**1.4**

Note. Newspaper sites in bold. From Barringer (2001, p. C6).

TABLE 1.4
Newspapers in the Media Metrix Top 10 General News Sites

Source	Site	Average Unique Visitors (Millions)
1. CNN	CNN.com	24.8
2. MSNBC	MSNBC.com	22.2
3. *Time* magazine	Time.com	9.5
4. ABC News	ABCnews.com	9.0
5. **New York Times**	**NYTimes.com**	**9.0**
6. **Washington Post**	**WashingtonPost.com**	**6.8**
7. **USA Today**	**USAToday.com**	**6.1**
8. Slate	Slate.com	4.7
9. Fox News	FoxNews.com	4.4
10. **Los Angeles Times**	**LATimes.com**	**3.2**

Note. At home and at work. Newspaper sites in bold. From Jupiter Media Metrix, 2001.

TABLE 1.5
Top 10 Parent Companies

Company	Average Audience (Millions)	Time per Person (hh:mm)
1. Microsoft	93.2	2:09
2. AOL Time Warner	90.1	6:41
3. Yahoo!	81.4	2:31
4. Google	44.7	0:27
5. U.S. Government	39.5	0:23
6. eBay	37.9	1:53
7. Amazon	35.3	0:19
8. Terra Lycos	33.1	0:18
9. RealNetworks	30.8	0:31
10. USA Interactive	30.4	0:21

Note. Combined at home and at work, May 2003. From "Nearly 40 Million Internet Users . . ." Nielsen/NetRatings, 2003.

11

TABLE 1.6
Top 10 Brands

Brand	Average Audience (Millions)	Time per Person (hh:mm)
1. MSN	82.1	1:53
2. Yahoo!	81.3	2:31
3. Microsoft	78.3	0:35
4. AOL	69.2	8:03
5. Google	44.7	0:27
6. eBay	36.4	1:50
7. Amazon	34.5	0:17
8. Real	30.6	0:30
9. About Network	25.8	0:13
10. MapQuest	23.8	0:11

Note. Combined at home and at work, May 2003. From "Nearly 40 Million Internet Users . . ." Nielsen/NetRatings, 2003.

However, the anticipated gold rush never came, mostly because the medium has not found an economic model to turn a profit. An economic downturn in the dot-com industry in 2000–2001 also contributed to the disappointment.

SEARCHING FOR THE BEST ECONOMIC MODEL

As already noted, one of the main hindrances to the growth of online news has been the lack of a successful economic model. As long as online newspapers do not generate profits (and most operate at losses), they will be seen as promotional vehicles for the cash cows—the print versions of the newspapers. In early 2003, there were indications that some online publishers were stabilizing and beginning to show profit. This was achieved following staff cutbacks and growth in advertising revenues (Miles, 2003). Naturally, newspaper editors and managers will be reluctant to give away too much free news online for fear of hurting their cash cows; but this is a shortsighted view. The online newspaper has a role to play in providing unique news in coordination with its print counterpart. However, the first task is to find an economic model for the success of the online newspaper. *New York Times* Company Chairman and Publisher Arthur Sulzberger, Jr., summarized the position of newspapers in the online age:

> If we're going to define ourselves by our history, then we deserve to go out of business. Newspapers cannot be defined by the second word—paper. They've got to be defined by the first—news. All of us have to become agnostic as to the method of distribution. We've got to be as powerful online, as powerful in TV and broadcasting, as we are powerful in newsprint. (Gates, 2002)

The two most obvious economic models for online newspapers are subscription fees and reliance on advertising (or some combination of the two). For a

TABLE 1.7
Leading U.S. Online Newspaper Sites

Major Metropolitan Dailies
1. Washington Post
2. Los Angeles Times
3. New York Times
4. Miami Herald
5. USA Today
6. New York Post
7. New York News
8. Atlanta Journal-Constitution
9. Dallas Morning News
10. Washington Times
11. Philadelphia Inquirer
12. Boston Globe
13. Chicago Tribune
14. Detroit Free Press
15. Phoenix Arizona Republic
16. San Francisco Chronicle
17. Tampa Tribune
18. Orlando Sentinel
19. Baltimore Sun
20. Charlotte Observer
21. Chicago Sun-Times
22. Cleveland Plain Dealer
23. St. Louis Post-Dispatch
24. Indianapolis Star
25. Fort Lauderdale Sun-Sentinel

Other Daily Newspapers
1. Columbia (SC) State (#41 overall)
2. Manchester (NH) Union Leader (#54)
3. Little Rock (AR) Democrat-Gazette (#59)
4. Albuquerque (NM) Journal (#61)
5. Charleston (SC) Post & Courier (#65)
6. Birmingham (AL) News (#70)
7. Portland (ME) Press Herald & Maine Sunday Telegram (#75)
8. Fargo (ND) Forum (#76)
9. Albany (NY) Times Union (#78)
10. Tallahassee (FL) Democrat (#81)

Business Newspapers
1. Wall Street Journal (#69 overall)
2. Financial Times (#152)
3. Investor's Business Daily (#215)
4. Atlanta Business Chronicle (#440)
5. Washington Business Journal (#530)

Alternative Newspapers
1. New York Village Voice (#111 overall)
2. American Reporter (#316)
3. Washington City Paper (#384)
4. Boston Phoenix (#398)
5. Nashville Banner (#497)

Specialty Newspapers
1. Washington Roll Call (#307 overall)
2. Army Times (#324)
3. Hollywood Reporter (#336)
4. Miami El Nuevo Herald (#715)
5. Washington Hill (#753)

Nondaily Newspapers
1. Pahrump (NV) Valley Times (#505 overall)
2. Jackson Hole (WY) News (#534)
3. Las Vegas View newspapers (#555)
4. Morehead City (NC) Carteret County News-Times (#622)
5. Chicago Pioneer Press newspapers (#625)

Campus Newspapers
1. Independent Alligator at Florida (#576 overall)
2. Lantern at Ohio State (#736)
3. Crimson White at Alabama (#745)
4. Illini at Illinois (#758)
5. State News at Michigan State (#768)

Note. May 2004. Based on 8,347,600 reader accesses through NewsLink, "Most-Linked-to Local News Sites in U.S. by Type," http://newslink.org/topsites.html, accessed May 12, 2004. For additional information about these lists and usage measurement, see http://newslink.org/topsitesfaq.html.

while in 1994 and 1995, some newspaper owners and managers felt they could charge for content and offered subscriptions. Repeated efforts to charge subscriptions for general-interest online news have failed, although recent efforts suggest that publishers may be returning to that model (Sullivan, 2003a, 2003b). Even the cutting-edge Mercury Center, after it severed its relationship with AOL in August 1996 and instituted a subscription, dropped the monthly fee in 1998 (the last Knight-Ridder newspaper to charge for its online edition). As of October 2001, only about two dozen U.S. newspapers, including the *Albuquerque Journal* (http://www.albuquerquejournal.com), the *Lewiston* (ID) *Tribune* (http://www.lmtribune.com), and the *Nashua* (NH) *Telegraph* (http://www.nashuatelegraph.com), charged a fee. A list of the leading daily newspapers that charged fees in 2003 is given in Table 1.8. Most of these offered reduced fees or no fees to print edition newspaper subscribers (Borrell & Associates, 2001; Palser, 2001; Sullivan, 2003a). There is increasing evidence that newspapers are using a registration model even if they do not charge fees. The registration process helps the online newspapers to profile their readers for advertisers and this, of course, boosts revenue (Sullivan, 2003b).

As for the advertising model, to date there simply has not been sufficient advertising volume and revenue to support online newspapers. There are numerous business models for Web content, including the failed videotext model, the failed paid Internet model, the failed free Web model, the failed Internet/Web ad push model, the current portals and personal portals model, and the evolving digital portals model (Picard, 2000). Within the various portal models, the failed subscription model may yet have a limited future for specialized newspapers. Commercial sites with valued content have already found this to work. *The Wall Street Journal* and its online site, for example, had more than 609,000 subscribers in 2002. "We already know that consumers will pay for highly valued, proprietary content that either makes or saves them money," stated *EContent* writer Steve Smith (2002b, p. 19). "For most other content brands, however, it gets more

TABLE 1.8
Top 10 Fee-Based Newspaper Web Sites

Newspaper	Circulation	Date Fees Began
Wall Street Journal	1,800,607	April 1996
Columbus Dispatch	251,557	October 2002
Arkansas Democrat-Gazette	185,709	October 2001
Tulsa World	139,383	June 2001
Albuquerque Journal	108,344	August 2001
Worcester Telegram & Gazette	102,978	July 2002
Cedar Rapids (IA) *Gazette*	64,504	October 2001
Santa Barbara News-Press	44,233	January 2002
Rochester (MN) *Post-Bulletin*	43,351	January 2002
Northwest Florida Daily News	37,389	August 2002

Note. January 2003. From Sullivan (2003a).

complicated. The fear of competition from free alternatives, the risks of severe traffic loss, and the overwhelming resistance among users have left the fee-based approach more of a pipe dream."

ONLINE NEWS SERVICE MODELS

Writing in 1996, when many news media outlets, particularly newspapers, were starting to put their content online, and fewer than 200 daily newspapers were available online, William Casey (1996), then the *Washington Post*'s director of computer-assisted reporting, observed that there were two audiences for online newspapers:

> The first group consists of newspaper readers with a need to see publications to which they normally don't have access. This involves displaced people who want to know what's going on back home, even years after they left, as well as business travelers. It's great for me to be able to read my *Washington Post* when I'm in Terre Haute or Telluride. And though I've been away from the upper Midwest for several years, keeping up on Minnesota news via the *Star Tribune* is a habit that's been easy to acquire. The second group consists of those with a specific interest in particular subjects or policy areas—policy wonks, if you will. Intensely committed, these are the kinds of folks who'll have the newspaper next to their computer monitor and will be posting their views on forums. (p. F17)

If this was the future model for online newspapers, the medium would have little to look forward to. The markets for travelers and "policy wonks" are small. If the market were confined to small niches, online news would not be a significant editorial force.

There seem to be at least four models for online newspaper functions. These include the 24-hours-a-day continuous news model, the community bulletin board site model, the supplementary news site model, and the exclusive news site model.

The 24-Hours-a-Day Continuous News Model

Like the wire services, online newspapers can be operated on an always-on-deadline condition (Farhi, 2000a, 2000b; T. Smith, 1999). Some authorities argue that for an online news operation, especially traditional newspapers that have gone online, to survive in the new century it must adopt a 24-hours-a-day news approach. Newspapers that offer constantly updated content must not only invest heavily in their Web sites, but provide both depth and ongoing effort to keep content current. They must be responsive to the peaks of their region (usually 10 a.m.—5 p.m. local time) and update most intensely during the heaviest traffic periods (Farhi, 2000a, 2000b). Some newspapers take this approach only when major breaking news occurs, such as the terrorist attacks on September 11, 2001. Many continue to fill their home pages and main news and feature sections with wire service content and not locally generated content. As portable news and information technologies, such as cellular telephones and handheld devices, become more common, newspapers must update often to remain competitive in the online world. Most daily newspapers make ongoing efforts to update their sites as news develops. The degrees to which these updates occur vary, of course, from major national and international stories or local stories to providing newswire feeds.

The Community Bulletin Board Site Model

Many online newspapers, however, have done more than rehash their print copy. Some have opted for what might be called the *community board site* model. The *Boston Globe* (http://www.boston.com/globe/), for example, was among the first major newspapers to design its online version to provide community information about events in the Boston and the New England area, featuring news about Boston's arts, weather, and commerce.[4] *The Globe* and *The New York Times* (http://www.nytimes.com), both owned by The New York Times Company, illustrate different paths that online newspapers can take. As a national and international newspaper, from the time *The Times* went online it decided to preserve its editorial appearance as an internationally prestigious newspaper in its online version (Shaw, 1997).

The Supplementary News Site Model

Some print and broadcast outlets also take advantage of the limitless space on the Web to add additional material to online news stories that appeared in their print and broadcast versions. In Miami, *Street* (http://www.miami.com/mld/streetmiami/) offers supplemental content to *The Miami Herald* in its online edition. *Street*, targeted to young adults, contains local music and entertainment, things to do, and celebrities in a depth and manner not possible in *The Herald*'s print edition. The content in these publications is often original or unique from other sources and is separate from the parent news organization. It means that the online subsidiaries provide additional content to their parent organization's stories. Many local newspapers have followed this model, serving as local equivalents of CNN, taking advantage of online timeliness by reporting local breaking

---

[4]University of Iowa media scholar Jane B. Singer (2001) argued that, despite the Web's worldwide reach, most online newspapers have their best chance to succeed by emphasizing local news content.

news stories that, if not covered online, would be reported on local radio or television before the newspapers (Heyboer, 2000).

The Exclusive News Site Model

One model that print and broadcast news organizations have not adopted is the exclusive news site model. By this, sites provide content not available elsewhere. Few if any online newspapers take this approach in deference to their parent print editions. In addition, such an approach is expensive and revenues do not support such newsgathering costs on a regular basis. To date, few newspapers or other news outlets have posted exclusives online.

CONNECTIVITY AND CONTENT MODELS

University of Amsterdam media researcher Mark Deuze (2001) offered a different perspective of online newspapers. He suggested four different models based on level of participation of individuals and the amount of control of content exerted by the newspaper. These are distinctions based on content and connectivity. His model provides excellent context in which to view the place of online newspapers within the larger framework of online news and information:

• *Mainstream sites*—These online newspaper sites tend to be closed in terms of participation levels by the public and exert the most control over content. They are typically linked to a parent news company and are exemplified by the CNN, MSNBC, and *The New York Times* sites.
• *Index and category sites*—These sites are less closed in terms of participation than mainstream sites. These sites also offer less concentration of content. They are separated from mainstream sites because they serve other functions in addition to providing news. This approach is not common among online newspapers and is more appropriate for other online news media, including search engine sites that provide news (e.g., Yahoo!).
• *Meta and comment sites*—These sites are more open in terms of public participation and offer even less control over their content. They focus primarily on the industry and specialized content about the news media and media issues and include the Poynter Institute, Freedom Forum, and *Editor & Publisher* Web sites.
• *Share and discussion sites*—Few online newspapers are devoted solely to sharing and discussion of the day's news and issues. More often than not, U.S. newspapers integrate this approach into their primary mainstream model. Newspapers that offer readers share and discussion interactivity offer the greatest amount of open public participation and the least degree of content control in

those sections of their sites. They provide platforms for discussion, exchange of ideas about current events, and basic online interaction.

ONLINE NEWSPAPER MARKETS

Newspapers on the Web often follow a market model that is based on geography despite the fact that the Web and Internet have disposed of such limitations. This is often the case because the original print edition of the newspaper is defined by a particular geographic orientation. There is much uncertainty about the economic and financial future of online newspapers. At the least, the success or failure of online newspapers depends on highly complex economics. Experts are unclear about whether online newspapers will become an economically viable business (Chyi & Sylvie, 2000). Some of this uncertainty and confusion is market related: What market does an online newspaper serve? Is a particular online newspaper local? National? Global? For print newspapers, the markets have almost always been defined by geography.

A recent study by Chyi and Sylvie (2000) noted that an online newspaper market is not a simple concept and that it has four potential dimensions. They determined orientations to content, advertising, marketing, and audience as important to market definition by online newspapers. Furthermore, they found that revenue models for online newspapers in their study were locally driven. By this, they meant that the online newspaper itself is "finding its own way toward profitability or failure" (p. 76).

For the most part, there are three or four levels of service: national/international, regional, and local-community (Chyi & Sylvie, 1999; Dibean & Garrison, 2001). In addition to those levels of geography, there are also specialized online newspapers that fill a niche that is often viewed as national and international.

National/International Model

These are exemplified by *USA Today* (http://www.usatoday.com), *The Washington Post* (http://www.washingtonpost.com), and *The New York Times* (http://www.nyt.com). *The New York Times'* online edition is often viewed as one of the best, if not the best, of the American newspapers on the Web (Shaw, 1997). This assessment, from the industry publication *Editor & Publisher*, praised its content. *USA Today* was the largest online newspaper in 2001 ("Missed What the Top Analysts," 2000). *The Washington Post* offers an award-winning site that attracted 3 million users and 120 million page views per month in 2001 (Lasica, 2001). It is a highly regarded site for national political news as well as other national and international coverage.

Regional Model

Some of the best regional examples are the *Chicago Tribune* (http://www. chicagotribune.com), *Los Angeles Times* (http://www.latimes.com), *The Miami Herald*'s Miami.com (http://www.miami.com and http://www.miami.com/ herald/), *Boston Globe*'s Boston.com (http://www.boston.com and http://www. boston.com/globe/), and the *Atlanta Journal-Constitution*'s Access Atlanta (http:// www.accessatlanta.com and http://www.accessatlanta.com/ajc/). The San Jose *Mercury News* (http://www.mercurynews.com and http://www.bayarea.com) co-hosts BayArea.com.

Local-Community Model

There are hundreds of these local and community-oriented Web sites in the United States. In Florida alone, there are several dozen quality dailies that serve small and well-defined markets with their sites. For example, the *Sarasota Herald-Tribune* emphasizes local communities such as Sarasota, Venice, Charlotte, North Port, Englewood, Bradenton-Manatee County, and even its portion of the greater Tampa Bay area in its west coast region of Florida (http:// sarasotaheraldtribune.com). The *Naples Daily News*' NaplesNews.com (http:// www.naplesnews.com), takes a similar highly localized approach. The *Key West Citizen* (http://www.keysnews.com) focuses only on news and tourism information for its 80,000-population Monroe County 100-mile stretch of islands known as the Florida Keys, with particular focus on 30,000 residents in the resort town of Key West.

Specialized or Niche Model

The *Wall Street Journal* online edition is perhaps the most significant example of the specialized online newspaper. It serves an international market of readers interested in financial and business information. The Journal Interactive Edition (http://public.wsj.com/home.html) offers expanded coverage and reports beyond what its traditional print edition provides. Often, these sites are restricted and available only to members willing to pay a monthly fee or other subscription. The site has a substantial subscriber base (Grimes, 2002). *The Financial Times* newspaper in London (http://news.ft.com/home/us/) is still another example of the financial or business publication that has a significant presence online. *The Financial Times* has recently explored options for charging for its specialized content (Grimes, 2002).

LEADING ONLINE NEWSPAPERS

Just as they have done in the print world, a handful of online newspapers have dominated online newspaper journalism. These have been identified typically by their traffic per day, but also because of their quality of content. In the following sections, we look at 10 of the industry leaders in the United States.

Boston Globe

The *Boston Globe* (http://www.bostonglobe.com), along with its companion site, boston.com (see Fig. 1.3), was among the first newspapers to go online and to create an intensely regional Web site that provided much more than an online version of the daily newspaper. The online newspaper and its larger city-oriented counterpart, boston.com, launched in 1995, and have become a Web portal for the greater Boston metropolitan area and the entire New England region, explained Eric Bauer, director of content of online news (E. Bauer, personal communication, April 8, 2002).

The *Globe*'s Web site does not emphasize the newspaper's name. Focusing on its local content, it calls itself boston.com. Turning the online newspaper into a local portal is now a common model for many newspapers (Miller, 2001). The model is great for local residents and visitors who want to learn about the city, explore local arts, or access restaurant reviews. The newspaper, meanwhile, is building a reputation as a good local corporate citizen (Shaw, 1997).

The popularity of boston.com is apparent in its traffic. The site receives an average of 80 million visits per month. The site offers most of the content of the daily *Globe*, but it does not include such tabular matter as stock charts. The site does not offer original reporting or other original content not found in the newspaper, Bauer (personal communication, April 8, 2002) stated. The site does buy a lot of content from other providers such as wire services and news syndicates, however. It includes much of the newspaper's wire or news service content, but this is generally breaking or daily spot news content and a few features. Bauer said the site is "principally a news site." The site also carries travel information, arts and entertainment news and information, business content , and sports news.

The site employs about 65 full-time and 10 part-time staff members in all areas of Web content production and site management. About 17 full-time and 4 additional part-time staff members are devoted to production of news content. Content producers are the most common positions and the site utilizes several "grades" of producers. There are two managers and several senior producers.

The online *Globe* breaks a news story before the printed editions when "it won't keep until the newspaper comes out the next day," Bauer (personal communication, April 8, 2002) explained. The sale of the Boston Red Sox baseball team and the merger of two major Boston banks are recent examples of these types of stories that broke first online. The site prides itself for breaking stories

FIG. 1.3. *The Boston Globe's* boston.com in August 2003.

21

such as these before local radio or television airs them. The newspaper has a long list of strengths—such as its international and national reporting desks and its sports department—and the online site takes advantage of them to enhance the online content when breaking stories occur.

The site's big local news story each April is the Boston Marathon. The internationally known long-distance race on Patriot's Day attracts thousands of running fans from around the world to the site. Site visitors before the race can find course video tours, the entrant database, race facts, previous results, local race-day traffic information and road closings, weather conditions, and dozens of links to other useful information. During the race itself, visitors can check course maps locating race leaders and they can get real-time race standings during the event. The site offers instant updates and quick, comprehensive results once the race has ended. However, Bauer felt the site could improve with a better, more useful, local calendar of events.

"On September 11, we were particularly terrific," Bauer (personal communication, April 8, 2002) offered. "We stayed up and the site did not crash. We had up-to-date information on all breaking news here. We do better than radio and that's a big thing."

Chicago Tribune

The *Chicago Tribune* Online Edition (see Fig. 1.4) was founded in March 1996 and serves an audience described by Ben Estes (personal communication, April 10, 2002), the editor of chicagotribune.com, as "half Chicago and half non-Chicago" readers. The site provides all of the content of the printed edition of the newspaper. One attraction is the site's devotion to providing breaking news on major stories. The site receives about 1 million hits per day. *The Tribune* was the first online newspaper service on AOL, beginning in May 1992, and one of the earliest electronic newspapers (Deuze, 2001; Palser, 2002).

Even such metropolitan online newspapers as the *Chicago Tribune* (http://www.chicagotribune.com) elect to carry much local and regional content (Barringer, 2001). Less than 10% of the site's content is original to the site and not available in the newspaper, Estes, who is responsible for editorial content, stated. The original content is usually breaking news stories. The site's content producers depend on the newspaper and its news and wire services for the bulk of content.

"*Chicago Tribune's* sites are number one in total market reach for Chicago news and information Web sites," the site notes (Chicago Tribune Media Kit, 2002). "Beating out popular national sites like CNN.com and MSNBC.com, Chicagoans choose to get their online news from a trusted, local brand. Attracting a young, educated, and affluent audience, the *Chicago Tribune* sites reach more than a million readers each month."

FIG. 1.4. *The Chicago Tribune's Online Edition in August 2003.*

23

There are eight full-time staff members at the Online Edition. All of these individuals are devoted to production of news content. The site is at its best when
breaking stories occur in the metropolitan Chicago area, Estes (personal communication, April 10, 2002) believes. "Any big news event in Chicago on weekdays,
we have broken it," he observed. "When the Democratic convention happened in
1996, we broke that story." The Web site's team feels its strength is in its immediacy and its easy-to-find content design. In addition to the newspaper content, the
site offers video and audio from CLTV, WGN-TV news, and WGN radio news.

The *Tribune* Online Edition is only one of a collection of sites produced by the
interactive side of the newspaper company. The newspaper also offers
chicagotribune.com special sections, such as those devoted to major annual
events. These include the Chicago Auto Show, NCAA college basketball tourna-
ments, National Football League previews, education, golf, real estate, dining,
and business. In addition to chicagotribune.com and its special sections, the
company produces ChicagoSports.com, metromix.com, CareerBuilder.com,
cars.com, apartments.com, newhomenetwork.com, and homes.com.

Dallas Morning News

The *Dallas Morning News* Web site (see Fig. 1.5) went online in November 1996.
It primarily serves the Dallas–Fort Worth metropolitan area market, but it also
serves the larger market of the state of Texas, according to Gerry Barker (personal
communication, April 8, 2002), general manager for Dallas Web operations, who
oversees business, marketing, financial, and partner relationships. The site records about 1 million page views per day, including approximately 100,000
unique visits per day.

Although the site intends to reflect the content of the printed newspaper, it is
enhanced with audio and video and about 5% to 10% original content. About
60% of site content originates from the printed newspaper. Another 30% or so is
built from wire services. The original content is often in the form of news and features and includes multimedia such as audio and video clips. In early 2002, the
online newsroom created a reporting desk for the site.

DallasNews.com has an online staff of about 40, but only 5 of those people are
reporters devoted to gathering news content. Content is managed by a senior editor for news and sports and a senior editor for presentation and multimedia. Another senior editor oversees lifestyles and entertainment content and one is responsible for technology and special projects. One senior editor is responsible for
coordination with the newspaper's sister television stations and other newspapers owned by the company.

The site's reporters and editors "deliver breaking local, national and international news throughout the day. In addition to providing news stories from the
newspaper, DallasNews.com also creates and edits stories specifically for the
Internet. The site also incorporates interactive features such as video and audio,

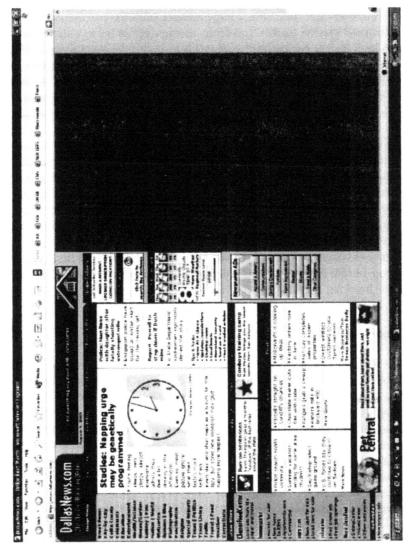

FIG. 1.5.   The *Dallas Morning News*' DallasNews.com in August 2003.

25

forums, polls, archives, and classifieds" ("Frequently Asked Questions," 2002). Some of the printed content, such as comics, wedding announcements, some sports results, and some Associated Press stories and headlines, is not available on the online site.

Staff members feel they offer a large amount of news, particularly content geared to their specific market. Producers are on duty 24 hours a day, 7 days a week to keep the site current. Although managers would like additional staff for more original reporting and for additional multimedia projects, they are proud of breaking the Timothy McVeigh story in 1996 and their coverage of the more recent Texas A&M University bonfire tragedy. Getting on top of news stories has become "routine" for the site (J. Banks, personal communication, April 25, 2002).

The site was recently redesigned to be more user friendly. Content organization is focused on simplicity. Redesign enhancements included "quicker and easier navigation, dynamic audio and video segments, and deeper, richer news and information" ("Frequently Asked Questions," 2002). The site's designers also plan "additional features such as enhanced search capabilities, personal technology features, and comprehensive business and sports news." The site offers user content preference personalization tools.

The site has never crashed or experienced a security breach in its first 6 years of operation, but the server slows down during heavy traffic periods such as on days of major breaking news stories and during football season.

Los Angeles Times

The *Los Angeles Times* is one of the world's leading newspapers and the dominant news source on the West Coast. Although it is internationally known, the newspaper seeks to serve Southern California with its online presence. Nonetheless, it has a significant audience of Californians as well as a national and international draw, according to Richard Core (personal communication, May 2, 2002), editor of latimes.com (see Fig. 1.6). Core has responsibility for overseeing the editorial production of the site. Core said about half of the site's visitors come from the print edition's primary circulation area of Southern California.

The site went on the Web in April 1995, but an earlier electronic edition known as Times Link was available in 1993 and 1994 on the proprietary Prodigy information service. The site has built a considerable amount of daily traffic. Core said there are about 1.7 million page views per day.

The site offers news, sports, business, and entertainment news stories that originate from the newspaper. This is supplemented with wire service content and video from KTLA-TV, an affiliated Los Angeles television station. However, the strength of the site is the newspaper's daily and weekend coverage. "We offer

FIG. 1.6. *Los Angeles Times'* latimes.com in August 2003.

27

the whole package that you would get from a metropolitan newspaper," Core (personal communication, May 2, 2002) explained.

Not all of *The Times'* print edition is included on its Web site. This includes display advertising, tables in the Business section such as CD interest rates or Sports section results and statistics, and syndicated content such as comics or advice columns. Almost all of *The Times'* news stories are posted, except in extremely rare cases. Some puzzles and some photographs are also not included, but the site producers plan to improve on this.

The site has no specific team of writers devoted solely to content for the online editions. However, there is content on the site that is not found in the printed editions of the newspaper and it is offered free. This includes the Calendar Live! Web-only entertainment coverage, guides on Southern California, special reports, a searchable restaurant guide, searchable classifieds, and audio and video content. Original content also includes multimedia such as interviews with reporters on major local stories, additional documents to support reporting (such as Adobe PDF files of indictments and lawsuit filings), and wire content. The site also presents affiliated television station video and audio clips and it offers graphics such as Macromedia Flash presentations.

There are approximately 20 full-time editorial persons and about 60 total individuals, including advertising and marketing, on the online staff. Editorial positions are mainly devoted to content production, video production, photo editing, news editing, and graphics.

The site has been involved in coverage of major international and national stories. Two of its most recent major efforts were the September 11, 2001, terrorist attacks and the 2000 presidential election, Core (personal communication, May 2, 2002) stated. The latimes.com staff is also proud of breaking the story about former President Clinton's brother, Roger, and his solicitation of payments for presidential pardons at the end of his brother's term in 2000–2001. The site has also been aggressively reporting about Catholic bishops who were encouraging Boston's Cardinal Law to resign during the church's child abuse problems in 2002. The site broke that story. In emphasizing local business and entertainment news, the site was the first to release results of the recent Screen Actors Guild election, information that was released after the deadline of the printed editions of the newspaper.

Core (personal communication, May 2, 2002) believes the strength of the site lies in the "quality of journalism" offered to readers. He also feels the site's coverage of breaking news, multimedia offerings, and usability and navigability are strengths. He would like to begin a writing team for breaking stories because his staff is forced to rely too much on wire coverage. He also seeks to "increase participation of print staff" with the online staff. The site is also trying to build user loyalty through newsletters and customizability and personalization features.

Miami Herald

For several generations of newspaper readers, *The Miami Herald*'s (http://www.miamiherald.com and http://www.miami.com) strengths have been in coverage of Florida, the Caribbean, and Latin America. *The Miami Herald* site is part of a larger site called Miami.com (see Fig. 1.7). In addition to *The Herald*, readers are able to access *El Nuevo Herald*, a Spanish-language daily newspaper that has content different from *The Herald*. Readers are also able to read the *Street*, an alternative newspaper with a South Florida entertainment focus, and the *Jewish Star Times*.

The Miami Herald went online in 1994. Part of Knight-Ridder, Inc., *The Herald*'s online site is similar in structure to that of the *San Jose Mercury News* and BayArea.com. Today, *The Herald*'s site is really two different sites that are produced at the same location and work together. There is *The Herald*'s content and then there is Miami.com's content. Managing Editor Jeordan Legón oversees content production of the site and says the staff's goal is "to be South Florida's home page" (J. Legón, personal communication, April 26, 2002). South Florida is a triethnic (Black, Hispanic, and White) and multicultural region. The community served by Miami.com includes both English and Spanish speakers and readers. As a result, the site serves both English-language and Spanish-language readers with *The Herald* and *El Nuevo Herald*. The site keeps servers busy with an average of 15 million page views per month (Legón, personal communication, April 26, 2002). Because it is a city and regional site and not solely a newspaper site, the operating model is a little different from other online newspapers.

Still, dominant content is that of the daily *Miami Herald*. Like other newspaper-based sites, the site also focuses attention on breaking news. The site supplements *Herald* content with wire content about breaking news. Other content is provided by additional Knight-Ridder newspapers, including metropolitan dailies across the nation and elsewhere in Florida, and other news properties such as weeklies owned by *The Herald* in the Florida Keys.

The site employs 27 persons, but they work mostly in advertising and marketing. Content producers maintain an important role and 6 individuals are assigned to producing and packaging news content, but these individuals do not write anything original. Producers work to prepare content packages and must be good with multimedia technologies, have bilingual skills, and be quality editors. The staff is small and close, but productive, Legón (personal communication, April 26, 2002) said.

The site was one of the first news organizations to break the story about anthrax at American Media in South Florida in fall 2001. It also provided readers with ongoing, in-depth coverage of the critical 2000 presidential election recount in Florida, particularly counties in South Florida where problems occurred. Readers could even look up county information by precinct. Another interna-

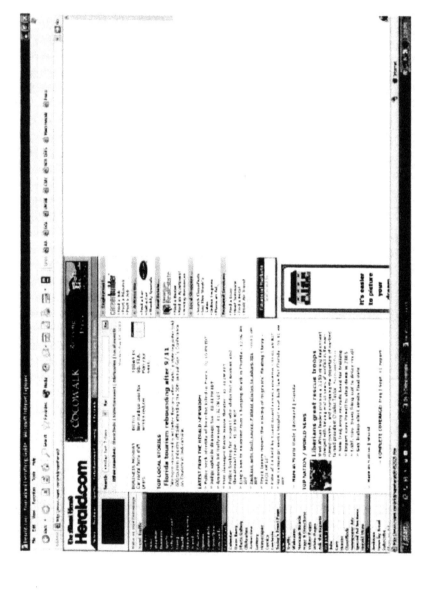

FIG. 1.7. *The Miami Herald's* miami.com in August 2003.

tional story the site has covered well, Legón stated, was the al Qaeda detainees at the U.S. Naval Base at Guantanamo, Cuba. The newspaper and its site also received attention for its local coverage of the Elián González situation just a few miles from the newsroom in 1999–2000.

Legón believes Miami.com's strength is its local coverage. "We really have more information about South Florida than any other site," Legón (personal communication, April 26, 2002) stated. Like other site managers, he would like additional staff members to report breaking news and to develop "unique" and original content for the site. "It would be nice to have people dedicated to online exclusively," he said.

The site continues to be secure, but it has experienced an occasional server crash. It does not offer much audio and video content compared to other online newspapers because managers feel site visitors do not use it and it is still difficult for some users to download and view or hear. "People just don't use it as much as we hoped," Legón stated.

Miami.com provides much more than just any of the newspapers it offers visitors. It seeks to be more than a newspaper with its metropolitan and regional content model. Its editors and producers continue to seek a better balance of local and nonlocal content and constantly seek "a way to present content that reflects Miami's flavor," Legón (personal communication, April 26, 2002) said.

The New York Times

The New York Times is one of the world's preeminent newspapers. Its online edition, called New York Times On The Web (http://www.nytimes.com), debuted on January 20, 1996 (see Fig. 1.8). The site truly serves the world. Its readers come from all over the globe. Editor Bernard Gwertzman (personal communication, April 10, 2002), who is in charge of the entire editorial operation online, determines the home page content each day. The site draws about one quarter of its audience from outside the United States. Another quarter of the audience is from the New York metropolitan area, and the rest are from other parts of the United States.

There are approximately 160 people working on the site. None, however, writes original content. The leadership roles at the site include an associate editor, news editors, a business editor, and a number of content and image producers. The site is not big on titles and, Gwertzman said, is "kind of egalitarian."

The site draws high audience numbers. There are about 1.5 million users per day visiting the site and about 300 million page views per month. All of this, of course, leads Gwertzman to be concerned about the servers' capacities at the newspaper. The content of the site varies, but reflects the general news standards of the company, Gwertzman said. All of the newspaper's National Edition is offered on the online site, although the Web site pays "a little more attention to entertainment," Gwertzman said. During the first 2 months of the war on terrorism in 2001, for example, *The Times'* site carried a photographer's journal from Af-

FIG. 1.8. *The New York Times* On The Web in August 2003.

32

ghanistan narrated by photographer Vincent Laforet. The site relies on newspaper reporters and wire services for most of the online content, but content at any given moment is a function of the time of the day.

The Times requires online users to register at no cost and it uses the demographic information it obtains to understand its market and attract advertisers. Users can subscribe to e-mail-based news alerts for major or breaking stories. These alerts were particularly valuable to readers in the aftermath of the attacks on the World Trade Center.

Major stories are a way of life at the site. The site's producers displayed the stories that won the newspaper a record seven Pulitzer Prizes in April 2002 for its coverage of the September 11, 2001, attacks, even though it is difficult to determine if online coverage had any impact (Kramer, 2001). The newspaper's Web site has also received considerable attention for coverage of the Enron scandals, the 2000 presidential election, the Monica Lewinsky scandal and investigation, and the government's seizure of Elián González in Miami to return him to his father in Cuba.

Gwertzman believes the site's main strengths are its ability to provide current and in-depth news 24 hours each day, seven days per week. He feels the newspaper's site is also strong in its use of images from *Times'* photographers and from wire services. It is also strong in use of multimedia, including video content. He said he wishes the site had its own reporters to generate original content.

The Times' online editor also pointed to the archives of the newspaper. Users can search and retrieve full-text of articles dating back to 1996. Users pay for the service on either a per-item or bulk plan. For the newspaper, as well as other dailies, online archives are a source of revenue (Grimes, 2002). However, for them to continue to provide revenues, such electronic content providers must provide more service (S. Smith, 2002a). Most of its revenue comes from advertising.

Like most other online newspaper editors, Gwertzman (personal communication, April 10, 2002) believes their biggest challenge is making a profit. The online operation, he noted, "is rather tight budget-wise." Although the site was hacked into several years ago, he feels security problems are behind them. He said he would like to continue offering "multimedia exclusives." These are offered when producers at the site interview *Times'* reporters on camera for elaboration on their published stories.

San Jose Mercury News

The *San Jose Mercury News* online edition is part of a larger portal site serving the San Francisco Bay region, known as BayArea.com (see Fig. 1.9). The site went online in 1995, but its online roots date to the early 1990s Mercury Center. BayArea.com calls itself the region's largest news site:

> Our coverage area ranges from Santa Rosa in the North Bay, to Gilroy in the South Bay; from Contra Costa and Alameda counties in the East Bay, to Santa Cruz in the

FIG. 1.9. *San Jose Mercury News'* BayArea.com in August 2003.

34

West. We're your source for the *San Jose Mercury News* and *Contra Costa Times* on-line, and feature content from other local sources, delivering the Bay Area's best news, entertainment, sports, business, health, travel, and home information. We're also home to the Bay Area's largest classified section online, teaming with CareerBuilder and Cars.com to bring you access to a robust database of local ads and information. (About BayArea.com, 2002)

The *Mercury News* site is dependent on the printed edition of the newspaper. About 95% of the *Mercury News* online site's text content comes from the news-paper, noted Rob Neill (personal communication, May 2, 2002), program man-ager for BayArea.com. Other content originates from wire services and newspa-pers such as *The New York Times* and the *Washington Post*. The site does not have individuals devoted solely to reporting for the online edition. "I don't think it makes sense having a specific team writing for online. It throws up a wall," Neill explained. "The newsroom is best suited for producing news and online produc-ers are best suited to put news online."

The recently redesigned site, which debuted in early 2002, does not require registration or subscription. It is searchable and information is easy to find, Neill (personal communication, May 2, 2002) said. Although the server has gone down on occasion, the site has not been hacked. To improve service to readers, the on-line production staff constantly refines site usability, Neill added. "You can al-ways work on usability. I don't think that's something that's ever perfect."

BayArea.com and the *Mercury News* managers and staff are searching for the right news model, Neill said. "Newsrooms have to redefine what they are, what a news story is," he said. "I am a big fan of newspaper reporters. I used to be one. I don't think we need to be sending other people to do their jobs."

USA Today

Gannett Corporation is one of the world's largest news businesses, with 95 news-papers and a combined daily circulation of about 7.7 million. It also owns and operates 22 television stations. Its flagship newspaper is *USA Today*, which has a daily circulation of 2.3 million and is available in 60 countries worldwide. The company also publishes *USA Weekend*, a weekly magazine of 24 million circula-tion in almost 600 newspapers (Company Profile, 2002).

The newspaper is internationally and nationally circulated 5 days per week and is one of the world's largest. Gannett is known for its corporate sharing and this benefits all of its newspapers, broadcast stations, and online sites. The online edition of *USA Today* (see Fig. 1.10) has won numerous national awards for its online journalism (Accolades, 2002).

The *USA Today* online edition has about 9.2 million readers per month. The average reader is affluent, mobile, and a decision maker. The typical reader is male, about 42 years old, possesses an undergraduate or graduate degree, is a

FIG. 1.10. USAToday.com in August 2003.

daily Web user, and is part of a family unit with a mean annual household income of $82,000 (Demographics, 2002). The Web edition is organized similar to the newspaper, with main sections devoted to news, sports, money, and life. News includes daily coverage from the newspaper as well as columns, opinion pieces, U.S. Supreme Court decisions, health and science, and local city guides. One of the newspaper's widely recognized strengths is its sports coverage. Baseball is one of the top attractions, drawing on Gannett's *Baseball Weekly*, but all other professional and amateur sports are also covered and updated regularly. The Money section offers business and financial news as well as interactive opportunities to create and manage investment portfolios online. Small business tips are offered and consumers seeking information about automobiles find the site useful. The site's Life section includes celebrities, television news and listings, movies and reviews, arts news, travel information, and a collection of columnists.

In addition to these sections, the site offers comprehensive and current weather information, a technology section, and a shopping section. Site visitors can take advantage of several interactive components of the site. These include "Talk Today," a chance for readers to chat online with experts and to subscribe to e-mail newsletters. Readers can subscribe to five different e-mail newsletters. These focus on the daily news briefing, daily technology report, weekly book publishing news, weekly automobile news and reviews, and weekly retail shopping deals and special offers. USAToday.com also provides wireless Internet users access to news and information through wireless telephones, personal digital assistants (PDAs) and handheld devices, and pagers. Site users may also search archives of the newspaper dating back to 1994.

Wall Street Journal

The *Wall Street Journal* introduced its online edition in 1995 (see Fig. 1.11). It has been designed to serve the business and financial communities in the United States and abroad, but it also focuses on general news, says managing editor Bill Grueskin (personal communication, April 18, 2002). Most of its content originates in the printed edition of the newspaper, but 2% or 3%, he said, is original. The original content, Grueskin described, is mostly additional feature content. From the printed *Journal*, the site uses news from its various editions. Although much comes from the U.S. edition, it also depends heavily on its European, Americas, and Asian editions. The site's producers also place news from the Dow Jones news service and other wires on the site.

There are approximately 60 full-time editors and producers on the online staff. Most of their time is spent preparing pages and updating stories for the 24/7 operation. The online site staff is proud of its success as a subscription site and boasts:

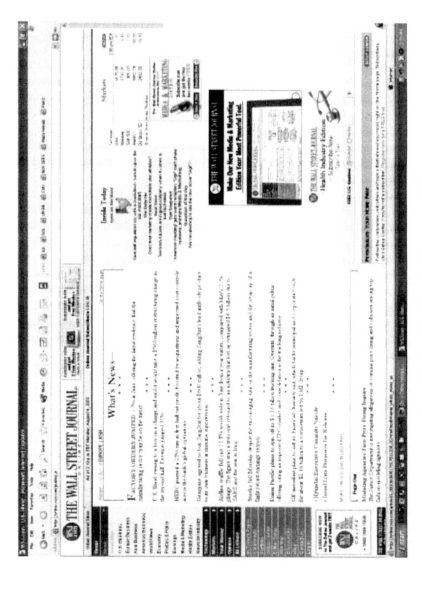

FIG. 1.11. *Wall Street Journal* Online in August 2003.

38

The Online Journal is the Web's most successful subscription-based site, providing more than one-half million subscribers with the most comprehensive coverage of global business and financial news. The Online Journal includes all of the regular columns and features from the print edition of *The Wall Street Journal* and more. The site's continuously refreshed pages include up-to-date markets and news coverage as well as special content written exclusively for the online edition. (About the Online Journal, 2002)

Subscriptions include access to the site's market news, research and charting, current and historical stock quotes, use of site personalization tools, e-mail and news alert services, access to the *Barron's* online edition, and access to the last 30 days of news archives.

The online site is organized somewhat differently from the print edition. For example, Marketplace, the second section of the printed edition, does not appear as an online section. Instead, articles from that section appear online by subject. The staff of about 80 full-time reporters and editors put the next day's edition of the newspaper on the site at about midnight the evening before publication. Early looks at coming stories are available as early as 7 p.m.

The site provides audio and video multimedia content and interactivity such as discussions and reader feedback. The site can also be personalized for users to select priorities and preferences for content display. Its ultimate strength, in the view of editor Grueskin, is the exclusive online content. Two years ago, the site gained attention for its coverage of the AOL/Time Warner merger. The site was the first news organization to break the story, posting it on its pages in the middle of the night.

Washington Post

The *Washington Post* (http://washingtonpost.com) has an international and national audience. Built on the reputation of the print brand of the national capitol's primary daily newspaper, the site has rapidly built a strong following since its debut in June 1996 (see Fig. 1.12). Douglas Feaver (personal communication, April 10, 2002), executive editor of washingtonpost.com, oversees the content of the site. He said the site does well providing online news and information to the Washington metropolitan area, including suburban Virginia and Maryland, as well as a large international market.

The *Washington Post* online, like *The New York Times*, has opted to present itself as a national and international online newspaper. The results have been impressive with 4 to 4.5 million unique visits a month, about 7 million page views on a typical weekday, and about half that amount on weekends.

Approximately 20% to 25% of the site's content is original. Feaver said about 60% to 75% of news content is original and about 33% of features are original to the site. Content is developed mostly by the newspaper's extensive staff, but also

FIG. 1.12. Washingtonpost.com in August 2003.

40

from online staff writers and Associated Press, Reuters, and Agence France-Presse wire services. There are about 240 persons employed at washingtonpost.com. Of that number, 5 writers are devoted solely to online content. A number of other part-timers contribute news, features, business, health, and entertainment content. "We have the entire *Washington Post* and additional information that compose our content," Feaver (personal communication, April 10, 2002) stated. "This includes wire services, exclusive Internet stories, restaurant reviews, and audio."

The Post's online edition has attracted considerable international attention because of a number of Washington-based stories in recent years. Coverage of the September 11, 2001, attack on the Pentagon is among the most recent. Despite the incredible demands for online news that day that crashed servers around the United States, *The Post* site remained online 95% of the time. Not only did the site develop its own content as the story unfolded throughout the day, but it also published the newspaper's multiple Pulitzer Prize-winning stories throughout the fall. The site also drew attention with its coverage of the Monica Lewinsky and Bill Clinton scandal and investigations in 1998 and it was among the first online sites to provide coverage of the seizure of Elián González in Miami—thanks to coverage from the newspaper's Miami bureau chief.

Having staff writers devoted to the Web site is one of the washingtonpost.com's strengths, Feaver stated. It also excels at multimedia content and photography. "We are very thorough," he said.

Like other online newspapers in its size and market category, the site's managers are struggling to design the best business model to keep it afloat. Editors are debating which content to charge for and which content to offer for free. The site's techies are also working very hard to keep the site secure. The technology is less than perfect, Feaver acknowledged, and it is a challenge for everyone. "Our bigger challenge is how to master this new style of storytelling—a true multimedia experience. It's an enormous challenge."

CONCLUSIONS

The Web and online newspapers can empower citizens with the information they provide in democracies (Fouhy, 2000). The importance of online newspapers and journalism is increasing today as technologies are evolving.

The online newspaper world is in transition. What it is today will not be the same online newspaper business in 5 years. Technology has too much impact on the medium for it to remain static. With technological advances such as the spread of broadband into homes and new multimedia opportunities, online newspapers will evolve as they have done in the first decade of the existence of the Web.

The impact of news media convergence will be significant. We already see evidence of this on newspaper, magazine, and television news Web sites. This results in the need for differently qualified staff. Students graduating into the job market are finding online newspapers and other online news media need combinations of skills not sought a decade ago. Today's content producers must be capable of working with text, images, audio, and video.

Despite the changing online newspaper industry, success will be measured not only by public service, but also by profits. Until a successful business model is found, the future of online newspapers will be in doubt. Access by and interaction with the audience seems critical. The more access is available through the wiring of the Internet world locally, nationally, and internationally, the greater the likelihood of a business model solution. Online newspapers must also be prepared for increased access through wireless technologies that are only beginning to emerge in this decade. The key, perhaps, is the financial viability of online newspapers. Who pays for it? If it is consumers who have to bear the financial burden, then how?

The financial future for online newspapers seems bright if a successful economic model can be found. Web and Internet technologies are opening new opportunities to communicate with audiences through new avenues. Online newspapers are only a decade old. Compared to other mass media, they are children waiting to mature.

The Form and Coloration Hypothesis: Arab and Israeli Online Newspapers During the 2002 Middle East Crisis

Michael B. Salwen

In a widely quoted passage from Siebert, Peterson, and Schramm's (1956) landmark *Four Theories of the Press*, the authors wrote that "the press always takes on the *form and coloration* [italics added] of the social and political structures within which it operates" (p. 1). The authors believed this assertion held in democratic nations with a free press as well as in totalitarian nations with a government-controlled or government-operated press.

When Siebert et al. (1956) made their observation, most people in most nations did not have easy access to international press reports. Today, with the availability of online newspapers from around the globe, people with access to the World Wide Web can test Siebert et al.'s assertion for themselves.

Siebert et al.'s (1956) prediction about news media coverage, as predicted by the form and coloration hypothesis, is especially likely to manifest itself in a nation's press when a nation is under assault. During times of crisis, social institutions, including the press, mobilize to defend the besieged state. The press becomes the cheerleader and propaganda arm for the state. In some states, such as Communist states with government-operated news media, this role is overtly advocated. In capitalist societies with privately operated news media, media owners support the besieged state in times of crisis out of sincere patriotic duty. They may not even believe they are cheerleaders, but merely objective transmitters of truthful information.

During mid-April 2002, world attention focused on the Mideast crisis. Israel was involved in the second week of a military incursion into parts of the West Bank under Palestinian Authority rule. The Israelis launched the offensive after experiencing a series of devastating suicide attacks. They claimed their aim was to destroy terrorist strongholds. They blamed Palestinian leader Yasser Arafat for— if not directly ordering the attacks—at least giving a nod and a wink to the terrorists and not clamping down on violence. The Israelis were trying to focus world attention on the suicide attacks. They wanted the world community to see the incursion as a justified response to terrorism. The Palestinians and Arab nations, on the other hand, were directing attention to the plight of the West Bank Palestinians. They wanted the world community to see the Israeli response as disproportionate to the suicide attacks.

The home page of Israel's *Jerusalem Post* featured the day's breaking news, of a Sabbath afternoon suicide bombing in Israel and of U.S. Secretary of State Colin Powell's visit to Israel. Scrolling down the page, however, a reader encountered stories that illustrated Siebert et al.'s (1956) statement that the press reflects the form and coloration of the structures in which it operates.[5]

An opinion piece claimed that Powell intended to warn Arafat that this was his "last chance" to make peace with Israel and that the United States might break relations with the Palestinians unless Arafat renounced terrorism. Another opinion story, relating what was portrayed as minor policy differences between the United States and Israel, was headlined "Bouncing the Ball Into Arafat's Court." Below that followed a series of news summaries, of which the headlines reflected the Israeli view:

- "Would-Be Woman Suicide Bomber Nabbed in Tulkarm"
- "IDF [Israeli Defense Force] Won't Withdraw Until Terrorists Surrender"
- "Seized Orient House Documents Link Arafat to Terrorism"
- "Wave of Attacks Expected After Pullout—Senior Officer"
- "PA [Palestinian Authority] Intelligence Chief Implicated in Terrorism"

How did the Arab press report the crisis?

The home page of Egypt's *Al-Ahram* Weekly Online[6] featured a photograph of Israeli Prime Minister Ariel Sharon sitting alone behind a desk, with a story caption of fewer than 40 words that managed to describe the Israeli incursion using the terms *monstrous, murder,* and *destruction*:

PARIAH, UNREPENTANT: People all over the world have shown their horror at the monstrous campaign of murder and destruction Israel is waging on the Pales-

---

[5]The newspaper *Ha'aretz* is generally considered more critical of the government.
[6]Many international media scholars regard this as the best newspaper in the Arab world.

tinians; but will governments heed their citizens' urging, buttress words with actions and isolate Ariel Sharon?

The home page of Saudi Arabia's *Arab News* featured a story with the headline "Unprecedented Show of Support for Palestinians." The story related how a marathon television campaign in the country had raised over $90 million to help the Palestinians. In a story headlined "Israel Buries Massacre," the online newspaper accused Israel of concealing a massacre of Palestinians in the West Bank town of Jenin. In another story headlined "Bush–Sharon Confrontation Looms," the Saudi publication claimed Israel was growing increasingly isolated, even from its patron the United States.

Online news users can log onto newspapers from around the world and get different perspectives regarding the same international events. The coverage in the Middle Eastern online newspapers reporting the Mideast crisis fell in line with national policies, just as the form and coloration hypothesis predicts. The Israeli press emphasized how Israel was a nation under siege and victim of terrorism, and how the Palestinian Authority was supporting the terrorism. It depicted the West Bank incursion as an act of self-defense and it portrayed its political differences with the United States as a minor disagreement between friends. It also reported captured Israeli documents linking the Palestinian Authority to terrorist attacks. The Arab press reported the suffering of the Palestinian people and the unity of the Arab world—and indeed, they claimed the entire world—in condemning Israel. It reported sharp policy differences between the United States and Israel that it suggested might lead to a permanent rift. It also reported stories of Israeli atrocities and a "massacre" in Jenin.

Nearly 50 years have passed since Siebert et al.'s (1956) observation about the world press. Yet, the observation remains as valid today as then. Only now online users can log on and see for themselves how world press reporting adheres to the form and coloration hypothesis.

REFERENCES

About BayArea.com. (2002). *About BayArea.com.* Retrieved April 15, 2002, from http://www.bayarea.com/mld/bayarea/contact_us/about/

About the Online Journal. (2002). *About the Online Journal/General Information.* Retrieved April 15, 2002, from http://online.wsj.com/help/0,4441,001-0,00.html#link_1

Accolades. (2002). *Accolades.* Retrieved April 15, 2002, from http://www.usatoday.com/a/adindex/omk/accolades.htm

Balding, T. (2002). *World press trends: Mixed fortunes for newspaper industry.* Paper presented at the World Association of Newspapers 9th World Editors Forum, Brugges, Belgium. Retrieved July 11, 2003, from http://www.wan-press.org/brugges2002/common/balding.html

Barringer, F. (2001, August 27). Growing audience is turning to established news media online. *The New York Times,* pp. C1, C6.

Borrell & Associates. (2001, October). *Newspapers report paid online subscribers.* Retrieved December 5, 2001, from http://www.naa.org/TheDigitalEdge/DigArtPage.cfm?AID=3225

Burgess, J. (1993, February 14). Firms face questions of technology's timing, cost. *The Washington Post,* p. H1.

Carlson, D. (2003). Dave Carlson's online timeline (1990 to present). *Dave Carlson's Virtual World.* Retrieved June 24, 2003, from http://iml.jou.ufl.edu/carlson/frames.htm

Casey, W. (1996, March 11). Provocative paperless papers; On-line journalism remains in transition. *The Washington Post,* p. F17.

Chicago Tribune media kit. (2002). *Target Chicago with the market leader.* Retrieved April 19, 2002, from http://mm2.advariant.com/mm/index.jsp?affiliate=chicagotribune

Chyi, H. I., & Sylvie, G. (1999, August). *Opening the umbrella: An economic analysis of online newspaper geography.* Paper presented at the annual meeting of the Association for Education in Journalism and Mass Communication, New Orleans, LA.

Chyi, H. I., & Sylvie, G. (2000). Online newspapers in the U.S.: Perceptions of markets, products, revenue, and competition. *Journal on Media Management, 2*(11), 69–77.

Company profile. (2002). *Company profile.* Retrieved April 19, 2002, from http://www.gannett.com/map/gan007.htm

Demographics. (2002). *Demographics.* Retrieved April 15, 2002, from http://www.usatoday.com/a/adindex/omk/demographics.htm

Deuze, M. (2001, October 18). Online journalism: Modeling the first generation of new media on the World Wide Web. Retrieved November 17, 2003, from http://www.firstmonday.dk/issues/issue6_10/deuze/index.html

Dibean, W., & Garrison, B. (2001). How six online newspapers use Web technologies. *Newspaper Research Journal, 22*(2), 79–93.

Farhi, P. (2000a, March). The dotcom brain drain. *American Journalism Review, 22*(2), 30.

Farhi, P. (2000b, September). Surviving in cyberspace. *American Journalism Review, 22*(7), 22–27.

Fouhy, E. (2000, May). Which way will it go? *American Journalism Review, 22*(4), 18–19.

Frequently asked questions. (2002). *Frequently asked questions.* Retrieved April 15, 2002, from http://www.dallasnews.com/registration/faqs.html#contentwebunique

Gates, D. (2002, May 1). The future of news: Newspapers in the digital age. *Online Journalism Review.* Retrieved May 2, 2002, from http://www.ojr.org/ojr/future/1020298748.php

Grimes, C. (2002, February 6). Premium payments may boost Web revenues. *Financial Times* (London), p. 3.

Heyboer, K. (2000, January–February). Going live. *American Journalism Review, 22*(1), 38–43.

Keefe, R. (1996, October 13). New *Tribune* president arrives during time of transition. *St. Petersburg Times,* p. 1H.

Kenworthy, T. (1997, March 2). Journalism: The McVeigh story and its impact; Publication of alleged bomb admission may alter course of trial. *The Washington Post,* p. A7.

Kramer, S. D. (2001, December 4). Crackerbox palace: When breaking news coverage becomes routine, it's time to raise the bar. *Online Journalism Review.* Retrieved December 6, 2001, from http://ojr.usc.edu/content/story.cfm?request=670

Kurtz, H. (1993, October 23). Click! On-line newspaper is a mixed read. *The Washington Post,* p. A1.

Lasica, J. D. (2001, September 20). A scorecard for Net news ethics: Despite a lapse related to the terrorist attack, online media deserve high marks. *Online Journalism Review.* Retrieved January 7, 2002, from http://ojr.usc.edu/content/story.cfm?request=643

Levins, H. (1997, January 4). Time of change and challenge (online newspapers). *Editor & Publisher, 130*(1), 58–60.

Miles, S. (2003, January 31). Web publishers see signs of profitability, stability. *The Wall Street Journal Online.* Retrieved February 21, 2003, from http://online.wsj.com

Miller, R. (2001, September 14). From niche site to news portal: How Slashdot survived the attack. *Online Journalism Review.* Retrieved December 6, 2001, from http://ojr.usc.edu/content/story.cfm

Missed what the top analysts are saying about our digital future? Catch up here. (2000, February 21). *The Guardian* (London), p. 62.

Palser, B. (2001, October). Pay-per-click. *American Journalism Review, 23*(8), 82.

Palser, B. (2002, November). We've only just begun. *American Journalism Review, 24*(9), 39–42.

Picard, R. (2000). Changing business models of online content services: Their implications for multimedia and other content producers. *The International Journal on Media Management, 2*(2), 60–68.

Quint, B. E. (1994, November). Extra! Extra! *Wilson Library Bulletin, 69*, 67–68.

Samoriski, J. (2002). *Issues in cyberspace: Communication, technology, law, and society on the Internet frontier.* Boston: Allyn & Bacon.

Shaw, D. J. (1997, June 17). The media.com: Revolution in cyberspace. *Los Angeles Times*, Home edition, p. A1.

Siebert, F. S., Peterson, T. B., & Schramm, W. (1956). *Four theories of the press.* Urbana: University of Illinois Press.

Singer, J. B. (2001, Spring). The metro wide web: Changes in newspaper's gatekeeping role online. *Journalism & Mass Communication Quarterly, 78*(1), 65–80.

Smith, S. (2002a, April). Content at your service. *EContent, 25*(4), 44–45.

Smith, S. (2002b, February). The free lunch is over: Online content subscriptions on the rise. *EContent, 25*(2), 18–23.

Smith, T. (1999, April 26). A new source of news. *Online Newshour.* Retrieved April 28, 1999, from http://www.pbs.org/newshour/bb/media/jan-june99/inews_4-26.html

Sullivan, C. (2003a, January 20). Information may want to be free, but even freedom has its limits. *Editor & Publisher, 136*(3), 22.

Sullivan, C. (2003b, January 20). Newspaper sites move to registration model. *Editor & Publisher, 136*(3), 10–12, 20–21, 23.

Weise, E. (1997). Does the Internet change news reporting? Not quite. *Media Studies Journal, 11*(2), 159–163.

CHAPTER TWO

Online News Trends

Michael B. Salwen

Online news sites operated by print and broadcast news organizations can contribute to public knowledge about news and public affairs issues by carrying original news of social consequence. These sites can be sources of exclusive news stories, investigative reports, and original commentaries, providing unique contributions to the marketplace of ideas. However, in most cases online news sites operated by print and broadcast news outlets have not made full and responsible use of their sites, seeing them as merely supplements or promotional vehicles for their original outlets, satisfied to reproduce their offline content online and carry wire service stories. Nonetheless, online news sites will have to offer original news if they are to evolve into more legitimate and original news resources in their own right and become more than promotional outlets for parent media outlets.

This is all easily said, but it would require commitment and some faith. It would also require separate budgets and editorial staffs for online sites, so they are separate editorial outlets in a corporation able to compete in the marketplace for original news. As things now stand, because of market considerations, news organizations have no incentives to produce original online news (Martin & Hansen, 1996; Thalhimer, 1994). They should, however, because news, unlike entertainment, mandates a greater degree of social responsibility. Producing original news is costly and labor intensive, requiring investments in bureaus, reporters, editors, graphics specialists, and content designers; and most publishers and general managers of news outlets find these expenditures unnecessary when they already have news from their offline outlets and the wire services. They also

47

fear that too much original online content could compete with and threaten the main offline organizations, their primary moneymakers. Most online news sites are free to users, unlike the printed versions. Efforts to create subscription-based news sites have largely failed, except for specialized services such as the *Wall Street Journal*. To date, most online news sites cannot subsist on advertising alone. Advertisers, for good reason, are leery about whether their online ads are being read. Thus, under present circumstances, we cannot expect online sites affiliated with print and broadcast organizations to establish reputations for editorial quality on their own. It is unlikely that they can provide much original online news as a public service obligation. Things may change, however, when and if market conditions change. Perhaps one of the major changes we can expect in coming years is fewer free news sites, despite public resistance to such a trend. Newspapers and magazines are finding it increasingly difficult to continue to give away information that they charge for in their hard-copy editions.

In Chapter 1, Garrison cited the example of the *Dallas Morning News'* online exclusive reporting Timothy McVeigh's confession as the Oklahoma City bomber. Although the story was lauded at the time as a harbinger of online newspaper exclusives, the story has thus far been an anomaly. By and large, news organizations subscribe to the common wisdom not to put much original material online, and certainly not exclusive stories, for fear of scooping themselves.[1] This makes sense economically, but it neglects the important public service component invested in any news organization, which is not merely some chimerical notion. Society would benefit from online news sites, in competition with other news outlets, with original news bringing more ideas and news into the marketplace.

Instances of original online news indicate that the medium can have a beneficial social influence. In 2000, Columbia University recognized the contribution of original online journalism with its first Online Journalism Awards. Many of the sites carried news unavailable anywhere else. *Salon*, a leading online magazine (or "zine") that is examined in length in this chapter, was the recipient of awards in two categories—enterprise journalism and general excellence. CNET.com, a technology news site, received the breaking news award for its reporting of the Microsoft antitrust ruling. BabyCenter.com was honored in the service award category. The judges lauded the site as a service for parents, describing it as "a complete guide to their baby's health for the first 12 months of life" (Christian, 2000, p. 5B). APB.com (All Points Bulletin), a site devoted to news about law and crime, was recognized in the category of creative use of the medium for its coverage of unsolved murders of nine women whose bodies were found in several Western states: "Audio, video, scanned police reports, maps, and photos of the victims make the stories come alive in a way that print publications couldn't do," the judges wrote (Christian, 2000, p. 5B).

---

[1]It remains a question whether online exclusives scoop the organization. Such online stories can be used to stimulate interest in receiving news from the offline organization.

These examples testify that online news sites can, if properly harnessed, contribute original information, stimulate public debate about issues, and emerge as important news media and social forces. Whether the news concerns a major antitrust ruling or infants' health, original news, rather than recycled news, contributes to public knowledge. However, as this chapter makes clear, online news sites have yet to find an economic model for success. Without such a model, it is unlikely that online news outlets will expend resources to obtain original online news when less expensive news is available. For example, the recognition of APB.com illustrates how even an award-winning online news site had not figured out how to make the medium financially successful. A few months before being honored, APB had filed for bankruptcy (Christian, 2000).

Some evidence suggests that online news sites are gradually moving away from the era of "shovelware"—of simply dumping wire service reports and their offline print and broadcast news to their online sites (Marlatt, 1999). Among other things, they report breaking news, such as accidents and disasters, and thereby compete against radio and television. They also provide additional content to their offline print or broadcast news stories and they coordinate their online and offline stories in original ways (Heyboer, 2000). For example, in the 2000 Online Journalism Awards, TimesUnion.com, the Web site of the Albany (NY) *Times Union*, was recognized in the category of collaborative coverage of its online and offline sites for its reporting in the Amadou Diallo police brutality case (Christian, 2000).

This chapter is concerned with whether online news outlets can become conveyors of original editorial content that contributes to the marketplace of ideas. To have this impact, online news sites must have editorial independence and not feel constrained by their parent print and broadcast outlets' concerns that original online news threatens the main news organizations. Online news sites have certain advantages over offline sites, including unlimited space and the ability to report the news at any time. It is also necessary to review online news trends during the past few years to get an idea where the medium is going and to provide context for the empirical studies that form the heart of this book.

This chapter briefly reviews whether Internet service providers (ISPs) and search engine portals, people's entry points to the World Wide Web, provide online users with original news and important news. It then reviews how "independent" online "webzines" (or "zines"), with no associations with traditional media outlets, have made an impact on online journalism, despite their relatively limited resources, by reporting original editorial content and occasional exclusives that attracted national attention.

The chapter concludes with two case studies in which online news had a social impact. First, it reviews the case of "Zippergate"—a defining moment in online journalism involving the revelation of President Bill Clinton's affair with a White House intern. The story quickly spread from a small online news site through the Washington news rumor mill to the mainstream news media. The chapter then reviews the case of online news coverage of the September 11, 2001, terrorist attacks on the World Trade Center and the Pentagon, when many people turned to online news sites to learn about the breaking news story.

NEWS ON SEARCH ENGINES

Where might we find original news online? Online sites without print or broadcast outlets do not have to be concerned with scooping themselves. Two potential sources of original news would be the portals that people use to go to the World Wide Web—search engines and ISPs. These sites often feature news lures, among other attractions, with varying degrees of prominence on their home pages. It is to the sites' advantage to keep users within these sites, rather than searching portals, so users read the sites' advertisements along with the various lures, including news lures.

However, these sites are not committed news organizations and, therefore, they have not provided original news. Nor do they see a reason to expend resources on obtaining original news when less expensive wire service or news agency news is available. Their news usually comes from established sources, mostly news agencies, such as the Associated Press or Reuters. In fact, one innovative search engine took its reliance on others for news to new heights. In September 2002 the search engine Google launched Google News, which used no editors or human intervention of any kind in selecting the news, including the headlines. Instead, Google News is run entirely by algorithms, pulling together related headlines and photographs from 4,000 Web sites worldwide. Story placement, too, is decided by algorithms, so the most salient news story in the media receives top placement in Google News. Clicking to a story takes the user directly to the original site of the news, going directly to the page with news and bypassing home pages. The people at Google concede that their algorithmic process makes for "some occasionally unusual and contradictory groupings" (from the Google Web site).

Still, many users access the Web through search engine sites, so the importance of search engines as an online news source cannot be dismissed. The home pages of leading search engines offer varying enticements on their home pages for users to click to news before typing search terms in the portals. Thus, news is not something most users search for when they go to search engines; rather, it is an enticement they encounter to grab their interest and keep them on the site. In most cases, the news is but one of many enticements on the crowded pages. Among other things, the sites typically offer online shopping, travel services, games, chat rooms, message boards, horoscopes, recipes, restaurant reviews, and yellow pages. The news could be easily drowned out among the choices. Think of the search engine home pages like a hard-sell sales environment for the user's attention. Think of a department store metaphor, where salespeople from various departments are pressing the customer to buy their products. The salespeople from different departments are pressing the user to sample their goods. All the salespeople are trying to keep the customer in the store (i.e., the Web site), in their various departments.

Many search engine home pages give at least modest prominence to news to push and pull users into clicking on news story icons. For example, on Sunday afternoon, December 9, 2001, during a period with more major international news than most ordinary times, with U.S. troops in Afghanistan routing Taliban forces and recent terrorist attacks against Israel, the search engine Yahoo! offered an "In the News" section on its opening page. This provided users the opportunity to click on two Afghanistan stories and, just below these stories, a story concerning a Palestinian suicide attack in Israel. Below this, the user was enticed to click on sports news, including the college football Heisman Trophy award announcement. With each click, the user was directed to different news pages, each with advertisements.

Excite's home page that day featured a top news story headline, "Anthrax Clues Emerge." Clicking on this headline took readers to an Associated Press story about how the recently opened anthrax-laced envelope sent to Senator Patrick Leahy might provide clues in the anthrax-by-mail attacks. Just below the anthrax story on the opening page, another icon offered users the opportunity to participate in an instant poll asking whether they believed that government efforts to crack down on terrorists threatened civil liberties. Sixty-three percent said "no." Clicking to respond to the poll or on any of the news stories on the home page took readers to another page with more opportunities to click on news, with these icons at the top of the page: AP, Reuters, AP U.S., Health, and Politics. As is apparent, the push and pull model could keep an interested user almost endlessly searching for more news.

It was difficult to find the news on the crowded Alta Vista home page. Users had to click on the small News icon above the search portal. Users who clicked on the icon were led to a page with boxed categories of news, starting with Top Stories. Below this, users could select from 13 other news categories in alphabetical order, ranging from Business and Companies to Travel and U.S. Regional.

On the one hand, interpreting search engine offerings of news seems merely a design issue matter. However, these pages reflect the designers' take on the importance of news and the users' use of online news. The news icon on the Lycos home page was even more difficult to find. The News icon was listed in alphabetical order in a left-side box of Lycos Topics, ranging from autos to travel, with an icon to click on more topics below.

The Ask Jeeves site had little news on its opening page, but what little was offered was prominently displayed on the relatively uncluttered page. Just under the search portal, set off against a light green background, it offered the icon: War on Terrorism: News and Resources.

Other search engines gave prominent attention to news on their home pages. Northern Light Search had one of the most conspicuous attractions to war news.

A large right-side box with a graphic of a newspaper and the headline "Today's News" had 10 news story icons below the image. Most dealt with Afghanistan and the Middle East, but sports stories and a More Headlines icon were also available. In addition, Northern Light also had a larger War on Terrorism icon with a U.S. flag on the left and a British flag on the right. Clicking on this icon brought users to news folders (e.g., Terrorism, North & Central America, etc.). This page also included icons for Special Collection stories from the wire services.

The department store model of search engine home pages (or ISP home pages) can be useful for designing studies to determine the likelihood of users going to news stories. It can be hypothesized that the more prominently news items are displayed on Web pages, the more likely users will click on those items. News is one of the many attractions used to lure users. Granted, much online news reading is fortuitous, when users are enticed to click on news stories while doing other things on the Web. However, people actively seek news online during breaking news stories. In this event, people treat online news much as they treat television news when they first hear of a breaking event—they search for more. Indeed, people may first learn of breaking news on television and then go online to search for more details. When Princess Diana died in a car crash, when the O. J. Simpson verdict was announced, and when terrorists destroyed New York's World Trade Center, online news use increased sharply. Online sites such as search engines recognize that people seek out news during such times and so the sites' home pages are redesigned to emphasize the breaking stories.

Thus far, we have noted that print and broadcast news organizations have not put much original content online. Our review of search engine portals indicates that these sites, too, have not been sources of original news information and that they often do not give prominent attention to news, even during a period when America is at war. What might we expect during less newsworthy times? Although search engines may use news to attract users, they are not primarily news organizations committed to providing the public with news and public affairs information. They thus rely on wire service news. This raises interesting questions about the future of online news. Any site, even a Wal-Mart site, may one day subscribe to and offer wire service news stories to attract users. Might such sites go further by offering original news, collected by editorial staff? For example, might Microsoft hire staff stationed in Silicon Valley to report technology news for its technologically adept users? Might General Motors hire staff to report automotive news on its Web site? This raises questions: Will the news favor the corporations that pay for the news and be, ultimately, uncritical fluff?

We mentioned earlier that some news organizations use their online news sites to provide additional information about news stories that appeared in their offline sites. We should not dismiss the supplemental nature of online news sites. Some online sites have supplemented their offline sites in original ways. When CNN Interactive was launched with much fanfare on August 31, 1995, it was one of the few places on the Web to provide constantly updated news. At the time, most of the 200 online newspaper sites updated their content only once, and sometimes twice, a day and those updates were often tied solely to publication deadlines. CNN Interactive was meant to provide news to news junkies who could not wait for their favorite stories on CNN (Sorensen, 1998).

Earning its name "interactive," the CNN site sought audience feedback. For example, after CNN's Bob Franken broke the story of District Judge Susan Webber Wright's decision to dismiss Paula Jones's lawsuit against President Clinton on the television network, CNN Interactive carried the news on a scrolling ticker and posted a brief story a minute later. In a nonscientific online poll, users cast 50,000 votes on Judge Wright's decision. An overwhelming 70% agreed with her decision. "Our message boards went wild, as well," a CNN spokesperson said. "In less than 24 hours, we had more than 3,000 messages on the topic" (Sorensen, 1998, p. A2).[2]

NEWS FROM ISPs

In addition to search engines, another potential source for original online news editorial content would be ISPs. As with search engines, ISPs are not primarily news organizations committed to reporting news. Nonetheless, 3 hours after the Oklahoma City bombing, online computer service providers were offering competition to cable television news, TV networks, and radio stations. In the community board tradition, they also offered message boards for subscribers to share their views and emotions in nationwide catharses.

By the mid-1990s, ISPs increased their staffs to improve news coverage by monitoring and managing news feeds around the clock. They also planned better ways to package their news with graphics and audio. Many critics decry these innovations as emphasizing bells and whistles over content (Cochran, 1995; Kenworthy, 1997). Although ISPs may rise to the occasion during major news events, critics do not believe that quality news reporting from ISPs is the norm. These critics fear that AOL's preference for "fluff news," such as diets and celebrity movie, CD, or book promotions, is contributing to the decline of quality news (Brendan, 2001; Houston, 2001).

THE ZINES

The mid-1990s witnessed the rise of sometimes audacious and brash independent online magazines, known as webzines, e-zines, and zines. These debuted with

---

[2]In January 2001, CNN Interactive announced a reorganization that would break down the barriers between the main organization and its online subsidiary. It required all its employees to be multiskilled reporters able to report for the cable network or any of its online sites. This, in fact, is becoming a trend in news companies.

names such as *Suck* and *Feed*. The zines offered original news and opinions and sometimes even news exclusives, often beating the better established and better financed traditional news media with scoops. Many observers praised the zines as among the most innovative and exciting news sites on the World Wide Web (Stein, 1999).

To understand the editorial success of the zines, it is worth looking back to the early 1990s, which brought praise to entrepreneur Ted Turner's variation on the existing medium of television—Cable News Network (CNN). CNN's 24-hour "real-time" news coverage of the 1990–1991 Persian Gulf War kept Americans—and many outside America—riveted on the war. Before this time, news of wars and far-off battles had to wait. Television coverage of the Vietnam War, the so-called "television war," consisted largely of delayed film coverage, even if it appeared live to many viewers. With CNN's coverage of the Gulf War, the stage was set for a 24-hour news cycle. Apparently there was a market for news junkies interested in 24-hour coverage of news as unfolding drama, as witnessed by the subsequent O. J. Simpson trials and the news media feeding frenzies with the deaths of John F. Kennedy, Jr., and Diana, Princess of Wales.

Even as cable television news became the dominant news medium to report 24-hour news, another medium—online news—was in the works, offering on-demand access to the news and the possibility for audience members to tailor their news needs and learn about any news story any time. By the mid-1990s, Internet stocks were the hottest market offerings. During the glory days of over-night dot-com millionaires, a bookseller named Amazon.com showed that in a short time it was possible to compete with industry giants such as Borders and Barnes & Noble. There was money to be made on the Internet, or so it appeared, and some media entrepreneurs and enterprising journalists saw a market for original online news.

The two most important zines in the short life of online journalism have been *Salon* and *Slate*. *Salon* comes from a humble background. Its origins date to the Newspaper Guild's bitter, 2-week strike at the *San Francisco Examiner* in late 1994. Striking Guild members decided to publish a strike paper on the Web, launching the *San Francisco Free Press*. After the strike, a group of the journalists, led by David Talbot, the *Examiner*'s arts and features editor, thought it had fortuitously found a way to make a profit on the Web and produce a high-quality, original journalistic product that would appeal to the public. At the time, the relatively few newspapers on the Web were dumping their offline content online. The group of journalists left the *Examiner* and launched *Salon*.

Salon made its debut on November 12, 1995, started by seed money from Apple Computer, Inc. The San Francisco-based zine began as a literary site, published once every 2 weeks. In April 1996, it went weekly. In early 1997, it began publishing every weekday. It originally featured book reviews and author interviews, gaining a reputation for cultural and political criticism with its lineup of distinguished writers, including humorist Garrison Keillor and literary social firebrand Camille Paglia (Piller, 2000). The words *irreverent, brash,* and *compelling* were often used to describe *Salon.*

By early 1997, *Salon* received informal reader feedback urging more news (Stein, 1999). The death of Princess Diana was pivotal in *Salon*'s direction as a news outlet. The zine was one of the first news organizations to blame the paparazzi reporters for Diana's death. As with its literary style, *Salon* developed an irreverent approach to news and political opinion. *Salon*'s editors claimed that its appeal and following was attributable to something newspapers once had—a discernible editorial voice. "In some ways a lot of *Salon* is very old-fashioned," said *Salon*'s managing editor, Andrew Ross. "There used to be a lot more voices in newspapers: Herb Caen, Mike Royko, Ambrose Bierce. But newspapers today tend to limit the range of debate. So, we're trying to bring back that kind of strong voice" (Lasica, 1998, p. 36).

Salon has also distinguished itself with scoops. Many of *Salon*'s scoops have been interviews, which the zine regards as one of its specialties and a low-cost means to procure original news stories. During the Clinton terms, *Salon* journalists had good relations with the administration and interviewed many Clinton-era figures. In 1998, a *Salon* journalist interviewed a terrorist sentenced to death for killing two CIA employees outside CIA headquarters in Langley, Virginia, in 1993. Major news organizations, including *The New York Times* and CNN, reported the story attributed to *Salon,* an important source of publicity for *Salon* and the entire online news industry (Lasica, 1998).

Salon gained national name recognition outside Web circles when it reported a scoop widely carried in the national media in late 1998. It reported U.S. Representative Henry Hyde's self-described "youthful indiscretion" of an extramarital affair during the 1960s.[3] At the time, Hyde was chairman of the House Judiciary Committee. The story was picked up by other news media and attributed to *Salon. Salon,* eager for publicity, sent out 250 faxes to media organizations to alert them of the coming scoop. For many Americans, this was the first they ever heard of *Salon* or the world of independent online magazines. "It's a milestone day for us," said Michael O'Donnell, *Salon*'s president and publisher. "People are calling, writing. We even had to put a security guard out in the lobby. . . . It's caused that kind of reaction. We've had a couple threats from some pretty extreme people" (Feeney, 1998, p. A21).

Not everyone was delighted by *Salon*'s scoop. When the Hyde story was exposed, Republican leaders, Hyde among them, were trying to impeach President Clinton for lying about his sexual relationship with White House intern Monica Lewinsky. *Salon*'s editors meticulously checked and verified the story. Hyde's office did not deny the story, but Republicans claimed that the Clinton White House manipulated *Salon*'s editors, furnishing *Salon* with information portray-

---

[3]The story was reported by Talbot. Hyde himself used the much-quoted term: "The statute of limitations has long since passed on my youthful indiscretions." Hyde was 41 when the 5-year affair began.

ing the Republicans as hypocrites.[4] *Salon*'s decision to carry the Hyde story was controversial, even within *Salon*. The zine already had a reputation as a Clinton defender in the (independent counsel Kenneth) Starr investigation of the president.[5] In addition to associating *Salon* with partisan politics, the Hyde scoop also connected *Salon* with tawdry sex stories. Online muckraker Matt Drudge had earlier fomented the Clinton scandal by reporting the news of Clinton's affair on his online site, the *Drudge Report*. *Salon*'s Washington bureau chief, Jonathon Broder, was forced to resign after he criticized his employer in the *Washington Post*. Broder said the decision to run the Hyde story made *Salon*'s staff appear like "sex-obsessed hypocrites" (Kurtz, 1998). On September 16, *Salon* ran an editorial explaining its decision to carry the controversial Hyde story. First, *Salon* refuted Republican charges that its editors were fed a White House propaganda story:

> Two weeks ago, *Salon* editor David Talbot received a phone call from a 72-year-old retiree in Aventura, Fla., named Norm Sommer. Sommer asserted that Henry Hyde, the chairman of the House Judiciary Committee, had between 1965 and 1969 carried on an extramarital affair with a married woman named Cherie Snodgrass.[6] At the time of the affair Hyde was an Illinois state representative, married and the father of four sons. Sommer was told of the affair seven years ago by Cherie Snodgrass' ex-husband, Fred Snodgrass. During a tennis game, Snodgrass, a friend and tennis partner, had blurted out the story of the affair and how it had ruined his family. Sommer said the story came to his mind again in January when the Monica Lewinsky scandal erupted and it was speculated that the affair might eventually end up before Hyde's committee.
> . . . Experience, however, has taught us that the favorite ploy of those who want to discredit our reporting is to accuse us of being a "pawn of the White House". . . . Therefore, it is important for us to state: The White House had nothing whatsoever to do with any aspect of this story. We did not receive it from anyone in the White House or in Clinton's political or legal camps, nor did we communicate with them about it. (from *Salon*'s Web site)

Then, *Salon*'s editorial bemoaned that such scandals should be news fodder, but it took a what's-good-for-the-goose-is-good-for-the-gander approach:

> In a different and better world, we would not have released this story. Throughout the tragic farce of the Clinton-Lewinsky scandal, we have strongly argued that the private lives of all Americans, whether they are public figures or not, should remain sacrosanct. . . . But Clinton's enemies have changed the rules. In the brave new world that has been created by the Clinton-Lewinsky scandal, the private lives of

---

[4]Some House Republicans even called for the FBI to investigate whether the White House helped plant the story. The White House denied the allegation.

[5]Earlier, *Salon* had run a story with the headline, "Kenneth Starr—Is a Crazed Sex Cop Running the U.S.?"

[6]Sommer said he had contacted 57 journalists over the past half-year. He also said he called the White House and Democratic National Committee but "nobody would speak to me."

public figures are no longer off-limits. . . . But in that case, what holds true for President Clinton must hold equally true of the august figure who leads the committee sitting in judgment upon him—Rep. Henry Hyde. (from *Salon*'s Web site)

The editorial gained attention in the news media, further enhancing *Salon*'s reputation. It became something of an online classic. *Suck*, an online zine, ran a tongue-in-cheek editorial satirizing *Salon*'s editorial, explaining why it did not run the Hyde story:

> After hours of crack-fueled discussion and extended consultation with our seven or eight sex columnists, we decided not to publish it. We feel that we owe you, our readers, an explanation of why we took this extraordinary step.
>
> Experience has taught us that the favorite ploy of those who want to discredit our reporting is to accuse us of being a "pawn of the Freemasons," "an ace in the hole for the Elders of Zion," and "a monopoly wheelbarrow for the International Potash Cartel." These organizations had nothing whatsoever to do with any aspect of this story.
>
> What was our motivation? In a different and better world, we would have released this story. Throughout the tragic farce of the Clinton-Lewinsky scandal, we have tirelessly searched our thesaurus for new ways to say "hummer." But in the brave new world that has been created by Idiotgate, there are some things the public does *not* need to know. Our critics will say we are fighting fire with pee, ascending to the ivory tower standards of those we deplore. Frankly, we are. But ugly times call for ugly tactics. When a pack of sanctimonious thugs bores you and your country with details of an affair where barely anybody got off, you have to show them that you can be a wicked little cocktease, too. (from *Suck*'s Web site)

More seriously, the Hyde story was so good that even *Salon*'s archrival, *Slate*, chided *The New York Times* for reporting the story and failing to sufficiently acknowledge *Salon*. Despite their differences, *Salon* and *Slate* shared a common interest in promoting zines. *The Times* was among several leading news organizations that were offered the Hyde story, but its editors decided not to carry the story for ethical reasons. In the brave new world of online journalism, after *Salon* went public with the story, the editors of *The Times* and other news media believed the story was now public knowledge and legitimate news. This was a case where an exclusive was declined. *The Times* did not want to be first with this seedy story, but it was willing to report the story after other news media ran it.

The journalistic practice of crediting online media with first breaking a news story became an ethical issue during the 2000 presidential campaign. *The New York Times* and *The Washington Post* carried stories that Republican presidential candidate George W. Bush had ignored the murder confession of a Texas inmate. Because of Bush's decision, two innocent men accused of the crime languished behind bars longer than needed. *Salon* carried the story first (Fost, 2000), but neither *The Times* nor *The Post* mentioned *Salon* in their stories. Both newspapers claimed they were already working on the story before *Salon* published its version, and therefore *Salon* did not deserve credit. The incident underscored how important *Salon* viewed favorable publicity that it was the original source of a major news story; all media desire such favorable publicity, but a relatively unknown online news organization would especially prize acknowledgments from prestigious newspapers as the source of exclusive news. It was interesting that *The Times* and *The Post* credited *Salon* as the original source of the seedy Hyde story, even though the newspapers knew about the Hyde story in advance (albeit they did not plan to publish the story). In the case of the Hyde story, crediting *Salon* was not so much a tip of the hat to *Salon*'s enterprise journalism as an excuse for carrying a story that they would not have otherwise run despite their knowledge of it.

The *Times*' Jim Yardley said he did not read the *Salon* piece about the Bush story. *Post* reporter Paul Duggan, the newspaper's Austin bureau chief, said that when he read *Salon's* article, "after five days of reporting, I had much more information in my notebook than the *Salon* story contained." The newspapers received complaints from *Salon*. In an e-mail to *Salon* News Editor Joan Walsh, Duggan wrote, "In this case, *Salon* or no *Salon*, my story would be in [Tuesday's] *Post*. For Walsh et. al to accuse me of an ethical breach suggests either no thought at all on *Salon*'s part, or a calculated cry for attention" (Fost, 2000, p. B1).

The Bush story represented yet another example of the problems that the brave new world of online news will have to confront. Online news services have no fixed deadlines; they could potentially put their notes or announcements of any ongoing news online. Must another news organization that runs a much fuller story than these notes then acknowledge the online news site's post? If every earlier mention must be acknowledged, would that stifle in-depth reporting, whereby news organizations release what little information they have to be first with news stories rather than developing stories in greater depth? Worse yet, might it lead to news organizations running undeveloped stories, or even rumors, without fully checking the stories' veracity?

There are other rare instances of online news exclusives, although few as important as *Salon*'s Hyde story. In 1999, a specialized online news site reported an exclusive based on government documents obtained through the Freedom of Information Act. The site, APBnews.com, then a year-old online service devoted to "crime, justice and public safety," reported new information on a sensational 1954 murder trial that was the O. J. Simpson criminal case of its day. APBnews reported that the FBI compiled a file on Cleveland Dr. Sam Sheppard, accused of murdering his wife, which it shared with prosecutors but not defense attorneys in the case. Sheppard was found guilty in 1954 and served 10 years in prison. He was acquitted in a 1966 retrial. In recent years, Sheppard's heirs have sought to have the state of Ohio declare Sheppard's innocence and sue the state for wrongful imprisonment (Ewinger, 1999). This case represents an excellent example of investigative reporting relying on public records to report an online exclusive.

A CONVENTIONAL ZINE

Other zines followed *Salon*, but *Salon* had established itself as the leader. The zines were not making a profit, but they predicted that profits would come soon. Microsoft Corporation, with a close eye on Web trends and a hunger to be ahead of the curve, launched a zine in a big way. Microsoft founder Bill Gates hired former *New Republic* editor Michael Kinsley to head the zine called *Slate*, launched on June 24, 1996. Kinsley resigned in February 2002. *Slate* stirred controversy even before its launch because of Kinsley's stated conventional approach to an unconventional news medium. Just as *USA Today* stirred controversy in the newspaper industry when it was introduced in the early 1980s as a bold, brash, breezy, and colorful publication at a time when most newspapers were serious, somber, and black and white, *Slate* was conventional where unconventionality was the norm. Kinsley promised "serious conventional journalism for people who are not cyberfreaks" (from *Slate*'s Web site). Other zines resented Kinsley and Gates's relatively late entry into their turf, after—as they saw it—they had laid the groundwork.

The question of whether online journalism requires a new journalism distinguishes the leading zines—*Salon* and *Slate*. Although it is difficult to compare online publications to anything in print, for the most part *Salon*'s Talbot opted for the cyberequivalent of short, breezy stories with colorful graphics. The tone, however, is decidedly brash and sometimes cheeky, and it does not shy away from sex. *Salon* devotes an entire section to what it describes as a mature approach to sex.[7] By contrast, *Slate*'s Kinsley advocated a more traditional tone with lofty thought pieces like in his *New Republic* days. In essence, he called for an electronic journal of opinion and commentary. Such comparisons are strained, and neither zine holds a monopoly on audacity or quality. *Salon*, for example, is rife with commentary. Over the years, Kinsley has conceded that the online medium is not suitable for the longer pieces that appear in *The New York Times Magazine* or the *New Yorker* that he saw as models (Stein, 1999). However, the editors' comments represent the journalistic philosophies of their founders. A month before *Slate*'s debut, Kinsley (1996) explained his philosophy of the new online journalism. His view was this: It was not much different from the old journalism in content, even if he reluctantly conceded that online stories must be shorter. Kinsley dismissed the view that the new medium required a new form of journalism:

> Yes, we'll have bulletin boards and discussion groups. Why not? But *Slate* will mainly consist of articles selected and presented in the traditional us-to-you manner. And while we will have a smattering of multimedia and interactivity and hyperlinks, many of those articles will take the familiar form of words combined into sentences merged into paragraphs—lots of paragraphs.
> . . . So why bother starting a magazine in cyberspace? One reason is economic: no costs for paper, printing, or postage. This alone has the potential to make

---

[7]Talbot is also the author of *Burning Desires: Sex in America*.

cyberspace a more democratic medium, and one goal of *Slate* is to demonstrate how the new technology can make serious journalism more easily self-supporting. (Kinsley, 1996, p. T15)

Soon after *Slate* was on the Web, other zines severely criticized Microsoft's entry into online news. It was natural for competitors to slam the competition, but with *Slate* the criticisms were particularly scathing because of animosity toward Microsoft and Gates and what the competition saw as Kinsley's haughty aspirations to quality journalism and his depiction of most Web users as "cyberfreaks."

From *Salon*: "To anyone who has spent much time on the Web over the last couple of years, it sounds as though Kinsley might be reinventing the wheel" (Kurtz, 1996, p. B1).

From *Feed*: "Kinsley's ideas are derivative ones—even more so with a company, like Microsoft, that has a long history of recycling other people's innovations" (Kurtz, 1996, p. B1).

From *Hot Wired*: "The selling of Kinsley . . . is a textbook case of how a company like Microsoft can buy its way into the journalism business and manipulate the so-called serious press to help it make over its corporate image" (Kurtz, 1996, p. B1).

Although conventional in content, from the beginning *Slate* planned to distribute its online content in an unconventional manner. Initially, *Slate* considered but quickly dropped plans to charge an annual fee for accessing the zine. "The market itself is not that big," Kinsley said from Microsoft's Redmond, Washington, headquarters. "You forget, working out here—most of the country is not on the Web yet" (Kurtz, 1997, p. C1). In time, however, when more of the country was wired, Kinsley made clear that *Slate* intended to resurrect its controversial plan for a subscription fee. As early as June 26, 1996, Kinsley told his readers, "We believe that expecting readers to share the cost, as they do in print, is the only way serious journalism on the Web can be self-supporting. Depending completely on advertisers would not be healthy even if it were possible" (from *Slate*'s Web site).

For Kinsley, the time to launch paid subscriptions came in March 1998, when some 20 to 25 million Americans were online. *Slate* introduced a $19.95 annual subscription. The decision to charge was long debated in industry circles. None of the zines was making a profit by relying on advertising alone. Online newspapers, in their formative years during the early and mid-1990s, experimented with online fees, but the trend was to drop them in favor of "free" advertising-supported content. The question facing *Slate* was this: Would Web users pay for a product that many users, as a matter of principle, believed should be free? Apparently not. In February 1999, *Slate* ended its yearlong experiment with a subscription fee. When it made this decision, it had only 25,000 to 30,000 paid subscribers, not enough to support the outlet and attract advertisers. "We never claimed to have found the one true path," Kinsley wrote in his "Readme" column of the decision to ditch paid subscriptions. "We tried one thing, now we're trying something else, and we'll keep trying until we figure it out" (Greene, 1999, p. D1).

ECONOMIC DOWN TIMES

In 2000, most general-interest online news outlets were not profitable, nor were any zines (Kurtz, 2001b). Both Talbot and Kinsley fought for bragging rights, debating which zine was better. When Talbot was quoted as saying "We have left them [*Slate*] in the dust," Kinsley responded that this was partly true—"*Salon* certainly has left *Slate* in the dust in terms of losing money" (from *Slate*'s Web site). However, all that Kinsley could argue in his favor was that *Slate* was losing less money than *Salon*. Even the mighty Bill Gates of Microsoft could not find a formula to make online news profitable.

Kinsley acknowledged *to Washington Post* media critic Howard Kurtz (2001b) that expectations were too high for online journalism:

Certainly the novelty has worn off. The news cycle makes it inevitable that "X is a big deal" is going to be followed by "X is a snooze." Five years is a pretty long run before you get to that. The mere fact that you're on the Internet is no longer anything for which you get cool points. We're part of the media landscape. (p. C1)

Indeed, *Salon*, *Feed*, and *Suck* started in 1995; *Slate* and *Word* started in 1996.

By 2000 and 2001, *Salon* was no longer giddy about a new form of independent online journalism that would compete against traditional news media outlets. *Salon* was still losing money even while garnering journalistic praise, receiving two Online Journalism Awards in 2000, including one for exposing how the television networks exploited a White House program to receive government favors for surreptitiously inserting antidrug messages into their programs.[8] *Salon* reported that the networks permitted the White House drug czar's office to review their prime-time scripts. If a show promoted an antidrug message, the networks would not have to air some public service announcements, allowing them to sell the time to advertisers (Lowry, 2000). Editorial success aside, many media pundits declared the deathwatch of *Salon*.

Salon was also a subject of controversy, hiring journalist Dan Savage to pose as a volunteer in conservative presidential candidate Gary Bauer's Iowa campaign during the 2000 election. Savage so detested Bauer's antigay policies that, when he had the flu, he wrote about how he licked doorknobs, pens, coffee cups, and office equipment to infect Bauer and other antigay workers in Bauer's office. Some readers were angered, but many chuckled at what they regarded as a tongue-in-cheek story:

---

[8]In addition to winning the award in the enterprise journalism category for the antidrug story, *Salon* also won in the category for general excellence.

Naked, feverish and higher than a kite on codeine aspirin, I called the Bauer campaign and volunteered. My plan? Get close enough to Bauer to give him the flu, which, if I am successful, will lay him flat just before the New Hampshire primary. I would go to Bauer's campaign office and cough on everything—phones and pens, staplers and staffers. I even hatched a plan to infect the candidate himself. I would keep the pen in my mouth until Bauer dropped by his offices to rally the troops. And when he did, I would approach him and ask for his autograph, handing him the pen from my flu-virus incubating mouth. (from *Salon*'s Web site)

Editor Talbot defended Savage's story as "very Hunter Thompson like" and fitting *Salon*'s unconventional appeal. "It was gonzo-style with an outrageous social point—that gays are fair game for whatever conservative political figure wants to beat up on them" (Farhi, 2001, p. 39).

However, the praise and controversy did not translate into profits. With its stock plummeting, the advertising market drying up, and the embarrassment of layoffs and wage cuts, *Salon* was frantically trying to survive. Advertising revenue was covering less than half its expenses; it had lost a staggering $68 million since its inception in 1995. *Salon* did what it once chastised its archrival, *Slate*, for doing—charging for access to its most important staff-written content. In May 2001, *Salon* introduced a $30-a-year "premium" version that allowed privileged readers to access special columns. *Salon* described its new site: "Salon Premium is a subscription service of *Salon.com* offering additional exclusive features and special 'Premium-only' content to Salon readers who pay an annual fee. Salon Premium helps support *Salon.com*'s unique brand of independent journalism" (from *Salon*'s Web site). To critics, the statement seemed similar to the remarks of *Salon*'s nemesis, Kinsley, several years earlier.[9]

Some readers signed up for the premium service, but many responded with angry e-mails. *Slate*'s Kinsley did not hide his glee at his rival's dire condition. "We're only human, and they were incredibly snotty about us, so it's hard not to feel some schadenfreude," Kinsley said. "*Salon* is cheap and sensationalistic. But the main reason they're in trouble is they spent too much" (della Cava, 2001, p. 1D).

ZIPPERGATE

In mid-January 1998, online gadfly journalist Matt Drudge, who fancied himself a modern-day Thomas Paine and Walter Winchell rolled into one, reported a scoop that would have political reverberations that threatened to topple a president. His story in his online newsletter, the *Drudge Report*, exposed President Clinton's sexual affair with White House intern Monica Lewinsky. *Newsweek* had done all the

---

[9]The practice of offering free online service for general coverage and charging for special stories or features or services without advertising represents a testable economic model for online news sites. To some extent, *The New York Times* does this by charging for archived stories—a valuable service for anyone doing research.

background research and was preparing to expose the story. Drudge found out about *Newsweek*'s coming scoop and reported it before the news magazine. The story that came to be known as "Zippergate" raised ethical problems, and it was a shabby way to introduce original online news to much of the public. It left the impression to many unfamiliar with online news that the medium was a source of tabloid trash and gossip. Say what you will of Drudge, though; the story affected public opinion and public policy—almost to the point of impeaching a president. Agence France Presse identified Zippergate as one of the 10 key dates in the media during the 20th century (Grossman, 1998). The story showed that an online news outlet could be a potent social force by putting a major issue on the public agenda.

It was ironic that Drudge's Zippergate scoop was based on the work of another magazine. To Drudge (2002), the news was *Newsweek*'s failure to immediately report the story, which he insinuated was attributable to the liberal press. Does a small online operation with limited resources such as the *Drudge Report* offer a model for online news success? Drudge, like Walter Winchell before him, exploited his connections to report rumors and gossip. In Washington, a connected insider is privy to cocktail circuit rumors and stories by sources with axes to grind.[10] Despite hard economic times in online news, Drudge's Web site is popular and, he says, financially successful. How successful? On the CNN program *Crossfire*, Drudge (2002) said his Web site earns him "nearly seven figures" annually after minimal operating costs. "It can be lucrative," he added. "This whole notion that the Internet is a dud is ridiculous. Otherwise, we all wouldn't have Web sites."

Not only Washington politics, but Hollywood politics, too, are bandied about on Drudge's site. In 2002, Drudge's Web site was a source of many behind-the-scenes criticisms directed against the Academy-Award-winning film *A Beautiful Mind*. Unattributed sources—some claimed representatives from competing studios—launched what some regarded as a smear campaign against the sentimental film based on a true story. The sources claimed the film overlooked the main character's adultery and anti-Semitism. The criticisms were not new and not false. Many film critics publicly made many of the same criticisms when the film was originally released several months earlier. The difference this time was that the criticisms were alleged to be an organized and covert campaign just before the awards aimed at wrecking the film's Oscar chances.[11] The film won the Academy Award for Best Picture.

---

[10]Likewise, many journalists know about the private lives of political figures, but they will not or cannot publish the stories for fear of losing their sources or because their publications will not report politicians' private lives. These journalists sometimes feed these stories to Drudge, and once disseminated by Drudge the journalists then claim the story is common knowledge and they then follow up on Drudge's stories with more information.

[11]On the eve of the awards, Drudge's site featured a story about the film's star, Russell Crowe, that depicted him as out of control. A story with the headline "Wild Man Crowe Did This to Me, Says Fan," alleged that Crowe bit into a fan's neck and surveillance video showed Crowe "kicking at a bouncer, spitting in a pub landlord's face and slamming his own brother's face first into a car."

Regarding Zippergate, Drudge's initial report about the sexual affair did not receive much attention, but the January 17 post made its way to various Internet news groups. Within a few days, the story was in major newspapers and on network news reports. From there, it became the subject of continuous coverage on outlets such as CNN and MSNBC.

Zippergate was a defining moment for online journalism, for both better and worse. On the positive side, the incident showed that even a small online media player could influence public opinion and public policy. To some, it seemed that no longer would a relatively small, elite group of media organizations set the news agenda for the public. On the negative side, the same positive was a negative. The incident augured the breakdown, or at least the erosion, of traditional media gatekeeping processes. Once one media outlet, no matter how small or obscure, exposed a juicy story, the story became "public" and fair game for all to report.

Stories rushed to publication without scrutiny are often erroneous. In this case, Drudge got his facts right (or at least *Newsweek* did). However, before the Lewinsky revelations, Drudge's previous moment of notoriety was for incorrectly reporting that Clinton White House aide Sidney Blumenthal was a "spousal abuser." Because of the false report, Blumenthal filed a lawsuit against Drudge and AOL, which carried Drudge's report at the time (Kurtz, 2001a). The suit, brought in 1997, was settled in early 2001, when Drudge retracted the story. Interestingly, AOL could not be sued because of a provision of the 1996 Telecommunications Act that states that "no provider or user of an interactive computer service shall be treated as the publisher or speaker of any information provided by another information-content provider." Based on this provision, AOL successfully argued that its service is comparable to that of a newsstand, not a publisher, and hence it was immune from libel prosecution.

Newsweek senior writer Michael Isikoff was checking the veracity of the Lewinsky story when Drudge learned of Isikoff's story and reported it. To conservatives, *Newsweek*'s decision to hold the story confirmed their beliefs about the liberal media. *Newsweek* editor Peter McGrath said the magazine did not run the story because it was still checking facts. "What bothered Drudge was that we [held] information on someone he didn't like," McGrath said. "Holding a story for a week isn't the same as killing it" (Deggans, 1998, p. 4A).

Before the year was over, Drudge's report would lead to Republican efforts to impeach Clinton. The Web was initially clogged as millions of users scrambled to download independent counsel Kenneth Starr's report on Congressional sites (Miller, 1998). At the time of Zippergate, the United States had approximately 23 million wired households and it seemed all of them wanted Starr's report at once. Starr's decision to post the report online gave citizens direct access to the source of news that, in the past, journalist gatekeepers would have culled through and decided which parts were newsworthy. This report, in particular, raised questions about newsworthiness and about taste because it had explicit descriptions of sex.

The *Chicago Tribune* generally avoided the phrase "oral sex." The *Christian Science Monitor* referred to semen as "residue." Meanwhile, critics of Internet regulation pointed out that the report's explicit sexual descriptions might have been banned from the Internet if the Communications Decency Act (CDA) that many Republicans supported had not been overturned in court (Scott, 1998). Users could even search for the salacious terms by keyword search subprograms.

Many critics viewed Starr's posting as a Republican ploy to embarrass and maybe unseat the president they intensely disliked—to, in effect, nullify the 1996 election. "I think this is being used by Republicans to spam the country before the president could even respond in an informed way," said *Salon*'s David Talbot, whom many conservatives pegged as a Clinton crony (Miller, 1998). The White House's online response to the report was not as widely circulated as the Starr report (Miller, 1998). Starr's decision to release the report also concerned the Clinton White House, which saw the dissemination of Drudge's story in the mainstream news media as fulfilling its prediction in a controversial 1995, 331-page report, *The Communication Stream of Conspiracy Commerce* (Miller, 1998). The report stated "the right wing has seized upon the Internet as a means of communicating its ideas to people" (Miller, 1998).

The Clinton presidency was tailor-made for conspiracy stories on the World Wide Web. *The Communication Stream of Conspiracy Commerce* report, the existence of which was acknowledged by the White House in 1997, alleged a right-wing conspiracy to smear President Clinton and his administration with Whitewater stories, the suicide of former White House Deputy Counsel Vincent W. Foster, Jr., and other sordid allegations.[12] Bennahum (1997), then the author of a forthcoming book on cyberspace, commented on the report in *The New York Times*:

> Such stories, of course, do not reflect a fine-tuned Republican conspiracy. Rather, they are symptomatic of an electronic "journalism," where clear authorship and editorial perspective are giving way to an era of multiple authors and collective, self-organized publishing. These sorts of on-line sites and discussion groups don't have mastheads to provide a signature of credibility. (p. A23)

In the White House's view, Drudge was a crony of the radical right. It was the Republicans' turn to cry foul and "liberal media bias" when *Salon* reported Hyde's "youthful indiscretion" during the Republican efforts to impeach Clinton.

For a time, Drudge's feat put online news on par with elite media of opinion. He had briefly succeeded in having online news influence public opinion and public policy, and he earned the authority to comment on politics and public af-

---

[12]In acknowledging the existence of the report, White House Press Secretary Michael D. McCurry said the purpose of the report, parts of which were shared with sympathetic journalists, was to "help journalists understand that they shouldn't be used by those who are really concocting their own conspiracies and their own theories" (Mitchell, 1997, p. A19).

fairs. Drudge became a media phenomenon. He appeared on respectable talk programs, such as *Meet the Press*. He spoke before the National Press Club, lauding the coming age as "an era vibrating with the din of small voices . . . a future where there'll be 300 million reporters, where anyone from anywhere can report for any reason" (Jurkowitz & Aucoin, 1999, p. A27).

Zippergate illustrated how quickly a sensational news story could spread from the political fringes to the mainstream media through the Web with little time for critical appraisal and for the victimized party to repair or at least respond to the news. Signs of the Web's ability to spread sensational news, both accurate and inaccurate, occurred earlier, before there were enough online users to make the impact of Zippergate. For example, minutes after a Los Angeles jury acquitted O. J. Simpson of murder, two of the biggest online news services declared Simpson guilty. Time Warner's now-defunct Pathfinder published the erroneous story.[13] The story also appeared on CNN Interactive, which had arranged to share Pathfinder's stories. The story was on the Web for only a few minutes before Pathfinder's editors caught the error and removed it. However, during the short time the story was up a user copied the image and sent it on the Internet. It was picked up by Delphi, a service owned by Rupert Murdoch's News Corp. Happy to disparage a competitor, Delphi reported the story under the headline, "A Pathfinder Loses Its Way" (Wilson, 1995).

The Oklahoma City bombing in 1995 provided an opportunity for the mainstream news media to be taken in by cyberhoaxes. It forewarned of the dangers of a future in which every person could be a journalist. Some news media, including *Newsday, USA Today,* and *The Dallas Morning News,* cited an inflammatory April 20 message about the bombing posted on what was said to be a militia group Web site. A journalism student at the University of Montana created the false site. Two days later, a user profile attributed to Oklahoma City bomber Timothy McVeigh—describing himself as the "Mad Bomber"—appeared on AOL. The British news service Reuters, among others, briefly picked up the story. That was enough for the story to spread like wildfire in Britain. "Hello. I'm the Mad Bomber—Boom!" the *Sunday Mirror* proclaimed. If reporters had checked the story, they would have discovered that the profile was created after McVeigh was arrested. AOL later distributed a press release stating that the profile was fictitious (Armstrong, 1995).[14]

In November 1996, the Web contributed to erroneous news stories about the crash of TWA Flight 800 in New York. Some news media reported the false story that the plane was downed by accidental "friendly fire" from a U.S. missile cruiser. Web message boards and chat rooms were rife with variations on the

---

[13]After spending more than $100 million on Pathfinder, in April 1999 Time Warner announced it was disbanding the financially failing service.

[14]In an attempt to stimulate internal criticism, in 2001 MSNBC.com became the first major online news service to employ an Internet news ombudsman (Garcia, 2001).

story.[15] At first, the missile story did not attract the mainstream news media. However, after former Kennedy White House Press Secretary Pierre Salinger publicly declared that he received documents from an unnamed French intelligence agent proving that a missile launched from a U.S. naval vessel accidentally downed the airplane, some news organizations carried the story because there was a credible source willing to be identified. Salinger later admitted he was wrong (Alter, 1997; Sancton, Shannon, & Zagorin, 1996).

Another story that was incorrect, at least in key aspects, was published in *Slate*. On June 8, 2001, *Slate* ran a piece on "monkey fishing" by local residents on a monkey-infested island in the Florida Keys, where a pharmaceutical company had released rhesus monkeys to breed. The author, Jay Forman, described how he had been part of an expedition using deep-sea fishing gear baited with apples and other fruits. Forman, a freelance writer who wrote a parody book titled *Chicken Pies for the Soul*, described the cruel method of expedition members "fishing" for monkeys: "The monkeys swarmed round the treat, and when the fisherman felt a strong tug he jerked the pole. I knew he had hooked one by the shriek it made—a primal yowl that set my hair on end. The monkey came flying from the trees, a juicy apple stapled to its palm" (from *Slate*'s Web site).

The *Wall Street Journal*'s online opinion page called the story "preposterous" and *The New York Times* later did some investigating. Among other sources, *The Times* contacted executives at the pharmaceutical company, local fishermen, and wildlife conservation officers and concluded that "the account itself appears to be a fairy tale" (Kuczynski, 2001, p. C1). *Slate* editors originally stood by the story. On June 25, however, editor Michael Kinsley claimed that the events described in the story did occur, but acknowledged that the story was "fiction in key aspects" and he apologized.[16]

Not all false stories on the Web are attributable to hoaxes. In June 1998, an erroneous Associated Press report of comedian Bob Hope's death set off a chain reaction of false stories through the news media. The AP's prewritten obituary had accidentally gone out over the Web. Many news organizations have obituaries of famous people ready so they do not have to clamor for facts to write the story under pressure. A sure sign that this was a prewritten story was the headline with *XX* in place of Hope's age to be filled in: "Bob Hope, Tireless Master of the One-

---

[15]There were many variations on the TWA flight 800 story. One version declared the plane was intentionally shot down to kill Henry Kissinger. Kissinger was not on the plane. Another version blamed the crash on a Russian "death ray." Other versions claimed the North Koreans and the Japanese religious cult Aum Shinrikyo operated the death ray. Another message blamed President Clinton for masterminding the crash, to stop former Arkansas state troopers from testifying about Clinton's sexual affairs.

[16]Kinsley claimed that even *The New York Times* article confirmed aspects of the story: "Despite suggestions by others that the entire episode was fiction, this excursion did take place. In fact, *The Times* story, by Alex Kuczynski, quotes the fisherman who took Forman and his friend on the trip. Contrary to allegations that no such practice ever existed, Kuczynski also confirms that monkey fishing occurred on other occasions before the one Forman describes" (from *Slate*'s Web site).

Liner, Dead at *XX.*" The AP quickly recognized the error and removed the story; but, as in the case of the O. J. Simpson story that had been picked up and spread while briefly on the Web, the Bob Hope story was picked up by other news media. In this case, an Arizona congressman was moved to eulogize Hope on the House floor. The eulogy had more to do with spreading the rumor that Hope, who was still very much alive at age 95, had died than did the AP story. Based on the Congressional eulogy, ABC News picked up the report and radio stations throughout the country spread the story. The nine phone lines rang incessantly at Hope's home in Toluca Lake, California, and Hope's daughter informed the press that her father was alive, having breakfast, and preparing to play golf. However, in the digital age it was hard to correct a false story that had been picked up and spread by so many news organizations (Rich, 1998). In April 2002, the Scripps Howard News Service made a similar error as the AP had with Hope's death, when it released a 12-page obituary of President Ronald Reagan. The story carried the imprint "Embargoed until Reagan's death." This story, however, was stopped before it spread through the news media.

THE SEPTEMBER 11, 2001, ATTACKS

To its credit, the mainstream news media are becoming more cynical about news tips traced to the Web. No major news organization picked up the ridiculous story that the 15th-century French spiritualist Nostradamus predicted the September 11, 2001, terrorist attacks on the World Trade Center and the Pentagon (Hardon, 2001). Nor did major news media pick up the bogus story that CNN footage of West Bank Palestinians celebrating the September 11 attack was old film video (Callahan, 2001).

During ordinary times, online users access news about the weather, science and health, and technology (a perennial favorite). The week after September 11, 2001, was no ordinary time, and online news sites became overwhelmed. Web news sites turned in a mixed performance during the aftermath of the attacks when people wanted raw information.[17] Minutes after American Airlines Flight 11 crashed into the World Trade Center's north tower at 8:45 a.m., millions of Americans, tried—most of them unsuccessfully at first—to log on to their favorite news sites.

The September 11 attacks showed that there was an audience for online national breaking news stories. Office workers, in particular, turned to the Web to learn about the major news story, indicating that online news could compete against their broadcast rivals in reporting real-time news. Office workers and others went online en masse, causing online traffic jams and crashing some

---

[17]Online news coverage of the Oklahoma City bombing presaged the ability of online newspapers to report breaking news (Cochran, 1995).

servers. However, after the first hour or two, most users could access news sites, and usage of news sites soared during the week after September 11. Online video news, in particular, enjoyed a surge of popularity in the aftermath of the attacks as stunned users wanted to see the planes striking the towers. Meanwhile, readers in the Arab world and many Americans could turn to the Qatar-based Al-Jazeera Web site for a uniquely Arab perspective on the attacks (Adams, 2001).

To their credit, to deal with the initial online logjam, a few popular news sites eliminated images and even advertisements to reduce the file sizes of page elements so that users could more easily and quickly access the sites. Sites such as CNN and the BBC stripped their front pages to a headline and added more servers, in addition to focusing the content to the attacks, but they still could not keep up with demand. *The New York Times'* NYTimes.com had a barren front page in stark black and white "except for the single story that mattered" (Palser, 2001, p. 50). NYTimes.com, which registers its users, also sent out e-mail alerts at 9 a.m., and more throughout the day, when its home page was inaccessible. It also sent out special alerts of local relevance to 200,000 Washington, DC, residents and to more than 1 million users in the New York City area.

The September 11 attacks also yielded original online news from the independent zine *Salon*. Based on an unnamed high-ranking news source, *Salon* reported that since America's success in eliminating Taliban and Al Qaeda terrorist forces in Afghanistan, American officials were meeting with senior exiled Iraqi military officials in Washington about arranging a possible successor to Iraq's President Saddam Hussein. The source described the meeting as "the first ever gathering of so many former Iraqi officers under one roof in Washington" (Allen-Mills, 2001, p. 1).

Following September 11, Americans turned to the Internet to learn about events in the Afghanistan and Iraq wars (Sorkin, 2003). During the war in Iraq, a Pew Internet & American Life project poll reported that 77% of Americans online used the Internet to monitor the short war. Most used it to keep up with the latest war events, but others used it to send prayers and to find alternative non-American and even Arab views of the fighting. Some, for instance, wanted information about Iraqi civilian deaths—something rarely reported in the American news media. Then there were those who just wanted to know what people in other nations thought about the war. Thanks to engines that translate non-English Web pages into English, Americans could read the op-ed pages in France and Germany. Perhaps a sign of early adopters, 4% of respondents in the Pew poll accessed online journals or diaries about the war, or so-called warblogs. Could this be a harbinger of future use of Internet news during major events?[18] Two

---

[18]Blogs are controversial because they are often untrue. They are uncensored and free for everyone to use. This may make them appear a desirable new outlet for news. However, blogs lack the checking for good journalism and are often regarded as personal views, rants, and responses.

thirds of the Pew poll respondents said the primary reason they went online was to get a variety of news sources; yet, ironically, most went to mainstream television and newspaper sites. Major events such as September 11, the war in Afghanistan, and the war in Iraq cause online news use to spurt. Although use declines after the event, it does not decline to previous levels. Many attracted to online news during the big event become addicted and regular users.

CONCLUSIONS

Online news is here to stay, but can it ever become a significant editorial force in its own right? Online news has extended the reach of news, making once difficult-to-obtain news accessible to many users. Online news has also made some strides in content during the last half-decade. Some news sites operated by print and broadcast outlets have added additional content not available in their offline stories. Increasingly, people are turning to online news sites to follow breaking news stories. In other words, online news is becoming an important news source for many Americans. With this greater reach comes the responsibility for online sites to report original news and contribute to the marketplace of ideas.

We also must acknowledge the multimedia advantages of online news, with audio and video and the ability to access related information and news stories. These medium characteristics may have consequences for how news is processed. However, contrary to media theorist Marshall McLuhan's assertion that the medium is the message and an extension of the human senses, content most definitely matters as far as news is concerned. Ultimately, online news organizations must provide original and important content that affects people's lives if they are to be taken seriously, have a social impact, and become prestigious news sources in their own right. Although many users turn to online news for news snippets—sports scores, stock quotes, weather reports, and so forth—online news has greater potential. Independent sites such as *Salon* and *Slate* show that there is an audience for in-depth, original online news.[19] Indeed, as this chapter has shown,

---

[19]This use of online news in passing snippets has led some researchers to suggest that online news use involves a good deal of incidental new exposure, from those attracted to news appeals while in search engine sites or logged on to their ISPs. Recently, communication scholars Tewksbury, Weaver, and Maddox (2001) investigated whether incidental news exposure on the Web contributes to an informed public. As they explained the rationale for their research:

Newsgathering has typically been seen as a purposeful, directed activity. Reading newspapers, listening to news on the radio, and watching television news programs are normally seen as the result of conscious choices. In the traditional media, news is relatively segregated from other content. Audiences can quite easily turn on the television, for example, without coming across news stories. In contrast, many of the most popular sites on the World Wide Web have integrated quite diverse areas of content on centralized services and pages. The Web may be unique in its ability to provide a typical user with an array of information choices that extend far be-

Salon, despite its relatively limited resources, has managed to acquire journalistic prestige through a number of scoops and to contribute to public understanding and social discourse about issues. There is no reason print and broadcast news organizations cannot make similar use of their online news sites. The organizations might give the sites names different from the main organizations to help distinguish them. Unfortunately, the zines have not succeeded financially, scraping to get by, and for this reason they may serve to discourage the development of sites with original online news.

In addition, portal sites such as search engines and ISPs might acquire reputations for news by hiring news staffs and reporting original news in addition to their usual fare of wire service news and links to established news sites. The subscriber who pays a monthly service fee to AOL or MSN might find value in AOL or MSN news exclusives to justify their monthly payments. In particular, technology-oriented subscribers to these sites may value exclusives about technology news, suggesting the need for ISPs to assign reporters to technology "beats." Similarly, search engines such as Yahoo! might attract people to their sites with original online news.

Online news has a long way to go if it plans to become a significant force in shaping public opinion and public policy. Drudge's report about Zippergate, no matter how seedy the story, had a major effect on public policy, and perhaps history. Drudge's story showed that online news could affect political discourse, even if not in the most constructive way. However, most online news media sites have not had significant impact. To his credit, Michael Kinsley, former editor of the *New Republic*, with mixed success, devoted his editorship at *Slate* (until his resignation in February 2002) to turning the zine into the online equivalent of the intellectual *New Republic*. Established news organizations would have an edge in starting the first prestigious online news sites, and those early in this endeavor would have a headstart.

Instead of becoming sources of news exclusives, another option for online news sites is to take advantage of their immediacy and compete against all-news cable television networks with real-time news. To some extent, they have already done this. The September 11, 2001, terrorist attacks showed that online news

---

yond what he or she intentionally seeks. News headlines are an almost constant feature of the most frequently visited sites on the Web, and there is some evidence that people encounter current affairs information when they had not been actively seeking it. Encounters of this sort may be called incidental exposure, and this may be an important contemporary avenue for citizen acquisition of current affairs information. (pp. 533–534)

Tewksbury and his colleagues (2001) used survey data from 1996 and 1998 to examine whether incidental news exposure was associated with current affairs knowledge. They found partial support for their hypothesis. In 1998, people who went online more often reported more incidental news exposure, and incidental news exposure was associated with greater current affairs knowledge. The researchers suggested that their failure to support the hypothesis in 1996 might have been attributable to changes in both the Internet audience and the online environment during the two periods.

could serve this function. Indeed, online news sites have an advantage over all-news cable television networks in that users do not have to passively wait for stories to unfold. They use different icons to access specific aspects of the breaking stories.

What little influence online news has had so far in affecting policy and influencing public opinion has been among independent online sites, taking editorial stands, establishing unique identities, and exposing occasional exclusive stories. For online news sites, the exclusive story—although rare—is necessary publicity for the online news organizations as well as the entire online news industry. *Salon*'s exclusive report of U.S. Representative Henry Hyde's "youthful indiscretion" helped make a large segment of the public aware of online news independents. In an award-winning investigative report, *Salon* reported that the television networks surreptitiously inserted antidrug messages into their scripts to win White House favors. The cases of *Salon* and *Slate* underscore the value of editorial independence. They are not online clones of print or broadcast media, nor are they restrained by a subservient role to any parent media organizations.

What might online news' significant impact involve? This chapter has focused on online news in the United States. However, a recent case in India, a democratic country with a free press rife with sensational newspapers, shows that online journalism has the potential to seriously influence policy and correct social problems. In March 2001, India's then 2-year-old online news outlet *Tehelka* (which means *sensation* in Hindi) reported a bribery scandal that resulted in the forced resignation of the defense minister and other government and military officials. *Tehelka* spent $40,000 over 8 months (a large sum for an investigative project in India) to have its dot-com journalists posing as defense contractors distribute bribes to senior Indian politicians and army officers in exchange for government contracts. It was all captured on videotape and later shown on television. Although the undercover journalistic deceit might raise eyebrows in the United States, Indians were not concerned about journalism ethics. India has a history of bribery scandals exposed in the press being dismissed by the courts. The irrefutable evidence captured on film caused a sensation. "This is a proud moment for Indian journalism," said Aroon Purie, editor-in-chief of the leading newsweekly magazine, *India Today*. "The basic purpose of journalism is to hold a mirror to society, however ugly the sight. That's what *Tehelka.com's* intrepid team has done" (Bahadur Kremmer, 2001, p. 6).

Most print and broadcast organizations view their online sites as supplements to their primary news products, even if there is some evidence that this situation is gradually changing. As supplements, the organizations see the job of their online news sites to whet interest in news so the public will turn to the offline sites to learn more. This may assure the existence of online news sites, but without original news and exclusive stories it does not bode well for their future. They will exist only as supplementary news sources so long as news organizations are unwilling to report online exclusives and investigative reports and grant their online news sites editorial independence. For those who care about journalism as a public service, rather than solely an economic enterprise, this is a sad fate. The only way for these online news sites to establish reputations and become recognized as vibrant news media in their own right, with original news, is for them to find a means of economic independence. With financial independence, they could hire news staffs and invest resources in correspondents and investigative reports.

It is enlightening to consider parallels as to how, in the early and mid-1930s, the young medium of radio became a major source of original news. At first, newspapers, through their powerful American Newspaper Publishers Association (now the Newspaper Association of America), used their collective power to press the leading wire services not to supply radio networks with news. The newspapers saw the radio networks as competition. CBS and NBC responded by hiring news staffs and establishing news bureaus. World War II stimulated their interest in obtaining original war news. Could online news services use a similar model, hiring news staffs and competing against conventional news media? Could they apply a different financial model, charging by daily usage rather than the tried models of subscriptions and the "free" advertising-supported model? Have market conditions changed such in recent years that they should consider reviving the failed subscription model? Could they focus on types of news, such as sports or business, that would attract interested readers and specialized advertisers willing to pay premium rates?

A successful working model of economic independence remains elusive. The rash of closings and cutbacks in online news (and the entire online industry) since 2000 do not augur well for online journalism's financial and editorial success. The news sites never appreciated the sizable costs involved in starting up and maintaining operations. Many sites are holding on during troubled times, despite their losses, hoping the audience for online news will grow and the appealing demographics of a larger online news audience will attract enough advertisers to sustain online news organizations' operations. Although the search for a viable economic model remains the first task, online news Web sites must also wrestle with other problems, such as finding ways to verify information in the time-pressed process to report the online news.

Convergence to the Web Is No Longer Just the Future
Bruce Garrison

The late MIT political scientist Ithiel de Sola Pool used the phrase "convergence of modes" in his book *Technologies of Freedom* in 1983. He was discussing the inevitable collapse of boundaries between delivery systems such as broadcasting, print, and common carriers.

He is probably smiling now.

Much has been said and written about media convergence in the past two decades. Countless panel discussions have taken place at conferences that focus on the Internet, the Web, the mass media, and journalism. Writers have addressed it in trade publications and popular media magazines.

Multimedia forms and media convergence have become much more common in the past decade. Convergence is now part of our mass media culture and language. It is very apparent on the Web. Convergence has moved rapidly from idea to usable product.

We frequently hear about new multimedia enterprises, such as Great Britain's Ananova, the real-time virtual newscaster (http://www.ananova.com) of the UK Press Association that debuted worldwide in April. We also see increased attention to video streaming of all sorts of content from newscasts to sports to movies.

Most serious Web sites—commercial, non-profit, government-military, educational, and otherwise—use some form of convergence that involves video, audio, group conferencing and individual forms of interactivity, or telephony. Convergence is also apparent in newer DVD media, in portable communication technologies such as cellular telephones and their growing Web applications, in motion picture production, and, of course, in just about any computer games.

Electronic mail, perhaps the most popular personal way of communicating on the Internet, has gone from its basic text form a decade ago to a multimedia format that is enhanced by colors, scalable fonts, embedded photographs, and attached audio-video clips.

With the introduction and widespread growth of the Internet and Web in the mid-1990s, convergence—that mixture of audio, video, graphics, interactivity, and print—gradually became a media content reality. The focus has been on the product itself and not the process or environment in which the multimedia end message is produced.

Convergence on the Web is also beginning to have a lasting impact on news and how news stories are told. Much has been written about how the non-linear nature of online story telling will change traditional journalism.

The truly hybrid nature of the Web has made it possible for traditional non-convergent news content such as newspapers, magazines, newsletters, radio, television, telephones, recorded music, movies, and other media to appear on the Web and in other forms such as CD or DVD.

Some forms of media convergence have only appeared in the past year or two, especially in mass markets. As media have converged and produced content reflecting the multimedia approaches taken (CNN Interactive, for example), convergence suddenly became one of the most important characteristics that made the Web different from other mass media.

Today there is a growing need to re-think and, perhaps, even re-organize the process and the location of individuals who produce content for these converging media. Originally, many new media were housed in their separate places, joined only in their final products. Even at large media corporations, it often meant separate buildings miles apart or separate buildings on the same corporate site. Creating a workspace for a Web production team and all that computer hardware was a problem that was not easily resolved.

This model has begun to change. As new facilities are created, new concepts in new media, multimedia, and media convergence are materializing. Designers are thinking about how media must work together in the new century. There is at least one good example of this approach in Florida.

Media General has developed a new facility in Tampa that should serve as an attention-getter for anyone involved in media, especially news. Media General is a large southeastern U.S. communications company that owns 21 dailies, 13 television stations, and more than 100 weeklies based in Richmond, VA (http://www.mediageneral.com).

With Media General's Tampa television, newspaper, and online companies, news media convergence was always a possibility. But it began for real in March. The complete operation includes the company's *Tampa Tribune* daily newspaper (http://www.tampatrib.com), WFLA-TV NewsChannel 8 NBC affiliate (http://wfla.com), and Tampa Bay Online (http://www.tbo.com) in the same News Center in downtown Tampa.

TBO is a Web portal site with a busy, but organized look. It includes news and numerous links for information. The site connects 15 "channels" of information. Among these are weather, sports, yellow pages, classifieds, careers, 8 On Your Side, beaches, money, entertainment, community, and health.

The Web site not only mixes content from the Tampa metropolitan daily newspaper and its sister television station, it also includes links to other TBO channels. These include *Hernando Today*, the Media General newspaper's Web site at http://www.hernandotoday.com that serves nearby Hernando County and Brooksville. It also includes the Web site for *Highlands Today*, the Media General newspaper that serves nearby Highlands, Hardee, and DeSoto counties at http://www.highlandstoday.com.

The News Center building is large and expensive—four floors, 120,000 square feet, and $30–$40 million—but it was designed to foster interaction and coordination among content developers and producers as well as, ultimately, a merger of the distribution means as well.

A circular multimedia assignment desk is the centerpiece. It is located on the second floor of a large two-story atrium area. Editors from the three news organizations sit and work together. Executives at the News Center like the design of one building and one goal of coordination.

The WFLA television production portion of the News Center is housed on the first floor. The television news staff is on the second floor. *The Tribune* and TBO.com staffs occupy the third floor. WFLA business operations are on the fourth floor.

According to one recent article in *The Tribune*, the News Center convergence has led to 10 additional positions for the three media, not a reduction. The final impact on positions and other news and content processes will not be known until the new construction dust settles there, of course.

However, the resulting convergence has already created other interesting needs. For example, still photographers must learn to shoot video; print reporters must become comfortable with appearing on television; television reporters will write print-oriented stories (instead of scripts) and generate other content for the online site. And, perhaps, someone will have to find additional time for the additional workloads.

"We're in this to serve our viewers and readers better," Deb Halpern, assistant news director at WFLA-TV stated in a recent *St. Petersburg Times* article about the new facility. "The three properties working together gives the journalism a greater reach."

Gil Thelen, executive editor of The Tampa Tribune, has written in his newspaper that Tampa area residents are broadening their use of media to find needed information. The converging News Center is an effort to catch up, he noted.

"A second factor is market competition and fragmenting audiences. Newspaper circulation is generally flat to down. Broadcast television news is experiencing a similar challenge as viewers scatter to a host of specialized cable sites such as MSNBC and CNN. Online news sites are also draining off readers and viewers," Thelen wrote in *The Tribune.*

"The multimedia efforts are designed to reaggregate the fragmented news audience to maintain Media General's news leadership in our community. We're betting that innovative, multimedia journalism will make business sense and will mean continued business success."

Perhaps college campuses can learn a lesson from the Tampa News Center experiment. As new facilities are imagined and developed, the plans should include interaction of traditional media for the future. Shared facilities, such as those for campus television and radio and newspapers and magazines, must be created to integrate with the online resources of Web sites.

Other cities are trying similar convergent multi-news media efforts, but they often are more promotional than anything else. And they certainly don't involve such a radical change as "living together" might require in addition to producing a common product.

Merger toward the Internet and the Web (or its next generation network form) is going to happen; it is just a matter of time. It might just be the broadband network we've been reading about in the past year.

Newer and high capacity forms of broadband communication are coming soon. Internet2 is under development. It and other new networks will offer a new form of broadband, the capability of transmission of multiple channels at the same time. With the increased capacity, the worldwide Internet network and its World Wide Web are given new and, perhaps, yet-to-be imagined potential.

Spend a little time visiting the CNN Interactive Web site (http://www.cnn.com) to see what some of the future for other news and media organizations might become. CNN has taken advantage of its own multimedia nature and integrated the Web with CNN's strengths in video and audio production. The result is a rather amazing mammoth Web site that provides a wide range of information sources for visitors. CNN Interactive is aiming at the next 20 years now that it has celebrated its first two decades on cable and satellite television systems.

Perhaps the irony in all this is that the media operations that will ultimately host the media are the smallest and require the least amount of space!... At least they are today. Compared to its older television side, CNN Interactive is tiny. And, similarly, the one room used by Tampa Bay Online is not much compared to the television and newspaper space . . . or the administrative space now in use.

We need to think about the impact of convergence on the media on our own campuses. Technology has changed how we deliver the news and other information. More changes are on the way. It's time to think about how and where we produce our media.

When new facilities are planned on campuses, the Media General News Center is a model worth considering. Not only should we think about housing student media in a single building—which is pretty common—we should consider the advantages and disadvantages of a single, shared work space. The technology, of course, does not require it. But high quality might.

Note. Originally published in *College Media Review*, Summer 2000, *38*(3), 28–30. Reprinted with permission of the author and editor.

REFERENCES

Adams, M. (2001, December 27). Seeking an Arab view of news; Alternatives: Many Arab-Americans and Muslims who don't trust U.S. press organizations go to Web sites and other news outlets to get a different perspective. *The Baltimore Sun*, p. 2A.

Allen-Mills, T. (2001, December 16). America plots overthrow of Saddam with Iraqi exiles. *The Times* (London), p. 1.

Alter, J. (1997, March 24). The age of conspiracism. *Newsweek*, *129*, p. 47.

Armstrong, D. (1995, September–October). Cyberhoax. *Columbia Journalism Review*, *34*, 12–13.

Bahadur Kremmer, J. (2001, March 27). India's new watchdogs bite back. *The Christian Science Monitor*, p. 6.

Bennahum, D. S. (1997, January 25). Techno-paranoia in the White House. *The New York Times*, p. A23.

Brendan, K. I. (2001, July–August). Click here for Britney! *The Washington Monthly*, *33*(7–8), 25–30.

Callahan, C. (2001, November). Anatomy of an urban legend. *American Journalism Review*, *23*(9), 46–48.

Christian, N. M. (2000, December 5). Columbia gives awards for journalism done online. *The New York Times*, p. 5B.

Cochran, W. (1995, June). A watershed event for online newspapers. *American Journalism Review*, *17*(6), 12–13.

Deggans, E. (1998, January 26). Clinton sex scandal. *St. Petersburg Times*, p. 4A.

della Cava, M. R. (2001, June 18). "Salon" does what it wants but what celebrated webzine needs is to survive wave of dot-com failures. *USA Today*, p. 1D.

Drudge, M. (2002, May 3). [Appearance on CNN's *Crossfire*].

Ewinger, J. (1999, November 17). File on Sheppard compiled by FBI posted on web. *Cleveland Plain Dealer*, p. 2B.

Farhi, P. (2001, March). Can Salon make it? *American Journalism Review, 23*(2), 36–40.

Feeney, M. K. (1998, September 18). Hyde story brings Internet magazine security. *The Hartford Courant*, p. A21.

Fost, D. (2000, October 19). Salon.com shows life with murder scoop; Also, male bastion Red Herring adds a woman's touch. *The San Francisco Chronicle*, p. B1.

Garcia, J. (2001, June). Online ombudsman. *American Journalism Review, 23*(6), 9.

Greene, J. (1999, February 12). Clean Slate: Webzine drops subscription fee. *The Seattle Times*, p. D1.

Grossman, L. K. (1998, July–August). From Marconi to Murrow to—Drudge? *Columbia Journalism Review, 38*(2), 17–18.

Hardon, A. (2001, September 23). The search for intelligent life on the Internet. *The New York Times*, Section 4, p. 2.

Heyboer, K. (2000, January–February). Going live. *American Journalism Review, 22*(1), 39–43.

Houston, F. (2001, July–August). AOL/TW spells big. *Columbia Journalism Review, 40*(13), 22–27.

Jurkowitz, M., & Aucoin, D. (1999, February 14). Questions still shadow scandal's impact. *The Boston Globe*, p. A27.

Kenworthy, T. (1997, March 2). The McVeigh story and its impact; Publication of alleged bomb admission may alter course of trial, journalism. *The Washington Post*, p. A7.

Kinsley, M. (1996, May 20). Dirt cheap and instant. *The Guardian* (London), p. T15.

Kuczynski, A. (2001, June 25). Tortured tale of journalism and monkeys. *The New York Times*, p. C1.

Kurtz, H. (1996, May 21). Housefly on the Web; Microsoft's precarious step into modem journalism. *Washington Post*, p. B1.

Kurtz, H. (1997, May 27). WWW.magazine; With giants' sights on their sites, little guys struggle to survive. *The Washington Post*, p. C1.

Kurtz, H. (1998, September 29). Bureau chief ousted over Hyde affair story; Disagreement rankles Salon editor. *The Washington Post*, p. D1.

Kurtz, H. (2001a, May 2). Clinton aide settles libel suit against Matt Drudge—at a cost. *The Washington Post*, p. C1.

Kurtz, H. (2001b, February 21). On its way out? Web sites struggle financially despite millions of visitors. *The Washington Post*, p. C1.

Lasica, J. C. (1998, June). Breakthrough on the Web. *American Journalism, 19*, 36.

Lowry, B. (2000, January 14). White House tie to anti-drug TV scripts criticized. *Los Angeles Times*, p. A1.

Marlatt, A. (1999, July 15). Advice to newspapers: Stop shoveling. Retrieved March 17, 2002, from http://www.iw.com/print/current/content/19990715-shoveling.html

Martin, S. A., & Hansen, K. N. (1996). Examining the "virtual" publication as a "newspaper of record." *Communication Law and Policy, 1*, 579–594.

Miller, G. (1998, September 12). The Starr Report; the Internet; Cyberspace's coming of age bittersweet for the faithful. *Los Angeles Times*, p. A1.

Mitchell, A. (1997, January 19). White House sees plotting behind unfavorable articles. *The New York Times*, p. A19.

Palser, B. (2001, November). Not so bad: The performance of online news sites on September 11 was better than the early reviews suggest. *American Journalism Review, 23*(9), 49–53.

Piller, C. (2000, December 11). The cutting edge: Focus on technology. Salon.com wins credibility online with intelligent and stylish content. *Los Angeles Times*, p. C1.

Rich, F. (1998, June 10). Journal; Bob Hope lives. *The New York Times*, p. A29.

Sancton, T., Shannon, E., & Zagorin, A. (1996, November 25). Shot in the dark? *Time, 148*, p. 44.

Scott, J. (1998, February 1). Scandal coverage crosses border of tabloid-land. *The New York Times*, p. A12.

Sorensen, E. (1998, April 8). News on the Web—The Internet gains with each big story. *The Seattle Times*, p. A2.

Sorkin, M. D. (2003, March 25). The war online; Away from TV, people turn to the web. *St. Louis Post-Dispatch*, p. A10.

Stein, N. (1999, January–February). Slate vs. Salon. *Columbia Journalism Review, 37*(5), 56–59.

Tewksbury, D., Weaver, A., & Maddox, B. D. (2001). Accidentally informed: Incidental news exposure on the World Wide Web. *Journalism & Mass Communication Quarterly, 78,* 533–554.

Thalhimer, M. (1994). High-tech news or just "shovelware?" *Media Studies Journal, 8,* 41–51.

Wilson, K. (1995, October 11). Murder, they (mistakenly) wrote. *Newsday*, p. A55.

CHAPTER THREE

Legal Issues in Online Journalism

Paul D. Driscoll

The foray by content providers into online distribution of news raises a myriad of legal and policy issues for both traditional news media outlets and a host of other news distributors. Although the application of First Amendment principles and tort rules to new technologies is not a novel issue, the newest communication medium, the Internet, presents an array of challenges to traditional communication law. This chapter begins with a discussion of media regulatory models that have evolved in response to the emergence of new communication technologies. It then examines how existing legal principles have been applied to the Internet in two areas critical to online news. First is the question of personal jurisdiction. Where in the world can news organizations and journalists be forced to defend themselves against lawsuits based on their online publications? The second issue discussed in the chapter is that of statutory immunity provided to interactive computer services for republishing on the Internet information provided by third parties.

MASS MEDIA REGULATORY MODELS

Each mode of expression has unique characteristics. Judges have long acknowledged the need to decide First Amendment questions by taking account of the particular medium of expression involved because "differences in the characteristics of new media justify . . . differences in the First Amendment standards applied to them."[1] When new technologies of mass communication emerge they are invariably subject to legal disputes, the resolutions of which eventually clarify their roles in our system of freedom of expression. The following discussion of how the First Amendment applies to existing media may assist in the analysis of how the Internet may be treated.

The Print Model

The ratification of the First Amendment and the rest of the original Bill of Rights in 1791 restricted the power of the new federal government to abridge freedom of speech and press. Legislators of the day had a rather limited view of the scope of the country's system of freedom of expression; their primary purpose in passing the amendment was to prevent prior restraints (censorship) by the newly created federal government. Although many states provided some protection for expressive activity in their individual constitutions, including specific protections for the press, the federal First Amendment did not restrict state abridgement of expression until 1925 when the U.S. Supreme Court finally recognized freedom of expression as a fundamental liberty protected from state encroachment.[2] Nonetheless, over the years the courts have expanded protection for newspapers and other print media into what is today referred to as the print model of First Amendment regulation.

The print model offers robust protection to an unlicensed printed press and incorporates a spectrum of well-established principles (e.g., the freedom to publish and protections against compulsory publication) that have resulted in the print medium being the least regulated of our outlets of mass communication. Although the First Amendment does not bestow absolute protection on the print media—they cannot, for example, escape punishment for the publication of obscenity or the legal responsibility for defamation—the print model is the gold standard against which the perimeters of First Amendment protection for other communication media are gauged.

The Broadcast Model

Soon after radio broadcasting emerged in the 1920s, the need for government coordination of the radio spectrum to check the widespread signal interference threatening the fledgling medium became apparent. The resulting licensing scheme limited the number of stations utilizing the airwaves and required by statute that broadcasters serve the public interest in return for the grant of a valuable license.[3] Thus, the "scarcity" of government-issued broadcast licenses to use

---

[1]Red Lion Broadcasting Co. v. FCC, 395 U.S. 367, 386 (1969).
[2]Gitlow v. New York, 268 U.S. 652, 666 (1925).

the public's airwaves became the justification for imposing regulations on broadcasting that would not survive First Amendment scrutiny if applied to print media. That broadcasting could be regulated under a reduced standard of First Amendment protection was first confirmed by the U.S. Supreme Court in 1943[4] and reaffirmed in 1969 when the Court said "[w]here there are substantially more individuals who want to broadcast than there are frequencies to allocate, it is idle to posit an unabridgeable First Amendment right to broadcast comparable to the right of every individual to speak, write, or publish."[5]

The number and scope of public-interest-based broadcast regulations have varied over the years but diminished substantially following a deregulatory trend beginning in the 1980s. Nevertheless, broadcasters' inferior First Amendment status compared to that of other media is illustrated by current regulations, such as the political broadcasting rules, limits on advertisements during children's television programming, a requirement for television stations to air educational and informational programming for children, a ban on tobacco advertising, and requirements to air programs designed to address community problems. Scarcity theory as a regulatory rationale has come under increased attack over the years as the number of broadcasting stations and other outlets of electronic mass communication proliferated. Despite its uncertain premise in modern times, scarcity remains a recognized legal theory, albeit one substantially weakened by an expanding world of electronic mass communication.

A second rationale for regulation of broadcasting emerged in the context of restrictions on the broadcast of indecent (but nonobscene) content. Government restrictions on indecent fare are unconstitutional when applied to print media but survive First Amendment review for broadcasting because of the "intrusive" nature of the medium and its unique accessibility to children. Because broadcast signals enter the home without invitation and a person may be unexpectedly assaulted by indecent content, restrictions on the times when such programming may be aired have been upheld by the U.S. Supreme Court,[6] despite the constitutionally protected nature of the material for adults.

The Cable Model

First Amendment protection of the cable television medium falls between the print and broadcast models; cable operations have more protection than broadcast stations but less than newspapers and other print media. Originally, cable television was regulated to ensure that "free" over-the-air broadcasting was not harmed by subscription-based cable services, a rationale that continues to be ap-

---

[3]Communications Act of 1934, 47 U.S.C. §§ 307(a)(d), 309(a), 310, 312 (1934).
[4]NBC v. U.S., 319 U.S. 190 (1943).
[5]Red Lion Broadcasting Co. v. FCC, 395 U.S. at 388.
[6]FCC v. Pacifica Foundation, 438 U.S. 726 (1978).

plied today even though only 16% of U.S. television households depend on over-the-air transmissions for their television service.

Reacting to broadcasters' concerns that cable television could fragment audiences and threaten the economic viability of the national system of free television, early cable regulations required cable systems to carry local television stations when requested and limited the number of broadcast television signals the local cable operator could import from distant markets. A version of the so-called must-carry rules remains in place today after the U.S. Supreme Court in 1994 narrowly upheld the must-carry and retransmission consent portions of the 1992 Cable Act against a First Amendment challenge.[7] Like broadcasters, cable operators are barred from advertising tobacco products, must follow the rules governing locally originated political content, and must adhere to advertising limits during children's programming. In addition to conforming to federal regulation, cable operators are also required to secure permission from local franchising authorities to build and operate their systems. Such agreements may require a cable system to dedicate some of its channel capacity to local public, educational, and governmental (PEG) programming. However, unlike in broadcasting, courts have rebuffed legislative attempts to ban indecent programming on cable television because adults in the household control, through subscription, the decision to allow sexually explicit but nonobscene fare into the home.[8]

Setting different First Amendment boundaries across media systems inevitably reflects considerations of the technological characteristics of a medium. The U.S. Supreme Court has recognized that "[e]ach medium of expression . . . must be assessed for First Amendment purposes by standards suited to it, for each may present its own problems."[9] For example, in *U.S. v. Playboy Entertainment Group*,[10] the Court struck down a section of the Telecommunications Act of 1996 that required cable companies to either fully scramble sexually oriented programming services on cable at times of the day when they were easily accessible to children—from 6 a.m. to 10 p.m.—or forgo offering such programming altogether during this time. Congress had passed the law in response to complaints that inadequate scrambling, known as *signal bleed*, was inadvertently exposing children watching basic cable programming to unwanted sexually explicit content. Rather than face the expense and technological challenges of completely scrambling both audio and video signals, many cable systems decided to drop sexually explicit cable programming services during the daytime hours.

In striking down the law as a content-based violation of the First Amendment, the Court relied on a key technical difference between cable and broadcasting: Cable television technology allows household-by-household blocking of un-

---

[7]Turner Broadcasting System v. FCC, 512 U.S. 622 (1994).

[8]Jones v. Wilkinson, 800 F.2d 989 (10th Cir. 1986), *aff'd without opinion*, 480 U.S. 926 (1987); Cruz v. Ferre, 755 F.2d 1415 (11th Cir. 1985).

[9]Southeastern Promotions, Ltd. v. Conrad, 420 U.S. 546, 557 (1975).

[10]592 U.S. 803 (2000).

wanted signals, whereas broadcasting does not. The ability of cable television operators to fully block a signal containing indecent content on request presented a less restrictive alternative than a requirement to scramble such content to all households, possibly cutting off access to programming adults had a right to view. Yet, an outright ban on indecent programming during this time of day presents no First Amendment violation when applied to the radio and television programs that enter the home or car unscrambled and without an effective blocking technology.

The Internet Model

As the newest medium of electronic mass communication, the Internet thus far has been regulated in a manner closely akin to the print model. The Internet lacks the characteristics of the broadcast and cable media used to justify expanded regulation. Unlike broadcasting, there is neither scarcity to justify a federal licensing scheme nor intrusiveness to justify indecency regulation, because Internet content is invited into the home. Unlike cable television, there is no substantial government interest to ensure that a system of free television remains available to the public.

To date, the U.S. Supreme Court's involvement in setting the boundaries of First Amendment protection for the Internet has developed exclusively against the backdrop of attempts by Congress to limit exposure to minors of sexually explicit media fare. With passage of the Communications Decency Act (CDA) of 1996,[11] Congress criminalized the knowing transmission over the Internet of obscene or indecent messages or child pornography that was patently offensive under contemporary community standards to any recipient under 18 years of age. The U.S. Supreme Court, by a 7–2 vote, struck down the Act's indecency provisions as unconstitutionally overbroad and therefore a violation of the First Amendment, while upholding the ban on obscenity and child pornography.[12] The Court acknowledged in *Reno v. ACLU* that the Internet is "a unique and wholly new medium of worldwide human communication."[13] It distinguished the Internet from the broadcast model, noting that neither the scarcity nor invasiveness rationale was applicable to the Internet, where affirmative steps are usually necessary to access specific material. The Court concluded that its prior decisions "provide no basis for qualifying the level of First Amendment scrutiny that should be applied to this medium."[14]

---

[11]Communications Decency Act of 1996, Public L. No. 104-104, § Sec. 502, 110 Stat. 133 (codified at 47 U.S.C. § 223).
[12]Reno v. ACLU, 521 U.S. 844 (1997).
[13]Id. at 850 (quoting ACLU v. Reno, 929 F. Supp. 824, 844 (E.D. Pa. 1996)).
[14]Id. at 870.

Reacting to the Court's decision in *Reno,* Congress passed the Child Online Protection Act (COPA) of 1998[15] in an attempt to rectify the CDA's numerous constitutional infirmities. Sometimes called "Son of CDA," the act levied criminal and civil penalties against commercial World Wide Web sites that knowingly and with knowledge of character of the material make available content that is harmful to minors. In addition to obscene content, material harmful to minors included indecent fare, as long as the indecency determination was made following guidelines that paralleled the U.S. Supreme Court's current test for obscenity found in *Miller v. California,*[16] as modified for minors. The statute defined material harmful to minors as:

> any communication, picture, image, graphic image file, article, recording, writing, or other matter of any kind that is obscene or that—(A) the average person, applying contemporary community standards, would find, taking the material as a whole and with respect to minors, is designed to appeal to, or is designed to pander to, the prurient interest; (B) depicts, describes, or represents, in a manner patently offensive with respect to minors, an actual or simulated sexual act or sexual contact, an actual or simulated normal or perverted sexual act, or a lewd exhibition of the genitals or post-pubescent female breast; and (C) taken as a whole, lacks serious literary, artistic, political, or scientific value for minors.[17]

In addition to restricting the law to only commercial Web sites, COPA also provided immunity for Internet service providers (ISPs) and other providers of telecommunication services. However, Web site operators were immune from prosecution only if they made good faith attempts to restrict access to minors by employing a method of age verification, such as credit cards, adult check services, or other reasonable measures.

With its goal of subjecting purveyors of sexually explicit materials to adopt age-verification schemes, COPA was quickly challenged as a violation of the First Amendment for allegedly banning constitutionally protected speech, not being the least restrictive means of accomplishing a compelling state interest, and of being substantially overbroad. A three-judge federal district court panel, concluding that the statute was unlikely to survive First Amendment review, granted a preliminary injunction.[18] The Third Circuit Court of Appeals affirmed[19] but based its decision entirely on the finding that the requirement to use putatively local contemporary community standards in determining what material is harmful to minors was overbroad. It was argued that Web publishers, unable to block Web site access to people living in the most conservative states and localities,

---

[15]Pub. L. No. 105-277, 112 Stat. 2681 (1998) (codified at 47 U.S.C. § 231).

[16]413 U.S. 15 (1973).

[17]47 U.S.C. § 231(e)(6).

[18]ACLU v. Reno, 31 F. Supp 2d. 473 (E.D. Pa. 1999).

[19]ACLU v. Reno, 217 F.3d 162 (3rd Cir. 2000).

would be forced to sweep all but the most puritan content behind the age-verification curtain.

On appeal, the U.S. Supreme Court vacated the judgment and remanded the case to the Third Circuit, concluding that the possible reliance on local community standards to identify material harmful to minors did not render the statute unconstitutionally overbroad on its face.[20] The Court pointed out that, technically, there is no requirement for judges to instruct jurors that the community standards to be applied under the statute should be those of the local community in a specific geographic area rather than the broader community standards of adults in general.

Although not lifting the injunction, the majority agreed that the application of local contemporary community standards did not make the law unconstitutional on its face but splintered on the question of whether community standards for the Internet should be national or local. Justice Thomas, joined by Chief Justice Rehnquist and Justice Scalia, viewed restrictions on sexually explicit content on the Internet in the same posture as regulations applied to telephone-delivered dial-a-porn[21] or the distribution of obscene materials through the mail:[22] "If a publisher chooses to send its material into a particular community, this Court's jurisprudence teaches that it is the publisher's responsibility to abide by that community's standards. The publisher's burden does not change simply because it decides to distribute its material to every community in the Nation."[23]

The rest of the Court, however, rejected the idea that the technological characteristics of a medium play no role in considering the operation of a statute affecting First Amendment values. In her opinion concurring in part, Justice O'Connor, although agreeing that there is no evidence that the use of local standards would automatically make the statute overbroad, nevertheless argued that a national standard should be applied to sexually explicit materials on the Internet. She distinguished material distributed nationally over the Internet from that delivered via telephones and mail where the speaker can control audience access based on geographic location. Justice Breyer also recognized the need for a national community standard for the Internet and, concurring in part, argued that such a standard could be found in the legislative history of the statute.

Justice Kennedy, joined in his concurrence by Justice Souter and Justice Ginsburg, contended that the question of community standards could not be properly analyzed without understanding the full construction of the statute, including the amount of speech covered and variations in community standards

---

[20]Ashcroft v. ACLU, 535 U.S. 564 (2002). The local contemporary community standards of Memphis, Tennessee, were applied in an obscenity prosecution when images were sent via an electronic bulletin board service from California to Tennessee. See U.S. v. Thomas, 74 F.3d 701 (6th Cir. 1996).

[21]Sable Communications of California, Inc. v. FCC, 492 U.S. 115 (1989).

[22]Hamling v. U.S., 418 U.S. 87 (1974).

[23]Ashcroft v. ACLU, 535 U.S. at 583.

with respect to the speech. In dissent, Justice Stevens concluded that regardless of how COPA's other provisions were construed, applying local contemporary community standards to the Internet "will restrict a substantial amount of protected speech that would not be considered harmful to minors in many communities."[24] That alone, Justice Stevens concluded, was sufficient to make the law unconstitutionally overbroad.

In March 2003, the Third Circuit again affirmed the District Court's preliminary injunction, this time examining other aspects of the lower court's decision rather than singularly relying on the community standards issue.[25] The court again found the law, although substantially narrower in scope than the CDA, remained too sweeping and therefore ran afoul of the First Amendment. Although acknowledging that the statute served a compelling interest in protecting the well-being of minors, it found that it was not sufficiently narrowly tailored or the least restrictive means of advancing the government's interest to survive constitutional strict scrutiny. Specifically, the court found that the statute was not narrowly tailored, particularly in its requirement to consider a work "as a whole," which is particularly difficult in an Internet context, where everything on the Web is connected to everything else. Examining the language of the statute, the court concluded that Congress unmistakably constructed the law to apply to isolated materials (e.g., a single picture, image, or article) and therefore would impermissibly burden a wide range of speech otherwise protected for adults.

The court was also troubled by the law's definition of a minor as someone age 17 or younger, because a particular work could have serious value or appeal to the prurient interest of an older teen but hold no serious value or prurient potential for a younger minor. Web site operators would have no way of determining whether their site would violate the Act if they were unable to determine to which minors, if any, their Web site contained harmful materials. The court also found that the definition of communication for "commercial purposes" reached well beyond the core of commercial pornographers the government intended to target, possibly including even nonprofit organizations. The court held that the affirmative defenses made available by using an age verification system placed too great a burden on speech that is protected for adults and could lead Web sites to self-censor their content. Finally, on the issue of less restrictive alternatives, the court found that software filtering systems would likely be at least as effective as the requirements of the Act, and at a much smaller First Amendment cost. In October 2003 the U.S. Supreme Court voted to review the Third Circuit's latest opinion.[26]

---

[24]Id. at 611.

[25]ACLU v. Ashcroft, 322 F.3d 240 (3rd Cir. 2003).

[26]ACLU v. Ashcroft, 322 F.3d 240 (3rd Cir. 2003), *cert. granted,* 72 U.S.L.W. 3266 (U.S. Oct. 14, 2003) (No. 03-218).

The passage in December 2000 of a third law dealing with the Internet and sexually explicit materials—the Children's Internet Protection Act (CIPA)[27]— completed Congress's statutory triad. The law requires public libraries receiving federal technology funds to install software capable of filtering obscenity, child pornography, and other material considered harmful to minors on all public computer terminals or forgo federal funds.

A three-judge District Court panel found the law facially unconstitutional and enjoined its enforcement,[28] concluding that the law forced libraries to violate their adult patrons' First Amendment rights and impermissibly required libraries to relinquish their First Amendment rights as a condition of the receipt of federal funds. The court found that filtering software resulted in thousands of Web pages containing protected speech being blocked and said that less restrictive alternatives were available to prevent the dissemination of sexually explicit materials to minors.

In June 2003 the U.S. Supreme Court in *United States v. American Library Association*[29] reversed the District Court by a vote of 6–3, holding that conditioning federal funds to libraries on the installation of filtering software did not violate the First Amendment. The differences in reasoning among the justices illustrate again the struggle to find the proper application of the First Amendment to the Internet.

The plurality opinion by Chief Justice Rehnquist, joined by Justice O'Connor, Justice Scalia, and Justice Thomas, rejected the idea that public libraries are traditional public forums where all Web publishers' viewpoints must be given access. Because it is not a public forum, the plurality reasoned, there is no requirement that the government engage in strict scrutiny to ensure that the least restrictive means have been applied to the government's restriction of speech. It is sufficient that ample alternative channels for communication of the information exist. Chief Justice Rehnquist attempted to ameliorate concerns about "overblocking" by pointing to the portion of the Act that allows librarians to disable a filter to allow adults access for bona fide research and other lawful purposes. The plurality dismissed concerns about the possible self-censorship by patrons too embarrassed to ask that a filter be disabled or a specific site unblocked: "[T]he constitution does not guarantee the right to acquire information at a public library without any risk of embarrassment."[30]

Although not part of its holding, the plurality opinion argued that CIPA could not place unconstitutional conditions on the receipt of federal funds because the

[27]Pub. L. No. 106-554, § 1701, 114 Stat. 2763A-335 (codified at scattered sections of 20 U.S.C. and 47 U.S.C.).
[28]American Library Ass'n v. U.S., 201 F. Supp. 2d 401 (E.D. Pa. 2002).
[29]U.S. v. American Library Ass'n, No. 02-361, 2003 U.S. LEXIS 4799 (June 23, 2003).
[30]Id. at *29.

First Amendment applies only to restrictions on private speech and not to speech of governmental actors such as public libraries. The opinion relies instead on the Court's 1991 decision in *Rust v. Sullivan*,[31] where it upheld a ban on abortion counseling in family planning clinics receiving federal funding, stating, "When the Government appropriates public funds to establish a program it is entitled to define the limits of that program."[32]

Justice Kennedy, in a concurring opinion, concluded there is little to the case if a librarian, on the request of an adult user, unblocks a site or disables a filter, thereby protecting the interests of adult patrons. In Kennedy's view, refusal of a librarian to do so, or a patron encountering a substantial burden, could lead to a challenge of the statute as it was applied.

Justice Breyer, also concurring in the judgment, took a position that, like the plurality opinion, demonstrated little interest in applying a print model of First Amendment regulation to the Internet, at least under these circumstances. Justice Breyer argued for an intermediate level of scrutiny, calling the filter requirement a kind of "selection" restriction akin to editing, which affects the kind and amount of materials that the library can present to its patrons. He favorably compared the intermediate level of scrutiny he would apply in this situation to decisions by the Court upholding regulations in the cable television and broadcasting area where "complex competing constitutional interests are potentially at issue or speech-related harm is potentially justified by unusually strong governmental interests."[33] The key question, he said, is one of fit.

In dissent, Justice Stevens bemoaned the vast restriction on adult access to protected speech resulting from the massive amount of overblocking inherent in current filter technology. He asserted that neither the government's interest in suppressing unlawful speech nor in protecting children from harmful materials justified such overly broad restrictions: "The Government may not suppress lawful speech as the means to suppress unlawful speech."[34] Justice Stevens argued that the statute would inevitably create a significant prior restraint on adult access to protected speech: "A law that prohibits reading without official consent . . . 'constitutes a dramatic departure from our national heritage and constitutional tradition.' "[35] In Justice Stevens's view, there are a variety of less restrictive alternatives available to local libraries.

Justice Souter, joined in dissent by Justices Ginsburg and Stevens, also took the position that the withholding of federal funds unless all public library computers attached to the Internet were filtered violated the First Amendment, because libraries deciding to take such actions on their own would themselves be vi-

---

[31]500 U.S. 173 (1991).

[32]U.S. v. American Library Ass'n at *31 (quoting Rust v. Sullivan, 500 U.S. 173, 194 (1991)).

[33]Id. at *41.

[34]Id. at *50 (quoting Ashcroft v. Free Speech Coalition, 535 U.S. 234, 255 (2002)).

[35]Id. at *53 (quoting Watchtower Bible & Tract Soc. of N.Y., Inc. v. Village of Stratton, 536 U.S. 150, 166 (2000)).

olating users' free speech rights. He also took issue with Justice Kennedy's assumption that filters would be unblocked on request, arguing that the statute does not specifically require such action. He rejected the plurality's claim that the filtering restrictions are analogous to acquisition decisions made everyday by libraries: "The proper analogy . . . is not to passing up a book that might have been bought; it is either to buying a book and then keeping it from adults lacking an acceptable 'purpose,' or to buying an encyclopedia and then cutting out pages with anything thought to be unsuitable for all adults."[36]

In sum, the Supreme Court's involvement to date with applying the First Amendment to the Internet suggests that the regulatory model to be applied is closest to the full protection model of the print media. The Court's decisions striking down the CDA and COPA were strong victories, suggesting full First Amendment rights for Internet speech. Even the Court's 2003 decision in *U.S. v. American Library Association* is moderated by the right of adult patrons to have the filter removed on request. Although the "negative option" (it is filtered unless you ask) is not typical of a full First Amendment protection model, it is not as serious as having no option at all to avoid filtering. Keeping in mind that the decision is limited in its impact to those situations where restrictions are conditioned as a trade-off for government funding, the most troubling aspect is the plurality's position that the government can assess the constitutionality of such restrictions using only a rational basis test—requiring only that the government has a legitimate (rather than a compelling) interest and that there are ample alternative channels for the communication (rather than requiring the least restrictive alternative to be employed). Justice Breyer's argument for intermediate-level scrutiny, although at least raising the government's bar a bit higher, still suggests that freedom of speech on the Internet may in some instances be subject to balancing against competing constitutional or governmental interests. His citations to Court precedents that upheld government restrictions on cable operators and broadcasters may be an ominous signal for those who count votes on the Court.

Medium-based models provide a useful beginning point for thinking about the application of the First Amendment to different communication technologies, but they cannot provide definitive answers to the myriad of contexts in which regulations impacting First Amendment values are ultimately expressed. For example, the U.S. Supreme Court held in 2003 that it is permissible for a state to criminalize cross burning if there is evidence that the act was performed with intent to intimidate, but cross burning as a purely expressive act has constitutional protection.[37] Would it be constitutionally permissible for a state or federal statute to proscribe burning a cross with intent to intimidate in cyberspace? Would sending an e-mail to a severely depressed teenager urging him to visit a Web site titled "How to Kill Yourself" be constitutionally protected expressive

---

[36]Id. at *74–*75.
[37]Virginia v. Black, 123 S.Ct. 1536 (2003).

activity or a violation of a state's criminal law against assisting someone to commit suicide?[38] Ultimately, it will fall to the courts to decide when government restrictions on Internet speech pass constitutional muster or traverse forbidden terrain. So far, the signs are mostly good.

PERSONAL JURISDICTION

A threshold question in examining the application of law to the Internet—and one left unresolved to date by the U.S. Supreme Court—concerns where a legal action can be maintained against a Web site operator for content made available in the borderless world of cyberspace. This legal determination, called *personal jurisdiction*, addresses the ability of a state to hale a nonresident defendant into court and make a binding judgment against the person. Traditionally a territorial-based concept, personal jurisdiction in the online context is more complicated because Internet content crosses both state borders and territorial sovereignties around the world.[39] For example, a resident of Texas may access a Web page housed on a server located in Florida and containing content written in New York allegedly defaming him in a story about his business operations in California. In which state or states could a plaintiff bring suit?[40] The complexity is compounded in jurisdictional battles stemming from online communication across international borders.

The question of jurisdiction is a critical one to online journalism, not only because of the expense and inconvenience involved in defending oneself in a far-flung location, but also because laws in areas such as libel and privacy may differ from state to state to the benefit of either the plaintiff or defendant. This could result in forum shopping by potential plaintiffs claiming to have been harmed by a news account made available on the Web. At the international level, other countries' laws often give significantly less protection to the press than that afforded in the United States, where the First Amendment often presents a formidable hurdle for those seeking damages against news organizations.

Domestic Jurisdiction

To ensure fundamental fairness under the due process clause of the Fourteenth Amendment, the U.S. Supreme Court has held that before a state can pull a non-

---

[38]See Rebecca Sinderbrand, *Point, Click and Die,* Newsweek, June 30, 2003, at 28.

[39]*See generally* Denis T. Rice and Julia Gladstone, *An Assessment of the Effects Test in Determining Personal Jurisdiction in Cyberspace,* 58 BUS. LAW. 601 (2003).

[40]Most lawsuits of this type are heard in federal court because Article 3, Section 2 of the U.S. Constitution provides for the jurisdiction of the federal courts in situations where residents of two different states sue one another.

resident into court there must be minimum contacts between the nonresident defendant and the forum state, thereby demonstrating that the potential defendant has purposefully availed himself or herself of the benefits and protections of the laws of the jurisdiction. In the landmark case of *International Shoe Co. v. Washington,*[41] the U.S. Supreme Court held that before exercising personal jurisdiction over a nonresident defendant there must be minimum contacts such that the suit does not offend "traditional notions of fair play and substantial justice."[42] The issue of what constitutes sufficient minimum contact in cyberspace becomes critical, especially because there is no practical way that a Web site can geographically limit its availability in the United States.

When jurisdiction is not limited by state long-arm statutes, a court's jurisdictional analysis first examines whether there is either general or specific jurisdiction. General jurisdiction can be asserted when a defendant has "systematic and continuous activities" in the forum state.[43] In such circumstances, personal jurisdiction can be asserted even when the defendant's specific actions in question are unrelated to the contacts in the state. However, if the nature of a defendant's contacts with a state precludes a finding of general jurisdiction, the court analyzes whether there have been sufficient minimum contacts arising from the particular claim that would warrant a reasonable finding of specific jurisdiction.[44] Such contacts need not be physical but can consist of commerce conducted exclusively through electronic communications, including the Internet.[45]

Federal courts have used primarily two approaches in determining whether there have been sufficient minimum contacts. The first is the so-called sliding scale test, employed by a Pennsylvania federal district court in *Zippo Manufacturing Co. v. Zippo Dot Com, Inc.*[46] The sliding scale test bases jurisdiction on the level of interactivity between the nonresident's Web site and the forum. On one end of the sliding scale is the passive Web site that does little more than make information or advertising available to interested persons. Such a site would not subject its operators to personal jurisdiction. On the other end of the scale, a defendant clearly conducts business in the forum state over the Internet. "If the defendant enters into contracts with residents of a foreign jurisdiction that involve

---

[41]326 U.S. 310 (1945). In World-Wide Volkswagen Corp. v. Woodson, 444 U.S. 286 (1980), the Court identified five factors considered important in questions relating to the exercise of personal jurisdiction: (a) the burden on the defendant; (b) the forum's interest in adjudicating the dispute; (c) the plaintiff's interest in obtaining convenient, effective relief; (d) the interest of the interstate judicial system in obtaining the most effective resolution of the controversy; and (e) the shared interest of several states in furthering fundamental social policies, *id.* at 291–292.

[42]International Shoe Co. v. Washington, 326 U.S. at 316 (quoting Milliken v. Meyer, 311 U.S. 457, 463 (1940)).

[43]Helicopteros Nacionales de Colombia, S.A. v. Hall, 446 U.S. 408, 414–16 (1984).

[44]International Shoe Co. v. Washington, 326 U.S. 310 (1945).

[45]Burger King Corp. v. Rudzewicz, 471 U.S. 462, 476 (1985).

[46]952 F.Supp. 1119 (W.D. Pa. 1997).

the knowing and repeated transmission of computer files over the Internet, personal jurisdiction is proper."[47] The tricky and somewhat subjective question of personal jurisdiction in the middle ground of the scale is assessed by the "level of interactivity and the commercial nature of the exchange of information that occurs on the Web site."[48] If there is enough interactivity, personal jurisdiction is appropriate. A sufficient level of interactivity may derive from interactions on the Internet or, in some cases, on the defendant's non-Internet contacts.

In the *Zippo* case, a Pennsylvania manufacturer of tobacco lighters sued a California company, Zippo Dot Com, in a trademark dispute involving the use of Internet domain names including zippo.com, zippo.net, and zipponews.com. The California company, which operated an Internet Web site and provided subscription-based sales allowing user access to newsgroups, contended that Pennsylvania had no rights of personal jurisdiction over the company. In deciding that Zippo Dot Com could be forced to defend itself in Pennsylvania, the court found that the company's actions went well beyond providing a passive Web site that could simply be viewed by others but had intentionally sought to do business in the state and indeed had contracted with 3,000 individuals and seven Internet access providers in Pennsylvania. In sum, the exercise of personal jurisdiction using the sliding scale approach focuses on the nature and quality of commercial activity undertaken by a content provider.

A second approach used by courts in determining personal jurisdiction is the "effects" test employed by the U.S. Supreme Court in the 1984 case of *Calder v. Jones*.[49] Rather than assessing the degree of interactivity, the effects test focuses on the impact of a tort (wrongful act) within a forum state by the defendant's intentional conduct. In *Calder*, a suit for defamation was brought in California by actress Shirley Jones against a reporter and an editor of *The National Enquirer*, a Florida-based national magazine. Although the paper and its distributor, present and conducting business in California on a regular basis, acceded to jurisdiction, the defendant reporter and editor claimed lack of jurisdiction, arguing that they had no control over where their employer distributed its product. In its unanimous opinion affirming jurisdiction, the Court did not stress the contacts of the defendants with the forum state but focused instead on the effects of the Florida defendants' conduct in California:

> The allegedly libelous story concerned the California activities of a California resident. It impugned the professionalism of an entertainer whose television career was centered in California. The article was drawn from California sources, and the brunt of the harm, in terms both of respondent's emotional distress and the injury to her professional reputation, was suffered in California. In sum, California is the focal point both of the story and of the harm suffered.[50]

---

[47]Id. at 1124.
[48]Id.
[49]465 U.S. 783 (1984).
[50]Id. at 788–89.

The plaintiff's claim was buttressed by the fact that California was the state with the largest circulation of the paper, more than 600,000 copies and twice the level of the next highest state. The Court concluded that under circumstances where the defendants intentionally aimed their harmful conduct at the forum they must reasonably anticipate being taken to court in California rather than forcing Jones to go to Florida to seek redress. Regarding the lack of contacts between the plaintiffs and the forum state, the Court concluded that: "The plaintiff's lack of 'contacts' will not defeat otherwise proper jurisdiction, but they may be so manifold as to permit jurisdiction when it would not exist in their absence."[51]

A recent study of Internet-based cases[52] concluded that federal appeals courts have employed "no consistent pattern for approaching personal jurisdiction among the circuits."[53] Appeals courts have applied both the sliding scale and the effects test, and sometimes a combination of both, in analyzing personal jurisdiction claims. The study's review of federal appeals court decisions, mostly trademark and domain name disputes, revealed a number of trends. For example, operating a purely passive Web site without "something more" to purposefully direct its activities to a forum state appears insufficient to trigger personal jurisdiction,[54] whereas a Web site that expressly aims its content at a state's residents and conducts business activities with them is likely to be subject to personal jurisdiction, a result that should be reasonably foreseen by the Web site owners. Less settled are the issues of what characteristics a Web site presents to render it completely passive and what level of interactivity between a Web site and a state's residents is sufficient to constitute "something more." Courts have generally ruled that the presence of a mailing address, an e-mail address, phone number, or printable mail-in form on a Web site advertising a business or service is insufficient to trigger personal jurisdiction if orders are not taken directly through the Web site. Yet even a passive Web site, if combined with other conduct, may lead to personal jurisdiction. For example, in a trademark infringement case, *Panavision Intern., L.P. v. Toeppen,*[55] the Ninth Circuit Court of Appeals held California properly exercised personal jurisdiction over an alleged "cyberpirate" who had registered the domain name *Panavision.com* in Illinois and established a Web site containing pictures of the city of Pana, Illinois. Using the effects test approach, the court held that Toeppen had intentionally directed his conduct at the

---

[51]Id. at 788 (citing Keeton v. Hustler Magazine, Inc., 465 U.S. 770, 779–781 (1984)).

[52]Amanda Reid, *Operationalizing the Law of Jurisdiction: Where in the World Can I Be Sued for Operating a World Wide Web Page?* 8 COMM. L. & POLICY, 227 (2003).

[53]Id. at 241.

[54]See Cybersell, Inc. v. Cybersell, Inc., 130 F.3d 414 (9th Cir. 1997). In *Cybersell,* the court found a lack of personal jurisdiction in Arizona when Cybersell AZ sued Cybersell FL in a trademark dispute over the latter's use of the domain name cybersell.com. In that case, the Ninth Circuit held that Cybersell FL only operated a passive Web site, had conducted no commercial activity in Arizona, and had not in any way aimed its activities at that state.

[55]141 F.3d 1316 (9th Cir. 1998).

California motion picture camera equipment company by asking for $13,000 to relinquish the domain name.

In *Panavision*, it was the request for payment directed at the California company that provided the "something more" needed for personal jurisdiction over an essentially passive Web site.[56] In November 2002, the California Supreme Court refused to grant personal jurisdiction over another essentially passive Web site in a misappropriation of trade secrets case where a Purdue University student posted on his Web site the software code of a program designed to bypass a copyright protection for DVDs.[57] The court found that the student had not intentionally targeted California because his sole contact with the state was through the posting on his passive Web site and that he was unaware that the licensing agent for the encryption code was a California company.

Evidence that a contract was able to be executed online would generally be sufficient to trigger personal jurisdiction, provided that at least some contract activity had actually taken place in the state. For example, shopping sites that allow customers to order online would generally trigger personal jurisdiction, at least when business has taken place in the forum state, even if such business is modest.[58] One federal district court has held that a Web site aggressively soliciting business would not be subject to personal jurisdiction in a state where it has been unsuccessful in attracting any business.[59]

Personal Jurisdiction and Online News

In the past, the boundaries of a court's jurisdiction generally extended no farther than a print publication's hard-copy circulation or a broadcasting station's service area. To date, there are few personal jurisdiction cases involving the online news media, although more can be expected in the future.

One of the earliest decisions addressing personal jurisdiction and online current affairs content involved an electronic rag called the *Drudge Report*. Matt Drudge, a self-defined "purveyor of gossip," electronically published the report from his Los Angeles apartment. The report was available on Drudge's Web site

---

[56]*See also* Nicosia v. De Rooy, 72 F. Supp. 2d 1093 (N.D. Cal. 1999) (Defendant's deliberate transmission of 11 e-mails inviting forum state residents to view passive Web site sufficient basis for jurisdiction in defamation case).

[57]Pavlovich v. Superior Court, 58 P.3d 2 (Ca. 2002).

[58]American Network, Inc. v. Access America/Connect Atlanta, Inc., 975 F. Supp. 494 (S.D.N.Y. 1997).

[59]See Millennium Enterprises, Inc. v. Millennium Music, LP, 33 F. Supp. 2d 907 (D. Or. 1999). In *Millennium*, the court held that defendants selling compact discs online could not reasonably anticipate being haled into an Oregon court until a business transaction had actually taken place with an Oregon resident. *See also* Bensusan Rest. Corp. v. King, 126 F.3d 25, 26 (2d Cir. 1997) (personal jurisdiction not recognized in New York in trademark dispute because Missouri nightclub had not solicited or conducted business through Web site with New York residents).

and distributed to 85,000 subscribers through his e-mail service. In his report on August 10, 1997, Drudge quoted anonymous sources accusing Washington, DC, resident and White House aide Sidney Blumenthal of spouse abuse. Blumenthal and his wife, who also worked at the White House, sued Drudge for defamation in U.S. district court in Washington, DC.

Drudge moved to have the case dismissed for lack of jurisdiction or, alternatively, transferred to California, his state of residence and the site of the publication. In *Blumenthal v. Drudge*,[60] the court rejected Drudge's motion and held that there were sufficient contacts between Drudge and Washington, DC, to maintain jurisdiction.

The court cited six reasons why Drudge had established the required "persistent course of conduct" under Washington, DC's long-arm statute:

(1) the interactivity of the Web site between the defendant Drudge and District residents; (2) the regular distribution of the Drudge Report via AOL; (3) Drudge's solicitation and receipt of contributions from District residents; (4) the availability of the Web site to District residents 24-hours a day; (5) defendant Drudge's interview with C-SPAN; and (6) defendant Drudge's contracts with District residents who provide gossip for the Drudge Report.[61]

That personal jurisdiction could be exercised against Drudge in Washington, DC, is an indication of how unsettled the law applying personal jurisdiction to the Internet was in 1998. A good case could be made that today personal jurisdiction would not be granted under a similar set of facts. The district court judge, citing the sliding scale approach developed in the *Zippo* case, characterized Drudge's site as the "epitome of Web site interactivity."[62] The evidence of this, the court held, was the fact that Drudge had a toll-free number that users could use to donate money and an e-mail address on his site allowing users to contact him and even add their names to his listserv to receive future reports. Such basic interactivity would likely not be determinative today. The second reason for jurisdiction, the accessibility of the report on America Online (AOL), might have some probative value regarding circulation but would be inadequate to establish sufficient contacts, especially because there was no way to document the number of *Drudge Report* readers in Washington, DC. Regarding solicitations to readers, the court seemed to place more value on the fact that the request for money was available 24 hours a day rather than the paltry $250 or so that had been contributed from the area. Drudge's travel to Washington, DC, to be interviewed by C-SPAN and his telephone calls to and from contacts in the District did not really establish persistent contact.

---

[60]992 F. Supp. 44 (D.D.C. 1998).
[61]Id. at 57.
[62]Id. at 56.

What really seemed to matter to the court was the 24-hour-a-day availability of the Web site to District residents, although it acknowledged that standing alone, this was insufficient to claim jurisdiction. Although Drudge might have been expected to know that "the primary and most devastating effects of the [statements he made] would be felt in the District of Columbia,"[63] it can also be argued that there was no evidence that Drudge intentionally targeted residents of the District.

The leading case involving online news and personal jurisdiction, *Young v. New Haven Advocate*,[64] was decided by the Fourth Circuit Court of Appeals in December 2002. It was the first case in which a federal appellate court reviewed the jurisdictional issue of whether Web site activity alone can force a news organization to defend itself in another state.

Stanley Young, warden of Virginia's Wallen Ridge State Prison, brought a defamation suit in that state against two Connecticut newspapers, the *New Haven Advocate* and *The Hartford Courant*, claiming that their articles accused him of racism and tolerance of inmate abuse. The allegedly defamatory comments concerned the treatment of Connecticut inmates who had been transferred to the Virginia "supermax" facility to relieve overcrowding, a public policy decision that had sparked considerable controversy in Connecticut. In addition to their traditional print publications, the newspapers also posted a number of the allegedly defamatory articles on their Web sites.

The federal district trial court ruled that Virginia could assert personal jurisdiction because the newspapers posted "allegedly defamatory articles on Internet Websites accessible twenty-four hours a day in Virginia,"[65] noting that a newspaper article published on the Internet can be physically present simultaneously in different locations and therefore subject to multistate jurisdiction.[66] The court relied heavily on the effects test analysis in *Calder*, concluding that the online articles had targeted a Virginia resident working at a state correctional facility and that the papers should have been aware that the harm suffered by Young would primarily occur in Virginia.

On appeal, the Fourth Circuit panel unanimously reversed, holding that the papers had insufficient contacts with Virginia to warrant the exercise of personal jurisdiction. The three-judge panel rejected the notion that just because the newspapers' Web site stories were available in Virginia the papers were intentionally directing their Web site content to a Virginia audience. The focal point of the articles, the court concluded, was the soundness of Connecticut's prisoner transfer policy, a discussion aimed at Connecticut readers, not at those in Virginia: "The newspapers do not have sufficient Internet contacts with Virginia to permit

---

[63]Id. at 57 (citing Telco Communications v. An Apple A Day, 977 F. Supp. 404, 407 (E.D. Va. 1997)).

[64]315 F.3d 256 (4th Cir. 2002), *cert. denied*, 71 U.S.L.W. 3721 (U.S. 2003).

[65]Young v. New Haven Advocate, 184 F. Supp. 2d 498, 508 (W.D. Va. 2001).

[66]Id. at 509.

the district court to exercise specific jurisdiction over them."[67] The appeals court distinguished the effects test applied in the *Calder* decision, noting that in *Calder* both the focal point of the story and the harm done occurred in California, a state where the plaintiff not only resided but one where *The National Enquirer* had its largest circulation.

Circulation of the Connecticut papers in Virginia had been negligible to non-existent; one of the papers had no Virginia subscribers and the other had only eight. Following the Ninth Circuit's decision in *Panavision* that "something more" is needed beyond the posting and accessibility of a Web site in another state, the panel presented a litany of reasons why there were insufficient links between the papers and Virginia residents to conclude that they had conceptually entered the state via the Internet for jurisdictional purposes: There was little or no circulation of the papers in Virginia; the papers did not solicit Virginia readership; the papers' Web site content and associated links addressed local matters; and the Web sites' advertisements, including classified ads, were local. The panel also noted that no one from either paper had traveled to Virginia to gather information for the articles and that neither paper had employees, offices, other assets, or business relationships in the state. Additionally, the newspapers did not derive any substantial revenue from goods used or services rendered in Virginia. The court concluded that even though the warden was a known resident of Virginia, the Web sites were not designed to attract or serve a Virginia audience. Focusing its analysis on the defendants' conduct rather than the plaintiff's residence, the panel refused to recognize personal jurisdiction in a circumstance where the news story was clearly targeted to Connecticut audiences, concluding that "Calder does not sweep that broadly."[68]

Questions of personal jurisdiction in domestic cases involving the Internet continue to evolve, and its application in cases involving online news remains in its earliest stages. Courts seem to employ elements of both the sliding scale and effects test in weighing claims of personal jurisdiction.

A recent analysis of current case law concluded that questions of jurisdiction could be better operationalized by establishing a two-pronged analysis. The first prong would be an analysis along the lines of the sliding scale. Evidence that a site is actively doing business on the Web would favor personal jurisdiction, but the

---

[67]Young v. New Haven Advocate, 315 F.3d 256, 264 (4th Cir. 2002). *See also* Schnapp v. McBride, 64 F. Supp. 2d 608 (E.D. La. 1998) (Louisiana police officer did not have personal jurisdiction in defamation suit in Louisiana based on story posted on Wisconsin newspaper's passive Web site where there were insufficient contacts with forum state, paper had minimal circulation in state, plaintiff was not focal point of story, and story targeted neither plaintiff nor Louisiana state residents); Falwell v. Cohn, No. Civ.A.6:02 cv 00040 (W.D. Va. Mar. 4, 2003) (Virginia does not have jurisdiction over Illinois resident operating anti-Jerry Falwell Web site where material targets a national audience and attacks a nationally known religious figure and does not manifest intent to expressly target a Virginia audience).

[68]Id. at 262.

defendant would have an opportunity to rebut such a presumption, such as in the case where there were few or no business contacts with residents in a particular forum state. Evidence that a Web site is passive would favor a decision against personal jurisdiction but standing alone would not be determinative where "something more" was evident. The second step would apply the effects test, examining whether the defendant had "engaged in intentional, and allegedly wrongful, conduct expressly aimed at the forum state."[69] In light of the *Young* case, future efforts to resolve personal jurisdiction claims in defamation cases involving online news reports may also include a determination of the "focal point of a story" in addition to considering where the plaintiff was harmed, as was the case in Calder.[70]

One commentator, decrying the "senseless morass into which the doctrine of libel law personal jurisdiction has fallen," called for dramatic reforms, especially a rethinking of the *Calder* decision as it applies in cyberspace.[71] Regardless of whether a set of bright lines ultimately evolves, decisions regarding personal jurisdiction should continue to follow the traditional principles of reasonableness and fairness.

Judicial consideration must begin with the assumption that personal jurisdiction cannot be granted simply because an online news story can be accessed from everywhere, including the state in which a plaintiff resides. It does not follow that just because a defendant knew a plaintiff resided in a state—and actually caused harm to the plaintiff in that forum—that the defendant had specific intent to cause such an effect in that forum. This is easily understood in the context of suits alleging trademark or breach of contract, where the defendant may not even know where the plaintiff resides. Even though by their very nature the harms associated with torts such as libel and invasion of privacy are likely to result in harm in the place where the plaintiff resides—at least when the plaintiff is an individual rather than a corporation[72]—personal jurisdiction should not be automatic simply because a news story can be accessed at the click of a mouse. Plaintiffs should also be required to demonstrate evidence of substantial circulation and intentional targeting by showing that the plaintiff was the focus of the story.

Traditional sliding scale analysis, with its focus on commercial interactivity, is not well suited when considering that news and information, not online sales of

---

[69]Reid, *supra* note 51, at 262.

[70]*Calder*, 465 U.S. at 788.

[71]See Julie Hilden, *Can a Libel Defendant Be Sued in Any and Every State for Material Published on a Website?* (June, 2002) http://writ.corporate.findlaw.com/hilden/20020604.html (last visited June 30, 2003).

[72]The Indiana appellate court in Conseco, Inc. v. Hickerson, 698 N.E.2d 816 (Ind. Ct. App. 1988), held that the jurisdictional analysis under the "effects test" is not readily applicable in cases involving national or international corporations and the Internet. Unlike individual harm, corporate harm is not generally located in a specific geographic area.

products and services, are the primary goal of Web-based journalism. Many newspaper and broadcast station Web sites are highly interactive and usually feature advertising, but they are not substantially focused on conducting online business. The wisest course may be a case-by-case approach where courts examine a multiplicity of factors in determining whether a news story posted on the Internet was done with the specific intent to target a state's residents, including whether a publication is generally recognized as a national, regional, or local news outlet; whether there were substantial sales of the news product in a state (in either hard copies or online paid subscriptions); whether the site's paid advertising is local or if advertising revenues are derived by interstate exposure; the presence of editorial offices or other business contacts within the forum state; and the nature and extent of newsgathering that took place within the forum state in preparing the story. The degree of interactivity, especially when manifested in business activity, would be an important consideration in some actions such as trademark and breach of contract claims. However, the degree of interactivity would have less relevance to traditional tort actions against online news sites, where interactions normally offer little in the way of direct online commerce yielding a significant commercial benefit to the news organization.[73]

The question of where the impact of the tort was felt the most cannot be ignored, especially if it can be shown that the defendant's news product regularly circulates to a considerable number of readers in the plaintiff's state of residence. However, simply knowing that theoretically someone could be hurt in a particular state, without something more, should not be sufficient for personal jurisdiction. Like the Fourth Circuit's decision in *Young*, a news story that allegedly libels a resident of a state should not open the door for personal jurisdiction in that state without sufficient evidence that the plaintiff was a focal point of the story, that the story was appreciably circulated in the state, and that the story was, at least by implication, calculated to cause injury in the state. This position was reflected in a December 2002 decision by the Fifth Circuit Court of Appeals in *Revell v. Libov*.[74] In *Revell*, a Texas resident and former associate deputy director of the FBI brought a defamation suit in Texas based on a posting to a bulletin board operated by the Columbia University School of Journalism in New York. The article, written by a Massachusetts resident, claimed that Revell and others in the Reagan Administration ignored warnings that could have avoided the terrorist bombing of Pan American flight 103 over Lockerbie, Scotland. The court did acknowledge that Texas residents could access the materials, but it concluded that there was insufficient contact with the forum state because the story did not refer to Texas and was not directed at Texas readers.

---

[73]The Sixth Circuit has held that a Web site is interactive to the degree that it reveals specifically intended interactions with residents of a state. See Neogen Corp. v. Neo Gen Screening, Inc., 282 F.3d 883 (6th Cir. 2002).

[74]317 F.3d 467 (5th Cir. 2002).

In *Keeton v. Hustler*, a non-Internet case, the Supreme Court observed that "[t]he tort of libel is generally held to occur wherever the offending material is circulated."[75] The extent of circulation is an important factor in assessing personal jurisdiction in cases involving online news. Lawsuits stemming from the content of Web sites with counterparts that are well-known national news outlets are likely to be considered appropriate subjects for personal jurisdiction in all states because the intent of these companies is to provide content to a national audience day after day. The Court's decision in *Keeton* held that regular circulation of a publication into a forum state is sufficient for asserting personal jurisdiction even when the plaintiff is not a resident.[76] Jurisdiction in all states would apply to the online editions of well-known national newspapers such as *The New York Times* (nytimes.com), *The Wall Street Journal* (wsj.com), and *USA Today* (usatoday.com), along with national television networks, like Cable News Network (cnn.com) and CBS (cbsnews.com; cbsmarketwatch.com). In such cases, evidence of substantial circulation into a state is easily available. Similarly, a local news outlet's lack of circulation in a state, like *The Hartford Courant* in the *Young* case, when combined with other indicators such as an orientation to local content and advertising, may be evidence that the online publication did not aim its content at another state. However, a free, online-only magazine with national aspirations but minuscule circulation would present a difficult question because, even with today's technology, it is impossible for Web site operators to know how many people in a particular state are reading their online product.

Web sites of local broadcast stations that clearly target only the residents of one state would not be likely candidates for personal jurisdiction outside of that state, whereas Web sites of those stations targeting audiences in several states would likely qualify for personal jurisdiction in those states targeted by the station but not necessarily in states that can fortuitously view their Web site but where they are not targeting audiences.

International Jurisdiction

The global nature of the Internet presents news organizations with an opportunity to make their products available throughout the world. However, due to the structure of the World Wide Web, even when the media would prefer to limit access to their products they are often unable to do so. For U.S.-based news organizations, the prospect of defending against a lawsuit in a far-off country conjures up nightmarish images of soaring expenses and exposure to foreign legal codes containing few if any of the statutory and constitutional protections provided the press in the United States. A recent libel case involving a news story written in the United States and published online illustrates the problem.

---

[75]Keeton v. Hustler, 465 U.S. 770, 777 (1984).
[76]Id. at 773.

In October 2000 an article entitled "Unholy Gains" appeared in *Barron's On-line*, the electronic edition of a printed financial magazine hosted by *The Wall Street Journal* and published by Dow Jones & Company. The online edition of the magazine was available on a subscription basis but had few subscribers (approximately 1,600) in Australia. The article made several references to Australian resident and Melbourne mining magnate Joseph Gutnick. Claiming that the article defamed him with accusations of money laundering and tax evasion, Gutnick sued the reporter and the publisher in the Supreme Court of Victoria, Australia, a country in which libel is a strict liability tort.[77]

Dow Jones argued that the Australian court should not exercise personal jurisdiction in the case because the article had been uploaded to the magazine's New Jersey server, making that state the publication site and therefore the appropriate venue for trying the case. However, the Victoria court rejected Dow Jones's claim, concluding that because damage to Gutnick's reputation would occur in his place of residence, the defamation had occurred there, making jurisdiction proper.

On appeal, the High Court of Australia in December 2002 unanimously upheld the exercise of personal jurisdiction.[78] It is a landmark decision in that it is the first court of final appeal in any country to address the issue of transnational civil liability based on Internet content.

The High Court took the position that the material was "published" not in New Jersey, but rather in the State of Victoria when downloaded by subscribers, concluding that damage to reputation occurs when the story is comprehended by the reader, the listener, or the observer. Because the harm occurred in Australia, the court reasoned, it may properly exercise jurisdiction. The court opined that Dow Jones's fears of global liability in virtually any court in the world "from Afghanistan to Zimbabwe" were unreal and said that publishers wishing to limit their liability in cyberspace could reasonably do so by considering the residence of the person they were writing about. The High Court did take note of the unique challenges posed by Internet publication, and one Justice, noting that the ruling was not wholly satisfactory, suggested that the issue may call for national and international discussion.

The decision in *Dow Jones* sent shock waves through the Internet publishing world, concerned that subjecting publishers of news on the Web to the vagaries of libel and other legal actions in every foreign country would threaten the flow of news and information around the world.[79] "Having to mount a defense in a for-

[77]Gutnick v. Dow Jones & Co., (2001) VSC 305.

[78]Dow Jones & Co. v. Gutnick, (2002) HCA 56, http://www.austlii.edu.au/au/cases/cth/high_ct/2002/56.html (last visited December 20, 2002).

[79]In April 2003, Bill Alpert, the financial reporter who wrote the offending article in the *Gutnick* case, filed a petition at the United Nations claiming that the Australian High Court is in breach of Article 19 of the U.N.'s International Covenant on Civil and Political Rights. As a signatory, Australia might be forced to change its country's libel laws if the U.N. finds that it unduly restricts the right of free speech.

eign state or country, where your only connection is access to a Web site, would be . . . daunting."[80] Publishers fearing a potential flood of litigation might begin to self-censor their Web publications to avoid civil liability or even criminal sanctions in those countries where libel is a criminal offense.

At greatest risk are publishers with assets that could be seized in a particular country to satisfy adverse judgments. Countries in the European Union could be especially threatening because their rules allow for enforcement of judgments in all member countries. However, if assets are not present, successful international plaintiffs will be forced to look to U.S. courts to enforce the foreign judgments.

It appears so far that U.S. courts are not inclined to enforce foreign judgments that conflict with the constitutional protections found in the First Amendment.[81] U.S. courts have taken this position in cases arising out of print publication, and there is little reason to expect a different result in the case of online defamation, especially with the Court's position in *Reno* that the Internet is entitled to full First Amendment protection. There are also indications that U.S. courts will refuse to hear cases for libel claims presented to U.S. courts by plaintiffs based on statements made in foreign online publications that fail to meet the exacting standards for libel required by the First Amendment.[82]

The laws of other countries limiting hate speech on the Internet have also been deflected by U.S. courts on First Amendment grounds. For example, a federal district court in California in 2001 issued a declaratory judgment that fines threatened by a French court against Yahoo! for failing to block listings of Nazi-related material offered for sale on its Web pages were not cognizable or enforceable under U.S. laws: "Although France has the sovereign right to regulate what speech is permissible in France, this Court may not enforce a foreign order that violates the protections of the United States Constitution by chilling protected speech that occurs simultaneously within our borders."[83] The case is on appeal to the Ninth Circuit.

News organizations, however, may be unable able to preempt litigation in a foreign country by seeking protection against an adverse judgment in a U.S. court. For example, in *Dow Jones & Company, Inc. v. Harrods*,[84] a federal district court judge for the Southern District of New York refused to issue a declaratory

---

[80]Kathleen Kirby, *Lawsuits from Half a World Away*, COMMUNICATOR, April, 2003, at 60.

[81]Kurt A. Wimmer & Joshua A. Berman, *United States Jurisdiction to Enforce Foreign Internet Libel Judgments*, 639 PLI/Pat 493 (2000) (Practicing Law Institute Patents, Copyrights, Trademarks, and Literary Property Course Handbook Series).

[82]Banamex v. Rodriguez, 30 Media L. Rptr. (BNA) 1129 (N.Y.S.2d 2002) (No. 603429/00). For a discussion of the case see Juanita Darling, *Forum Shopping and the Cyber Pamphleteer: Banamex v. Rodriguez*, 8 COMM. L. & POLICY, 361 (2003).

[83]Yahoo v. League Against Racism and Anti-Semitism [LICRA] and the Union of Jewish Students, 169 F. Supp. 2d 1181, 1192 (N.D. Cal. 2001).

[84]237 F. Supp. 2d 394 (S.D.N.Y. 2002).

order stating that any libel judgment against Dow Jones by an English court would be unenforceable in the United States. Dow Jones had argued that any judgment against it in the case, which resulted from an April Fool's Day joke gone awry, would violate the First Amendment's protection of opinion. It had asked the U.S. court for a declaratory judgment, arguing that the time and expense of defending itself in London, as well as the threat to First Amendment values, warranted such an order. The court refused, concluding that Dow Jones's claims before any trial were too remote, abstract, and hypothetical to constitute an actual controversy qualifying for declaratory relief.[85] Harrods, as part of what appeared to be preparation to filing a suit for defamation, demanded that Dow Jones turn over print circulation figures for *The Wall Street Journal* in the United Kingdom, the number of online subscribers in the country, and the number of hits to WJS.com since the publication of the article in question.

Despite initially favorable treatment in U.S. courts, the ultimate scope of protection for materials posted on the Web remains murky, especially given the strikingly different attitudes toward issues such as libel, hate speech, and sexually explicit content by different countries around the world. One commentator sums up the dilemma: "[I]f France can prevent an American company from displaying Nazi memorabilia in France, does that mean that Iraqi courts can prevent the display of the Victoria's Secret Web site in Iraq? On the other hand, does the First Amendment give us the right to inflict our way of life on another country or willfully violate another country's laws?"[86]

One option that has considerable support is to develop an international body of law harmonizing the treatment of speech on the Internet. There have been numerous calls for such international cooperation,[87] but even if such international agreement is possible, it is unclear whether participation by the United States in such treaties would pass constitutional review where restrictions are placed on speech originating within the United States that was protected by the First Amendment. As one commentator put it:

> International treaties and agreements have begun to cluster, if not fully unify, countries' practices on consumer protection, intellectual property, taxation, and to some extent, privacy. But these shifts are incremental, and often the inking of a treaty—or even, within the European Union, the promulgation of a directive left for individual countries to implement—is only a starting point that tests individual

---

[85]Id. at 408–409.

[86]Samuel Lewis, *Have Web Site, Will Travel—Despite the Legal Limits*, BROWARD DAILY BUSINESS REVIEW, February 5, 2003, at A7.

[87]Matthew Fagin, *Comment: Regulating Speech Across Borders: Technology vs. Values*, 9 Mich. Telecomm. Tech. L. Rev. 395 (2003). *See also* David Grant, *Defamation and the Internet: Principles for a Unified Australian (and World) Online Defamation Law*, 3:1 JOURNALISM STUD., February 2002, at 115.

countries' and cultures' mettle to actually enforce that which has been abstractly agreed to.[88]

Whether such international agreements can significantly reduce transnational legal tensions remains unknown.

It has also been suggested that employing technology to make Web site information available based on geographic location may hold some promise in resolving international conflicts over Internet content. A chip could be embedded in each computer allowing its geographic location to be determined by interaction with the already-established global positioning system.[89] Service providers using a check-off system could determine by country user access to particular content on its system.

The filtering of Web site content is already implemented on a countrywide basis by repressive governments attempting to limit what their citizens can see or read on the Internet. As part of an ongoing study of Internet filtering worldwide,[90] Jonathan Zittrain and Benjamin Edelman of the Berkman Center for Internet and Society at Harvard Law School reported that China regularly denies its citizens access to more than 19,000 Web sites that the government deems threatening and has even temporarily blocked access to the popular Google search engine.[91] Their study also found that Saudi Arabia banned 86% of the most popular sexually explicit sites.[92] Google itself has removed sites that may conflict with local laws from the German and French versions of its index to avoid legal liability, declaring it a common practice among search engines to block sites from appearing in search results at the request of partners, users, and government agencies.[93] Although the emerging geolocation technology could go a long way in solving "the objection that one jurisdiction's residents will be de facto subject to another's laws because of a Web site's all-or-nothing exposure to the Net's masses,"[94] its widespread application might substantially decrease the undifferentiated reach that makes the Internet medium such a democratic and revolutionary force in human communication.

---

[88]Jonathan Zittrain, *Be Careful What You Ask For: Reconciling a Global Internet and Local Law,* Harvard Law School, Public Law Working Paper No. 60 (May 2003), at 10. (http://ssrn.com/abstract_id=395300 (last visited July 3, 2003)).

[89]Id.

[90]Jonathan Zittrain and Benjamin Edelman, *Documentation of Internet Filtering Worldwide* (April 2003) (http://cyber.law.harvard.edu/filtering (last visited July 18, 2003)).

[91]Joseph Kahn, *China Has World's Tightest Internet Censorship, Study Finds,* N.Y. Times, Dec. 4, 2002, at A13.

[92]Id.

[93]John Schwartz, *Study Tallies Sites Blocked by Google,* N.Y. Times, Oct. 25, 2002, at C8.

[94]Zittrain, *supra,* note 87, at 11.

IMMUNITY FOR INTERACTIVE COMPUTER SERVICE USERS AND PROVIDERS

It is impossible to fully comprehend the transformation of news in an age of technological and ownership convergence. As the Internet celebrates its 30-something birthday with its 12-year-old progeny, the World Wide Web,[95] the laws governing who should face responsibility for harms stemming from information published in cyberspace remain unsettled. For example, can a Web site such as news.google.com, which presents computer-selected current events information from the online content of more than 4,500 news organizations around the world, ever be held legally responsible for the content?

In legal terms, a printed newspaper's counterpart on the Web is still considered a newspaper, albeit one that may offer moderated chat sessions, unmoderated discussion boards, commercial links, and a wide range of other services. However, what is the correct legal description of a *Drudge Report*? Is it news, and is its publisher a journalist? The following discussion examines Section 230 of the Communications Decency Act, which grants legal immunity to "interactive computer services" for information provided by third parties placed on the Internet. Until now, courts have interpreted the statute almost exclusively against a backdrop of legal claims for injury to reputation and privacy, but ultimately it may be present at many of the crossroads where journalism and law intersect.

Under common law principles, someone who repeats or republishes the defamation of another is as responsible as the original publisher, reflecting the adage that tale bearers are as bad as tale makers. Someone who communicates the defamatory content of another is therefore liable for the harm suffered as though he or she had originated the information.[96] For purposes of assigning liability for defamation, courts have traditionally divided republishers into three categories: (a) Publishers, such as newspapers, magazines, and broadcast stations, are liable for any republication of defamatory materials, a result stemming from the extensive editorial control exercised by these media; (b) distributors, such as newsstands, bookstores, and libraries, face liability only if they know or have reason to know of the defamatory material contained in the materials they distribute; and (c) common carriers, such as telephone and telegraph companies, that function as a conduit for an enormous number of messages sent over their communication facilities normally without regard to content. Common carriers are free from liability as long as they do not participate in the preparation of content. These traditional categories work well when applied to established media but blur when applied to the technological and communication structures found on the Internet.

---

[95]Katie Hafner, *The Net Is 30-Something, But the Web Is a Child*, N.Y. Times, Dec. 10, 2001, at C4.
[96]*See, e.g.*, W. Page Keeton et al., PROSSER AND KEETON ON THE LAW OF TORTS § 113, at 799 (5th ed. 1984).

Two early Internet libel cases revealed a dilemma facing Internet service providers (ISPs) that ultimately triggered Congressional action. In the 1991 case of *Cubby, Inc. v. CompuServe Inc.,*[97] a U.S. district court characterized interactive computer service CompuServe as nothing more than a distributor of a third-party's online newsletter, *Rumorville USA,* which had allegedly defamed the plaintiffs who operated a rival newsletter called *Skuttlebut.* In granting summary judgment, the court found that CompuServe simply offered its subscribers an electronic library of news publications and said that, like any other distributor:

> A computerized database is the functional equivalent of a more traditional news vendor, and the inconsistent application of a different standard of liability to an electronic news distributor such as CompuServe than that which is applied to a public library, book store, or newsstand would impose an undue burden on the free flow of information. Given the relevant First Amendment considerations, the appropriate standard of liability to be applied to CompuServe is whether it knew or had reason to know of the allegedly defamatory *Rumorville* statements.[98]

The court found CompuServe was shielded from liability because there was no evidence that it had knowledge or reason to know of the allegedly defamatory statements.

A different result emerged in *Stratton Oakmont, Inc. v. Prodigy Services Co.,*[99] when the New York Supreme Court decided in 1995 that a financial bulletin board operated by the interactive computer service Prodigy should be treated like an original publisher when allegedly defamatory comments made by an unidentified party were placed on its bulletin board. In rejecting Prodigy's claim that it should be treated like a distributor, the court noted the company claimed to actively screen and edit messages before posting them, ran software screening programs, and published content guidelines. Such active editorial control, the court reasoned, pointed to a publisher, not a distributor.

The paradox between the two decisions was not lost on either the interactive computer service providers or the U.S. Congress. An interactive service provider could seemingly avoid liability only by eschewing any monitoring of the content available on its service, even if it desired to do so. Congress, on the other hand, wanted service providers to monitor their content, especially in regard to sexually explicit materials unsuitable for minors. When Congress passed the Communications Decency Act of 1996, it provided immunity for "Good Samaritan" blocking and screening of offensive material.

The Communications Decency Act collapsed under First Amendment review, but the protection against liability from third-party content remained in effect. Section 230(c)(1) says that "No provider or user of an interactive computer ser-

---

[97]776 F. Supp. 135 (S.D.N.Y. 1991).

[98]Id. at 140–141.

[99]23 Media L. Rep. (BNA) 1794, 1995 N.Y. Misc. LEXIS 229 (N.Y. Sup. Ct. May 25, 1995).

vice shall be treated as the publisher or speaker of any information provided by another information content provider."[100] Although interactive computer services were now free from liability for affirmatively restricting access to or the availability of objectionable material provided by third parties,[101] it appeared they were also protected from failing to do so. The statutory protection for ISPs and other interactive computer services[102] for posting information from other information content providers[103] removed a succulent target for attorneys representing plaintiffs claiming they were harmed by communications posted on the Internet. Compounding plaintiffs' frustrations, many if not most original publishers of harmful information on the Internet are anonymous or lack the financial assets to make a lawsuit worthwhile. Whether it's a Web site, chat room, bulletin board, listserv, or newsgroup, the interactive computer service would appear to have complete immunity as long as it did not itself author or aid in the development of the material.

Courts interpreting the plain meaning of the statute soon began to rebuff attempts by plaintiffs to hold ISPs legally responsible for third-party content. One of the first cases testing the new federal immunity was brought by Kenneth Zeran, the victim of a cruel prank perpetrated by a person using an AOL bulletin board. The bulletin board carried the postings of an unidentified person offering for sale "Naughty Oklahoma T-Shirts" bearing tasteless and offensive slogans related to the infamous bombing of the Murrah Federal Building in Oklahoma City, telling interested purchasers to call "Ken" and listing Zeran's phone number. Variations of the original posting were repeated for 5 days. Not surprisingly, Zeran faced a large number of angry and derogatory messages, including death threats. Zeran repeatedly contacted AOL and was told that the account from which the messages were posted would soon be closed. AOL did remove two notices, but they continued to reappear.

In April 1996 Zeran sued AOL in federal district court, arguing that, like any other distributor, the ISP had a responsibility to immediately remove the postings from its service and was negligent in its delays. AOL responded that Section 230 provided an affirmative defense against any claims for liability, and the dis-

---

[100]47 U.S.C. § 230(c)(1).

[101]47 U.S.C. § 230(c)(2) provides that "No provider or user of an interactive computer service shall be held liable on account of—(A) any action voluntarily taken in good faith to restrict access to or availability of material that the provider or user considers to be obscene, lewd, lascivious, filthy, excessively violent, harassing, or otherwise objectionable, whether or not such material is constitutionally protected."

[102]47 U.S.C. § 230(f)(2) defines "interactive computer service" as "Any information service, system, or access software provider that provides or enables computer access by multiple users to a computer server, including specifically a service or system that provides access to the Internet and such systems operated or services offered by libraries or educational institutions."

[103]47 U.S.C. § 230(f)(3) defines "information content provider" as: "Any person or entity that is responsible, in whole or in part, for the creation or development of information provided through the Internet or any other interactive computer service."

trict court agreed.[104] On appeal, the Fourth Circuit upheld the decision,[105] noting that Zeran's claim that Section 230 protected only publishers and not distributors did not apply because libel law deals only with material that is published and that, under traditional standards of distributor liability, the refusal to remove material in a timely manner once notified of its defamatory content transforms the distributor into publisher, making distributor liability nothing more than a subset of publisher liability.[106]

A similar result occurred in 1997 when Sidney Blumenthal and his spouse sued a Walter Winchell wannabe named Matt Drudge and AOL over accusations of wife-beating contained in his electronic publication called the *Drudge Report.* At the time, Sidney Blumenthal was a presidential assistant in the Clinton Administration. The report was available through a link on Drudge's Web site, which also contained hyperlinks to other online news publications. Drudge also distributed his report to 85,000 subscribers free of charge through his e-mail service. At the time of the alleged defamatory publication, Drudge had a written agreement with AOL allowing its subscribers access to his report. AOL paid Drudge a royalty of $3,000 monthly under its 1-year contract and reserved the right to remove content that was in violation of its terms of service. There was no evidence, however, that AOL had ever exercised such control or played any role in creating and developing material for the report. A few days after publication of the allegedly libelous statements, Drudge published a retraction that was also carried by AOL. The report was also removed from AOL's archives. In the defamation suit that followed, the federal district court in Washington, DC, held that AOL was immune from liability because it was an interactive computer service and Drudge was an information content provider, concluding that Section 230 applied to AOL.[107] Such immunity, the court held, was a policy choice made by Congress that distinguished the treatment of third-party information placed on the Internet from its treatment in other media: "Congress could have made a different policy choice; it opted not to hold interactive computer services liable for their failure to edit, withhold or restrict access to offensive material disseminated through their medium."[108] The fact that AOL's contract with Drudge allowed for editorial control does not seem to have made a difference, at least when such control had not been exercised.

---

[104]Zeran v. America Online, Inc., 958 F. Supp. 1124 (D.D.C. 1997).

[105]Zeran v. American Online, Inc., 129 F.3d 327 (4th Cir. 1997), *cert. denied,* 524 U.S. 937 (1998).

[106]The 1977 *Restatement (Second) of Tort* § 577 definition of "publication" states: "(1) Publication of defamatory matter is its communication intentionally or by a negligent act to one other than the person defamed. (2) One who intentionally and unreasonably fails to remove defamatory matter that he knows to be exhibited on land or chattels in his possession or under his control is subject to liability for its continued publication."

[107]Blumenthal v. Drudge, 992 F. Supp. 44 (D.D.C. 1998).

[108]Id. at 49.

The immunity provided by Congress in Section 230 has evolved into a durable defense for traditional ISPs[109] and other types of interactive computer service providers, including auction sites such as eBay and sales sites such as Amazon.com.[110] Interactive computer service providers retain Section 230 immunity even when they structure their sites in a way that limits an information provider's selection of content through the use of multiple-choice questions, closed-end response categories, and specific essay questions. For example, in *Carafano v. Metrosplash.com, Inc.*[111] a dating service doing business as *Matchmaker.com* was sued by actress Chase Masterson after a fraudulent dating profile using her name and personal information was created in the company's database. Reactions to the licentious profile resulted in harassing and obscene phone calls, e-mails and other disturbing correspondence. Masterson sued Metrosplash in federal district court for invasion of privacy, misappropriation of right of publicity, defamation, and negligence.

Metrosplash sought immunity under Section 230 as an interactive computer service provider, which was granted by the court. However, the district court also held that Metrosplash, in addition to being an interactive computer service provider, was potentially subject to publisher liability as an information content provider because unlike a bulletin board service, the company used a lengthy questionnaire to solicit information from prospective customers, including multiple-choice and forced-choice questions, the answers to which were an integral part of an individual's dating profile made available to prospective suitors. The court found that Section 230 immunity did not apply when the interactive service provider was also an information content provider, but granted company's motion for summary judgment on other grounds. On appeal, the Ninth Circuit concluded that the Internet matchmaker was not transformed into an information content provider because no profile has any content until the user actively creates it.[112] The panel held unanimously that although Metrosplash may have facilitated

---

[109]*E.g.,* Ben Ezra, Weinstein, and Co., Inc. v. America Online, Inc., 206 F.3d 980 (10th Cir. 2000), *cert. denied,* 531 U.S. 824 (2000) (AOL's e-mail requests to third-party content providers to correct stock quotation errors insufficient to overcome Section 230 immunity); Green v. America Online, 318 F.3d 465 (3rd Cir. 2003) (ISP immune from tort claims under Section 230 for defamation occurring in chat room).

[110]*E.g.,* Gentry v. eBay, Inc., 99 Cal. App. 4th 816 (2002) (online auction Web site an interactive computer service immunized by Section 230 against claims under California law for negligent misrepresentation when eBay did not sell or offer to sell sports collectibles); Schneider v. Amazon.com, 31 P.3d 37 (Wash. Ct. App. 2001) (Online Web site operator and bookseller is interactive computer service provider and not liable under Section 230 for allegedly defamatory comments in book review supplied by third party or breach of contract for failing to remove comments from its site); Patentwizard, Inc. v. Kinko's, Inc., 163 F. Supp. 2d 1069 (S.D.S.D. 2001) (Copy center serving as interactive computer service provider not liable under Section 230 for allegedly defamatory comments made in chat room by customer using copy center computer).

[111]207 F. Supp. 2d 1055 (C.D.C.A. 2002).

[112]Carafano v. Metrosplash.com, Inc., 339 F.3d 1119 (9th Cir. 2003).

the expression of information, the selection of content was left exclusively to the user.

The cracks in judicial equanimity regarding Section 230 immunities first appeared in a 2001 decision by the Florida Supreme Court.[113] The case concerned a number of negligence claims against AOL brought by a mother alleging that the ISP had allowed its chat rooms to be used to market photographs and videotapes of child pornography involving her son, even after having been notified of such activities. The Florida trial court[114] and the state's Fourth District Court of Appeal[115] held that AOL was entitled to immunity under Section 230 and that the federal law necessarily superseded the various state causes of action.

In a 4–3 decision, the Florida Supreme Court upheld the lower courts' decisions. The majority opinion closely tracked the Fourth Circuit Court of Appeal's decision in *Zeran*, tracing the history of the Section 230 and the Congressional intent behind its passage. Like *Zeran*, it relied on Section 577 of the *Restatement (Second) of Tort (1997)* as imposing publisher liability on a "speaker who fails to take reasonable steps to remove defamatory statements from property under her control."[116] Concluding that the publication of obscene literature or computer pornography is analogous to the defamatory publication in *Zeran*, the Court upheld the lower courts' application of Section 230 immunity.

The three judges in dissent claimed that the majority's reasoning led to a "totally unacceptable interpretation . . . that should not be followed."[117] In a blistering opinion written by Judge Lewis, the dissenters took issue with the majority's reliance on what they claimed was the wrong section[118] of a manifestly outdated[119] *Restatement*, rejecting the proposition that "the law treats as a publisher or speaker one who fails to take reasonable steps to remove defamatory statements."[120] They argued that it is erroneous to conclude that distributors are merely an internal category of publishers, and maintained that some form of distributor liability is appropriate under Section 230. They rejected the position that "an ISP can never be subject to liability based upon its own patently irresponsible role as a distributor who has allegedly been given actual notice of materials pub-

---

[113]Jane Doe v. America Online, 783 So.2d 1010 (Fla. 2001).

[114]Jane Doe v. America Online 2001 WL 228446 (Fla. 2001).

[115]Jane Doe v. America Online, 718 So.2d 385 (Fla. 4th DCA 1998).

[116]Jane Doe v. America Online, 783 So.2d at 1016.

[117]Id. at 1019.

[118]Id. at 1022. Rejecting the application of §577(2) ("One who intentionally and unreasonably fails to remove defamatory matter that he knows to be exhibited on land or chattels in his possession or under his control is subject to liability for its continued publication.") the dissent looked to §581(2) of the *Restatement*, which says that "one who only delivers or transmits defamatory matter published by a third person is subject to liability if, but only if, he knows or has reason to know of its defamatory character."

[119]Id. at 1021, n.11 (The *Restatement (Second) of Torts (1977)* does not address the role of Internet presences.)

[120]Id. at 1021 (quoting Zeran v. America Online Inc., 958 F. Supp. 1124, 1133 (E.D. Va. 1977)).

lished on its service by a specified customer (in furtherance of criminal conduct as defined by Florida law) by soliciting the purchase and sale of explicit child pornography, yet has done absolutely nothing about it."[121]

The dissenters reviewed Congressional intent in granting immunity under the Communications Decency Act. They argued that the plain language of Section 230 provides for publisher immunity but not distributor immunity, claiming that if Congress had meant to extend protection to distributors it would have done so. Comparing the legislative intent for the Good Samaritan provisions—protecting minors from inappropriate sexual content—to the results in case, the dissenters asked: "What conceivable good could a statute purporting to promote ISP self-policing efforts do if . . . an ISP which is specifically made aware of child pornography . . . may, with impunity, do absolutely nothing, and reap the economic benefits flowing from the activity?"[122] In its view, Congress never meant for such a broad immunity to apply.[123]

A second dissenting judicial opinion against the application of blanket immunity under Section 230 came in a June 2003 decision by the Ninth Circuit Court of Appeals. In *Batzel v. Smith*,[124] Section 230 immunity was again extended beyond ISPs to Web site operators and e-mail listserv moderators who publish information provided by third-party information content providers. Bob Smith, a handyman working at entertainment attorney and art collector Ellen L. Batzel's home in North Carolina, sent an e-mail message to the operator of the Amsterdam-based Museum Security Network Web site. In the e-mail, Smith claimed that Batzel had bragged to him about being the granddaughter of Heinrich Himmler, one of Adolf Hitler's right-hand men. Noting the hundreds of older looking European paintings in Batzel's home (that Batzel allegedly said she had inherited), Smith expressed his belief that the paintings were looted from homes of Jewish people during World War II.

Tom Cremers, a museum security professional and the operator of the Museum Security Network, received Smith's e-mail message and after some minor editing posted the message on the Network's Web site and included it in the Network's listserv, also noting that he had sent Smith's information to the FBI. When Smith became aware that his e-mail had been published, he contacted Cremers, complaining he never intended his e-mail to become part of an international message board because he had sent it to Cremers's personal e-mail, and not to the e-mail address through which messages for posting were sent by subscribers.

Batzel, learning of the post 3 months after it appeared, denied ever saying she was a descendant of a Nazi official or that she had inherited her artwork and claimed that Smith had defamed her over a billing dispute and because she re-

---

[121]Id. at 1024.
[122]Id. at 1025.
[123]Id. at 1026.
[124]Batzel v. Smith, 333 F.3d 1018 (9th Cir. 2003).

fused to show his screenplay to her Hollywood contacts. She sued Smith, Cremers, and the Museum Security Network for defamation in U.S. District Court in California. In an interlocutory appeal to the Ninth Circuit based on California's anti-SLAPP (Strategic Lawsuit Against Public Participation) statute, the panel held that Cremers was entitled to Section 230 immunity because the Web site and listserv fell under the definition of a user (and perhaps a provider) of an interactive computer service under Section 230(c)(1) of the Communications Decency Act, a category the court concluded was not limited to only ISPs. The court also rejected the argument that Cremers's decision to add Smith's e-mail to his Web site and listserv and providing some minor editing should result in making the information lose its status as third-party information "provided by another information content provider."[125]

The decision clearly recognized protection under Section 230 for Web site operators and listservs, but the panel remanded the case to the district court to determine whether, because Smith never intended his e-mail to be distributed, he could be considered another information content provider, potentially undercutting Cremers's claim of immunity under the statute.

Judge Gould, dissenting in part, took issue with the majority's interpretation of the statutory language "information provided by another information content provider." His concern was the difficulty that may be entailed in determining if information provided by another was done for the purposes of making it available (or further available) on an interactive computer service, a determination that must usually be made by the receiver of the information. Determining an author's intentions is difficult and would be impossible in those cases when the information provider is anonymous. "Laypersons may not grasp that their tort liability depends on whether they reasonably should have known that the author of a particular communication intended that it be distributed on the Internet."[126]

This was exactly the predicament facing Cremers; Smith denied any intention of having his communication to Cremers posted on the Internet. Judge Gould's solution was to hold that "the CDA immunizes a defendant only when the defendant took no active role in selecting the questionable information for publication. If the defendant took an active role in selecting information for publication, the information is no longer 'information provided by another' within the meaning of §230."[127] However, as the majority opinion pointed out, such a solution would only serve to undermine the primary reason for granting immunity—users or providers should have the ability to select information without fear of triggering liability.[128]

---

[125]47 U.S.C. § 230(c)(1). The panel points out that the legislative purpose in creating publisher immunity in the Act was to allow for such editorial decision making.

[126]*Batzel*, 333 F.3d at 1038.

[127]Id. at 1038.

[128]Id. at 1032.

In passing the Communications Decency Act, Congress found that "[t]he Internet and other interactive computer services have flourished, to the benefit of all Americans, with a minimum of government regulation."[129] It declared that it is the policy of the United States to "preserve the vibrant and competitive free market that presently exists for the Internet and other interactive computer services, unfettered by Federal or State regulation."[130] Such pronouncements, however, were not made in a vacuum. Congress passed the CDA with the intention of curtailing children's access to inappropriate material and to deter trafficking in obscenity, stalking, and harassment by means of computer. These goals are also reflected in the statute.[131]

Every court that has ruled on the issue so far has concluded that Section 230 grants broad immunity to users or providers of third-party content. The goal, of course, is to balance protection for the Internet medium with the interests of those victimized by it in gaining vindication and adequate compensation while deterring similar conduct by others. As illustrated in the *Zeran* case and others, broad application of Section 230 immunity often leaves victims without an effective remedy. Matt Drudge, for example, had an annual income of $36,000 at the time he was sued by Sidney Blumenthal and his spouse. An October 2003 decision by the Seventh Circuit bemoans the fact that Section 230 bears the title "Protection for 'Good Samaritan' blocking and screening of offensive material," while its principal effect is to induce ISPs to do nothing about the distribution of indecent and offensive materials via their services.[132]

Outcomes based on fact situations such as those found in the Florida Supreme Court's decision in *Doe,* where it appeared that a truculent ISP would do nothing about child pornography on its system, suggest that the expansive judicial interpretations of Section 230 might be on a collision course with the U.S. Supreme Court, the U.S. Congress, or both.

Yet to apply traditional notification-based distributor liability to interactive computer services could trigger an avalanche of unintended consequences. A sufficient number of lawsuits against interactive service providers, or even the chilling effect from potential liability, could shut off a substantial amount of material available on the Web today. The Fourth Circuit Court's opinion in *Zeran* described one possible scenario:

> Each notification would require a careful yet rapid investigation of the circumstances surrounding the posted information, a legal judgment concerning the information's defamatory character, and an on-the-spot editorial decision whether to risk liability by allowing the continued publication of that information. Although this might be feasible for the traditional print publisher, the sheer number

---

[129]47. U.S.C. §230(a)(4).
[130]47 U.S.C. §230(b)(2).
[131]47 U.S.C. §230(b)(4–5).
[132]Doe v. GTE Corp., 347 F.3d 655 (7th Cir. 2003).

of postings on interactive computer services would create an impossible burden in the Internet context. Because service providers would be subject to liability only for the publication of information, and not for its removal, they would have a natural incentive simply to remove messages upon notification, whether the contents were defamatory or not.[133]

Even properly motivated ISPs and other interactive computer service providers may be unable to scratch the surface of complaints about illegal or harmful content. One 1998 study estimated that the Web has about 320 million pages; the number is surely much larger today.[134] If even a minute fraction of the 7 billion domain requests made each day triggered complaints, the reviewing task could be overwhelming.[135]

The continuing convergence of technology also raises questions that need to be addressed. For example, a broadcast radio station, traditionally held liable for the content of third-party information, would clearly face liability for airing a syndicated program containing defamatory remarks provided by an independent third-party programmer. However, suppose an Internet-only "radio station" like Beethoven.com carried the same program. Would the Web stream operator be entitled to Section 230 immunity as an interactive computer service providing third-party content? A similar situation could occur if a local television station aired defamatory comments in a prepackaged story supplied by a public relations company in a so-called video news release. Clearly the station would face potential liability. Yet a Web site placing the same content on the Internet, at least one unaffiliated with a recognized news organization, would apparently not face liability. In fact, in litigation stemming from the T-shirt postings at issue in *Zeran*, radio station KRXO in Oklahoma City was forced to defend itself against charges of defamation, false light invasion of privacy, and intentional infliction of emotional distress after its morning show announcers read from and discussed the AOL postings on the air.[136]

It seems reasonable that the Web sites of established news organizations face potential tort liability for third-party content because they share in and benefit from the mantle of credibility that comes from a news organization's commitment to accuracy through rigorous fact-checking. It is also logical that online news sites face liability when they alter third-party content to such an extent that they can be considered central to its creation and development. However, to impose liability whenever an interactive computer service provider functions as a gatekeeper by selecting material for inclusion, and immunize only those operat-

---

[133]*Zeran v. America Online, Inc.*, 129 F.3d 327, 333 (4th Cir. 1997), *cert. denied*, 524 U.S. 937 (1998).

[134]Paul Recer (AP), *Computers Can't Access Vast Number of Web Sites*, Detroit Free Press, April 3, 1998, www.freep.com/tech/qnet3.htm (last visited July 1, 2003).

[135]Thomas L. Friedman, *Is Google God?* N.Y. Times, June 29, 2003, sec. 4, at 13.

[136]*Zeran v. Diamond Broadcasting, Inc.*, 19 F. Supp. 2d 1249 (W.D. Okla. 1997).

ing as common carriers of all information without regard to content would create serious chilling effects on most Internet content providers.

Wherever the lines are ultimately drawn, it is clearly time to rethink the appropriate standards of liability and advance the law further into the Internet age. As one commentator put it, "The law rolls in because it must, to meet a demand inherent in human affairs, the demand for predictability and limits."[137] As is often the case, technology has leapt ahead of the law, but like the media systems preceding it, the law of the Internet will evolve from the venerable but dated doctrines of a brick-and-mortar world to accommodate the unique technological attributes of the newest medium of mass communication.

---

[137]Deckle McLean, *Internet Defamation*, COMMUNICATION AND THE LAW, December 2002, at 22.

PART TWO

STUDIES OF ONLINE NEWS
AUDIENCES AND CONTENT

The Baseline Survey Projects: Exploring Questions

Michael B. Salwen
Bruce Garrison
Paul D. Driscoll

News on the World Wide Web and other forms of the Internet is still a relatively new way of finding out what is going on in the world. Scholars and professionals alike are still finding their way through the newest technological means of distributing news. Countless questions persist as to how and why people use online news. Still other questions pertain to the effects of those uses. There is a need for basic information.

This chapter investigates practical and basic online news use questions. It is the presentation of what we call our baseline research about online news use by adults in the United States. We wondered: Is the lack of use simply a matter of access, or is it much deeper? What about those who consume online news? Among individuals who have access to online news, for example: How do people use online news in conjunction with other, more traditional news media? Why do people use online news? How do people interact with online news stories? What do people think of the advertisements on online news sites?

Most of the empirical findings in this chapter come from research designed to address simple questions. Although fundamental, these intriguing questions raised in the professional and academic literature pertain to online news reading and related behaviors. Answering these basic questions can form a benchmark for additional research, future research designs and approaches, as well as the foundation for theoretical developments.

BASELINE STUDY METHODS

The baseline data in this chapter and data presented in several other chapters of this book represent findings from five national telephone survey studies conducted in 2001 and 2002 at the University of Miami in Coral Gables, Florida. The studies were conducted in the Communication Research Center, part of the School of Communication's Center for the Advancement of Modern Media. In addition to the baseline survey itself, we also drew on the other four more theoretically based surveys when comparable analyses were possible. More details about each survey's methodology are provided in the subsequent chapters in which theoretical aspects of the surveys are presented.

The national telephone surveys were based on samples drawn using stratified designs. This permitted each of the 50 states and the District of Columbia to be represented roughly proportionate to their populations according to the 2000 U.S. Census (http://www.census.gov). For the baseline survey, random residential telephone numbers were drawn from the Fall 2001, Winter 2002, Spring 2002, and Summer 2002 editions of the national Select Phone telephone software package on compact disc and database published by InfoUSA (Select Phone, 2001). The numbers were generated on a state-by-state basis from the database of more than 100 million residential and commercial telephone numbers (excluding the commercial numbers) using a table of random numbers and the random number selection function built into the Select Phone software. Each state roster of chosen numbers was then adjusted using a one-up and one-down last digit method to include unlisted numbers and newly assigned numbers not in the database. If there was no answer, a busy signal, or an answering machine reached during an attempted call, up to two more attempts were made later that evening or on other evenings to reach the number.

One of the national surveys was devoted solely to gathering baseline data on online news use. In this particular survey, conducted February 25 through 28, 2001, 511 respondents were contacted (for the complete questionnaire, see the Appendix). The response rate, excluding invalid contacts, was 61%. The completion rate here and in the other four national surveys reported in this volume was measured as completed calls relative to refusals.

A fundamental aspect of this book involved defining online news users. An October 2002 survey by the Pew Internet & American Life Project (2002b) found that 82 million Americans (or 70% of Internet users) had gone online for news; on an average day, about 26% of people with Internet access said they get news online. This series of studies used a more restricted criterion for news users. In most of the telephone surveys conducted in the series of studies, respondents were categorized as one of three user types:

- Nonuser—Those individuals contacted who stated they were not on the World Wide Web or not users of other online resources on the Internet on any days during an average week.
- Web user—Those who were on the Web or Internet, but did not use the Web for reading news on any days during an average week.
- News user—Those who were online and read online news at least 1 day in an average week.

We intentionally used slightly different operational measures of "users" in the surveys. We felt that we could contribute to understanding online news use and to future methodological development by examining whether slightly different versions of key questions yielded similar results, suggesting evidence for their reliability. In general, this level of reliability was confirmed.

In the baseline survey, respondents were considered nonusers if they responded zero to the question asking how many days a week, if any, they went online to use the Internet or World Wide Web (see Question 8 in the Appendix for this questionnaire). If they responded 1 or more days to this question, they were then asked a series of three questions (Questions 10, 11, and 12 in the questionnaire) to determine if they were online news users or Web users:

→*Many newspapers, news magazines, television stations, and cable television network stations have news sites on the World Wide Web. How many days a week, if any, do you read online Web sites offered by one or more of these conventional news media outlets? [NOTE: IF LESS THAN 1 DAY PER WEEK, CIRCLE "ZERO"]*

<u>→0</u> 1 2 3 4 5 6 7 DK REF

→*Internet service providers, such as America Online, Netscape, or Microsoft Network also have online news. How many days a week, if any, do you read the news from any of these or other Internet service providers? [NOTE: IF LESS THAN 1 DAY PER WEEK, CIRCLE "ZERO"]*

<u>→0</u> 1 2 3 4 5 6 7 DK REF

→*Search engines, such as Yahoo!, Lycos, or Alta Vista also have online news. How many days a week, if any, do you read the news from any of these or other search engines? [NOTE: IF LESS THAN 1 DAY PER WEEK, CIRCLE "ZERO"]*

<u>→0</u> 1 2 3 4 5 6 7 DK REF

If a respondent answered 1 day a week or more to any one or more of these questions, the person used the Web for news and was categorized as a news user. If a respondent answered zero to all three questions, the person was categorized as a Web user. We generally made no distinctions in magnitude of news users (beyond a minimum estimate of 1 day per week) and did not distinguish between the different questions that determined news users. We felt the different questions were not valid measures of different online news use, although we felt they all measured online news use. For example, respondents may have accessed online news sites on Time.com (Question 10), but reached the site through their Internet service provider (ISP; Question 11). For this reason, we treated the use of multiple questions to distinguish Web users from news users as additional questions to increase the likelihood of determining whether respondents were news users.

TABLE 4.1
User Variable in the Miami National Surveys

Survey	N	Valid N	Nonuser	Web User	News User
Baseline	511	507	194 (38.3%)	146 (28.8%)	167 (32.9%)
Survey 1	619	616	229 (37.2%)	152 (24.7%)	235 (38.1%)
Survey 2	512	508	211 (41.2%)	184 (35.9%)	113 (22.1%)
Survey 3	536	536	256 (47.8%)	118 (22.0%)	162 (30.2%)
Survey 4	792	781	313 (40.1%)	207 (26.5%)	261 (33.4%)

Note. Survey field dates: Baseline survey (February 25–28, 2002), Survey 1 (November 11–15, 2001), Survey 2 (November 15–16, 18–20, 27, 2001), Survey 3 (February 4–7, 2002), and Survey 4 (November 11–13, 2002).

In the baseline survey, 313 respondents went online (Web user). Of these, a little more than half (*n* = 167) used the medium for news (news user). The percentages of nonusers, Web users, and news users were remarkably similar in the different surveys, providing a reliability check to the slightly different wording sometimes used in the user variable measure.

The baseline sample was 56% female and 44% male. More than 80% of the sample was White (*n* = 417), about 10% were Black (*n* = 52), and 3% were Asian (*n* = 14). Politically, the typical respondent described himself or herself as middle of the road (*n* = 191, 39.8%). A total of 126 respondents described themselves as somewhat conservative (26.3%) and 74 (15.4%) as somewhat liberal. The demographic profile of the user variable indicated some noteworthy differences among different users. These differences are explored in this chapter. In general, Web users and news users were generally younger, better educated, and in higher household income brackets than nonusers.

Table 4.1 reports the percentages of the user variable in the five telephone surveys from the Coral Gables campus.

Although the data in Table 4.1 reveal some disparities among survey waves, they indicate that use of the online medium for news is substantial. The combined percentages for Web users and news users hover at about 60%, a statistic inline with recent national data in early 2003. In the future, we can expect the use of online news to increase as accessibility increases through wired access to the Web, but also through wireless access, such as with cellular telephones and handheld devices. Furthermore, existing Web users not using news sources may discover news content as they find new and expanded uses for the Web.

USER DEMOGRAPHICS

Understanding online users requires investigation into the characteristics of the respondents who defined themselves as online users. This section examines three of the most common demographic variables associated with socioeconomic status—age, education, and income. We did not measure occupation.

Age was measured as a ratio variable. Education and income were measured as categorized ordinal variables. For education, we used a 7-point scale: 1 = *no high school*; 2 = *some high school or in high school*; 3 = *high school degree*; 4 = *some college or in college*; 5 = *college degree*; 6 = *some graduate work or in graduate school*; and 7 = *graduate degree* (including law and medicine). Income was measured at the household, not individual level, because computer access is often a household rather than a personal matter. Annual household income was measured as a graduated 5-point scale: 1 = *under $25,000*; 2 = *$25,001 to $50,000*; 3 = *$50,001 to $75,000*; 4 = *$75,001 to $100,000*; and 5 = *more than $100,000*.

Analysis of variance (ANOVA) indicates that age is a significant discriminator among the three groups, as shown in Table 4.2. Nonusers tend to be much older (early and mid-50s) than Web users (late 30s and early and mid-40s) and Web news users (early 40s). Post hoc analyses at $p < .05$ support this observation. However, in four of the five national studies, there were no statistically significant differences between the mean ages of Web users and Web news users. In Survey 1, the mean age of Web news users was significantly younger than that of Web users. However, in Survey 3 and Survey 4 the mean age of Web users was lower than Web news users, but the difference was not statistically significant.

TABLE 4.2
ANOVAs of User Types by Age

User Type	N	M	SD	F	p
Baseline survey					
Nonuser	192	53.49[a]	17.74	35.74	.001
Web user	143	42.78[b]	15.73		
News user	160	40.05[b]	13.30		
Survey 1					
Nonuser	219	56.57[a]	17.71	63.69	.001
Web user	148	44.44[b]	15.07		
News user	229	40.35[c]	13.78		
Survey 2					
Nonuser	209	52.38[a]	17.92	26.62	.001
Web user	182	43.32[b]	15.18		
News user	112	40.43[b]	11.76		
Survey 3					
Nonuser	235	52.43[a]	16.19	34.08	.001
Web user	117	39.44[b]	14.40		
News user	158	41.78[b]	13.63		
Survey 4					
Nonuser	293	56.73[a]	18.79	69.90	.001
Web user	209	41.76[b]	15.36		
News user	257	42.88[b]	13.84		

Note. Means with different superscripts differ significantly at $p < .05$ by the Fisher least significant difference (LSD) test.

TABLE 4.3
ANOVAs of User Types by Educational Categories

User Type	N	M	SD	F	p
Baseline survey					
Nonuser	193	3.44[a]	1.24	51.02	.001
Web user	144	4.40[b]	1.46		
News user	163	4.82[c]	1.30		
Survey 1					
Nonuser	223	3.71[a]	1.46	33.94	.001
Web user	151	4.36[b]	1.38		
News user	231	4.80[c]	1.40		
Survey 2					
Nonuser	210	3.51[a]	1.19	47.79	.001
Web user	184	4.33[b]	1.30		
News user	112	4.86[c]	1.23		
Survey 3					
Nonuser	241	2.78[a]	1.18	34.36	.001
Web user	118	3.46[b]	1.15		
News user	151	3.70[b]	1.09		
Survey 4					
Nonuser	305	3.69[a]	1.37	44.77	.001
Web user	209	4.50[b]	1.37		
News user	257	4.74[b]	1.40		

Note. Means with different superscripts differ significantly at $p < .05$ by the Fisher LSD test.

In looking at educational level, nonusers tend to be less well educated than both Web users and Web news users. As shown in Table 4.3, nonusers are generally high school educated, but Web users and Web news users at least had some college. In all of the studies the Web news users had, on average, the greatest amount of formal education and, in three of the five studies, had significantly higher education levels than Web users. In all of the studies, nonusers reported significantly lower educational accomplishments.

Those who use the Web, and especially those who use the Web for news, tend to be younger and better educated than nonusers. Over 40% of nonusers cited the lack of a computer, an inadequate computer, or cost as their reasons for not going online (UCLA Internet Report, 2003). It is not surprising, then, that nonusers also report smaller household incomes compared with Web users and Web news users. As shown in Table 4.4, income is also an indicator of Web use and Web news use. Non-Web users, on average, typically have household incomes in the $25,001-to-$50,000 range, whereas Web users are much closer to, or in, the $50,001-to-$75,000 range. Web news users, on the other hand, earn $50,001 to $75,000 per household. The difference in the household incomes of Web users and Web news users—although Web news users' household incomes were somewhat higher throughout—was statistically significant in two of the five surveys.

TABLE 4.4
ANOVAs of User Types by Household Income Categories

User Type	N	M	SD	F	p
Baseline survey					
Nonuser	167	2.20[a]	1.08	34.48	.001
Web user	125	2.89[b]	1.31		
News user	147	3.31[c]	1.21		
Survey 1					
Nonuser	189	2.12[a]	0.99	46.54	.001
Web user	135	3.10[b]	1.24		
News user	220	3.16[b]	1.29		
Survey 2					
Nonuser	182	2.23[a]	1.12	33.39	.001
Web user	163	3.04[b]	1.31		
News user	107	3.32[b]	1.19		
Survey 3					
Nonuser	202	2.31[a]	1.10	21.20	.001
Web user	96	3.01[b]	1.37		
News user	143	3.10[b]	1.27		
Survey 4					
Nonuser	244	2.31[a]	1.11	45.15	.001
Web user	174	3.07[b]	1.25		
News user	224	3.33[c]	1.25		

Note. Means with different superscripts differ significantly at $p < .05$ by the Fisher LSD test.

USERS AND MEDIA USE

Because the focus of this book is online news use, it is worth examining whether online news users differ in relevant ways from those who are not online and those who are online but do not use online news. In this section we address whether news users differ from other respondents in their media use, primarily news media use. The question is important because as online news use becomes more common, researchers will want to investigate whether online news use supplements or displaces other news media use (Lin, 2001).

Table 4.5 reports a series of ANOVAs comparing nonusers, Web users, and Web news users in terms of news media use and overall television viewing. We included interpersonal discussion of news as a form of news acquisition. The first analysis examines the number of days per week respondents reported discussing with others issues in the news. The following four analyses examine differences in the number of days per week respondents estimated that they engaged in various news media activities by user category. Finally, the last analysis examined the amount of time spent watching television each day (converted into minutes). Because this is an exploratory analysis, we set significance at the liberal $p < .10$ standard and tested for post hoc differences among groups using LSD tests. All but one of the analyses, watching TV news, attained significance.

TABLE 4.5
Media Use Among User Groups

Activity	N	M	SD	F	p
Discussing news					
Nonuser	189	4.52[a]	2.54	10.77	.001
Web user	145	4.74[a]	2.27		
News user	166	5.58[b]	1.82		
Newspaper reading					
Nonuser	193	4.12[a]	2.84	2.87	.058
Web user	146	4.04[a]	2.84		
News user	167	4.71[b]	2.63		
Watching all-news cable TV					
Nonuser	189	2.69[a]	2.91	4.76	.001
Web user	145	2.72[a]	2.72		
News user	164	3.52[b]	3.52		
Watching TV news					
Nonuser	194	5.50	2.40	1.72	.180
Web user	144	5.05	2.37		
News user	167	5.43	2.17		
Listening to radio news					
Nonuser	193	4.61[a]	2.85	2.30	.100
Web user	144	3.96[b]	2.92		
News user	167	4.44[ab]	2.62		
Reading newsmagazines					
Nonuser	194	0.56	1.33	1.93	.146
Web user	143	0.45	1.18		
News user	164	0.74	1.39		
Watching television					
Nonuser	191	221.45[a]	143.18	45.15	.001
Web user	144	133.78[b]	89.96		
News user	160	128.22[bc]	81.99		

Note. Means with different superscripts differ significantly at $p < .05$ by the Fisher LSD test.

As can be seen in Table 4.5, online news users discussed issues in the news with others more days per week than nonusers or Web users. Nonusers and Web users did not significantly differ in their daily discussion of news. Table 4.5 also reports that online news users read a newspaper more days per week than their nonuser and Web user counterparts. The difference between nonusers and Web users was not significant. In Table 4.5, once again we see that online news users differed from their nonuser and Web user counterparts in estimated number of days each week they spend viewing all-news cable TV. The difference between nonusers and Web users was not significant. Table 4.5 reports no significant differences among the three groups of users regarding their overall noncable TV news viewing.

Radio news listening yielded somewhat different results from the pattern observed thus far, as shown in Table 4.5. Interestingly, nonusers appeared to listen to radio news more days per week, although the difference between nonusers and news users was not significant. Nonusers, however, listened to significantly more radio news than Web users. As with TV news, news magazine reading yielded no significant differences among groups. Table 4.5 shows a sharply different picture of nonusers regarding time in minutes spent daily watching television. The nonusers watched much more television than their Web and news user counterparts.

News users differed from other users, especially nonusers, in several ways. In discussing issues in the news, news users differed from the other users by discussing news with others more often, about 5.5 days per week compared to about 4.5 days week for nonusers and 4.75 days per week for Web users. The difference between nonusers and Web users was not significant. Concerns have been expressed about the link between increased Internet use and social isolation (Nie & Erbring, 2000), but these data suggest that, at least in the news context, those who use the Internet to acquire news also have a marked proclivity to discuss news events with others (albeit in a discussion format possibly mediated by the same Internet technology). Similarly, in reading a printed newspaper, Web news users read a newspaper more days per week (about 4.7 days) than nonusers (4.1 days) and Web users (4.0 days). The difference between nonusers and Web users was not significant. Additionally, Survey 2 in this series asked respondents to estimate the number of minutes per day spent reading a printed newspaper. No statistically significant differences were found between user groups, with each group averaging a little over a half-hour per day of newspaper reading (M nonuser = 35 min, M Web users = 31 min, M Web news users = 39 min), $F = 1.47$, ns. Although this finding perhaps bodes well for subscriptions to printed newspapers, it should be noted that a number of studies have found evidence for a significant decrease in the amount of time spent reading printed newspapers as time spent online increases (Nie & Erbring, 2000). A survey conducted by the Pew Internet & American Life Project (2002c) found that 14% of Internet users say the Internet has decreased the time they spend reading newspapers; the estimate rises to 21% for veteran Internet users. Waldfogel (2002) also found evidence of consumer substitution between the Internet and daily newspapers for news consumption. Nevertheless, 75% of Internet users also reported reading a printed newspaper in the last 7 days (Newspaper Association of America, 2002).

In watching an all-news TV cable channel, news users again differed from nonusers and Web users. News users watched an all-news cable channel about 3.5 days per week, compared to about 2.7 days for nonusers and Web users.

In these three important news media use activities, news users were discriminated as different from other users. A picture comes across of news users as news junkies, engaged in relatively heavy usage of the traditional news media of newspapers and all-news cable news channels. They also discussed issues in the news more than nonusers or Web users.

The picture was different for radio news listening. In this case, nonusers used the news medium more than Web users and there was no difference between Web users and news users. Perhaps this was because radio, unlike newspapers and all-news cable TV networks, is not a medium primarily associated with news. With radio, people who might not otherwise get as much news through traditional news sources might get their news in passing reports while using the medium for its primary function of entertainment. Nonusers may also listen to more radio because they are more disposed to entertainment media and then get news snippets between the entertainment-seeking activities.

Two other news media usage measures did not attain significance: television news and news magazines. Television (excluding all-news cable TV networks), like radio, is not primarily a news medium, which may have partly accounted for this finding. Also, television news use approached a ceiling (group means of 5–6 days per week), whereas newsmagazine reading was low among all groups, reaching a floor, making it difficult to test for significance. Differences in television news media use by user groups were found, however, in Survey 2, where respondents estimated the minutes of overall TV news use (cable and broadcast) on an average day. Nonusers reported watching significantly more television news compared to Web users or Web news users (nonusers $M = 97$ min; Web users $M = 69$ min; Web news users $M = 77$ min), $F = 6.58$, $p < .01$. Post hoc analysis showed no significant difference between Web users and Web news users ($p < .37$, LSD). A study by the Pew Research Center for the People and the Press (2000) also documents a significant decline in viewership of broadcast television news and a concomitant rise in use of the Internet for news, and concludes that the Internet is sapping broadcast news audiences. The Pew study also noted that Internet use is having less of a direct negative impact on cable TV news, radio, and print outlets.

Interestingly, overall television viewing (without regard for news) was far greater among nonusers, about 3.5 hr per day. Both Web users and news users watched a little more than 2 hr of television per day. The difference between Web users and news users was not significant. This finding supports other research suggesting a displacement effect on overall television viewing resulting from time spent online (Waldfogel, 2002).

NEWS SITES USED

Much evidence suggests that people get a good deal of their online news exposure as a consequence of general Web searching, attracted to enticements to click to news stories offered by their ISPs when they log on and off their computers or when searching for nonnews information on search engines such as Yahoo! and Lycos. Andrew Kohut, the director of the Pew Research Center in Washington, DC, said the Center often finds that many hits at news Web sites are serendipitous.

A presidential election offers an opportunity to examine the news audience's use of online news when people are interested in political candidates and the candidates' positions on issues. The Pew Research Center examined online election news use during the 1996 and 2000 presidential elections (The Pew Research Center for the People and the Press, 2000). The Pew report found that people sought "convenience" rather than original news as their primary motive for searching the Web for election news. This, the report noted, led many users to read established and "mainstream" news media on the Web. Comparing the findings to 1996 election data, Pew reported that online news users increased from one-fifth (22%) of the public to one-third (33%). Pew also compared the percentages of convenience versus searching for original news in 1996, showing an obvious trend toward greater convenience. Why should this be the case? As the report noted:

> Convenience is the Internet's main appeal as a campaign news source. More than half of those who went online for election news (56%) cited convenience as their main reason for doing so, up from 45% in 1996. During that campaign, when the Internet had yet to fully emerge as a news medium [1996], a majority of election news consumers (53%) said they went online because they weren't getting all the news they wanted from traditional media; just 29% cited that factor in the current survey. (The Pew Research Center for the People and the Press, 2000)

Based on a subsample of 186 online news users, Pew reported that a leading news organization, CNN, was the most frequently accessed site for election news. MSNBC, *The New York Times,* local news sites, and other traditional news sites also ranked high, although the data must be examined with caution because they are based on small numbers. Still, they suggest that a few leading branded news sources were already emerging as dominant, findings further supported in our studies. The data from the Pew Research Center for the People and the Press also indicated that many people turned to their ISPs (AOL ranked Number 2 and MSN ranked Number 5) and to search engine portals (Yahoo! ranked Number 3) for news. There is reason to suspect that people's exposure to news from ISPs and search engine portals were often chance encounters. People saw an enticement for an interesting news story, and they clicked it.

In the baseline survey, respondents who used online news named 161 news sites where they get most of their news online. Table 4.6 shows the top eight sites that received eight or more mentions. After the top eight, no site received more than three mentions, including three mentions of non-U.S. newspaper Web sites. The data indicate no dominant news site, with the top three receiving about equal mentions and Number 4, America Online, not far behind. These top four sites were national news sites. After this, the fifth most mentioned news site was the local newspaper (which would have received 15 mentions had local radio and television news sites been included). The considerable number of mentions of local news sites underscores that there will probably always be a place for local news online, especially online newspapers. A study by the Newspaper Association of America (2002) found that 62% of Internet users looking for local news turned to online newspapers.

TABLE 4.6
Top Eight News Sites

Site Name	%
Yahoo!	17
MSN	16
CNN	15
AOL	12
A local newspaper	9
MSNBC	6
New York Times	6
Fox News	5

Note. n = 161.

TABLE 4.7
Survey 3 Top 10 News Sites

Site Name	%
Yahoo!	18
CNN	17
AOL	15
MSN	9
Miscellaneous	9
International news site	7
Local newspaper	3
MSNBC	3
New York Times	3
USA Today	2
Drudge Report	2

Note. n = 148.

Survey 3 in the project, which focused on online news credibility, was conducted on February 4 through 7, 2001. This study included a number of baseline
questions as well. In this study, 148 respondents named 26 different categories of
sources of online news, as shown in Table 4.7. For this survey, online news readers preferred Yahoo!, CNN, and AOL as the dominant sources. However, MSN
was also highly ranked. It is interesting that local television news sites were not
more frequently mentioned, considering that local television news is often cited
as having a great deal of credibility with local audiences.

In summary, our findings are consistent with other research findings that a
few large, established, branded news sites have emerged as people's main sites
for news. People use sites associated with offline news organizations as well as
ISPs and search engines, which often feature news provided by the Associated
Press. Local newspapers are heavily used for learning about activities in the
community.

AUDIENCE INTERACTIVITY

There are differing levels of interaction or interactivity on the Internet and World Wide Web and different approaches to the term's meaning in the context of online news media (Massey & Levy, 1999). Pavlik (1999) defined interactivity as a two-way communication process of reciprocal influence. Interactivity is an interchange of information and action. It is not usually measured as a matter of speed and involves more than just making a choice (Kaye & Medoff, 1999; Lewis, 1999).

Most research approaches the concept of interactivity in terms of the audience. Scholars generally feel interactivity empowers the audience (Massey & Levy, 1999; Morris & Ogan, 1996). Web site interactivity is a positive attribute sought by most online news organizations (for more information, see the Dibean & Garrison discussion of the different forms of interactivity of online newspapers in Chapter 11). The inclusion of interactivity as part of an online news site serves to grab the attention of readers and increase the amount of time spent on the Web site. Some authorities maintain that interactivity is essential to the success of a site and has become mandatory for site design and for the overall reader experience. It has been viewed to delight visitors, to motivate them to initiate two-way and group communication, and to become more involved with the site and its goods and services (Kaye & Medoff, 1999).

Interactivity can be a user interacting with a computer program on the other end of the network connection or it could be an interaction with another person. For most online news organizations, audience interactivity is most often viewed as a matter of interaction with the software or programs of the Web site. The Web extends beyond the potential of interactive television and has emerged as a system of informative delivery.

Massey and Levy (1999) conceptualized interactivity in four dimensions for online newspapers. They looked at the complexity of choices available, responsiveness to the user, ease of adding information, facilitation of interpersonal communication, and immediacy as primary dimensions of interactivity of online news. Their analysis of Asian online newspapers, however, found online newspapers provided readers with complex choices of news content, but did not fare well on the other four levels.

Newhagen (1997) studied the perception of interactivity in mass media and computer networks. He found that respondents who had e-mailed comments to a network news program rated traditional mass media to be less interactive, less important, and of lower quality than respondents in a random national sample. Although interactivity ratings did not predict mass media credibility, respondents who had e-mailed the program and those who defined interactivity as "cybernetic feedback" found computer communication to be more credible than those who did not.

The baseline project investigated whether respondents interact with online news by "doing something" with accessed news. The project posed seven inter-

TABLE 4.8
Online Interactivity Behavior

Behavior	A Lot or Sometimes	Rarely or Never
Read online news to learn more about a news story that you learned about elsewhere (*n* = 166)	89.1%	10.8%
Bookmark or set one or more favorite Web sites that are news sites (*n* = 166)	54.2%	45.8%
Participate in online polls about issues in the news (*n* = 163)	21.1%	78.9%
Listen to audio news stories online (*n* = 163)	19.3%	80.7%
Watch streaming video of news stories online (*n* = 166)	19.3%	80.7%
Post or read messages about issues in the news that you subscribe to through your e-mail service, commonly known as a "listserv" or "alert list" (*n* = 166)	13.2%	86.7%
Post or read messages in message boards or chat rooms that concern events or issues in the news (*n* = 166)	12.6%	87.4%

activity questions, asking respondents whether they perform each activity a lot, sometimes, rarely, or never (see Table 4.8). As a group, the online news users did little interacting with online news stories. With five of the questions, large majorities said they rarely or never interacted with online news stories. The two interactive behaviors for which majorities said they participated did not require much activity.

To explore possible underlying dimensions of online interactive behaviors involving news content, a principal component analysis (Varimax rotation) of the seven interactivity items was conducted. As shown in Table 4.9, three separate and intuitively logical dimensions emerged, accounting for 62.35% of the variance in online interactive behaviors involving news content. The two items that

TABLE 4.9
Factor Analysis of Interactivity Behavior Items

Behavior	Multimedia	Listing	Searching
Listen to audio news stories online	.87	.02	.17
Watch streaming video of news stories online	.84	.25	.02
Post or read messages about issues in the news that you subscribe to through your e-mail service, commonly known as a "listserv" or "alert list"	.16	.84	.01
Post or read messages in message boards or chat rooms that concern events or issues in the news	.09	.84	.14
Bookmark or set one or more favorite Web sites that are news sites	.03	.17	.70
Read online news to learn more about a news story that you learned about elsewhere	.01	−.13	.69
Participate in online polls about issues in the news	.24	.18	.51
Variance explained	31.64%	16.08%	14.63%

loaded on Factor 1 both dealt with multimedia aspects on online news. The two items that loaded on Factor 2 both dealt with message listing activity, either by listservs or message boards and chat rooms. Finally, the three items that loaded on Factor 3 dealt with online news searching.

Because the factor analyses indicated a degree of construct validity, summated scales were created. For the multimedia and listing dimensions, the reliabilities were deemed acceptable for exploratory analysis (Cronbach α reliability coefficients .69 and .66, respectively). Reliability of the searching scale was unusually low (.33).

ATTITUDES TOWARD ONLINE NEWS ADVERTISING

Most online operations are "bleeding money from their parent companies," and to partly offset these losses online news sites rely heavily on advertising. "But what are those e-dollars buying?" one media critic asked. "When a Nielsen saleswoman recently gave me numbers for ads on well-trafficked sites, I was stunned. The 'click-through' rates, which reveal how many users click onto the ads, weren't even 1 percent. They were tenths, even hundredths, of 1 percent" (Fouhy, 2000, p. 19). Attitude toward online advertising is a practical concern relevant not only to the advertising and media industries, but also to the online consumers, facing a tsunami of irritating pop-up ads and, increasingly, longer form ads.

In our baseline study, a total of 115 news users (71.4%) said they noticed advertisements when they were online for news. Still, a surprising 28.6% ($n = 46$) said they did not notice the ads. Among those who noticed the ads, 46 (40%) said the online ads were just as annoying as conventional advertising and an equal number said they were more annoying than advertisements in conventional news media. Only 7 respondents (6.1%) said the online ads were less annoying than those in conventional news media and 16 (13.9%) said the ads were not annoying at all.

Notwithstanding issues of effectiveness and annoyance, Internet advertising revenues rarely cover the cost of providing content for online news sites. A marked downturn in online advertising in the last few years, along with the bursting of the dot-com bubble, has compounded the problem. Online advertising revenues tumbled an estimated 12% in 2001 and again by about the same amount in 2002 (eMarketer, 2002, p. 43). Internet revenue forecasts for 2003—although noticeably wide-ranging—are predicted to be somewhere between $5 and 10 billion, a relatively minor category comprising between 2% and 3% of total media spending (eMarketer, 2002).

Part of the common wisdom is that online users will not pay a fee to use a general-interest online news site. Palser (2001), who writes "The Online Frontier" column for the *American Journalism Review*, believes it's time to question the common wisdom. "We're not talking about decades of indoctrination," she contended. "Most sites and surfers have only been online a few experimental years. . . . Nobody wants to pay, but the premise that users would boycott online news out of indignation underestimates its value" (p. 82).

A few companies have been successful in persuading users to pay for news content. Dow Jones, for example, has been selling an online version of its printed newspaper, *The Wall Street Journal*, since 1996, and is nearing profitability. At the end of 2002, *The Wall Street Journal Online* had 650,000 subscribers. More than 20 other daily newspapers now restrict most of their online editorial content to paying customers, often letting print subscribers access the online content for free.

A hybrid revenue strategy has been adopted by many news organizations searching for a sustainable business model to fund their online presence. Increasingly, news sites allow access to some site information but require some form of payment for full access. For example, CNN.com sells access to its video streams (both directly to the consumer and indirectly to third-party distributors/bundlers like AOL) but provides the bulk of its news coverage without charge. The online magazine, *Salon,* teetering on the edge of bankruptcy, offers users a choice of accessing the bulk of its news content by either paid subscription or by agreeing to watch an advertisement in return for a 1-day pass.

One strategy for struggling sites may be the offering of fee-based ancillary services, such as access to archival material, to boost the revenue stream. More important may be generating revenue through a variety of small online content purchases (usually under $5) known as *micropayments* to supplement news site revenues. Popular ISPs and portals that provide substantial news coverage (often from the Associated Press and other news wires) but not considered traditional news media, are beginning to offer services like Internet radio and music downloading in addition to regular advertising links. For example, Yahoo! hopes to lessen its dependence on advertising revenue by increasing the number of premium services it can sell to the 200 million people who use its portal each month, including services designed specifically for users with broadband connections. One of the anticipated offerings is a premium service focusing on video broadcasts of sports, entertainment, and news programming (Hansell, 2003).

There are some indications that consumers are beginning to acclimate themselves to paying for online content. The Online Publishers Association (2002) noted the rapid growth in paid online content, estimating that 1 in 10 online users in the United States now pay for some form of online content, generating almost $1 billion in revenue in the first three quarters of 2002, much of it in the personal or dating and business or investment categories. General news sites generated 84% of their paid online content revenues by subscriptions (mostly monthly) and 16% through single purchases. Simply stated, original news and editorial coverage is unlikely to flourish on the Web unless consumers are convinced that paying for content is reasonable. Whatever its form—micropayments, monthly fees, or annual subscription fees—most news sites will need a hedge against insufficient advertising revenues.

One appeal of fee-based news sites is the possibility of avoiding or receiving reduced advertising, an approach already being tested by some Web services

(Yaukey, 2002). Particularly controversial are pop-up ads that appear suddenly in the browser window. Many users are thought to find these ads particularly annoying because they interrupt online searches. They are also controversial in media measurement because it is not clear whether a "hit" is a valid measure of ad exposure. Still, Charles Buchwalter, vice-president of the Internet media research firm Jupiter Media Metrix, said advertisers like them because they believe it is "a great way to get recognition and increase impact" (Ross, 2001, p. E3).

Precisely because consumers do not actively seek pop-up ads and because it is questionable whether they are read or whether they are closed before they are readable, in late December 2001 Jupiter Media Metrix decided to no longer include them as hits, or "unique visitors."[1] The decision had a significant impact on the firm's ratings data. As a result, x10.com, which promotes wireless cameras and ranked as the fourth most popular advertising site in October, with 39 million users, did not rank among the top Internet advertising sites after the new policy went into effect. "We don't think it makes sense to include traffic due to pop-ups in our top rankings because . . . there's a difference between voluntary and involuntary traffic," Buchwalter said (Ross, 2001, p. E3). In February 2003, some of the nation's largest online newspaper publishers settled a dispute with Gator, a company that distributes pop-up ads over Web sites visited by Gator users, including those of the newspapers' sites (Associated Press, 2003). Details of the agreement were sealed, but the company had been ordered by Federal District Court to stop delivering pop-up ads at sites run by the newspaper companies.

USER COMPUTER SKILLS AND INTERNET ACCESS

Survey 3 sought to determine baseline data on respondents' computer skills and access to the Internet and World Wide Web in early 2002. In Survey 3, a total of 536 individuals were asked whether they used a computer. A total of 341 (63.6%) said they used a computer at some level. Of those using a computer, 90.2% said they had some sort of Internet access. Most used the computer at home (65.2%), but another 31.6% used a computer at work or at school. A small proportion (3.2%) accessed a computer at a library or elsewhere. Broadband access, such as Digital Subscriber Line (DSL) and cable modem, is clearly growing. Estimates are constantly under revision, but there were approximately 15.6 million broadband, high-speed Internet subscribers in the United States in September 2002 (Leichtman Research Group, 2002). A survey conducted by the UCLA Center for Communication Policy from April to June 2002 reported that 17% of households subscribed to a high-speed service (UCLA Internet Report, 2003). The Pew Internet and American Life Project (2002a) reported that 24 million users had access to

---

[1] *Unique visitors* is a term of art in Internet ratings that refers to each user's visit to a site only once, no matter how many times the person visits the site during a sampling period.

high-speed Internet access at home. Many users, of course, have high-speed access at work or school. In this survey ($n = 143$), as many online users were connecting through broadband services (49.7%) as were dial-up services (50.3%), although an additional small number ($n = 15$) admitted not knowing their connection speed. Although this proportion of broadband to dial-up seems very high, it may be explained in terms of high-speed business and school access, but not home access. Users with high-speed access to the Internet not only spend significantly more time online each week but also outpace telephone dial-up users across a wide variety of online activities (UCLA Internet Report, 2003). More broadband users characterize the Internet as a very important or extremely important information source (78%) compared to 58% of dial-up users (UCLA Internet Report, 2003). The Pew Internet and American Life Project (2003a) found that broadband users distinguish themselves from telephone dial-up users in three major ways. Broadband users (a) become creators and managers of online content, (b) satisfy a wide range of queries for information, and (c) engage in multiple Internet activities on a daily basis.

In terms of use skills, most online news users in the survey felt they were intermediate-level computer users, as shown in Table 4.10.

Respondents, in general, were not what could be considered frequent online users. Although some computer users did not access the Internet and Web, access to an ISP was, on average, 1.03 days per week. The mean does not include nonusers, who did not answer the question. Characterizing the overall sample, respondents could not be considered frequent online users. Data in Table 4.11 show ISP and portal site access was also minimal among all computer users. Online users, however, were devoting considerable time online. Among people with computers and Internet access who accessed their ISP from 1 to 7 days a week, use was reasonably heavy ($M = 3.36$ days). These respondents spent more than an hour and a half (101 min) per day using the Internet. Use ranged from just 1 or 2 min per day to as much as 480 to 600 min or 8 to 10 hr per day. This measure is influenced, of course, by individuals with "always-on" high-speed broadband service such as those provided by DSL and cable modem companies. Internet and Web use for online news was about a half-hour per day (27 min). Online news use ranged from just a couple of minutes to as much as 300 min per day for one respondent.

TABLE 4.10
Perceived Computer Skills Levels of Online News Users

Level	%
Beginner	12
Intermediate	56
Expert	32

Note. $n = 154$.

TABLE 4.11
Access to Online News

Level	n	M	SD	Mdn
Days per week accessing ISP	281	1.0	1.9	0.0
Days per week accessing portals	275	1.0	1.9	0.0
Minutes per day using Internet or Web	160	101.1	115.4	60.0
Days per week spent using e-mail	157	5.5	2.1	7.0
Days per week spent reading online news	312	1.7	2.4	0.0
Minutes per day spent reading online news	152	26.8	31.2	20.0

REASONS FOR USING ONLINE NEWS

The baseline project asked respondents about their level of agreement with 16 possible reasons for following news on the World Wide Web. Respondents answered these questions on a 5-point scale with responses *strongly agree, agree, neither agree nor disagree, disagree,* and *strongly disagree*. The responses to these questions are reported in Table 4.12, where the agreement and disagreement responses are collapsed (interviewers were instructed to emphasize the words in bold). As a group, respondents tended to agree with most of the reasons for using online news, with only two questions not eliciting majority agreement.

Because the baseline study was exploratory, it will be helpful to explore whether the 16 reasons for using online news reflected underlying dimensions. To this end, a principal component factor analysis with Varimax rotation was run. This yielded a four-factor solution that accounted for 57.67% of the variance. The factors generally made intuitive sense and can be refined by future researchers wishing to replicate the findings (see Table 4.13).

The three items on Factor 1 pertained to the convenience of using online news. As the bolded words and phrases that were emphasized by the interviewers indicate, these respondents evaluated online news as convenient and easy. The five items that loaded on Factor 2 dealt with the quantity and quality of online news. In addition to finding more news online, these respondents also evaluated online news as different, reliable, and more in-depth than conventional news. The two items on Factor 3 can be conceived as a more extreme case of the quantity–quality factor. Here, respondents evaluated online news in terms of major differences. Online stories were either unusual or presented different points of view. Finally, the two items on Factor 4 dealt with serendipitous chance encounters with the news. Here, respondents came on news while doing other things online or perhaps while searching for specific news stories.

Four other items on the bottom of the table did not clearly load on any single factor. They either did not load well on any factor or loaded high on two or more factors. The one item that was a close call dealt with respondents' evaluations of news "that directly interests you." This loaded high on the difference factor, but it also loaded high on the convenience factor.

TABLE 4.12
Reasons for Following News Online

Reason	Agree	Disagree	Neither
Because you can go online to the World Wide Web to get the news **any time you want** (n = 162)	95.1%	1.8%	3.1%
Because you can **go directly** to the news that interests you (n = 163)	90.8	3.7	5.5
Because news on the Web is a **quick and easy way** to keep up with the news (n = 161)	87.6	8.1	4.3
Because getting news on the Web is **convenient** for you (n = 163)	84.0	6.1	9.8
Because you can go to the Web to **learn more about breaking news stories** (n = 163)	81.6	12.9	5.5
Because getting news on the Web is **easier** than getting it from conventional news sources (n = 163)	70.5	20.2	9.2
Because the Web offers news that reflect your **interests** (n = 163)	68.1	18.4	13.5
Because you find interesting **news stories** by chance while you are on the Web doing other things (n = 163)	67.5	24.5	8.0
Because news on the Web offers the ability to get **different viewpoints on news stories** (n = 161)	65.2	22.4	12.4
Because news stories catch your attention when **logging on or logging off** the computer (n = 163)	60.1	33.2	6.7
Because you find **unusual** news stories online (n = 163)	60.1	27.5	12.5
Because you can get **news** on the Web that is not available elsewhere (n = 162)	59.9	32.1	8.0
Because you can get **more news** on the Web than from conventional news sources (n = 163)	57.1	34.9	8.0
Because news on the Web is **more in-depth** than news from conventional news sources (n = 161)	51.6	35.4	13.0
Because news on the Web is **different** from conventional news sources (n = 161)	41.6	41.6	16.8
Because news on the Web is more **reliable** than news from conventional news sources (n = 160)	16.3	55.0	28.8

Note. Interviewers were instructed to emphasize the words in bold.

Having at least partly established construct validity of sets of items through factor analysis, the next step involved establishing the reliability of summated scales to determine how important respondents evaluated each of the dimensions. The scales of the first two factors achieved acceptable reliability (Cronbach α coefficients of .79 and .75, respectively). The other factors, each based on two items, yielded low reliability (.48 and .59, respectively). Normally, analyses might not be run on the low-reliability scales, especially when below .60, but because the analysis is exploratory to aid future researchers, the analyses continued.

As Table 4.14 indicates, five of the six paired sample t tests were significant. Respondents viewed convenience of online news as its primary strength, significantly more so than the other three factors ($p < .001$). On the 5-point scale, respondents evaluated convenience as almost 4. They viewed the quantity–quality factor as the least important dimension of online news—barely above the 3.0

TABLE 4.13
Factor Analysis of Reasons for Using Online News

Reason	Convenience	Quantity/ Quality	Different	Serendipity
Because getting news on the Web is **convenient** for you	**.86**	.12	−.03	.19
Because news on the Web is a **quick and easy** way to keep up with the news	**.78**	.03	.16	−.15
Because getting news on the Web is **easier** than getting it from conventional news sources	**.78**	.16	−.09	.14
Because news on the Web is **different** from conventional news sources	.22	**.74**	.06	−.03
Because news on the Web is **more in-depth** than news from conventional news sources	.11	**.70**	.27	−.25
Because you can get **more news** on the Web than from conventional news sources	.32	**.68**	.18	.08
Because news on the Web is more **reliable** than news from conventional news sources	−.09	**.64**	.02	.02
Because you can get **news** on the Web that is not available elsewhere	.10	**.58**	.26	.30
Because you find **unusual** news stories online	.02	.21	**.69**	.31
Because news on the Web offers the ability to get **different viewpoints on news stories**	.11	.37	**.63**	−.15
Because you find interesting **news stories** by chance while you are on the Web doing other things	.25	−.03	−.03	**.77**
Because news stories catch your attention when **logging on or logging off** the computer	−.04	−.08	.13	**.77**
Because you can **go directly** to the news that interests you	.40	.03	.63	.07
Because you can go online to the World Wide Web to get the news **any time you want**	.60	.05	.52	−.07
Because the Web offers news that reflect your **interests**	.07	.32	.41	.45
Because you can go to the Web to **learn more about breaking news stories**	.42	.14	.24	.21
Variance explained	27.65%	13.11%	10.36%	6.55%

midpoint. Respondents did not discriminate their evaluations of the difference and serendipity factors, rating both reasonably high.

TYPES OF NEWS ACCESSED

As illustrated in Survey 3, online news users show a distinct preference for national and international news, whereas newspaper and television users seek primarily local news. Data in Table 4.15 indicate that some respondents could not

TABLE 4.14
Paired Sample *t* Tests of Reasons for Using Online News

Reason	M	SD	N	r	t
Convenience	3.95	.79		.31**	11.72**
Quantity–Quality	3.10	.75	159		
Convenience	3.94	.79		.05	5.66**
Difference	3.45	.82	160		
Convenience	3.94	.79		.16*	5.27**
Serendipity	3.46	.97	161		
Quantity–Quality	3.10	.75		.48**	5.43**
Difference	3.45	.82	159		
Quantity–Quality	3.10	.75		.05	3.86**
Serendipity	3.46	.96	159		
Difference	3.45	.82		.12	0.07
Serendipity	3.45	.97	160		

*$p < .05$. **$p < .001$.

TABLE 4.15
Type of News Read by Medium Preference

	Respondent Primary News Source		
Type of News Preferred	Newspaper	Television	Online
Local	53%	43%	14%
National	26	32	49
International	6	9	25
Local and national equally	5	7	2
Local and international equally	1	1	1
National and international equally	2	2	8
All three types equally	7	6	1
Totals	100	100	100

Note. Newspaper $n = 424$; television $n = 484$; online $n = 381$.

determine a single category of preference. Most read national news (49%) or international news (25%) online. Another 8% preferred both equally. Local news, which apparently is still served by newspapers and television adequately for these respondents, was read by 14%. The study did not determine if respondents meant local news near where they lived or local news from another geographic location that was considered "local" by the respondent.

In the fourth survey ($n = 792$) we asked the 264 news users to assess their use of 11 types of online news, using 5-point scales ranging from *all the time* to *never*. The collapsed categories are shown in Table 4.16. The most frequently accessed news was the weather. Two other categories were accessed all the time or often by at least 50% of the online news users: local news and international news. Least ac-

TABLE 4.16
News Subject Category Preferences of Online News Users

Type	All/Often	Sometimes	Rarely/Never
Weather	61.7%	20.5%	17.8%
Local news	54.9	15.5	29.6
International news	50.0	31.1	18.9
Domestic politics	44.3	30.7	25.0
Business	36.4	31.1	32.6
Sports	35.6	22.0	42.4
Crime news	35.4	30.4	34.2
Health/fitness	23.9	38.3	37.9
Science news	22.3	31.8	45.8
Opinion	16.0	27.1	56.9
Celebrity news	12.9	21.6	65.5

TABLE 4.17
Preferences for General and Important News Seeking

News Medium	General	Important Story
Television news	54%	76%
Print news	17	4
Radio news	3	6
Online news	26	14

Note. $n = 376$ for General (the question asked: If you have a choice of news media for information about a news story, which would you choose? Would it be television, radio, print, or online news?); $n = 377$ for Important Story (the question asked: Which single news medium do you first turn to when you learn about an *important* news story? Is it television, radio, newspapers, or online news?).

cessed were news about celebrities, opinion, and—perhaps surprisingly for a technologically sophisticated audience—science news.

When news reports were available online and in other news media, respondents to Survey 3 expressed a strong preference for television, as shown in Table 4.17. More than half (54%) identified television as the top choice. The proportion increased to three quarters (76%) of respondents when the decision involved an "important story." The most interesting observation here, perhaps, is the decline of use of print news media for important stories. Readers clearly seek immediacy for important stories and turn to television. Although online news sites offer immediacy as well, readers still turn to television when important stories are developing.

Online readers in Survey 3 also believed that the familiarity of a news organization that they used online was significant. In Table 4.18, data show more than half (57.3%) of those responding felt the familiarity of a new brand name was extremely important or very important.

TABLE 4.18
Perceived Importance of Familiarity of News Organization

Site Name	%
Extremely important	21%
Very important	37
Somewhat important	28
Not very important	9
Not important at all	6

Note. n = 150.

TABLE 4.19
Perceived Online Privacy Safety

Type	%
Very safe	22%
Somewhat safe	43
Neither safe nor unsafe	14
Somewhat unsafe	17
Very unsafe	5

Note. n = 155. Respondents were asked, "How safe do you feel regarding your privacy when using the Internet?"

ONLINE PRIVACY ISSUES

Use of online news and information and the interactive nature of most Web sites has led to an increase in the amount of concern individuals have for their privacy online. These matters will be addressed elsewhere in this book, but the baseline research looked at perceived privacy "safety" levels of online information and online commercial activity. As shown in Table 4.19, nearly two thirds of online users in Survey 3 felt somewhat safe (43%) or very safe (22%) online.

When it came to making purchases online, confidence increased slightly. A total of 68% of respondents (n = 155) said they had made at least one online purchase in the past with a credit card.

REFERENCES

Associated Press. (2003, February 8). Publishers settle with Gator in fight on Web pop-up ads. *The New York Times*, p. 2C.

eMarketer. (2002). Media spending outlook 2003: A review of the latest projections, survey data and trends in the online/offline media landscape. Retrieved February 4, 2003, from http://www.emarketer.com

Fouhy, E. (2000, May). Which way will it go? *American Journalism Review, 22*(4), 18–19.

Hansell, S. (2003, February 13). Yahoo outlines plans for adding premium services. *The New York Times*, p. C6.

Kaye, B. K., & Medoff, N. J. (1999). *The World Wide Web: A mass communication perspective.* Mountain View, CA: Mayfield.

Leichtman Research Group. (2002, November). Broadband Internet tops 15.6 million in the U.S. Retrieved February 24, 2003, from http://www.leichtmanresearch.com/press/1107release.htm

Lewis, M. (1999). *Definition of interactivity.* University Library Karolinska Institutet, Stockholm, Sweden. Retrieved January 20, 2003, from http://netsim.kib.ki.se/interactivity.cfm

Lin, C. A. (2001). Audience attributes, media supplementation, and likely online service adoption. *Mass Communication & Society, 4,* 19–38.

Massey, B. L., & Levy, M. R. (1999). Interactivity, online journalism, and English-language Web newspapers in Asia. *Journalism & Mass Communication Quarterly, 76,* 138–151.

Morris, M., & Ogan, C. (1996). The Internet as mass medium. *Journal of Communication, 46,* 39–50.

Newhagen, J. (1997). The role of feedback in the assessment of news, information processing and management. *Information Processing & Management, 33,* 583–594.

Newspaper Association of America. (2002). *Facts about newspapers 2002.* Retrieved February 24, 2003, from http://www.naa.org/info/facts02/index.html

Nie, N. H., & Erbring, L. (2000). *Internet and society: A preliminary report.* Stanford, CA: Stanford Institute for the Quantitative Study of Society.

Online Publishers Association. (2002, December). *Online paid content: U.S. market spending report.* Retrieved February 4, 2003, from http://online-publishers.org/opa_paid_content_report_122002_final.pdf

Palser, B. (2001, October). Pay-per-click. *American Journalism Review, 82.*

Pew Internet & American Life Project. (2002a, June). The broadband difference: How online Americans' behavior changes with high-speed Internet at home. Retrieved November 11, 2002, from http://www.pewinternet.org/reports/toc.asp?Report=63

Pew Internet & American Life Project. (2002b, December). Counting on the Internet. Retrieved February 14, 2003, from http://www.pewinternet.org/reports/toc.asp?Report=80

Pew Internet & American Life Project. (2002c, March). Getting serious online. Retrieved February 14, 2003, from http://www.pewinternet.org/reports/toc.asp?Report=55

Pew Research Center for the People and the Press. (2000). Youth vote influenced by online information: Internet election news audience seeks convenience, familiar names. Retrieved December 2, 2001, from http://www.people-press.org/online00que.htm

Ross, R. (2001, December 28). Window closed on pop-up ads. *Toronto Star,* p. E3.

UCLA Internet Report. (2003). Surveying the digital future: Year Three. Retrieved February 5, 2003, from http://www.ccp.ucla.edu

Waldfogel, J. (2002, September). Consumer substitution among media: Federal Communications Commission Media Ownership Working Group. Retrieved November 14, 2002, from http://www.fcc.gov/ownership/studies.html

Yaukey, J. (2002, April 15). *End of free: As Web sites struggle toward profitability, consumers are paying the price in the form of new fees for popular service.* Gannett News Service.

CHAPTER FIVE

Online News Credibility

Rasha A. Abdulla
Bruce Garrison
Michael B. Salwen
Paul D. Driscoll
Denise Casey

The number of adults using the Internet to find and read news online is on the rise. One national study by the Pew Research Center reported that weekly use of online news tripled from 11 million to 36 million people in the United States between 1996 and 1998, which the center called "astonishing" (Pew Research Center for People & the Press, 1998). Other studies have shown similar growth in use of the Internet, the World Wide Web, and other online information resources (see, e.g., Jupiter Media Metrix, 2001; Nielsen Media Research, 1999).

Multiple concerns about online news and information have emerged in the past decade. These include fear about public access to private information, but also about publication of rumors online, inclusion of personal and institutional biases, the general levels of trust of online news, and the accuracy of information rapidly posted to Web sites during the cycles of breaking news stories. One issue that has emerged because of this growth is the credibility of new information technologies and new media news delivery systems. One analysis reported that barely one in three media Web sites posted privacy policies for information provided both voluntarily (e.g., personal electronic mail addresses or other information taken from user registration forms) and involuntarily (e.g., Web browser cookies or tracking specific page visits and clicks within a Web site) by users (Pryor & Grabowicz, 2001). Even when they are posted, online statements of privacy policy are often lengthy and nearly incomprehensible. They tend to serve more as a legal alibi for the Web site owner than an actual information source for site users.

This study investigated the similarities and differences of user perceptions of the credibility of traditional news media delivery systems—newspapers and television news—and the credibility of Web-based online news. Specifically, this chapter investigates news credibility in an attempt to determine the components of news credibility across traditional and new online news media.

CREDIBILITY OF ONLINE NEWS

Because of content accuracy, reliability, and other related concerns, some observers have predicted a troubled future for online news. Johnson and Kaye (1998) reminded us that one of the basic characteristics of the Internet, its potential free access to everybody to upload information without much scrutiny, might affect the credibility of the medium as a source of information. Flanagin and Metzger (2000) noted that whereas newspapers, books, and television undergo a process of information verification before they reach the public, Internet sites do not always use such measures. The lack of editorial and gatekeeping rules similar to those in the traditional print and broadcast news media is central to the problem. This, of course, is likely to increase the importance of branded online news sites such as CNN.com and perhaps emphasize the value of the so-called halo effect of an existing print or television news organization to its online equivalent (e.g., *Time* magazine and its Web counterpart, *Time Online*).

Schweiger (1998) pointed out that credibility becomes an important heuristic for content selection at a time of information overload. Credibility may also influence the journalistic and commercial success of a medium (Schweiger, 2000). Online news industry observers and newspaper editors have expressed similar concerns over credibility, believability, ethical lapses, newsgathering techniques, and news presentation (Arant & Anderson, 2000; Lasica, 2001). These and numerous other professional issues are frequent topics of discussion and debate on the pages of the *Online Journalism Review* (http://ojr.usc.edu).

Studies conducted in recent years have analyzed the dimensions of the Internet, the Web, and, to a lesser extent, online news credibility. Flanagin and Metzger (2001) observed that much media credibility research has ignored online news and that the bulk of research was conducted prior to online news development. There are differences, these scholars argued, between online news and other more established news media such as television, radio, and newspapers. Online news can be reported at any time. The newspaper, by contrast, is limited to when people obtain the hard copy. Thus, the dimension of timeliness must be considered in studying credibility of the Internet as a medium.

Flanagin and Metzger (2001) concluded that the Internet is a "multidimensional technology used in a similar manner to other more traditional media" (p. 153). They found online conversational uses such as chat rooms, electronic mail, and the telephone that paralleled traditional media. They also determined information-retrieval and information-giving similarities. They concluded that "needs fulfilled by these channels cluster in ways consistent with past research, regardless of the technologies employed to meet them" (p. 153).

In an earlier study, Flanagin and Metzger (2000) investigated perceptions of Internet information credibility in comparison to other media. They concluded that the Internet was as credible as television, radio, and magazines, but not newspapers. They found that credibility varied by medium among different types of information sought by audiences, such as news and entertainment. Respondents reported that they did not verify information found on the Internet, but this finding also varied by the type of information needed. The amount of experience using the Internet and how an individual perceived the information were associated with efforts to verify online information.

Schweiger (2000) found newspapers in Germany were rated ahead of the Web and television on 9 of 11 credibility items. He also found that Web users and nonusers alike rate the credibility of the Web as remarkably similar to television and newspapers.

Sundar (1996) determined that individuals rated stories with direct quotations from sources to be significantly higher in credibility and quality than those without quotations. The use of direct quotations did not appear to affect subject ratings of liking for online news or perceptions of representativeness or newsworthiness of the online news.

Kiousis (1999) found news credibility perceptions to be influenced by media use and interpersonal discussion of news. He found general skepticism about news, but people rated newspapers as more credible than online news or television. Online news, however, was rated more credible than television. Like other studies of print and broadcast news media, Kiousis found the credibility rating of a medium was associated with its use. He also found links between discussion of news and perceptions of television news, but not for online news or newspapers. He offered evidence of links between media use and public perceptions of credibility for newspapers and television news, but not in the assessment of online news.

Using credibility as their focus, Johnson and Kaye (1998, 2000) concluded that online news media and online candidate literature were perceived to be more credible than traditional print and broadcast news media, even though both online news and traditional news media were perceived to be somewhat credible. No differences were found for news magazines and issue-oriented sources.

Finberg, Stone, and Lynch (2002; see also Online News Association, 2001) found one main concern about online news credibility was the perceptions of other journalists, who do not hold it in high regard. The national study determined that online news was a supplementary news source for most users. They also observed that the public has accepted online news as a credible news option, and that many readers did not feel online news credibility was an issue.

MEDIA CREDIBILITY MEASURES

Researchers have utilized a variety of measurements and statistical procedures in their quest to understand media credibility. Bivariate and multivariate approaches have been used, including regression analysis (Mulder, 1980, 1981) and factor analysis (Flanagin & Metzger, 2000; Newhagen & Nass, 1989). Many have used traditional data collection methods such as telephone surveys and laboratory and field experiments. New technologies such as online surveys and other experiments are beginning to be used as well (Johnson & Kaye, 1998; Sundar, 1998). Online surveys using electronic mail and the Web, however, have unresolved methodological issues such as low response rates, self-selection bias, and access (Couper, Traugott, & Lamias, 2001; Schaeffer & Dillman, 1998).

Media credibility and believability are closely related and used interchangeably at times in the literature. In conventional use, *credibility* is typically defined as a facility for inspiring or instilling belief. Something that is credible is thought to offer reason or evidence to be believable or within the range of possibility. If it is believed, it is considered to be true or honest. *Believability* is a factor in the credibility of a source or medium. Meyer (1973), for example, narrowly defined credibility as whether or not a newspaper was believed by its readers. Robinson and Kohut (1988) found that believability levels for an information medium are not closely related to political and demographic variables that had been found to divide American public opinion. They observed that although the public groups news media according to believability, the resultant groupings are not the same as the differences usually drawn between television and print journalism, although respondents did say that local TV is less likely to be factual than the nation's major dailies. They concluded that, in 1988 at least, there was "no believability crisis for the press" (p. 188). The study also found that opinions about believability were not associated with one particular medium and, although personality was a factor in believability of individual journalists, it was mostly a factor of organizations and not people or celebrity.

Numerous researchers have developed media credibility scales. Despite the diversity of scales, the various scale items are highly similar and measure the same underlying dimensions. Rather than searching for a single scale, researchers often create ad hoc scales to tap into hypothesized "dimensions" of credibility.

Sundar (1999) developed a credibility scale applicable to both print newspapers and online newspapers. He found "striking similarity between the factor structures underlying receivers' perceptions of print and online news" (p. 382). He claimed this similarity made it possible to use the same scales for different media, which he described as a "boon" to researchers (p. 382).

Johnson and Kaye (1998, 2000) employed believability, fairness, accuracy, and depth of information in their study. Sensationalism was one of six dimensions used by Sundar (1996). He also used accuracy, believability, bias, fairness, and objectivity. Kiousis (1999) measured online news credibility by asking respondents to assess whether online news is factual, is concerned with making profits, invades people's privacy, is concerned about the community's well-being, and cannot be trusted on a 5-point Likert-type scale ranging from *strongly agree* to *strongly disagree.*

Flanagin and Metzger (2000) used single-item measures in studying the credibility of Internet information. They operationalized credibility as a multidimensional concept built from five traditional components found in the literature: believability, accuracy, trustworthiness, bias, and completeness.

Trustworthiness, fairness, bias, completeness, respect for privacy, representation of individual interests, accuracy, concern for community well-being, separation of fact and opinion, concern for public interest, factual foundations of information published, and qualifications of reporters were used as one set of credibility measures by Rimmer and Weaver (1987). The study's second set of measures was derived from traditional Roper-style media use and preference questions.

Ognianova (1998) utilized nine semantic differential items to measure online news story credibility. They were factual–opinionated, unfair–fair, accurate–inaccurate, untrustworthy–trustworthy, balanced–unbalanced, biased–unbiased, reliable–unreliable, thorough–not thorough, and informative–not informative. A separate 4-item scale was used to measure advertisement credibility.

Wanta and Hu (1994) used believability and affiliation indexes to evaluate media credibility. The believability index was built around media manipulation of public opinion, getting facts straight, dealing fairly with all sides of an issue, and separation of fact from opinion. Affiliation was measured with concern for community well-being, watching out for reader interests, and concern for public welfare.

Gaziano and McGrath (1986) identified 12 dimensions of newspaper and television news credibility in a national telephone survey. These were fairness, bias, telling the whole story, accuracy, respect for privacy, watching out after people's interest, concern for community, separation of fact and opinion, trustworthiness, concern for public interest, factuality, and level of reporter training.

Furthermore, Gaziano's (1987) analysis of four major mid-1980s credibility studies found 12 different groupings of operationalizations of credibility. These included (a) believability; (b) accuracy, completeness, and covering up facts; (c) trustworthiness and reliability; (d) being unbiased, balance of coverage, fairness, objectivity; (e) other characteristics of press performance, such as invasion of privacy, covering up stories; (f) overall evaluations of how well media do their jobs; (g) confidence in media institutions, comparisons of media with other institutions; (h) independence of media from special interests, other organizations, institutions; (i) power/influence of media in community or society; (j) relationship of news media to government; (k) honesty and ethical standards; and (l) professionalism, training of people in the media. She noted that these measures had also been used in studies by Hovland and Weiss (1951–1952), Meyer (1973), and others.

Claiming that the Gaziano and McGrath (1986) scale lacked face validity and theoretical grounding, Meyer (1988) developed an index for newspaper credibility composed of five dimensions: fairness, bias, telling the whole story, accuracy, and trustworthiness. He argued that face validity was evident in his scale because the items pointed toward believability (Rubin, Palmgreen, & Sypher, 1994).

Semantic differential scales have been widely used in measurement of source credibility. Infante (1980) used three dimensions to measure source credibility: trustworthiness, expertise, and dynamism. For trustworthiness, he used honest–dishonest, trustworthy–untrustworthy, and sincere–insincere. For expertise, he used skilled–unskilled, qualified–unqualified, and informed–uninformed. For dynamism, he used bold–timid, active–passive, and aggressive–meek.

RESEARCH QUESTIONS

This study investigates the credibility of news across traditional and online media. It examines the dimensions of news credibility as a threshold to what predicts news credibility. Online news credibility is investigated against use patterns and user demographics using the orientation of the Gaziano and McGrath (1986) credibility scale.

Credibility research comparing the Internet to traditional news sources has not been conclusive or consistent (Flanagin & Metzger, 2000). Research about print newspapers and online newspapers suggests additional, perhaps new, dimensions may exist. For example, print newspapers are regarded as a serious news medium. Newspapers, after all, by their very name are committed to news. Television news, by contrast, is regarded as less serious because the medium of television is not primarily associated with news, and credibility studies have shown television credibility to be more based on individual on-air personalities such as news anchors than the news organization or station (Newhagen & Nass, 1989). Television news is often viewed as an addendum to the entertainment medium. Similarly, the Internet and the Web are not solely devoted to news. Thus, the "entertainment" dimension must be considered when print and online newspapers are compared.

The following research questions guided this study:

1. What are the primary components of newspaper, television news, and online news credibility?
2. What similarities and differences are found in the credibility dimensions of newspapers, television news, and online news?

METHODS

This study employs a representative national sample. As such, it has certain advantages and disadvantages over experimental studies. The most obvious advantage is external validity, in that the findings can be generalized from the sample to the population. The most obvious disadvantage is in internal validity because re-searchers cannot control all the unknown external variables that might affect the dependent variable of credibility.

The national probability sample was drawn from the 50 states and the District of Columbia. Data were collected using a telephone survey of adults age 18 or older, conducted February 4 through 7, 2002. A total of 536 interviews were com-pleted. The response rate was 41%. The response rate was computed after exclud-ing business telephone numbers, fax machines, and any numbers contacted that were not in service. The remaining dialed numbers were cataloged and tracked. The response rate was computed by dividing the completed calls by the amount of usable telephone numbers that had been attempted. At least two callback at-tempts were made for numbers with busy signals, answering machines, or no an-swers to attempt to complete interviews. Interviewers were communication un-dergraduate students trained and supervised by the authors.

The sample was drawn using a stratified design, proportionate to the popu-lation of the United States. Population figures were obtained from the 2000 U.S. Census (http://blue.census.gov/population/www/cen2000/respop.html). Using proportions equal to each state's population, interviewers were assigned to complete calls to residents utilizing a modified random digit dialing model. Residential telephone numbers were drawn from the fall 2001 edition of the na-tional Select Phone telephone software on compact disc and database published by InfoUSA (Select Phone Pro CD database, 2002). Random residential tele-phone numbers were generated on a state-by-state basis from the database of more than 100 million telephone numbers using a table of random numbers and the random number function built into the Select Phone software. Each state roster of chosen numbers was adjusted using a one-up and one-down last digit method to include unlisted and other numbers not included in the pub-lished CD database. Business and other commercial numbers were categorically eliminated from the sample.

Prior to asking respondents to evaluate a particular news medium using the scale, interviewers "qualified" responses by establishing use of the medium. Me-dia use was defined as at least 1 day per week of newspaper readership; at least 1 day per week of television news viewing; and, for online news users, at least 1 day per week of either (a) use of online news on the Web, (b) use of online news through an Internet service provider (ISP), or (c) use of online news through an Internet search engine portal.

The survey instrument included a news credibility scale adapted from Gaziano and McGrath (1986). The scale was chosen because of its high reliability (Cron-bach α of .92 was reported by Newhagen & Nass, 1989). Rubin et al. (1994) also reported that most news credibility research has used a variation of this scale. The Likert-type scale had 12 items, focusing on traditional credibility components (trustworthiness, currency, bias, fairness, reporting the whole story, objectivity, honesty, up-to-date, believability, balance, accuracy, and timeliness). Respondents rated items on a 5-point scale ranging from *strongly agree* to *strongly disagree*, with *neutral* as the midpoint. Respondents who used each news medium were asked

> I'd like to know what you think about [newspapers, television news, or online news] as a source of news and information. I'm going to mention some descriptive words . . . and, after I read each word, please tell me whether the word describes your feelings. Give me your answer in terms of whether you strongly agree, agree, disagree, strongly disagree, or whether you are neutral. Do you think [newspapers, television news, or online news] is. . . .

After checking for the reliability of each of the three credibility scales, a summated mean was computed and the scales were analyzed for similarities and differences. Scales were factor analyzed to determine underlying dimensions of each scale utilizing a 1.0 eigenvalue factoring criterion, the Varimax rotation, and the principal component analysis extraction method.

FINDINGS

The demographics of the sample showed that females were overrepresented and minorities were underrepresented, but not so severely as to indicate serious problems in sample representativeness. As shown in Table 5.1, the survey sample was 54% female ($n = 291$), 9% Hispanic ($n = 46$), and 11% African American ($n = 56$). The median age was 45. About four fifths of the respondents had either a high school degree ($n = 136$), some college education ($n = 131$), or a college degree ($n = 119$). The median annual family income category was $50,001 to $75,000. Respondents had spent long periods of time in their communities as well (median of 15 years).

More than half of respondents were newspaper subscribers, but more than four in five were cable or satellite television subscribers, as shown in Table 5.2. Furthermore, most news was consumed at home (82.3%), instead of at work, school, or other possible locations. News media use habits varied across news media, as shown in Table 5.2, but television was the primary source of information among respondents in this study. Respondents read newspapers a mean of 3.76 days per week ($n = 535$, $Mdn = 3.0$) and watched television news a mean of 5.11 days per week ($n = 532$, $Mdn = 7.0$). Online news use was measured three ways: (a) in terms of days of access of news sites on the Web per week ($n = 312$, $M = 1.65$, $Mdn = 0.00$); (b) days of access through an ISP per week ($n = 281$, $M = 1.03$, $Mdn = 0.00$); and (c) days of access through a Web portal site per week ($n = 275$, $M = 0.98$, $Mdn = 0.00$).

As shown in Table 5.3, the type of news preferred varied by news medium used. Newspaper readers and television viewers preferred local and national

TABLE 5.1
Sample Demographics

Demographic Variable	n	%
Gender		
Male	241	45.0
Female	291	54.3
Race		
White	422	78.7
Black	56	10.4
Asian	15	2.8
Native American	3	0.6
Other	21	3.9
Hispanic ancestry		
Yes	46	8.6
No	469	87.5
Don't know or refused	21	3.9
Education		
No high school	34	6.3
High school or vocational school	136	25.4
Some college (no degree)	131	24.4
Undergraduate degree	119	22.2
Graduate school (degree or no degree)	100	18.7
Household income		
$25,000 and under	82	15.3
$25,001–$50,000	133	24.8
$50,001–$75,000	112	20.9
$75,001–$100,000	56	10.4
Above $100,000	58	10.8
Don't know or refused	95	17.7
Time living in community	Mdn = 15.0 years	M = 20.4 years
Age	Mdn = 45.0 years	M = 46.2 years

TABLE 5.2
General News Consumption

Variable	n	%
Newspaper subscriber		
Yes	282	52.6
No	241	45.0
Cable TV or satellite TV subscriber		
Yes	438	81.7
No	85	15.9
Primary location of news consumption		
Home	441	82.3
Work or school	59	11.0
Other	20	3.7
Days per week reads newspaper	Mdn = 3.0	M = 3.8
Days per week watches television news	Mdn = 7.0	M = 5.1
Days per week accesses online news sites	Mdn = 0.0	M = 1.7
Days per week accesses ISP news sites	Mdn = 0.0	M = 1.0
Days per week accesses portal news sites	Mdn = 0.0	M = 1.0

TABLE 5.3
Types of News Most Read and Medium Most Often Used

Type of News	Newspaper Users	Television Users	Online Users
Local	53.3%	43.4%	13.8%
National	26.4	31.8	49.3
International	6.1	8.5	25.0
Local–national	5.0	6.8	2.0
Local–international	0.7	1.0	0.7
National–international	1.9	2.3	7.9
All	6.6	6.2	1.3
n	424	484	152

news, whereas online news users preferred national and international news. Few used online news sources for local information.

Internet users were, by far, most interested in international news. Among online news users, 25% chose international news as the type of news they read most often, as opposed to 8.5% of television viewers and 6.1% of newspaper readers. A smaller proportion of news users were most interested in combinations of news and refused to be categorized as interested in a single level of news. These also varied by type of news used most often. About 6% of newspaper and television users were interested in local, national, and international news combinations. About 8% of online news users, however, were interested in national and international news combinations, with the least combined interest level involving local news.

Overall, respondents rated online news highest in credibility. Data in Table 5.4 indicate that online users rated online news more positively. The scores should be understood as reflecting only individuals who were self-described users of the

TABLE 5.4
Perceived News Credibility by Medium

	Newspapers		Television		Online	
	M	SD	M	SD	M	SD
Trustworthy	0.51	0.88	0.51	0.94	0.70	0.74
Current	1.03	0.68	1.08	0.57	1.11	0.68
Biased	−0.60	0.95	−0.44	1.02	0.01	0.89
Fair	0.22	0.91	0.34	0.90	0.52	0.76
Report the whole story	−0.15	1.03	−0.19	1.04	0.18	0.98
Objective	0.25	0.95	0.19	0.97	0.43	0.81
Dishonest	0.44	0.88	0.43	0.87	0.57	0.79
Up-to-date	0.97	0.57	1.03	0.57	1.07	0.62
Believable	0.62	0.72	0.67	0.75	0.75	0.66
Balanced	0.17	0.95	0.20	0.98	0.41	0.89
Accurate	0.34	0.89	0.43	0.85	0.65	0.72
Timely	0.86	0.64	1.00	0.56	1.09	0.61

Note.   Data range from −2 (strongly disagree) to +2 (strongly agree).

media evaluated. This means that television news users who did not use online news did not evaluate online news. Thus, some respondents offered perceptions of only one news medium (newspaper only, $n = 36$; television only, $n = 50$; online only, $n = 3$), some offered perceptions of two news media (newspaper and television only, $n = 251$; television and online only, $n = 29$; newspaper and online only, $n = 7$), and some evaluated all three news media ($n = 95$).

Newspaper readers rated newspapers highest on three variables directly associated with their timeliness (current, 1.03; up-to-date, 0.97; and timely, 0.86) and they rated newspapers lowest in terms of bias (-0.60) and completeness (-0.15). Television viewers responded similarly, rating television news highest for timeliness (current, 1.08; up-to-date, 1.01; and timely, 1.00). They also perceived television to be weakest in terms of bias (-0.44) and reporting the whole story ($-.019$). Online news users saw their news source similarly, but with a more positive perspective. Online news users felt the same about the strengths of online news and its timeliness (current, 1.11; up-to-date, 1.07; and timely, 1.09) and about the weakness of bias (0.01) and completeness (0.18).

Factor analysis of the newspaper credibility scale resulted in a three-factor solution emphasizing balance, honesty, and currency of information that accounted for 56.0% of variance. Factor analysis of the television credibility scale resulted in a two-factor solution emphasizing fairness and currency, which accounted for 53.1% of variance. Factor analysis of the online news credibility scale resulted in a three-factor solution focused on trustworthiness, currency, and bias that accounted for 60.0% of variance.

Table 5.5 displays the newspaper credibility factor analysis. The three-factor solution reveals distinct dimensions of credibility focusing on balance, honesty, and currency. The balance factor is dominated by balance and reporting the whole story. Objectivity, fairness, and accuracy also load on the factor. Honesty is the second component, made up of dishonest, believable, and trustworthy. Currency, the third factor, is built around up-to-date, current, and timely.

As shown in Table 5.6, the television news credibility factor analysis emphasizes fairness and currency. The dominant factor centers on fairness. Other strong-loading scale items are balance, trustworthy, accurate, and objective. The remaining items in the factor were report the whole story, believable, biased, and dishonest. The second factor is similar to the currency factor in newspapers. The strongest loaded item was current (.808), but up-to-date and timely also strongly loaded. This certainly relates to literature about television news credibility that suggests credibility is more individually than institutionally oriented (Newhagen & Nass, 1989).

The online news credibility factor analysis in Table 5.7 has 3 primary dimensions: trustworthiness, currency, and bias. Trustworthy is the highest loaded item for the 7-item Factor 1, but believable and accurate were also strong. Other items for this factor included report the whole story, balanced, and fair. Factor 2, currency, is similar to the factors found for newspapers and television news. For each

TABLE 5.5
Newspaper Credibility Factor Analysis

Factor	Balance	Honesty	Currency
Balance			
Balanced	.767	.103	.035
Report the whole story	.732	.090	.231
Objective	.669	.110	.122
Fair	.598	.430	.019
Accurate	.575	.410	.139
Summated mean		0.168 (SD = 0.687)	
Cronbach's reliability		.78	
Honesty			
Dishonest	.031	**.812**	.039
Believable	.224	**.665**	.224
Trustworthy	.413	**.632**	.175
Summated mean		0.528 (SD = 0.637)	
Cronbach's reliability		.65	
Currency			
Up-to-date	.115	.128	**.781**
Current	.060	.069	**.765**
Timely	.129	.084	**.749**
Summated mean		0.957 (SD = 0.495)	
Cronbach's reliability		.70	
Not Used			
Biased	**.403**	.365	−.264
Eigenvalue	4.04	1.68	1.00
Variance explained	33.7%	14.0%	8.3%

Note. Data range from −2 (*strongly disagree*) to +2 (*strongly agree*). Boldface type represents the highest factor loadings.

of the three factor solutions, currency was composed of the same items. Timely is the dominant item, but current and up-to-date also load well. The bias factor in this scale, not apparent in the newspaper or television news factor solutions, points to an interesting difference in this solution when compared to the other two. Biased and objective form this 2-item factor, suggesting important perceived differences by users of online news compared to newspapers and television news.

DISCUSSION

Media credibility is a complex concept. Researchers have used a wide range of approaches to evaluate it and understand its components. The addition of online news to the list of sources of information available to the public has led to concerns about its credibility as well as its perception by the public as a news source in relation to established, more traditional news sources. As access and availabil-

TABLE 5.6
Television Credibility Factor Analysis

Factor	Fairness	Currency
Fairness		
Fair	.819	.074
Balanced	.738	.037
Trustworthy	.719	.238
Accurate	.701	.285
Objective	.701	.033
Report the whole story	.676	.150
Believable	.621	.300
Biased	.563	−.208
Dishonest	.456	.277
Summated mean	0.305 (SD = 0.525)	
Cronbach's reliability	.85	
Currency		
Current	.073	**.808**
Up-to-date	.121	**.798**
Timely	.111	**.769**
Summated mean	1.036 (SD = 0.459)	
Cronbach's reliability	.74	
Eigenvalue	4.57	1.81
Variance explained	38.1%	15.1%

Note. Data range from −2 (strongly disagree) to +2 (strongly agree). Boldface type represents the highest factor loadings.

ity of online news grow, the concern for quality of information found online will also increase. News consumers concerned about sources of information and its trustworthiness, believability, currency, and other characteristics will demand and seek sources of news that are reliable and credible.

Even when individual credibility dimensions by news medium are standardized, it is apparent that researchers who wish to compare across media will still need some form of compromise in selecting their dimensions for analysis. This study has revealed differences in how Americans perceived the credibility of newspapers, television news, and online news in early 2002.

The dimensions of currency, timeliness, and up-to-date remain important in the credibility of all three news media studied. For newspapers, the dominant aspect of currency is that it is perceived to be up-to-date. Television news is thought to be current, but also up-to-date and timely. Online news is seen to be timely, but also current and up-to-date. These subtle differences suggest further research to determine their importance.

Newspaper credibility is seen to be based in balance, honesty, and currency. However, newspapers, to offer credibility, must be perceived to be balanced in storytelling, complete in providing information, objective, fair, accurate, and unbiased. They must also be honest in their presentation of news, believable, and

TABLE 5.7
Online Credibility Factor Analysis

Factor	Trustworthiness	Timeliness	Bias
Trustworthiness			
Trustworthy	.783	.255	-.019
Believable	.750	.185	.015
Accurate	.727	.164	.125
Report the whole story	.684	.106	.032
Balanced	.623	-.068	.486
Fair	.595	-.051	.373
Summated mean		0.543 (SD = 0.563)	
Cronbach's reliability		.83	
Currency			
Timely	.148	.898	.024
Current	.221	.867	-.065
Up-to-date	.121	.772	.125
Summated mean		1.093 (SD = 0.550)	
Cronbach's reliability		.84	
Bias			
Biased	-.062	.062	.846
Objective	.482	.191	.592
Summated mean		0.220 (SD = 0.667)	
Cronbach's reliability		.37	
Not used			
Dishonest	.337	.180	.046
Eigenvalue	4.28	1.82	1.09
Variance explained	35.7%	15.2%	9.1%

Note. Data range from −2 (*strongly disagree*) to +2 (*strongly agree*). Boldface type represents the highest factor loadings.

trustworthy. Television news credibility is anchored in fairness, respondents have shown. Viewers want news that is fair and balanced, but also see trustworthiness, accuracy, objectivity, completeness, believability, lack of bias, and honesty as elements of fairness. These respondents felt that online news credibility is built on trustworthiness. For online news to be credible, it must be trustworthy and believable. It must also be accurate, complete, balanced and fair, and honest.

The online findings seem to relate to the nature of the Internet as a medium that transcends borders and time zones. It also has the potential to be explained by an acculturation process of Internet users (who are usually more educated), which makes them more aware of, more interested in, and/or more receptive to, international news. In this regard, the Internet could be serving as an eye-opener to its users, at least in the sense of making them aware of a more diverse news menu available to them.

Perhaps the most interesting element of online news credibility, however, is the apparent concern for bias expressed by online news users. The existence of a separate factor for bias and objectivity suggests a strong focus for this component of credibility of online news and reflects, perhaps, experiences by online users that have led to biased and less-than-objective reports at online news sites. This could be due to the relative difficulty of assessing the objectivity, or biases, of Web-based news when compared to a newspaper's content or that of a television newscast. Internet users are aware of the ease of uploading a page on the Web, and with a little design experience, making it look like the output of a well-established, professional organization. This seems to underline the importance of branding in online news. Readily identifiable news organizations that have moved to a Web presence or Web sites that use existing and known news brands (e.g., CNN, the Associated Press, or other news services) have this advantage over news sites that are only on the Web and do not offer branded news.

Readers understand that editing and other forms of editorial screening occur in newspaper and television newsrooms. Whereas it is easy to find out who publishes or edits a newspaper or holds the license and edits a television newscast, it is sometimes much harder to determine who publishes a Web site. This might be a factor that leads to more concern among online news users regarding the objectivity, or lack thereof, of an online news site, and consequently, its overall credibility.

There is clearly need for additional analysis of these three credibility scales and public perceptions of the performance of newspapers, television news, and online news. Furthermore, it would have been valuable, for example, to have asked respondents about the credibility of newspapers, television, and online news simultaneously. It is clear from the data that asking only regular users about a particular medium gives only one perspective on this complex issue. A side-by-side-by-side comparison of newspapers, television, and online news may yield insights into nonusers and their views of each of the three news media relative to each other.

This analysis has laid the groundwork for additional investigation. Further analysis based on demographic characteristics of respondents is needed. This should include news consumption preferences, gender, high- and low-level users, computer literacy levels, online access, education, race and ethnicity, and income. It would also be valuable to analyze only individuals who responded to each of the three scales to determine their comparative ratings of newspapers, television news, and online news. There is additional need to determine why fewer people use online news: Is it solely an Internet access issue or is it access combined with perceptions of lower online news credibility? In-depth analysis of nonusers may provide the insight needed to better understand the findings presented in this study.

REFERENCES

Arant, M. D., & Anderson, J. Q. (2000, August). *Online media ethics: A survey of U.S. daily newspaper editors.* Paper presented to the Newspaper Division, Association for Education in Journalism and Mass Communication, Phoenix, AZ.

Couper, M. P., Traugott, M., & Lamias, M. J. (2001). Web survey design and administration. *Public Opinion Quarterly, 65,* 230–253.

Finberg, H. I., Stone, M. L., & Lynch, D. (2002, January 31). *Digital journalism credibility study.* Online News Association. Retrieved February 1, 2002, from http://www.onlinenewsassociation.org

Flanagin, A. J., & Metzger, M. J. (2000). Perceptions of Internet information credibility. *Journalism & Mass Communication Quarterly, 77,* 515–540.

Flanagin, A. J., & Metzger, M. J. (2001). Internet use in the contemporary media environment. *Human Communication Research, 27,* 153–181.

Gaziano, C. (1987). News peoples' ideology and the credibility debate. *Newspaper Research Journal, 9*(1), 1–18.

Gaziano, C., & McGrath, K. (1986). Measuring the concept of credibility. *Journalism Quarterly, 63,* 451–462.

Hovland, C. I., & Weiss, W. (1951–1952). The influence of source credibility on communication effectiveness. *Public Opinion Quarterly, 15,* 635–650.

Infante, D. A. (1980). The construct validity of semantic differential scales for the measurement of source credibility. *Communication Quarterly, 28,* 19–26.

Johnson, T. J., & Kaye, B. K. (1998). Cruising is believing: Comparing Internet and traditional sources on media credibility measures. *Journalism & Mass Communication Quarterly, 75,* 325–340.

Johnson, T. J., & Kaye, B. K. (2000). Using is believing: The influence of reliance on the credibility of online political information among politically interested Internet users. *Journalism & Mass Communication Quarterly, 77,* 865–879.

Jupiter Media Metrix. (2001). *U.S. online users, 2000–2006: Industry projections.* Retrieved March 27, 2002, from http://www.jmm.com/xp/jmm/press/industryProjections.xml

Kiousis, S. (1999). *Public trust or mistrust? Perceptions of media credibility in the information age.* Paper presented to the Mass Communication and Society Division, Association for Education in Journalism and Mass Communication, New Orleans, LA.

Lasica, J. D. (2001). *How the Net is shaping journalism ethics.* Retrieved August 14, 2001, from http://www.well.com/~jd/newsethics.html

Meyer, P. (1973). Elitism and newspaper believability. *Journalism Quarterly, 50,* 31–36.

Meyer, P. (1988). Defining and measuring credibility of newspapers: Developing an index. *Journalism Quarterly, 65,* 567–574.

Mulder, R. (1980). Media credibility: A use-gratifications approach. *Journalism Quarterly, 57,* 474–477.

Mulder, R. (1981). A log-linear analysis of media credibility. *Journalism Quarterly, 58,* 635–638.

Newhagen, J., & Nass, C. (1989). Differential criteria for evaluating credibility of newspapers and TV news. *Journalism Quarterly, 66,* 277–284.

Nielsen Media Research. (1999, May). *TV viewing in Internet households.* Retrieved August 18, 2001, from http://www.nielsenmedia.com

Ognianova, E. (1998, August). *The value of journalistic identity on the World Wide Web.* Paper presented to the Mass Communication and Society Division, Association for Education in Journalism and Mass Communication, Baltimore, MD.

Online News Association. (2001, July 21). *ONA's digital journalism credibility study overview.* Retrieved August 14, 2001, from http://www.journalist.org/Programs/Research2Text.htm

Pew Research Center for People & the Press. (1998, June 8). *Internet use takes off: Event-driven news audiences: Pew Research Center biennial news consumption survey.* Retrieved August 18, 2001, from http://www.people-press.org/med98rpt.htm

Pryor, L., & Grabowicz, P. (2001, June 13). Privacy disclosure on news sites low: Detailed study suggests new media needs to work on public trust. *Online Journalism Review.* Retrieved August 14, 2001, from http://ojr.usc.edu/content/story.cfm?id=595

Rimmer, T., & Weaver, D. (1987). Different questions, different answers? Media use and media credibility. *Journalism Quarterly, 64,* 28–36.

Robinson, M. J., & Kohut, A. (1988). Believability and the press. *Public Opinion Quarterly, 52,* 174–189.

Rubin, R., Palmgreen, P., & Sypher, H. (1994). *Communication research measures: A sourcebook.* New York: Guilford.

Schaeffer, D. R., & Dillman, D. A. (1998). Development of a standard e-mail methodology: Results of an experiment. *Public Opinion Quarterly, 62,* 378–397.

Schweiger, W. (1998). Wer glaubt dem World Wide Web? Ein experiment zur glabwurdigkeit von nachrichten in tageszeitungen und im World Wide Web [Who believes in the World Wide Web: An experiment about the reliability of news in daily newspapers and in the World Wide Web]. In P. Rossler (Ed.), *Online contributions to the uses and effects of communication* (pp. 123–145). Opladen, Germany: Wesduetscher Verlag.

Schweiger, W. (2000, March 1). Media credibility—Experience or image?: A survey on the credibility of the World Wide Web in Germany in comparison to other media. *European Journal of Communication, 15,* 37–59.

Select Phone Pro CD database, version 2.1. (2002). Omaha, NE: Info USA.

Sundar, S. (1996, August). *Do quotes affect perception of online news stories?* Paper presented to the Communication Technology and Policy Division, Association for Education in Journalism and Mass Communication, Anaheim, CA.

Sundar, S. (1998). Effect of source attribution on perception of online news stories. *Journalism & Mass Communication Quarterly, 75,* 55–68.

Sundar, S. (1999). Exploring receivers' criteria for perception of print and online news. *Journalism & Mass Communication Quarterly, 76,* 373–386.

Wanta, W., & Hu, Y. (1994). The effects of credibility, reliance, and exposure on media agenda-setting: A path analysis model. *Journalism Quarterly, 71,* 90–98.

CHAPTER SIX

Public Fear of Terrorism
and the News Media

Paul D. Driscoll
Michael B. Salwen
Bruce Garrison

This chapter is based on a research investigation undertaken approximately 9 weeks after the terror attacks of September 2001. It focuses on the public's fear of terrorism and its relationship to three issues of interest to communication researchers. First, we look at the relationship between feelings of fear about terrorism and public attitudes toward restrictions on civil liberties and the news media. Next, we explore the relationship between feelings of fear about terrorism and news media use. The third focus is an examination of whether self-reports estimating an affective state—fear of terrorism—result in a perceptual bias similar to that repeatedly found in the literature of the so-called third-person effect theory. The latter issue is dealt with in much more depth in Chapter 7, and specifically in the context of the online news user, but some preliminary observations derived from the data set collected for this investigation may lend some additional insight. The chapter concludes by presenting descriptive data about online news readers and their uses and perceptions of online news media coverage of the war on terrorism.

In mid-November 2001, daily life for many Americans was at least moving on, if not exactly back to normal. The public continued to struggle with the psychological stresses of adjusting to a world that suddenly appeared to be a great deal more dangerous than the one encountered before September 11. During this time period, the news media gave fervid and exhaustive coverage to the war in Afghanistan, anthrax attacks, and anxiety. As one Federal Bureau of Investigation (FBI) agent told Newsweek, "Although anthrax is not contagious, fear of it was epidemic" (Begley & Isikoff, 2001, p. 30). Fears that the country had suffered another terror attack were raised on November 12, 2001, when American Airlines Flight 587, bound from New York to Santo Domingo, crashed in a Queens neighborhood, killing 265 people.

A nationwide survey of 1,000 adults by the Pew Research Center, conducted from October 31 to November 7, 2001, provides some general impressions of Americans' attitudes toward the threat of terrorism during this time (Pew Research Center for People and the Press, 2001). The Pew Center study found that 89% of Americans reported following news stories about terrorism in the United States either very closely (63%) or somewhat closely (26%). Twenty-four percent said they felt depressed because of their concerns about terrorist attacks or the war against terrorism, a sharp decline from the 71% reported in mid-September, immediately following the attack. Forty percent reported being either very worried (13%) or somewhat worried (27%) about themselves or someone in their family becoming a victim of a terrorist attack, with people living in major coastal cities more worried (50%) than Americans living elsewhere (38%). Finally, 47% of the respondents felt the news media were giving just the right amount of coverage to the spread of anthrax story, whereas 40% said the news media were giving it too much coverage. Seven percent felt the news media were not giving the story enough coverage (Pew Research Center for People and the Press, 2001). It is against this backdrop that the data in this study, a representative U.S. telephone survey of 512 adult respondents conducted during the evenings from November 15 to 20, 2001, and the evening of November 27, 2001, were collected.

RESTRICTIONS AND FEAR

In times of great crisis, governments reflexively turn to measures of increased social control, hoping to diminish dangers and lessen fears. For example, in the ongoing campaign against terrorism, the government has established laws such as the U.S.A. Patriot Act, designed to facilitate law enforcement's antiterrorism efforts. The Patriot Act and other government antiterrorism initiatives have sparked concern for the perceived erosion of civil liberties.

Americans in principle support protecting individual freedoms from government abridgment, but the historical record is replete with examples of excesses, especially during unusual and intense "pathological periods," when shifting public attitudes toward basic liberties threaten to undermine the normal impulse to restrain government power (Blasi, 1985). One such period occurred during World War II when 120,000 persons of Japanese ancestry, many of them American citizens, were forced into relocation camps. Civil liberties were also curtailed during the U.S. Civil War, as they were by the Sedition Act during World War I and "Red Scares" of the 1920s and the 1950s. Such ignominy does not occur often, but fear of terrorism could again foster public attitudes leading to a contraction in civil liberties. Altheide and Michalowski (1999) noted that, "The prevalence of fear in public discourse can contribute to stances and reactive social policies that promote state control and surveillance. Fear is a key element of creating 'the risk society,' organized around communication oriented to policing, control, and prevention of risks" (p. 476).

It is generally accepted that although the American public supports freedom of expression in the abstract, there is little concrete tolerance for expressions of disliked and offensive opinion. A large body of research, developed mostly since Stouffer's (1955) seminal study of tolerance for nonconformity, has found the American public generally unwilling to extend civil liberties to objectionable groups, although such positions fluctuate and have many moderators (Davis, 1975; McClosky, 1964; Nunn, Crockett, & Williams, 1978; Prothro & Grigg, 1960; Sullivan, Piereson, & Marcus, 1979, 1982).

The tendency to support freedom of expression in principle is also found in public opinion toward the news media (Becker, Cobbey, & Sobowale, 1978; First Amendment Center, 2002). Yet support for freedom of the press and the First Amendment on the whole has been declining (First Amendment Center, 2000, 2001, 2002). In a national survey conducted in 2002, 49% of the respondents said they thought the First Amendment goes too far in the rights it guarantees; the same percentage thought the First Amendment gives Americans too much freedom (First Amendment Center, 2002). There is also a disturbing trend in public opinion favoring the placement of restrictions on the news media. For example, 40% of respondents in a 2002 study said newspapers should not be allowed to freely criticize the U.S. military (First Amendment Center, 2002). Because the pathological approach would suggest that fear may be an important component in support for increased government restrictions, it is hypothesized that:

H₁: Feelings of fear about terrorism will be positively associated with a willingness to restrict civil liberties and support for government restrictions on the news media.

FEAR AND NEWS MEDIA EXPOSURE

For almost three decades, the relationship between fear and media exposure has been the subject of numerous social science research investigations, focusing mostly on whether exposure to violence on television is related to fear of crime. For example, some theorists argued that television viewing caused fear of crime and perceptions that the world was a scary place (Bryant, Carveth, & Brown, 1981; Gerbner & Gross, 1976; Gerbner, Gross, Morgan, & Signorielli, 1980). Hirsch (1980, 1981) argued that there was no consistent evidence of such a relationship in the Gerbner data, and Doob and MacDonald (1979) reported that the relationship between the amount of television viewed and fear of crime was insignificant after controlling for the actual amount of crime in respondents' neighborhoods.

Other researchers focused on a possible reverse direction of causality, where increased fear of crime leads people to greater amounts of television viewing (Tamborini, Zillmann, & Bryant, 1884; Zillmann, 1980). A stronger correlation between media exposure and fear of crime has also been found when societal—rather than personal level—fear is measured (Tyler & Cook, 1984) and when fear is measured in urban areas rather than rural areas (Zillmann & Wakshlag, 1985). In a review of the fear of crime research, Heath and Gilbert (1996) concluded that there is evidence of a positive relationship, although there are many moderators, including characteristics of the message, the audience, and the operationalization of fear of crime.

There are a number of reasons to expect a significant positive relationship between fear of terrorism and the amount of exposure to news media. Individuals experiencing high levels of fear might selectively expose themselves to news reports about the fight against terrorism in an effort to gain reassuring information or obtain information that may be useful in reducing threat. Alternately, an individual's level of fear may also be elevated by the highly arousing nature of news coverage about terrorism, especially if additional threatening information is reported. Newhagen and Lewenstein (1992), studying the effects of 1989 Loma Prieta earthquake, found increased exposure to television news was positively related to increased levels of fear. Kubey and Peluso (1990) reported a significant positive relationship between strength of emotional reaction and time spent viewing television coverage of the *Challenger* space shuttle tragedy.

More frequent exposure to highly arousing news about terrorism may also trigger an availability heuristic, causing individuals to believe that terror attacks are more likely or frequent because they are easier to imagine or recall, thus increasing fear (Slovic, Fischoff, & Lichtenstein, 1979). Exposure to terrorism news may also distort the risk interpretation process and intensify feelings of fear, just as watching the motion picture *Jaws* caused irrational fear of shark attacks in many people (Slovic et al., 1979). Newhagen (1998) found that news stories using images that evoke anger and fear had higher approach ratings on an approach–avoidance scale and were better recalled than news images evoking disgust. Lang, Newhagen, and Reeves (1996) reported that responses to negative video of news events included higher negatively valenced arousal, higher short- and long-term attention, and increased memory of content during and after exposure.

However, a case can also be made for a negative relationship between feelings of fear about terrorism and exposure to news. People with high fear of terrorism might avoid exposing themselves to news reports that could exacerbate an already fearful emotional state. Most news reports at this time contained threat cues that could have intensified a person's level of fear. An individual may seek to control his or her level of fear by avoiding such threat cues (Leventhal, 1970). People at high fear levels may engage in defensive avoidance, actively avoiding thinking and hearing about both the original attacks and newer threats such as the anthrax attacks. Brashers (2001) pointed out that, "Avoidance can shield people from information that is overwhelming and distressing and can provide escape from a distressing certainty by maintaining uncertainty" (p. 483).

There is also evidence that individuals actively use media to adjust mood state (Potts & Sanchez, 1994; Zillmann, 2000; Zillmann & Bryant, 1985). A person wishing to reduce the noxious affect associated with fear of terrorism would putatively not select news content about terrorism, or at least expose himself or herself to less of it compared with someone at a lower fear level. Individuals experiencing high levels of fear should consider news reports aversive and selectively choose to limit exposure. Potts and Sanchez (1994) found that depression was clearly associated with a variety of negative feelings reported to result from watching news programs, and concluded that news programming may exacerbate depressive moods.

Biswas, Riffe, and Zillmann (1994) found an interaction effect between gender and the appeal of bad news stories for individuals in a negative mood state. As predicted by mood management theory, women in a negative affective state selectively exposed themselves to less bad news (or more good news) than women in a positive affective state. However, men in a negative affective state tended to select more bad news than did men in a positive affective state. It was suggested that such an effect may be related to male anger and a motivation to maintain a negative affective state to facilitate retaliation against the source that induced the negative affect. Such a gender effect may also be apparent in this study because of the intermingling of anxiety about terrorism and anger directed toward those attacking the United States.

It is likely that surveillance needs in times of national crisis would tend, at least to some extent, to override psychological motivations to avoid news. For example, Vincent and Basil (1997) found a significant positive relationship between college students' needs for surveillance and newspaper reading and broadcast news media use. In the days immediately following the September 11 attacks, people attended to the news media at very high levels, even though such national tragedies are known to elicit deep sorrow, anger, and worry (Sheatsley & Feldman, 1965). People may find exposure to news about terrorism especially efficacious in reducing fear if news reports show that steps are being taken by the government to ensure security, or contain information about precautions that can be taken to avoid danger. Such high-utility information may dominate hedonistic motivation (Zillmann, 2000). Nevertheless, because there are competing explanations for the possible relationship between fear of terrorism and amount of exposure to news, it is hypothesized that:

H_2: There will be a significant relationship between feelings of fear about terrorism and the amount of time spent with news media.

Exposure to information about the terror attacks prompted many individuals to take precautions to avoid dangerous situations. News coverage at that time carried stories about how people were coping with terrorism threats including canceling or postponing trips, checking suspicious mail, purchasing antibiotics to ward off anthrax, avoiding public places, and shopping for gas masks and protective suits. It is logical to think that the greater the level of a person's fear about terrorism, the more danger-avoiding behaviors he or she would perform. It is hypothesized that:

H$_3$: The number of danger-avoiding measures taken will be positively associated with feelings of fear about terrorism.

FEAR AND THIRD-PERSON EFFECTS

The phenomenon of so-called third-person effects was identified by Davison (1983) in an article relating anecdotes and "four small experiments." His observations led him to speculate that media messages may have their greatest behavioral effects not on the intended audience, but rather on those who anticipate the message to have deleterious effects on others—the third persons. For example, Davison related how White military officers during World War II misjudged the persuasive influence of Japanese propaganda messages directed at Black U.S. soldiers on the island of Iwo Jima. The Japanese leaflets urged the Black soldiers to desert rather than fight a "White-man's war." Although there was no evidence the propaganda was effective in influencing the Black soldiers, the White officers nonetheless reshuffled personnel in the Black units to reduce the likelihood of desertion.

Davison's (1983) observations launched an extensive line of inquiry by mass communication researchers resulting in hundreds of research reports regarding third-person effects (e.g., Davison, 1996; Gunther, 1991; Lasorsa, 1989; Paul, Salwen, & Dupagne, 2000; Perloff, 1996, 1999). The theoretical approach is usually divided into two components: perceptual bias and behavioral outcomes. The perceptual component is tested by comparing an individual's estimate of the impact of a media message on himself or herself to a parallel estimate made by the individual about the effects of the same message on specified or generalized "others." There is robust support for the perceptual bias component of the theory under specified conditions, but especially when a media message's persuasive effect is thought to be undesirable.

Given the robust nature of perceptual biases, a key concern is whether such psychological distortions actually affect behavior or, as it is usually measured, behavioral intentions. The evidence for behavioral effects is mixed (e.g., Gunther, 1995; Price, Tewksbury, & Huang, 1998; Rojas, Shah, & Faber, 1996; Rucinski & Salmon, 1990; Salwen & Driscoll, 1997).

Chapter 7 presents a study of the third-person effect and fear about terrorism, moving from the tradition of examining third-person effects from a mostly cognitive domain to the affective realm. Because comparable data were collected in this investigation, some preliminary hypotheses testing is presented here.

Based on the existing literature, it would seem logical that perceptual biases should be evident when asking about the fear effects of news media terrorism coverage. It is therefore hypothesized that:

H_4: Respondents will demonstrate perceptual bias by estimating significantly higher fear effects resulting from news exposure about terrorism on others compared to themselves.

One of the possible confounding variables when examining self-reports about fear is the tendency for males to give lower fear estimates than females, despite physiological evidence of an equally strong arousal effect on both sexes. This long-acknowledged problem with gender differences in self-reported measurement of fear may stem from a social desirability bias (Cantor, 1999; Sparks, 1991). If this is the case, the magnitude of perceptual bias should be higher for males, unless males who underestimate the fear effect on themselves also underestimate it for specified others. Such a result seems unlikely. Therefore, it is hypothesized that:

H_5: There will be a significantly higher magnitude of perceptual bias by males than by females.

The final hypothesis is a test for a behavioral effect. Consistent with some other findings in third-person research, it is hypothesized that:

H_6: The magnitude of perceptual bias will be positively related to support for government restrictions on civil liberties and restrictions on the news media.

METHODOLOGY

A representative U.S. telephone survey gathered data from 512 adult respondents during the evenings from November 15 to 20, 2001, and the evening of November 27, 2001. Interviewing was not conducted during the Thanksgiving holiday period of that month. The sample was drawn using a stratified design to represent the 50 states and the District of Columbia roughly proportionate to their populations in the 2000 U.S. Census. Residential telephone numbers were drawn from the latest available edition of the national Select Phone telephone software package on compact disc and database published by InfoUSA (Select Phone Pro CD Database, 2001). Random residential telephone numbers were generated on a state-by-state basis from the database of more than 100 million telephone numbers using a table of random numbers and the random number selection function built into the Select Phone software. Each resulting state roster of random numbers was then adjusted using the one-up and one-down last digit method to include unlisted numbers not included in the database. If there was no answer, a busy signal, or an answering machine, up to two more attempts were made later that evening or during another evening to reach the number. The response rate, excluding invalid contacts, was 52%.[1]

Variables analyzed in this study are conceptually and operationally defined next.

Feelings of Fear About Terrorism

This concept was measured by asking respondents to assess "how they felt today about the threat of terrorism" on a scale ranging from 1 (*doesn't describe at all*) to 5 (*very accurately describes*). The words were: *scared, anxious, calm, worried, frightened,* and *unconcerned.*

Respondents' scores were combined by summing individual item scores and calculating the mean. Although reliability for the scale was acceptable ($\alpha = .82$) the low item-to-total correlation for the term *unconcerned* ($r = .33$) prompted its removal. A scale composed of the remaining 5 items was used ($\alpha = .84$, $M = 2.67$, $SD = 1.10$). A higher score reflects greater feelings of fear about terrorism. The previously discussed concern about gender differences in self-reports of fear did manifest itself in this study. Men reported a significantly lower level of fear ($M = 2.34$, $SD = 1.04$) compared to women ($M = 2.92$, $SD = 1.07$), $t(501) = 6.00$, $p < .01$. Because of differences in self-report by gender, the fear scale measure is controlled for gender when correlated with other variables in this study.[2]

Willingness to Restrict Civil Liberties

This concept was measured by asking respondents to react to six statements about government activities involving restrictions on civil liberties that might facilitate terrorism investigations. Responses to the statements were measured on a 5-point scale from 1 (*strongly disagree*) to 5 (*strongly agree*). Each statement was prefaced with the phrase "It should be made easier for the government to . . ." or

---

[1]Completion rate used in this study was computed by completions divided by completions + refusals.

[2]It was thought that feelings of fear about terrorism may also differ significantly between persons living in urban areas and those in less populated areas (Pew Research Center for People and the Press, 2001). There was not a significant difference in fear, however, between respondents who lived in or near a large urban area ($M = 2.64$, $SD = 1.08$) and those who did not ($M = 2.71$, $SD = 1.12$), $t(496) = .63$, $p > .05$.

"The government should be allowed to . . ." The proposed restrictions on civil liberties were (a) monitor telephone calls, (b) read people's e-mail, (c) track people's credit card purchases, (d) detain people indefinitely if there is reason to believe they know something about terrorist attacks, (e) secretly search someone's property without a warrant or judge's approval, and (f) issue national identification cards to better keep track of people.

A restriction on civil liberties scale was created by summing the six individual item scores and calculating the mean ($\alpha = .81$, $M = 3.33$, $SD = .93$). A higher score represents a greater willingness to allow government conduct that infringes on civil liberties in the fight against terrorism.

Willingness to Restrict the News Media

This concept was measured by asking respondents to react to five statements about government activities in the fight against terrorism that would restrict the news media. Responses were measured on a 5-point scale ranging from 1 (*strongly disagree*) to 5 (*strongly agree*). Each statement was prefaced with the phrase "The government should have the legal right to . . ." or "The news media should be allowed to . . ." The statements reflecting restrictions on the media were (a) stop broadcast or publication of a news story if the government believes it is necessary to fight terrorism, (b) force journalists to reveal their confidential sources of information if the government believes it is necessary to fight terrorism, and (c) ban access to World Wide Web sites if the government believes a site contains enemy propaganda. The two statements reflecting expansive rights for the media were (a) news media should be allowed to broadcast or publish stories about government incompetence in fighting terrorism even if it hurts public morale; and (b) news media should be allowed to cover stories about people or groups that believe United States policies were to blame for the terrorist attacks.

After recoding for uniform direction, a willingness to restrict news media scale was created by summing the five individual item scores and calculating the mean. Examination of the item correlation matrix revealed that the three items that directly referenced allowing the government to place restrictions on the press did not correlate well with the two items that referenced an expansive role for the press in reporting on terrorism activities. A factor analysis of the five items revealed two separate components: the three questions on government restrictions loaded on the first component and the items on the behavior of the press loaded on a separate second component. Because the concept of interest is willingness to restrict the news media, an alternative scale was constructed using only the three items directly asking about government regulation of the press ($\alpha = .70$, $M = 3.38$, $SD = 1.00$). A higher score reflects an increased willingness to restrict the news media.

Danger-Avoiding Behaviors

Respondents were asked whether or not they had taken certain behaviors to protect themselves from possible new terrorist attacks. The behaviors asked about
were (a) whether respondent had inquired about obtaining or actually purchased
antibiotics for possible use against anthrax infection; (b) put off or canceled taking a trip; (c) avoided shopping malls, sporting events, or other public places; (d)
examined mail looking for suspicious letters or packages; and (e) shopped for or
purchased a gas mask or protective suit.[3] The variable measure was the number of
positive responses (K–R 20 = .40, M = .71, SD = .84). Because of the low reliability, the two individual danger-avoiding behavior items with the highest frequency of occurrence—examine mail for suspicious letters or packages (n = 226)
and putting off or canceling a trip (n = 81)—were used to test the hypothesis.

Time Spent Attending to News Media

Respondents were asked to estimate about how much time during an average day
they spend reading newspapers, watching television news, and reading news online.[4] The variable measure was calculated by adding the total time spent each day
with all three sources of news. The mean estimate of total news exposure (n =
496) was just over 2 hr per day (2 hr, 4 min). Those who read newspapers (n =
385) spent an average of 45 min with the paper; those viewing television news (n
= 468) spent 90 min per day viewing. Those reading news online (n = 108) spent
an average of 36 min per day reading news.

Perceptual Bias

Following the tradition of third-person effects research, perceptual bias was
measured using two items: the respondent's self-assessment of how exposure to
terrorism coverage in the news had affected himself or herself and the respondent's assessment of how exposure to terrorism coverage in the news media had
affected the public's level of fear. The paired measurements, rotated to avoid order effects, were asked for each news medium that the respondent said he or she
used on an average day (newspapers, television, or online). Perceptions of fear
generated by exposure to the news media were measured on a scale ranging from
1 (*decreased a lot*) to 5 (*increased a lot*). The measurement of the magnitude of

---

[3]Of the five possible behaviors queried, 48% (n = 242) reported taking none of the actions; 37%
(n = 187) reported taking one of the actions; 11% (n = 53) took two of the actions; 4% (n = 19) took
three of the actions; 1 respondent reported four actions; and 1 respondent reported taking all five
actions.

[4]Respondents were instructed not to include any Internet or other online newspaper reading in
their estimates of time spent reading newspapers.

perceptual bias for each respondent was calculated by subtracting perceived fear effects on others from perceived fear effects on self.

Online News User Behaviors

A number of online news use behaviors were measured. Online news users were asked to react to a series of statements about online news coverage of terrorism on a 5-point scale ranging from 1 (*strongly disagree*) to 5 (*strongly agree*). The statements were whether they thought online news coverage of terrorism (a) has been overly sensationalized, (b) helps reassure the public that the real risks of terrorism are small, (c) has been believable, and (d) has been accurate. Online news users were also asked whether they had communicated with others about terrorism or learned about terrorism by (a) sending e-mails to family, friends, or co-workers; (b) using instant messaging; (c) reading comments on a Web site, bulletin board, chat room, or e-mail listserv; (d) posting comments on a Web site, bulletin board, chat room, or e-mail listserv; and (e) listen to online audio news stories or watch online video news stories. Responses were measured on a 4-point scale ranging from 1 (*never*) to 4 (*often*).

Other Demographics

Other demographic data collected in this study included age, gender, race, ethnicity, education, urban area residency, household income, and political liberalism or conservatism.[5]

FINDINGS

The sample was 57% female (*n* = 289) and 43% male (*n* = 221). With regard to ethnic and racial composition, 8% of the sample identified themselves as having an Hispanic ethnic origin, and racial breakdowns were 84% Whites, 8% Blacks, 2% Asians and 5% other. The median age was 45. About one third of the respondents had a high school degree (*n* = 166) with approximately one quarter report-

---

[5] Age was measured in years. Gender was coded 1 for male and 2 for female. Race was: White, Black, Asian, or other. Hispanic or Latino ancestry was coded 1 for yes and 2 for no. Education was ranked in seven categories: (a) no high school, (b) some high school, (c) high school or vocational degree, (d) some college, (e) college degree, (f) some graduate work, and (g) graduate degree. Urban residency was a dichotomous measure of whether the respondent reported living in or near a large urban area: 1 for yes and 2 for no. Household income was ranked in five categories: (a) under $25,000, (b) $25,001 to $50,000, (c) $50,001 to $75,000, (d) $75,001 to $100,000, and (e) more than $100,000. Political liberalism or conservatism was measured by asking respondents to place themselves into one of the following political categories: (a) very conservative, (b) somewhat conservative, (c) middle-of-the-road, (d) somewhat liberal, and (e) very liberal.

ing some college ($n = 133$) and one quarter reporting having earned a college degree ($n = 123$). The median annual household income category was $50,001 to $75,000. Sixty-three percent reported living in or near a large urban area.

Slightly over three fourths (76.5%) of the respondents reported reading a newspaper on an average day, with estimates ranging from 2 min per day to 4 hr, 30 min. Newspaper readers spent an average of 35 min per day with the newspaper. Ninety-three percent of the respondents watched television news on an average day, with estimates ranging from 7 min to 12 hr per day. On average, respondents who watched television news watched for 2 hr, 23 min per day. Twenty-one percent of the respondents reported reading news online during an average day, with estimates ranging from 2 min to 3 hr, 30 min. Those who read news online averaged 36 min per day. Overall, news consumption was quite high but consistent with the high degree of information seeking characterizing this period.

As predicted in Hypothesis 1, a significant positive relationship was found between the level of fear about terrorism (controlling for gender) and a willingness to place restrictions on both news organizations ($sr = .10$, $n = 478$, $p < .01$) and civil liberties ($sr = .12$, $n = 447$, $p < .01$).

Support was also found for Hypothesis 2. There was a significant positive correlation between estimates of total news exposure and feelings of fear about terrorism ($sr = .16$, $n = 487$, $p < .01$). There were also significant positive relationships between feelings of fear about terrorism and television use ($sr = .13$, $n = 497$, $p < .01$) and newspaper use ($sr = .14$, $n = 497$, $p < .01$). For those who read news online, there was no significant relationship between time spent reading news online and feelings about fear of terrorism ($sr = .10$, $n = 105$, $p > .05$).[6]

Partial support was found for Hypothesis 3. Although the hypothesis could not be directly tested, there is some evidence that engaging in danger-avoidance behaviors is significantly related to levels of fear about terrorism. There was a significant positive relationship between examining mail for suspicious letters or packages and fear about terrorism ($sr = .22$, $n = 500$, $p < .01$). Similarly, putting off or canceling a trip was also positively related to fear about terrorism ($sr = .23$, $n = 498$, $p < .01$).

Hypothesis 4 predicted that respondents would demonstrate perceptual bias by estimating significantly higher affective message effects resulting from news exposure about terrorism on others compared to themselves. As shown in Table 6.1, across the three media examined, there were significant differences in the perceptual estimates about the perceived effect of exposure to news media about terrorism on fear of terrorism. Respondents consistently made higher estimates of a fear effect from news media coverage on others compared to themselves. This

---

[6]It was assumed that because of the widespread availability of both newspapers and television, a respondent's nonexposure on an average day was a meaningful observation. However, because individual access to online news remains somewhat limited, only those who actually reported reading some news online during an average day were included in the correlation between fear of terrorism and amount of news read online.

TABLE 6.1
Paired Sample t Tests on Perceived Fear Effect Estimates
From Exposure to Terrorism by Medium

Source	M	SD	df	t
Newspaper readers				
Self	3.38	.67	355	20.08*
Others	4.24	.74		
TV news viewers				
Self	3.52	.68	439	20.81*
Others	4.34	.70		
Online news readers				
Self	3.33	.74	93	5.71*
Others	3.89	.85		

Note. Judgments were made on a 5-point fear scale: 1 = *decreased a lot*; 2 = *decreased some*; 3 = *no change*; 4 = *increased some*; and 5 = *increased a lot*.
*$p < .01$.

finding extends a well-documented phenomenon into the area of affective perceptions.

Hypothesis 5, which predicted a significant difference in the magnitude of perceptual bias between men and women, was supported in only one of the three media comparisons. No significant difference was found between men and women in the magnitude of third-person effect estimates for newspaper reading (male $M = .90$, $SD = .81$; female $M = .85$, $SD = 75$), $t(352) = .57$, $p > .05$. Nor was a significant effect found for television viewing, although the mean difference did approach significance (male $M = .91$, $SD = .82$; female $M = .76$, $SD = .83$), $t(436) = 1.90$, $p = .058$. Interestingly, a significant effect was found for online news readers (male $M = .82$, $SD = .83$; female $M = .29$, $SD = 1.00$), $t(92) = 2.76$, $p < .01$. A review of the frequencies revealed that men (a) made lower estimates of the effects of exposure to online news on themselves than women did, and (b) made higher estimates than women about the effects of exposure on others.

No support was found for Hypothesis 6, which predicted that the magnitude of perceptual bias would be positively related to support for restrictions on civil liberties and the news media. The only significant relationship between magnitude of perceptual bias and support for restrictions on civil liberties was in the television condition and in the opposite direction from what had been hypothesized ($r = -.13$, $n = 400$, $p < .01$). The more respondents estimated fear effects from television news on others compared to themselves, the less likely they were to support government restrictions on civil liberties. A similar result occurred with newspapers and support for restrictions on the news media. Higher respondent estimates for fear effects on others compared to themselves was related to less support for restrictions on the news media ($r = -.10$, $n = 339$, $p < .05$).

Online News Users and Terrorism News

Research conducted in the aftermath of September 11 showed that people made extensive use of the Internet to find information about the attacks and communicate with others (Pew Internet and American Life Project, 2001a, 2001b; Varisco, 2002). Not surprisingly, the Internet played a supplemental role to television and telephone; only 3% of Internet users say they received most of their information about the attacks or their aftermath from online sources and many initially reported difficulties getting to online news sites (Pew Internet and American Life Project, 2001a). In the month following the attacks, about 22% of Internet users reported reading news online during an average day (Pew Internet and American Life Project, 2001b). About half of all American Internet users consulted online news sites during the first 3 weeks after the attacks, often using search engines to find information (Pew Internet and American Life Project, 2001b).

This study compared online news users' perceptions of terrorism news coverage across media. As shown in Table 6.2, online news users reported online news to be less sensational than both television and newspapers in their terrorism coverage. Online news was also reported to be more reassuring about the real risks of terrorism, more believable, and more accurate than either newspapers or television. At least in the context of news coverage of terrorism, the concerns about bias in online news content identified in Chapter 5 were not apparent here.

Table 6.3 shows the mean frequency of online behaviors used to communicate with others about terrorism and the use of video or audio streams. In the aggregate, online news users engaged in relatively few ancillary communication activities relating to terrorism information. The highest rated activity was sending e-mail to others about terrorism subjects, although the mean was barely higher than the "seldom" category. Almost 10% reported that they often sent e-mails about terrorism to others, and 32% said they sometimes sent such e-mails. Five percent reported often listening to online audio or video stories about terrorism, and almost 28% said they sometimes listened to or viewed streamed material.

TABLE 6.2
Attitudes Toward Terrorism Coverage by Online News Users

	Mean Agreement			SD		
	Newspapers	Television	Online	Newspapers	Television	Online
Sensational	3.13	3.45	2.73	1.14	1.33	1.02
Reassuring about risk	2.62	2.48	2.69	1.06	1.11	.99
Believable	3.79	3.64	3.81	.80	.84	.67
Accurate	3.50	3.28	3.55	.95	1.01	.90

Note. Judgments were made on a 5-point scale where 1 = *strongly disagree*; 5 = *strongly agree*. Includes only respondents who read news online.

TABLE 6.3
Terrorism-Related Behaviors of Online News Users

Activities	Mean	SD
Send e-mail messages to family, friends, or coworkers about terrorism	2.05	1.09
Listen to online audio news or watch online video news stories about terrorism	1.88	.98
Read comments on a Web site bulletin board, chat room, or by listserv about terrorism	1.73	1.00
Use instant messaging to communicate about terrorism	1.41	.82
Post comments on a Web site bulletin board, chat room, or by listserv about terrorism	1.30	.77

Note. Judgments were made on a 4-point scale where 1 = never, 2 = seldom, 3 = sometimes, 4 = often. Includes only respondents who read news online.

DISCUSSION

This investigation revealed fear as a significant variable in a number of areas of interest to communication researchers. However, many of the significant associations found between fear of terrorism and the variables under study were decidedly small and must be interpreted with caution. As with any correlation, there could be uncontrolled variables that may have an impact on the observed effects.

One possible explanation for the weak relationships between feelings of fear and other variables might be the substantial presence of "repressors" in the survey sample, or those who report low levels of negative affect when, in fact, they are much more emotionally reactive (Sparks, Pellechia, & Irvine, 1999). It has also been suggested that personality variables may affect both the selective exposure level of individuals to negative media fare and the effects of such fare on individuals' emotional states (Sparks & Spirek, 1988). It is unknown how such phenomena are distributed in the general population. It has also been suggested that biologically based individual differences in temperament may relate to media use motivations (Sherry, 2001).

The positive relationships between fear of terrorism and willingness to restrict civil liberties and the news media are not surprising. It may be that fear of terrorism is leading many Americans toward an increased willingness to trade their civil liberties for safety. In such perilous times, Benjamin Franklin's (1759) observation that "They that can give up essential liberty to obtain a little temporary safety deserve neither liberty nor safety" may ring hollow to many fearful citizens. It may also be that Americans have little regard for either their civil liberties or the role of the press in a democracy. Mueller (1988) argued that the public's grasp of and self-interest in civil liberties is seemingly so minimal that it may not be tangibly measurable. The public's apparent disregard for First Amendment principles, found in the research of the First Amendment Center (2002), increases the possibilities of government excesses in the war on terrorism.

The significant correlation between feelings of fear about terrorism and over-all news media exposure suggests that news reports may either exacerbate fears of terrorism or that people at higher levels of fear seek out news more than others. The direction of causality remains undetermined. Higher levels of fear may trigger selective exposure to news for surveillance, information uncertainty reduction, reassurance, or some other gratification. Additionally, in the deluge of terrorism news dominating the media at the time were stories of heroism, patriotism, and the government's dogged determination in prosecuting the war against terror. Such news content is certainly positive in hedonic value. One of the limitations of this study was the inability to collect measures of other news media exposure. It may be that adding measures of exposure to radio newscasts, news magazines, and other news sources would have helped to clarify the relationship between level of fear and news media use. However, of the news media studied, the relationship between fear and exposure to news, in addition to being significant overall, was also significant for both television and newspapers. The relationship did not hold for users of online news media. One possible explanation is the high level of control available to online users in the selection of content. Such control can facilitate ongoing mood management.

Of interest to third-person effect theorists is the evidence that perceptual bias appears to extend into estimates about the emotional impact of media messages. Although no support was found for gender-based differences in the magnitude of third-person effects for mainstream media, the fact that male online news users make lower estimates of effects on themselves and higher estimates about others is a curious finding worthy of further study.

Finally, it would appear that online news users, at least in the context of news reports about terrorism, may find online information more favorable than that found in newspapers or on television newscasts. Perhaps it is the user's almost unlimited choice of news content, and not the content itself, that ultimately shapes attitudes about the credibility of news on the Web.

REFERENCES

Altheide, D. L., & Michalowski, R. S. (1999). Fear in the news: A discourse of control. *The Sociological Quarterly, 40*, 474–503.
Becker, L. B., Cobbey, R. E., & Sobowale, I. A. (1978). Public support for the press. *Journalism Quarterly, 55*, 421–430.
Begley, S., & Isikoff, M. (2001, October 22). Anxious about anthrax. *Newsweek*, pp. 28–35.
Biswas, R., Riffe, D., & Zillmann, D. (1994). Mood influence on the appeal of bad news. *Journalism Quarterly, 71*, 689–696.
Blasi, V. (1985). The pathological perspective and the first amendment. *Columbia Law Review, 85*, 449–514.
Brashers, D. E. (2001). Communication and uncertainty management. *Journal of Communication, 51*(3), 477–497.
Bryant, J., Carveth, R. A., & Brown, D. (1981). Television viewing and anxiety: An experimental examination. *Journal of Communication, 31*(1), 106–119.

Cantor, J. (1999). Comments on coincidence: Comparing the findings on retrospective reports of fear. *Media Psychology, 1*, 141–143.

Davis, J. A. (1975). Communism, conformity, cohorts, and categories: American tolerance in 1954 and 1972–73. *American Journal of Sociology, 81*, 491–513.

Davison, W. P. (1983). The third-person effect in communication. *Public Opinion Quarterly, 47*, 1–15.

Davison, W. P. (1996). The third-person effect revisited. *International Journal of Public Opinion Research, 8*, 113–119.

Doob, A. N., & MacDonald, G. E. (1979). Television viewing and fear of victimization: Is the relationship causal? *Journal of Personality and Social Psychology, 37*, 170–179.

First Amendment Center. (2000). *State of the First Amendment 2000.* Nashville, TN: The Freedom Forum.

First Amendment Center. (2001). *State of the First Amendment 2001.* Nashville, TN: The Freedom Forum.

First Amendment Center. (2002). *State of the First Amendment 2002.* Nashville, TN: The Freedom Forum.

Franklin, B. (1759). Historical review of Pennsylvania. In *Bartlett's Familiar Quotations, 348* (Emily Morison Beck ed., 1980).

Gerbner, G., & Gross, L. (1976). Living with television: The violence profile. *Journal of Communication, 26*(2), 173–199.

Gerbner, G., Gross, L., Morgan, M., & Signorielli, N. (1980). The mainstreaming of America: Violence profile No. 11. *Journal of Communication, 30*(3), 10–19.

Gunther, A. (1991). What we think others think: Cause and consequence in the third-person effect. *Communication Research, 18*, 355–372.

Gunther, A. (1995). Overrating the x-rating: The third-person perception and support for censorship of pornography. *Journal of Communication, 45*(1), 27–38.

Heath, L., & Gilbert, K. (1996). Mass media and fear of crime. *The American Behavioral Scientist, 39*, 379–386.

Hirsch, P. (1980). The "scary world" of the nonviewer and other anomalies: A reanalysis of Gerbner et al.'s findings on the cultivation analysis, Part I. *Communication Research, 7*, 403–456.

Hirsch, P. (1981). On not learning from one's mistakes: A reanalysis of Gerbner et al.'s findings on the cultivation analysis, Part II. *Communication Research, 8*, 3–37.

Kubey, R. W., & Peluso, T. (1990). Emotional response as a cause of interpersonal news diffusion: The case of the space shuttle tragedy. *Journal of Broadcasting & Electronic Media, 34*, 69–76.

Lang, A., Newhagen, J., & Reeves, B. (1996). Negative video as structure: Emotion, attention, capacity, and memory. *Journal of Broadcasting & Electronic Media, 40*, 460–477.

Lasorsa, D. L. (1989). Real and perceived effects of "Amerika." *Journalism Quarterly, 66*, 373–378, 529.

Leventhal, H. (1970). Findings and theory in the study of fear communication. In L. Berkowitz (Ed.), *Advances in experimental social psychology* (Vol. 5, pp. 119–186). New York: Academic.

McClosky, H. (1964). Consensus and ideology in American politics. *American Political Science Review, 58*, 361–382.

Mueller, J. (1988). Trends in political tolerance. *Public Opinion Quarterly, 52*, 1–25.

Newhagen, J. E. (1998). TV news images that induce anger, fear, and disgust: Effects on approach-avoidance and memory. *Journal of Broadcasting & Electronic Media, 42*, 265–276.

Newhagen, J. E., & Lewenstein, M. (1992). Cultivation and exposure to television following the 1989 Loma Prieta earthquake. *Mass Comm Review, 19*(1–2), 49–56.

Nunn, C. A., Crockett, H. J., & Williams, J. A. (1978). *Tolerance for nonconformity.* San Francisco: Jossey-Bass.

Paul, B., Salwen, M. B., & Dupagne, M. (2000). The third-person effect: A meta-analysis of the perceptual hypothesis. *Mass Communication & Society, 3*, 57–85.

Perloff, R. M. (1996). Perceptions and conceptions of political media impact: The third-person effect and beyond. In A. N. Crigler (Ed.), *The psychology of political communication* (pp. 177–197). Ann Arbor: University of Michigan Press.

Perloff, R. M. (1999). The third-person effect: A critical review and synthesis. *Media Psychology, 1,* 353–378.

Pew Internet and American Life Project. (2001a, September 15). *How Americans used the Internet after the terror attack.* Retrieved October 4, 2001, from http://www.pewinternet.org/reports/toc. asp?Report=45

Pew Internet and American Life Project. (2001b, October 10). *How the Internet was used by millions after the terror attacks to grieve, console, share news, and debate the country's response.* Retrieved November 28, 2001, from http://www.pewinternet.org/reports/toc.asp?Report=46

Pew Research Center for People and the Press. (2001, November 8). *Worries about terrorism subside in mid-America.* Retrieved November 13, 2001, from http://people-press.org/reports/display. php3?ReportID=142

Potts, R., & Sanchez, D. (1994). Television viewing and depression: No news is good news. *Journal of Broadcasting & Electronic Media, 38,* 79–90.

Price, V., Tewksbury, D., & Huang, L.-N. (1998). Third-person effects on publication of a Holocaust-denial advertisement. *Journal of Communication, 48*(2), 3–26.

Prothro, J. W., & Grigg, C. W. (1960). Fundamental principles of democracy: Bases of agreement and disagreement. *Journal of Politics, 22,* 276–294.

Rojas, H., Shah, H. D., & Faber, R. J. (1996). For the good of others: Censorship and the third-person effect. *International Journal of Public Opinion Research, 8,* 163–186.

Rucinski, D., & Salmon, C. T. (1990). The "other" as the vulnerable voter: A study of the third-person effect in the 1988 presidential campaign. *International Journal of Public Opinion Research, 2,* 345–368.

Salwen, M. B., & Driscoll, P. (1997). Consequences of third-person perception in support for press restrictions in the O. J. Simpson trial. *Journal of Communication, 47,* 60–78.

Select Phone Pro CD Database, version 2.1. (2001). Omaha, NE: InfoUSA.

Sheatsley, P. B., & Feldman, J. J. (1965). A national survey on public reactions and behavior. In B. Greenberg & S. Parker (Eds.), *The Kennedy assassination and the American public: Social communication in crisis* (pp. 149–177). Palo Alto, CA: Stanford University Press.

Sherry, J. L. (2001). Toward an etiology of media use motivations: The role of temperament in media use. *Communication Monographs, 68,* 274–288.

Slovic, P., Fischoff, B., & Lichtenstein, S. (1979). Rating the risks. *Environment, 21*(3), 14–20.

Sparks, G. G. (1991). The relationship between distress and delight in males' and females' reactions to frightening films. *Human Communication Research, 17,* 625–637.

Sparks, G. G., Pellechia, M., & Irvine, C. (1999). The repressive coping style and fright reactions to mass media. *Communication Research, 26,* 176–177.

Sparks, G. G., & Spirek, M. (1988). Individual differences in coping with stressful mass media: An activation-arousal view. *Human Communication Research, 15,* 195–216.

Stouffer, S. (1955). *Communism, conformity, and civil liberties.* New York: Doubleday.

Sullivan, J. L., Piereson, J., & Marcus, G. (1979). An alternative conceptualization of political tolerance: Illusory increases 1950s–1970s. *American Political Science Review, 79,* 781–794.

Sullivan, J. L., Piereson, J., & Marcus, G. E. (1982). *Political tolerance and democracy.* Chicago: University of Chicago Press.

Tamborini, R., Zillmann, D., & Bryant, J. (1984). Fear and victimization: Exposure to television and perceptions of crime and fear. In R. Bostrom (Ed.), *Communication yearbook* (Vol. 8, pp. 492–513). Beverly Hills, CA: Sage.

Tyler, T. R., & Cook, F. L. (1984). The mass media and judgments of risk: Distinguishing impact on personal and societal level judgments. *Journal of Personality and Social Psychology, 47,* 693–708.

Varisco, D. M. (2002). September 11: Participant webservation of the "war on terrorism." *American Anthropologist, 104,* 934–938.

Vincent, R. C., & Basil, M. D. (1997). College students' news gratifications, media use, and current event knowledge. *Journal of Broadcasting & Electronic Media, 41*, 380–392.

Zillmann, D. (1980). Anatomy of suspense. In P. H. Tannenbaum (Ed.), *The entertainment functions of television* (pp. 133–163). Hillsdale, NJ: Lawrence Erlbaum Associates.

Zillmann, D. (2000). Mood management in the context of selective exposure theory. In M. E. Roloff (Ed.), *Communication yearbook 23* (pp. 103–123). Thousand Oaks, CA: Sage.

Zillmann, D., & Bryant, J. (1985). Affect, mood, and emotion as determinants of selective exposure. In D. Zillmann & J. Bryant (Eds.), *Selective exposure to communication* (pp. 157–190). Hillsdale, NJ: Lawrence Erlbaum Associates.

Zillmann, D., & Wakshlag, J. (1985). Fear of victimization and the appeal of crime drama. In D. Zillmann & J. Bryant (Eds.), *Selective exposure to communication* (pp. 141–156). Hillsdale, NJ: Lawrence Erlbaum Associates.

Third-Person Perceptions of Fear During the War on Terrorism: Perceptions of Online News Users

Michael B. Salwen
Paul D. Driscoll
Bruce Garrison

The September 11, 2001, terrorist attacks on the World Trade Center and the Pentagon traumatized Americans. Two weeks later, Attorney General John Ashcroft confirmed that Americans had reason to panic. Terrorists lived among us, he announced. Our borders and coastlines were vulnerable. Most chilling of all, he warned that new attacks could come within the week. A month after the attacks, *The Washington Post* reported that, during a classified briefing, FBI and CIA officials informed select Congress members that new attacks were "100 percent" likely (Milban & Slavin, 2001).[1] Meanwhile, new anthrax attacks were in the news, and administration officials were giving conflicting messages about the dangers of anthrax and whether the anthrax attacks were linked to the September 11 attacks.[2] *The Post*'s science and medicine writer wrote that public officials' delicate balancing act of "trying to express uncertainty and reassurance at the same time" was "sowing chaos and confusion" (D. Brown, 2001, p. B3). A *New York Times*/CBS News Poll reported that a majority of Americans believed another terrorist attack was very likely, that the government was not doing enough to prepare for a biological attack, and that government officials were not telling Americans everything they needed to know about anthrax (Berke & Elder, 2001).

This study examined public fear after the attacks and the United States led invasion against Taliban government forces and Al Qaeda terrorists in Afghanistan.

---

[1]The leaked reports of this story angered Bush administration officials, who threatened to restrict Congressional members' access to classified reports.

[2]Subsequent FBI investigations concluded that the anthrax attacks were probably acts of domestic terrorism unrelated to the September 11 attacks.

185

The study, grounded in principles of perception, focused on individuals' estimations of their own fears and their perceptions of the public's fears. It also examined people's perceptions of the fears of a specific segment of the public—Web users who used the medium to learn about the war on terrorism. By examining perceptions of Web users' fears, we consider how a new news medium affected public perceptions of media in society.

This study drew on the third-person effect hypothesis, which asserts that individuals judge the news media to exert greater persuasive influence on other people than on themselves—a cognitive effect. By expanding the range of the perception from persuasive influence to the visceral response of fear, we consider whether the third-person effect operates in the realm of perceived emotional affective responses. It seems reasonable to surmise that, just as people estimate others to be less perceptive than themselves and therefore more susceptible to media influence, they also judge other people to be more susceptible to irrational emotional responses attributable to threatening media reports. Both perceptions of cognitive and affective effects provide self-serving, ego-enhancing boosts for individuals. This study also investigated the third-person effect behavioral hypothesis, examining whether individuals who judged news media coverage of the war to have greater fear effects on others would exhibit increased support for wartime restrictions on media coverage of terrorism.

THE NEW MEDIA ENVIRONMENT

New media, or new applications of existing media, can affect how individuals acquire and process the news. Ten years before the war on terrorism, during the Persian Gulf War, the television networks and especially Cable News Network (CNN) received kudos for their real-time coverage of the war. Correspondents in Israel, outfitted in military gear and gas masks, reported Iraqi Scud missile attacks, and CNN's Peter Arnett in Baghdad gained fame and generated controversy reporting the allies' bombing of the Iraqi capital. Because almost all Americans had access to television, television viewing of the war was a shared national experience.

In the war on terrorism, a relatively new news medium, little more than 5 or 6 years old, came to the fore—online news. The importance of online news in the war on terrorism was apparent when, on first learning of the attacks, millions of Americans logged on to online news sites, causing a logjam and temporary access problems (Palser, 2001). In the period between the Persian Gulf War and the attacks on New York and Washington, access to and use of the World Wide Web and Internet grew astronomically around the world, but especially in the technologically advanced portions of the world, such as the United States. Online news has the potential to change the way the audience learns about and processes the news (Hacker & van Dijk, 2000). The World Wide Web offers the potential for users to keep abreast of news at their convenience, to exercise more control over the news stories they read, and to select from an almost limitless number of online news media outlets around the nation—and even around the world. For example, during the war on terrorism the online site of the Qatar-based Al Jazeera satellite television network, the source of video messages from Osama bin Laden, acquired a following in the United States (Miller, 2001).

However, a digital divide existed. Little more than half the American public had access to the Web (Coombs & Cutbirth, 1998; Sefton, 2000). The most obvious implication of the divide is that some people have greater access to news and public affairs information, exacerbating knowledge gaps (van Dijk, 2000). From a person-perception perspective, another implication is that people form groups or "communities" with ingroups and outgroups, and they form beliefs about ingroup and outgroup members. Duck, Hogg, and Terry (1995) examined the third-person effect from social identity theory and self-categorization theory, arguing that group members see outgroup members as less discerning about media influence than themselves and other ingroup members. Their results were consistent with predictions derived from the theories. Other studies indicate that perceptions of others in different reference groups can affect third-person perceptions (Duck, Hogg, & Terry, 2000; Matera & Salwen, 1999; Neuwirth & Frederick, 2002).

A growing body of perceptual research in mass communication examines how people judge media effects on themselves and on other people. Even people without access to the Internet and Web know about these new forms of communication, and they have ideas about the people who use these new media. Did Web users' easy access to news about the war mean that they were deluged with more frightening news, and that they therefore were more terrified? Those who were not wired often thought of Web users this way—as paranoid and delusional. Stories of cyberhoaxes related to the September 11 attacks—such as the Web rumors that the 15th-century French mystic Nostradamus predicted the attacks and that the face of devil could be seen in the billowing smoke of the World Trade Center's rubble—seemed to confirm that Web users were an eccentric and paranoid group (Bruce, 2001; Hardon, 2001). However, individuals online who used the medium for news probably felt they were better informed than those not online, and that they were more composed during unpredictable times. In summary, it is easy to see how people judge themselves and people like themselves as smarter and more composed than most other people during troubled times.

THE THIRD-PERSON EFFECT

The considerable body of research on the third-person effect perceptual component or perceptual hypothesis provides compelling evidence that people judge the news media to wield greater persuasive influence on other people (Lasorsa,

1992; R. M. Perloff, 1993, 1996, 1999; see Paul, Salwen, & Dupagne, 2000, for a meta-analysis of third-person effect findings). Some studies that examined the third-person effect behavioral component or behavioral hypothesis report that third-person perception is associated with greater willingness to endorse restrictions on perceived harmful media messages (Gunther, 1995; Rojas, Shah, & Faber, 1996).[3] Thus, those who see themselves as perspicacious and relatively invulnerable to harmful media effects see others as susceptible to these effects. As a consequence, they support censorship to "protect" other people from harm (Salwen, 1998). After the September 11 attacks, well-meaning people might have believed that the deluge of frightening news reports threatened other individuals more than themselves. Frightened individuals, they reasoned, might panic and take uncalled-for actions, such as hoarding goods and avoiding crowded places.

Support for the behavioral hypothesis is especially evident in those cases where the messages are particularly harmful.[4] Support or partial support for the behavioral hypothesis comes from studies on pornography (Gunther, 1995; Gunther & Hwa, 1996; Lee & Yang, 1996; Rojas et al., 1996) and television violence (Gunther & Hwa, 1996; Rojas et al., 1996). The research with support for censorship of public issues and political messages is less clear and less often studied. Rucinski and Salmon (1990) failed to find support for the third-person perception to predict restrictions of presidential campaign messages, although the relationship was in the hypothesized direction. Salwen and Driscoll (1997) failed to find support for censorship in a third-person effect study of a high-profile trial. Salwen (1998), on the other hand, found a relationship between third-person perception and support for censorship of manifestly "unfair" political campaign messages during the 1996 presidential campaign. This study examines the relationship between third-person perception and support for government censorship during wartime. History shows that the U.S. government has imposed severe restrictions on civil liberties and the press during wartime, often with public approval (Blanchard, 1992; Graham-Yooll, 1993; Newhagen, 1994; Seigenthaler, 1991).

Some third-person effect scholars have drawn on the psychological theory of optimistic bias to explain the third-person effect. Optimistic bias posits that people judge themselves less likely than other people to experience negative life events (Brosius & Engel, 1996; Chapin, 2000; Gunther & Mundy, 1993). In the context of the third-person effect, susceptibility to media influence is regarded as a negative event. Both optimistic bias and third-person perception provide self-serving functions for individuals, such as reinforcing self-esteem (Banning, 2001; J. D. Brown, 1986; Duck, Terry, & Hogg, 1995; Gunther, 1991; Gunther &

---

[3]Several studies failed to support the behavioral component hypothesis (Price, Tewksbury, & Huang, 1998; Rucinski & Salmon, 1990; Salwen & Driscoll, 1997).

[4]We refer to the behavioral hypothesis to support censorship here, but we must add the behavioral hypothesis can include other behaviors (e.g., Atwood, 1994). Still, the majority of behavioral hypothesis studies has concerned support for censorship.

Mundy, 1993; Hoorens, 1993; Huang, 1995; Kennemer, 1990; L. S. Perloff, 1983; L. S. Perloff & Fetzer, 1986; Shapiro & Dunning, 2000; Weinstein, 1980; Weinstein & Klein, 1996; Wills, 1981) and sustaining illusions of control (Atwood, 1994; Duck, Terry & Hogg, 1995; McKenna, 1993; Taylor, 1983). Some third-person effect scholars, taking a cue from Davison's (1983) proposition that people judge themselves less vulnerable because they believe they possess greater subject matter expertise than most other people, have advanced a self-knowledge hypothesis. The self-knowledge hypothesis proposes that as people judge themselves more knowledgeable about subject matter than other people, third-person perception increases (Driscoll & Salwen, 1997; Lasorsa, 1989; Salwen & Dupagne, 2001; White & Dillon, 2000). Davison (1983) wrote:

> In a sense, we are all experts on those subjects that matter to us, in that we have information not available to other people. This information may not be of a factual or technical nature; it may have to do with our own experiences, likes and dislikes. Other people, we reason, do not know what we know. Therefore, they are more likely to be influenced by the news media. (p. 9)

Researchers have conceived of harmful media effects in terms of the media's persuasive influence. According to this view, simply being persuaded is undesirable, and all the more so when the communication concerns undesirable-to-believe messages (Salwen & Dupagne, 1999). When posed with a desirable-to-believe message, the effect is often negated and sometimes reversed as a "first-person effect" tendency to exhibit greater perceived media influence on oneself (Andsager & White, 2001; Atwood, 1994; Chapin, 2000; Duck & Mullin, 1995; Gunther & Thorson, 1992; Innes & Zeitz, 1988). The notion that one can be persuaded by a mass media message suggests that one is gullible. However, as we have stated, in the weeks after the September 11 attacks, the overwhelming theme of news coverage was fear. As with persuasive influence, it may be undesirable to be frightened by news coverage of crises and tragedies and desirable to be calm and collected. Perhaps there may be social differences in willingness to acknowledge fear. For example, given gender norms (Lo & Wei, 2000), perhaps women may be more fearful (or more willing to admit their fear) than men.

SOCIAL DISTANCE

The third-person effect social distance corollary asserts that third-person perception increases as the others who are supposedly more susceptible to media influence become more dissimilar to the self. According to this view, people reason that those who are like them are more likely to share their views, their critical abilities to appraise media coverage, and their superior ability to resist harmful media influence. Early social distance studies typically had student samples estimate media influence on themselves and on different groups of geographically more distant others, such as fellow students, other people in the state, and other Americans (Cohen, Mutz, Price, & Gunther, 1988; Gunther, 1991; White, 1997). Eveland, Nathanson, Detenber, and McLeod (1999) noted that not all studies exhibit "an increasing pattern of perceived effects as the comparison group shifted from people in your home state to people from your region of the country to people in the U.S. in general" (p. 278). They concluded that "research on the role of social distance in perceptions of media influence actually appears to provide only a limited picture of social distance" (p. 279).

If the social distance research provides a limited picture, perhaps it is because researchers have focused too much attention on distance and not on the social aspect of the concept. Using geographic distance to substitute for social distance can be problematic. R. M. Perloff (1996) explicitly conceived of social distance as a social-psychological variable ranging from "people just like me" to "people not at all like me" (p. 186). Some social distance studies narrowly defined the others (i.e., the specified others), whereas most third-person effect studies described the others in broad, unspecified terms, the most general being "the public" or "most other Americans" (i.e., the generalized others). Presumably, people see themselves as socially distant from generalized others because it is easy to distance oneself from nameless, faceless others. Attaching faces to the others changes the dynamics of the perception. People may see themselves as distant or close to the specified others depending on the social relationships between themselves and the specified others. For example, Gibbon and Durkin (1995) reported increased third-person effects as the similarity of the others grew more socially distant from family members, to neighbors, to members of the state, to other Australians, to others in general.

Gibbon and Durkin's (1995) first two measures of others, in particular, concerned others within one's sphere of interpersonal relations. After that, social distance was more problematic. There was a presumption that others in the state were closer to the individual than others in the nation. It is questionable whether people can always make such fine distinctions once people are outside the realm of the interpersonal relations and the community. In the digital era, a community need not be conceived in terms of geographic distance. Researchers have conceived of the World Wide Web as a community, with smaller communities within the community (Dahlgren, 2000; Fitzgerald, 1996). Geographic distance is of little importance on the Web. At a finer level, those within the Web community who use the medium for news represent another gradation of community. Using the third-person effect as a theoretical framework and the social distance corollary to conceive of the Web as a community, hypotheses were advanced.

First, the study tested the general third-person effect hypothesis:

H_1: Respondents will estimate greater media-induced fear effects about the war on terrorism on the generalized others of "the public" than on themselves.

This study also asked respondents to estimate media fear effects on people who were getting their news about the war through the Web. Based on the social distance corollary, we hypothesized:

H₂: Non-Web users will estimate greater fear effects on those who use the Web for news about the war on terrorism than those who do not use the Web for news about the war.

Furthermore, the study tested the behavioral hypothesis:

H₃: Third-person perception of war coverage on fear will predict support for wartime media restrictions.

METHOD

A representative U.S. sample of 619 adults (age 18 and older) was surveyed by telephone using a stratified design, so that each state and the District of Columbia were represented proportionate to the national population in the 2000 U.S. Census. Respondents were surveyed during the evenings of November 11 to 15, 2001. Residential telephone numbers were drawn from the Fall 2001 edition of the national Select Phone telephone software package on compact disc and database published by InfoUSA (Select Phone Pro CD Database, 2001). Random residential telephone numbers were generated on a state-by-state basis from the database of more than 100 million telephone numbers using a table of random numbers and the random number selection function built into the Select Phone software. Each resulting state roster of random numbers was then adjusted using the one-up and one-down last digit method to include unlisted numbers not in the database. If there was no answer, a busy signal, or an answering machine, up to two more attempts were made later that evening or during another evening to reach the number. The response rate, excluding invalid contacts, was 56%.

Because changes in the news could affect opinion, efforts were made to keep the survey fieldwork interval short. Nevertheless, news events during the survey that might have affected the results should be noted. On Monday morning, November 12, 2001, American Airlines Flight 587, bound for the Dominican Republic, crashed in New York City's urban Rockaway Beach area a few minutes after takeoff from John F. Kennedy International Airport. Although aviation officials quickly discounted terrorism, focusing on a massive mechanical failure, the crash exacerbated the nerves of a jittery nation. Competing for the top news that day, Taliban forces abandoned Afghanistan's capital of Kabul en masse but still held several strategic centers, including Kandahar. The next day, anti-Taliban Northern Alliance troops captured the ethnic Pashtun tribe homeland of Jalalabad. As important as these events were individually, they were part of an ongoing larger story during turbulent times.

Operational Measures

Effects. There were three measures of fear effects attributable to media coverage of the war on terrorism. The 5-point scale measures assessed respondents' judgments of (a) their own level of fear attributable to media coverage of the war on terrorism, (b) estimates of the public's level of fear attributable to media coverage of the war on terrorism, and (c) estimates of Web users' level of fear attributable to their Web use regarding the war on terrorism.[5]

Support for Restrictions. Support for wartime media restrictions consisted of respondents' agreement or disagreement (*strongly agree, agree, neither agree nor disagree, disagree*, or *strongly disagree*) with what they were told were seven proposed laws "that would make it easier for the government to place restrictions on journalists and the Internet." A factor analysis indicated that the scale was unidimensional.[6] Respondents were asked whether "the government should have the legal right to" do the following:

- Stop journalists from interviewing persons that the government labels as terrorists.
- Force journalists to disclose their confidential news sources when the government believes that the information will help it fight the war on terrorism.
- Stop journalists from broadcasting or publishing news stories that it believes will hinder its fight in the war on terrorism.
- Require journalists to report official government information in their news stories that the government believes will help it fight the war on terrorism.
- Close down Web sites on the Internet that the government believes spread enemy propaganda.

---

[5]The questions were:

- Do you think that, due to the news coverage of the war on terrorism, the public's level of fear has increased a lot, increased somewhat, decreased somewhat, decreased a lot, or would you say it has not changed?
- Do you think that, due to the news coverage of the war on terrorism, your own level of fear has increased a lot, increased somewhat, decreased somewhat, decreased a lot, or would you say that your own level of fear has not changed?
- Regardless of whether you use the Internet, do you think that, due to the Internet coverage of the war on terrorism, that the level of fear among most Internet and World Wide Web users has increased a lot, increased somewhat, decreased somewhat, decreased a lot, or would you say that most Internet users' levels of fear have not changed?

[6]Initially, based on student sample pretests, we suspected the scale might break down into two dimensions of general restrictions and restrictions on the Web.

- Monitor the Internet and Web use activities of people that it considers dangerous.
- Require Internet companies, on request, to give government agencies information about subscribers.

Users. To measure online news use, respondents were asked whether they used the Internet or the World Wide Web. If they were Web users, they were then asked how many days a week, if any, they read an online news media outlet and then how many days a week they accessed news through their Internet service provider (ISP).[7] If they read online news at least 1 day per week on either a news media outlet site or through their ISP, they were coded as Web news users. We conceived of the user variable as ranging from those who were not on the Web (non), to those on the Web who did not use the Web for news (Web), to those who were on the Web and used the medium for news (news).

Other Variables. Other variables included a series of demographics and self-reported political orientations: gender, age in years, race collapsed as White and Black, Hispanic ethnicity (yes or no), a 5-point scale of income categories, a 7-point scale of education level categories, and a 5-point political orientation scale ranging from *very conservative* to *very liberal* with *middle-of-the-road* as the midpoint.

FINDINGS

Women were overrepresented and minorities were underrepresented, but not so severely as to indicate serious problems in sample representativeness. The sample was 58% female ($n = 357$), 9% Hispanic ($n = 55$), and 9% African American ($n = 55$). The median age was 46.5. About three quarters of the respondents had either a high school degree ($n = 156$), some college education ($n = 140$), or a college degree ($n = 169$). The median annual family income category was $50,001 to $75,000.

Almost two thirds of the 616[8] respondents classified in the user variable said they used the Internet or Web ($n = 387$, 62.8%), a finding congruent with or

---

[7]The questions were:

- Many newspapers, news magazines, television stations, and cable television network stations have online news sites. How many days a week, if any, do you read Web sites offered by one or more of these news media outlets?
- Internet service providers, such as America Online, Netscape, or Microsoft Network also have news sites. How many days a week, if any, do you read the news from any of these or other Internet service providers?

[8]Three respondents did not answer the questions to be classified.

somewhat higher than most U.S. adoption level estimates.[9] Among this group of Web users, 152 (24.7% of the total sample and 39.3% of Web users) were nonnews users (i.e., did not read either an online media outlet or an online news site provided by their ISP at least 1 day a week). A total of 235 respondents (38.1% of the total sample and 60.7% of Web users) read news online.

The alpha reliability coefficient of the support for media restrictions scale was .78. To the dismay of many media scholars and journalists, public support for media restrictions is surprisingly high. It was particularly high in this study, probably because the wartime atmosphere heightened public anxiety and willingness to endorse government restrictions.[10] The mean level of support of the media restrictions scale was above the 3.0 midpoint ($M = 3.74$, $SD = .91$). Self-reported fear levels were high, too. Although, as we note later, respondents judged a third-person effect to attribute greater fear on others than on themselves, the public's own self-reported fear level was above the 3.0 midpoint ($M = 3.45$, $SD = .79$).[11]

The Perceptual Hypothesis

Difference of means tests on fear levels indicated support for the perceptual hypothesis (Hypothesis 1). Respondents estimated greater media fear effects on most other members of the public than on themselves (Self $M = 3.45$, $SD = .80$;[12] others $M = 4.15$, $SD = .89$), $t(592) = 19.39$, $p < .001$. The difference between self and other Web users was also significant (Self $M = 3.46$. $SD = .78$; Web news users $M = 3.72$, $SD = .85$), $t(503) = 6.10$, $p < .001$.[13]

The Social Distance Corollary

To test the social distance corollary (Hypothesis 2), the results of three one-way analyses of variance by the "effects" measures (self, public, Web news users) and the "users" measures (nonusers, Web users, and Web news users) are reported in

---

[9]The Internet ratings service Nielsen/NetRatings (2001) reported that in October 2001 62% of Americans had access to the Internet.

[10]Salwen (1998), for example, reported high levels of support for government restrictions on "unfair" media messages during a presidential election, the exemplar case of when the media should enjoy considerable freedom to inform the public.

[11]Our findings were congruent with a Pew Research Center for People and the Press (2001) report that found strong support for censorship of media coverage during the war on terrorism. In the Pew study, as of mid-October nearly three quarters of respondents rated press coverage of terrorism as good or excellent. Nevertheless, 79% supported censorship of news coverage from Afghanistan and even a solid 62% said censorship of domestic coverage of anthrax attacks was a "good thing."

[12]The standard deviation changed slightly from the .79 reported earlier in this section because it was based on a slightly smaller sample size, among those respondents who answered both the self and others effects questions.

[13]The difference between the two groups of others, the public ($M = 4.17$, $SD = .87$) and Web users ($M = 3.71$, $SD = .86$) was also significant ($t = 11.23$, $p < .001$).

TABLE 7.1
Nonusers, Web Users, and Online News Users' Perceptions of Fear

Perception	Users	N	M	SD	F
Own fear of news	Non	225	3.48	.75	0.44
	Web	147	3.40	.75	
	News	234	3.44	.85	
	Total	606	3.45	.79	
Public's fear of news	Non	216	4.22	.88	1.24
	Web	148	4.16	.90	
	News	234	4.08	.90	
	Total	598	4.15	.89	
Web news users fear of news	Non	167	3.98	.93	12.84*
	Web	122	3.62	.82	
	News	218	3.55	.78	
	Total	507	3.71	.86	

$^*p < .001$.

Table 7.1. The hypothesis predicting that Web nonusers would perceive greater effects on Web news users was supported. The Scheffé post hoc tests indicate two significant pairwise differences, both involving nonusers' perceptions of Web news users' fear. As predicted, nonusers ($M = 3.98$, $SD = .93$) were significantly more likely than Web users ($M = 3.62$, $SD = .82$, $p < .001$) and news users ($M = 3.55$, $SD = .78$, $p < .001$) to judge those who got war news on the Web to be frightened. This perception was wrong, if we accept respondents' self-reports of their own fear levels (Non, $M = 3.48$, $SD = .75$; Web, $M = 3.40$, $SD = .75$; News, $M = 3.44$, $SD = .85$), $F(603) = .04$, ns.[14]

It is worth noting the smaller sample size ($n = 507$) of the perceptions of the Web news users' fear than for estimations of self and perceptions of the public (Self, $n = 606$; Public, $n = 598$). This was attributable to the inordinately large number of "don't know" responses among the nonusers ($n = 105$, compared to only $n = 18$ on perceptions of public fear and $n = 6$ of estimations of own fear). This interesting finding, confirmed in other studies, underscores that people typically feel they can judge media effects on themselves better than on others. They also feel they could judge media effects on the public, of which they are a part. However, for a sizable number of Web nonusers, it is difficult to estimate media

---

[14]Another point worth noting here is that online news users judged online news to devote less coverage to the war on terrorism than conventional news media. Among all respondents, when asked to estimate the percentage of news in the news media devoted to the war on terrorism, the mean response was 66.18% ($SD = 26.55$, $N = 602$). Online news users were also asked to estimate the percentage of news devoted to the war on terrorism in online news. Overall, they saw little difference with other users regarding the news media in general, but they estimated online news to devote less news to the war (media in general, $M = 66.65\%$, $SD = 24.54$; online news, $M = 54.35\%$, $SD = 30.62$; $n = 234$; $t = 5.90$, $p < .001$).

fear effects on Web news users; so much so that 38.6% of Web nonusers felt so socially distant from those who use the Web for news that they volunteered a "don't know" response rather than hazard a guess.

The Behavioral Hypothesis

To test the behavioral hypothesis (Hypothesis 3), congruent with much past research we report regression analyses. Table 7.2 reports two hierarchical regression models predicting support for media restrictions. The models are the same except for the last block. The last block of the model on the left includes the others-minus-self effects measures that comprise third-person perceptions (the total model explaining 8% of variance). The last block of the model on the right has the three fear effects measures (explaining 9% of variance). Separate regressions were computed because the fear effects measures are not independent from the third-person effects measures.

The behavioral hypothesis was partly supported. One of the two third-person effect variables, on the generalized others of the public, predicted support for restrictions ($p < .05$). However, third-person perception of other Web news users was not significant. The best predictor in the model was political orientations. Not surprisingly, the more conservative the respondents' orientations, the greater their support for media restrictions ($p < .001$). The only other significant

TABLE 7.2
Hierarchical Regressions Predicting Support for Media Restrictions

	Beta			Beta
Block 1				
Gender	.14**			.10*
Education	−.09			−.13*
Age	−.02			.00
Race	.02			.02
Hispanic	.01			.03
Income	−.01			.02
R^2	.02			.03*
Block 2				
Politics	.21***			.24***
R^2	.04***			.05***
Block 3				
TPE Public	.14*	Own fear		.03
TPE Web	−.02	Public fear		.11*
		Web fear		.06
R^2	.02*			.01
Total R^2	.08***			.09***

Note. Among the dummy variables, gender was 1 = male and 2 = female; race was 1 = White and 2 = Black; Hispanic was 1 = yes and 2 = no.
*$p < .05$. **$p < .01$. ***$p < .001$.

predictor in the model was gender, with women endorsing restrictions more than men ($p < .01$).

The other model in Table 7.2 shows how the individual effects affected support for restrictions. In the last block, only perceived effects on other members of the public predicted support for restrictions ($p < .05$). This underscored the findings in the first regression—that people's perceptions of generalized others' fear predicted support for restrictions. Again, the other significant predictors in the model were conservative political orientations ($p < .001$) and female gender ($p < .05$), and education was a significant negative predictor ($p < .05$). As level of education decreased, support for wartime media restrictions increased.

Why should perceived greater fear effects on generalized others, not specified others, explain support for wartime media and Internet restrictions? Perhaps because the consequences of effects on the general public are so much greater, and so much more dangerous, than on a niche of the public segment of Web users. When just about everyone else is affected by fear, and from the person's perspective he or she is among the few unaffected, this calls for a severe response to restrict dangerous messages.

To flesh out these findings, Table 7.3 reports regressions predicting support for restrictions among the three user categories. These findings indicate that perceptions of media fear effects on the general public among non Web users (Non) accounted for the strong support for restrictions ($\beta = .26$, $p < .01$). By contrast,

TABLE 7.3
Hierarchical Regressions Predicting Support for Media Restrictions by Users

	Non Beta	Web Beta	News Beta
Block 1			
Age	−.20*	.10	.01
Race	−.12	.32**	−.05
Income	.11	.07	−.12
Education	−.07	−.15	−.09
Gender	.04	.34**	.07
Hispanic	−.04	−.11	.02
R^2	.04	.19**	.05
Block 2			
Politics	.20*	.13	.27***
R^2	.03*	.01	.07***
Block 3			
TPE Public	.26**	−.01	.11
TPE Web	−.13	.01	.07
R^2	.06*	.00	.02
Total R^2	.13***	.20***	.14***

Note. Among the dummy variables, gender was 1 = male and 2 = female; race was 1 = White and 2 = Black; Hispanic was 1 = yes and 2 = no.

*$p < .05$. **$p < .01$. ***$p < .001$.

Web users' (Web) and Web news users' (News) perceptions did not predict support for censorship. These findings seem contrary to theory. In line with the paternal explanation for censorship in the third-person effect, one might expect the most sophisticated users to endorse censorship to "protect" others judged more vulnerable than themselves. However, in this case, it may be that non Web users' stereotypes of Web users as more fearful than themselves explains this finding. That is, people who do not use the Web may think of those who use the Web as paranoid, fearful, and prone to believing wild rumors disseminated on the Web.

Table 7.3 also indicates that the significant findings could be attributed to different groups of users. Female Web users supported restrictions. Conservative respondents who were non Web users and news users supported restrictions. Not too much should be made of this finding because conservative Web users exhibited a directional tendency to support restrictions, but it was not statistically significant ($p < .23$). In the demographics block, younger non Web users supported restrictions and African American Web users supported restrictions. Overall, Table 7.3 reports higher levels of total explained variance than Table 7.2, underscoring the importance of measuring people's use of the Web in studies of perceived Web news effects.

CONCLUSIONS

The news media are often criticized for spreading fear during times of crisis, such as during terrorist attacks.[15] Terrorists, of course, initiate the acts that are intended to spread fear, but terrorists would be impotent without the media to publicize their actions. The September 11, 2001, attacks and their aftermath provided an unparalleled opportunity to examine the affective impact of news reports about the war on terrorism using a representative national survey in a wartime setting with strong external validity.

The purpose of terrorism is to terrorize. To some extent the terrorists succeeded in spreading fear: Even self-reported fear levels were high. So, too, was support for wartime media and Internet restrictions. If another purpose of terrorism is to drive democracies to rein in their freedoms, thereby undermining them, here, too, the terrorists at least partly succeeded by creating a public mood sympathetic with restrictions on civil liberties. However, the findings also indicated that perceptions of fear and support for restrictions were complex. Although people were genuinely frightened, most people overestimated the fear in society, thinking other people were more fearful than themselves. Thus, although fear levels were high, they were not as high as most people thought. It is this self–other distinction in people's judgments about the media's impact on fear,

---

[15]Perhaps the classic study in fear contagion concerns Orson Welles's Halloween eve radio broadcast of *War of the Worlds*, depicting a Martian invasion of the earth (Cantril, 1940).

and the possible consequences of these judgments, which is ripe for media effects theory development.

The extension of the third-person effect to fear effects proved rewarding. The findings in this study indicated that the third-person effect, usually measured as cognitive effects of persuasive media influence, manifests itself with affective media influence. It seems likely that the same processes—of people deriving self-serving, ego-enhancing needs by attributing greater persuasive media influence to others—hold with people attributing greater fear effects to others. People may judge being afraid as a negatively valenced outcome, despite the legitimacy of a fear response to a devastating attack, possible future attacks, and an ongoing anthrax threat. However, people did not deny their own fear. People acknowledged high levels of fear in this study, underscoring the threatening times, although they overattributed fear to others. Individuals may equate being afraid with weakness or a lack of courage; others may equate it with taking foolish actions, such as hoarding goods. Some people may be unwilling to disclose the depths of their fear.

The findings also indicated the value of examining perceived media effects on narrowly specified others who may be exposed to the messages, in this case on people who used the Web for news about the war on terrorism. We drew on the much-used analogy of the Web as a community to conceive of Web news users and nonusers as social groups with ingroup and outgroup members. Members of a community would be expected to see outgroup members as unlike themselves. This proved to be the case: As predicted, non-Web users estimated significantly greater fear effects for those who used the Web for news about the war on terrorism. It is possible to attribute the predicted differences exclusively to one's social category in the digital divide, especially because no evidence was found for a significant difference in media-induced fear estimates between Web users who read news online and those who do not. It is also possible that non Web users have ideas about the amount, content, and context of news reports available online that would explain the findings. Much popular lore depicts heavy computer users as paranoid and delusional, although this stereotype may be fading as online use becomes the norm. Still, a sizable segment of the public that is not online may continue to hold such views. This is an intriguing proposition, and further research might fruitfully examine public perceptions about users of online news.

The regression analyses provided partial support for the role of third-person effects in explaining support for media restrictions. The magnitude of perceptual bias between media-induced fear estimates on self versus the generalized public made a modest contribution to explaining support for restrictions, especially in the regression model examining only non Web users. Still, other variables were better predictors than third-person perception. Because gender is a predictor of fear (with women more fearful than men), it is not surprising that female gender is also a significant predictor in explaining support for wartime press restrictions, especially when the restrictions are supposedly employed to target the terrorist threat. Gender proved to be a particularly important variable in this third-person effect study of media effects on fear. Our society deems it more acceptable for women to exhibit—or at least acknowledge—fear.

Other variables sometimes associated with support for restrictions, including age and political orientation, were significant predictors. However, importantly, as our findings indicated, the relationship between perceptions of fear and these variables was dependent on respondents' online use. Interestingly, race was a significant predictor of support for restrictions, but only with Web users who do not use the Internet for online news.

Further research examining perceptual biases in estimating affective media influences might be facilitated by a clearer understanding of the measurement of affect. It may be important to understand the variable concept of media-induced fear. A language-based self-appraisal of fear might better be measured as a multidimensional concept, perhaps including an assessment of generalized anxiety, anger, and arousal. This study supports the extension of the third-person effect to estimates of media-induced affect in both its perceptual and behavioral components. Further research should examine contingent conditions, such as the valence of the affective estimate, and other conditions under which the outcomes predicted by theory may be manifested.

REFERENCES

Andsager, J. L., & White, H. A. (2001, August). *Message credibility and congruence in first- and third-person estimations.* Paper presented at the annual meeting of the Association for Education in Journalism and Mass Communication, Washington, DC.

Atwood, L. E. (1994). Illusions of media power: The third-person effect. *Journalism Quarterly, 71,* 269–281.

Banning, S. A. (2001). Do you see what I see? Third-person effects on public communication through self-esteem, social stigma, and product use. *Mass Communication & Society, 4,* 127–147.

Berke, R. L., & Elder, J. (2001, September 25). A nation challenged: The poll; Poll finds support for war and fear on economy. *The New York Times,* p. A1.

Blanchard, M. A. (1992). Free expression and wartime: Lessons from the past, hopes for the future. *Journalism Quarterly, 69,* 5–17.

Brosius, H. B., & Engel, D. (1996). The causes of third-person effects: Unrealistic optimism, impersonal impact, or generalized negative attitudes towards media influence? *International Journal of Public Opinion Research, 8,* 142–162.

Brown, D. (2001, November 4). How do we treat this outbreak of uncertainty? *The Washington Post,* pp. B1, B3.

Brown, J. D. (1986). Evaluations of self and others: Self-enhancement biases in social judgments. *Social Cognition, 4,* 353–376.

Bruce, I. (2001, September 20). Online: Working the web: Gossip: The web is a goldmine of information but beware, says Iain Bruce it is also a minefield of disinformation. *The Guardian* (London), p. 6.

Cantril, H. (1940). *The invasion from Mars: A study in the psychology of panic.* Princeton, NJ: Princeton University Press.

Chapin, J. R. (2000). Third-person perception and optimistic bias among urban minority at-risk youth. *Communication Research, 27,* 51–81.

Cohen, J., Mutz, D., Price, V., & Gunther, A. (1988). Perceived impact of defamation: An experiment on third-person effects. *Public Opinion Quarterly, 52,* 161–173.

Coombs, W. T., & Cutbirth, C. W. (1998). Mediated political communication, the Internet and the new knowledge elites: Prospects and portents. *Telematics and Informatics, 15,* 203–217.

Dahlgren, P. (2000). The Internet and the democratization of civic culture. *Political Communication, 17,* 335–340.

Davison, W. P. (1983). The third-person effect in communication. *Public Opinion Quarterly, 47,* 1–15.

Driscoll, P. D., & Salwen, M. B. (1997). Self-perceived knowledge of the O. J. Simpson trial: Third-person perception and perceptions of guilt. *Journalism & Mass Communication Quarterly, 74,* 541–556.

Duck, J. M., Hogg, M. A., & Terry, D. J. (1995). Me, us and them: Political identification and the third-person effect in the 1993 Australian federal election. *European Journal of Social Psychology, 25,* 195–215.

Duck, J. M., Hogg, M. A., & Terry, D. J. (2000). The perceived impact of persuasive messages on "us" and "them." In D. J. Terry & M. A. Hogg (Eds.), *Attitudes, behavior and social context: The role of norms and group membership* (pp. 265–291). Mahwah, NJ: Lawrence Erlbaum Associates.

Duck, J. M., & Mullin, B. A. (1995). The perceived impact of the mass media: Reconsidering the third-person effect. *European Journal of Social Psychology, 25,* 77–95.

Duck, J. M., Terry, D. J., & Hogg, M. A. (1995). The perceived influence of AIDS advertising: Third-person effects in the context of positive media content. *Basic and Applied Social Psychology, 17,* 305–325.

Eveland, W. P., Nathanson, A. I., Detenber, B. H., & McLeod, D. M. (1999). Rethinking the social distance corollary: Perceived likelihood of exposure and third-person perception. *Communication Research, 26,* 275–302.

Fitzgerald, M. (1996, November 23). Building newspapers and communities. *Editor & Publisher, 130,* 26–27.

Gibbon, P., & Durkin, K. (1995). The third person effect: Social distance and perceived media bias. *European Journal of Social Psychology, 25,* 597–602.

Graham-Yooll, A. (1993). New dawn for press freedom? A personal and prejudiced opinion. *Media Studies Journal, 7*(4), 21–27.

Gunther, A. (1991). What we think others think: Cause and consequence in the third-person effect. *Communication Research, 18,* 355–372.

Gunther, A. (1995). Overrating the x-rating: The third-person perception and support for censorship of pornography. *Journal of Communication, 45*(1), 27–38.

Gunther, A. C., & Hwa, A. P. (1996). Public perceptions of television influence and opinions about censorship in Singapore. *International Journal of Public Opinion Research, 8,* 248–265.

Gunther, A. C., & Mundy, P. (1993). Biased optimism and the third-person effect. *Journalism Quarterly, 70,* 58–67.

Gunther, A. C., & Thorson, E. (1992). Perceived persuasive effects of product commercials and public service announcements: Third-person effects in new domains. *Communication Research, 19,* 574–596.

Hacker, K. L., & van Dijk, J. (Eds.). (2000). *Digital democracy: Issues of theory and practice.* London: Sage.

Hardon, A. (2001, September 23). The search for intelligent life on the Internet. *The New York Times,* section 4, p. 2.

Hoorens, V. (1993). Self-enhancement and superiority biases in social comparison. *European Review of Social Psychology, 4,* 113–139.

Huang, L. (1995, August). *The role of the self in the third-person effect: A view from cognitive and motivational perspectives*. Paper presented at the annual meeting of the Association for Education in Journalism and Mass Communication, Washington, DC.

Innes, J. M., & Zeitz, H. (1988). The public's view of the impact of the mass media: A test of the "third person" effect. *European Journal of Social Psychology, 18*, 457–463.

Kennemer, J. D. (1990). Self-serving biases in perceiving the opinions of others: Implications for the spiral of silence. *Communication Research, 17*, 393–404.

Lasorsa, D. L. (1989). Real and perceived effects of "Amerika." *Journalism Quarterly, 66*, 373–378, 529.

Lasorsa, D. L. (1992). Policymakers and the third-person effect. In J. D. Kennamer (Ed.), *Public opinion, the press and public policy* (pp. 163–175). New York: Praeger.

Lee, C., & Yang, S. (1996, August). *Third-person perception and support for censorship of sexually explicit visual content: A Korean case*. Paper presented at the annual meeting of the Association for Education in Journalism and Mass Communication, Anaheim, CA.

Lo, V., & Wei, R. (2000, April). Third person effect, gender, and pornography on the Internet. *Journal of Broadcasting & Electronic Media, 46*, 13–33.

Matera, F., & Salwen, M. B. (1999). Issue salience and the third-person effect: Perceptions of illegal immigration. *World Communication, 28*(3), 11–27.

McKenna, F. P. (1993). It won't happen to me: Unrealistic optimism or illusion of control? *British Journal of Psychology, 84*, 39–50.

Milban, D., & Slavin, P. (2001, October 10). Bush edict on briefings irks Hill; White House stems information flow. *The Washington Post*, p. A1.

Miller, B. (2001, October 12). Richardson Internet provider hosts site for Arab TV network. *Fort Worth Star-Telegram*, p. 10.

Neuwirth, K., & Frederick, E. (2002). Extending the framework of third-, first-, and second-person effects. *Mass Communication & Society, 5*, 113–140.

Newhagen, J. E. (1994). The relationship between censorship and the emotional and critical tone of television news coverage of the Persian Gulf War. *Journalism Quarterly, 71*, 32–42.

Nielsen/NetRatings. (2001, November). More Americans online [Reprint of a *New York Times* article citing Nielsen/NetRatings data]. Retrieved December 23, 2001, from http://www.nielsennetratings.com/newsletter/newsletter_netupdate/press_clips.htm#1

Palser, B. (2001). Not so bad: The performance of online news sites on September 11 was better than the early reviews suggest. *American Journalism Review, 23*(9), 49–53.

Paul, B., Salwen, M. B., & Dupagne, M. (2000). The third-person effect: A meta-analysis of the perceptual hypothesis. *Mass Communication & Society, 3*, 57–85.

Perloff, L. S. (1983). Perceptions of vulnerability to victimisation. *Journal of Social Issues, 39*, 41–61.

Perloff, L. S., & Fetzer, B. K. (1986). Self–other judgments and perceived vulnerability to victimization. *Journal of Personality and Social Psychology, 50*, 502–510.

Perloff, R. M. (1993). Third-person effect research, 1983–1992: A review and synthesis. *International Journal of Public Opinion Research, 5*, 167–184.

Perloff, R. M. (1996). Perceptions and conceptions of political media impact: The third-person effect and beyond. In A. N. Crigler (Ed.), *The psychology of political communication* (pp. 177–197). Ann Arbor: University of Michigan Press.

Perloff, R. M. (1999). The third-person effect: A critical review and synthesis. *Media Psychology, 1*, 353–378.

Pew Research Center for People and the Press. (2001, November 28). *Terror coverage boosts media's image*. Retrieved December 1, 2001, from http://www.people-press.org/112801s1.htm

Price, V., Tewksbury, D., & Huang, L.-N. (1998). Third-person effects on publication of a Holocaust-denial advertisement. *Journal of Communication, 48*(2), 3–26.

Rojas, H., Shah, H. D., & Faber, R. J. (1996). For the good of others: Censorship and the third-person effect. *International Journal of Public Opinion Research, 8*, 163–186.

Rucinski, D., & Salmon, C. T. (1990). The "other" as the vulnerable voter: A study of the third-person effect in the 1988 presidential campaign. *International Journal of Public Opinion Research, 2*, 345–368.

Salwen, M. B. (1998). Perceptions of media influence and support for censorship: The third-person effect in the 1996 presidential campaign. *Communication Research, 25*, 259–285.

Salwen, M. B., & Driscoll, P. (1997). Consequences of third-person perception in support for press restrictions in the O. J. Simpson trial. *Journal of Communication, 47*, 60–78.

Salwen, M. B., & Dupagne, M. (1999). The third-person effect: Perceptions of the media's influence and immoral consequences. *Communication Research, 26*, 523–549.

Salwen, M. B., & Dupagne, M. (2001). Third-person perception of television violence: The role of self-perceived knowledge. *Media Psychology, 3*, 211–236.

Sefton, D. (2000, March 22). The big online picture: Daily Web surfing now the norm. *USA Today,* p. 3.

Seigenthaler, J. (1991). The First Amendment: The first 200 years. *Presstime, 13*(2), 24–30.

Select Phone Pro CD Database, version 2.1. (2001). Omaha, NE: InfoUSA.

Shapiro, M. A., & Dunning, D. A. (2000, August). *Self-serving bias and self-esteem in estimating risk.* Paper presented at the annual meeting of the Association for Education in Journalism and Mass Communication, Phoenix, AZ.

Taylor, S. E. (1983). Adjustment to threatening events: A theory of cognitive adaption. *American Psychologist, 38*, 1161–1173.

van Dijk, J. (2000). Widening information gaps and policies of prevention. In K. L. Hacker & J. van Dijk (Eds.), *Digital democracy: Issues of theory and practice* (pp. 166–183). London: Sage.

Weinstein, N. D. (1980). Unrealistic optimism about future life events. *Journal of Personality and Social Psychology, 39*, 806–820.

Weinstein, N. D., & Klein, W. M. (1996). Unrealistic optimism: Present and future. *Journal of Social and Clinical Psychology, 15*, 1–8.

White, H. A. (1997). Considering interacting factors in the third-person effect: Argument strength and social distance. *Journalism & Mass Communication Quarterly, 74*, 557–564.

White, H. A., & Dillon, J. F. (2000). Knowledge about others' reaction to a public service announcement: The impact of self-persuasion and the third-person perception. *Journalism & Mass Communication Quarterly, 77*, 788–803.

Wills, T. A. (1981). Downward comparison principles in social psychology. *Psychological Bulletin, 90*, 245–271.

CHAPTER EIGHT

Under Construction: Measures of Community Building at Newspaper Web Sites

Cassandra Imfeld
Glenn W. Scott

The successful local paper of today has gone far toward, and is prophetic of, the larger local journalism which will parallel the needs of the primary unit of democracy, the small town. But it has only begun to realize the possibilities of its field from the standpoint of intensive cultivation, both on the news and business sides. In the town today, there is a growing need for intercommunication between people.

—Harris and Hooke (1923, p. vii)

More than 80 years ago and a time well before the age of Internet, Harris and Hooke (1923), authors of the preceding quotation (1923, p. vii), recognized the value of interaction between community members and the newspaper. They claimed, "The paper of the past has been passive, the paper of the future must be active and aggressive" (p. 303). According to the entrepreneurial pair, a newspaper's failure to engage citizens in dialogue and respond to its community's needs would lead to its demise.

In this information era, Harris and Hooke's (1923) words still ring true. Newspapers today still need to engage members of their community in a dialogue and provide relevant news to readers. However, with the advent of the Internet and the popularity of the World Wide Web, the traditional relationship between newspapers and readers is changing. According to a recent government study, more than 143 million Americans—or roughly 54% of the population—use the Internet, and 2 million Americans go online monthly (*A Nation Online*, 2002). Of these 143 million users, more than 90 million Americans have participated in on-line communities, a cyberspace feature quickly becoming a staple of online communication (Horrigan, 2001). Further, a recent report by the Center for Media Research (2003) found that Americans, while at work, "depend heavily on the Internet for breaking news and information compared to traditional media." Moreover, studies have demonstrated that online newspaper sites attract a substantial audience from their local markets. *The Washington Post's* online site, for instance, was found to attract 40.2% of the adults in its immediate market (Greenspan, 2002).

These statistics provide a clear and urgent message to print newspapers that have been struggling through a decade of declining readership. As Surman and Wershler-Henry (2001) noted, "[T]he printing press has always lent itself to one-to-many communication. . . . Print doesn't lend itself to massive dialogues between groups of people, or even two-way conversations" (p. 46). The Internet changes this dialogue. By embedding digital features such as discussion boards into news sites to promote communal online discourse, newspapers have an opportunity to create a steady and relevant dialogue involving readers in ways that heed Harris and Hooke's (1923) early call for what they termed *intercommunication*.

This study, seeking to explore this issue, uses a quantitative content analysis to examine an interactive feature that today offers perhaps the most potential for active and shared public discourse, discussion boards. Such boards are locations on the Internet offering templates where users can read and post messages. They are known by many names including forums, boards, and groups. They range from the primitive to the sophisticated, depending on software applications and skills of the users. In most cases, discussion boards are employed to share and discuss information and opinions. As for online newspaper sites, most boards invite comments about issues in the news. Why do boards exist at all on news sites? First, as Greenspan (2002) noted, they attract Internet-oriented readers, drawing more audience members to eyeball articles, images, and advertisements. Second, they keep readers on the sites longer. Finally, and less commercially, they offer a means for newspapers to perform the public service of engendering democratic discourse through communities of users.

At issue in this study is how and whether the structure of such discussion boards may serve to promote a kind of familiar intercommunication—or, in modern parlance, interactivity—that some researchers suggest may come to characterize news consumption as this information age matures. In this study, we analyzed newspaper online sites in an attempt to gather baseline data to begin exploring the determinants of online community building around the delivery of daily news.

COMMUNITIES, NEWS, AND THE NET

Scholars and futurists have in the past decade begun to see the productive uses of community building as a worthy achievement of computer-mediated communication (Rheingold, 2000; Surman & Wershler-Henry, 2001; Wellman, 2001;

Wellman & Gulia, 1999). If the benefits derived from social intercourse—often today termed *social capital*—can be obtained in interpersonal experiences, some have maintained, so too can people expect to gain from personal interactions across cyberspace (N. Lin, 2001). Some theorists claim that the Internet promises to increase social rewards by providing infinitely greater linkages promoting everything from the trade in ideas to commerce. Said N. Lin (2001), "I suggest that indeed we are witnessing a revolutionary rise of social capital, as represented by cybernetworks. In fact, we are witnessing a new era in which social capital will soon supersede personal capital in significance and effect" (p. 215).

Oldenburg (1999), a sociologist, observed that people need "third places" away from the responsibilities and hierarchies of work and home to commune in horizontal, supportive social structures for pleasure and often playful, unconstrained discourse. Rheingold (2000) and Kim (2000) extended that notion to the Internet, where they find the same opportunities and functions at play. The difference is that such communing occurs not in pubs and civic plazas but across space and time, often through Web sites (Lesser, Fontaine, & Slusher, 2000).

Kim (2000) said that discussion boards (or forums) are among the most common types of online features for fostering interaction that can last "over a period of days, weeks, even months" (p. 34). These online gathering places need not harbor people for lifetime commitments. When no longer useful, they may simply "fold up or simply fade away" (Surman & Wershler-Henry, 2001, p. 25). Although no real scholarly consensus has emerged on the semantic distinctions between online "networks" and "communities," it is sufficient for this chapter to look on online communities as gatherings of people who are united by similar interests, willing to share in ongoing discussions, and likely, as Kim (2000) said, to "enhance their sense of belonging" (p. 34). Certainly, differences exist among online community sites in terms of function and longevity. An online community associated with a news site would seem to favor transient uses more than, say, sites designed for long-term support or relationship building such as a site for cancer survivors.

Scholarly investigations into online news applications have lately provided rich layers of information. These studies have looked at areas such as credibility and perception (Flanagin & Metzger, 2000; Sundar, 1999, 2000), agenda setting (Althaus & Tewksbury, 2002; Roberts, Wanta, & Dzwo, 2002), geographic orientations (Chyi & Sylvie, 2000; Singer, 2001) and the applications of technical features (Dibean & Garrison, 2001; C. A. Lin & Jeffres, 2001; Massey & Levy, 1999). One important study about popular Web sites in general—but not about news sites in particular—helped to establish a foundation for this study by finding significant relationships between home-page structure and site traffic. That study, by Bucy, Lang, Potter, and Grabe (1999), involved a content analysis of 496 Web sites, both commercial and non-commercial, and found that structural complexities in site design did influence use.

Researchers have just begun to explore connections between news sites and interactive features. Zeng and Li (2003) drew on previous work on news-site interactivity (Gubman & Greer, 1997; Schultz, 1999), and found that circulation size of newspapers predicted the degree of interactivity on their online sites. Using an index of interactivity encompassing several kinds of features, from e-mail to discussion boards to hypertext, Zeng and Li's analysis of 106 newspaper sites suggested that larger-circulation papers offered more interactive features than others. That study differs from this one in the range of examined features. Zeng and Li constructed an index joining various interactive elements. This study chose to isolate just one, the discussion board, and to code for specific elements that, taken together, might help to identify determinants of a news site's capacity to foster a community of users. As for examining distinct types of interactive features, Garrison (2003) began to isolate factors explaining reporters' use of e-mail. One of the few studies to look specifically at discussion boards (Schultz, 2002) found a "disconnect" between the discussions on the boards and the practices of journalists at *The New York Times*.

The works of prominent journalism professionals and critics have offered similar findings. Palser (2002), online news editor at the Poynter Institute, described discussion forums as "well-suited for catharsis, conversation and companionship," but they rarely provide information that "jumps the fence" into the newsroom (p. 58). These works suggest that the worth of interactivity provided through discussion boards remains unresolved. Whether such boards will become viable parts of electronically delivered news is the key question that motivates studies such as this one. Clearly, technical aspects are still being sorted out. In a somewhat encouraging approach, the new media critic for *Editor & Publisher* magazine offered a list of features for making discussion boards salient to online sites (Outing, 2000). One key bit of online advice was to use active monitors to guide discussions: "One of the most common mistakes is to open a discussion board on a topic and expect users to make it work," Outing said. "The person 'behind the curtain' is all important."

This is theory put in very plain terms. That person behind the curtain can be seen, for the purposes of this chapter, as a gatekeeper—one operating in the fluid circumstances of cyberspace. As Outing's (2000) comment suggests, the gatekeeping function serves to explain a process in which managers of the news organization make decisions that affect the opportunities of site visitors to take part in interactive conversations and in the construction of online communities. The gatekeeper also has some role in determining, as Palser (2002) said, whether discourse on discussion boards built into news sites will indeed have any effect on the news itself. As Singer (1998, 2001) noted, the gatekeeping taking place with interactive media forces an expansive definition of the process. If some of the benefits and delights of community building arrive in the unintended consequences, as Rheingold (2000) asserted, then gatekeepers must be as intent on the free flow of interaction as the controlled flow of information.

If the notion of creative feedback is good, though, so is the idea that gatekeepers must have the means to promote useful interactivity. That can mean imposing rules or providing other sorts of features that serve to maintain expression at socially acceptable levels. As Ogdin (2002) noted, "With no enforceable rules, any behavior is acceptable. If any behavior is acceptable, there are no norms, no mores, no taboos unique to the community. In that case, what is called community is probably merely an [sic] loosely-knit group of people with some common interest." Others have warned that under assumed identities in cyberspace, the threat of real consequences for one's behavior seems obscure. Rules are thus a mechanism for sites to prevent inappropriate behavior while encouraging a communal environment. Rules can ensure the vitality and longevity of online communities (Depew, 2001), but they should be kept to a minimum and based on everyday human courtesy (Rheingold, 1998).

This chapter considers the combined suggestions of theorists and critics alike and finds that virtually all of them offer the same general beginning: Gatekeepers, in their fluid roles, remain critical to the successful operation of online interactivity related to the delivery of news. Gatekeepers are the guardians and the benefactors of structure. Although it may be true, as Palser (2002) argued, that the largest papers have the best resources for structuring discussion boards in ways that promote useful discourse, it also would seem to be true that interactivity is built less of hard bricks than of pliable software programs and the time taken to add text and participate in discussions. The willingness of site managers and staffers to provide structures to guide online discussions, then, would seem to dictate some important degree of usefulness and vitality that might give discussion boards worthy roles in the overall delivery and consumption of online news.

The previous discussion leads to the following research questions:

- What kinds of structural features exist today on the discussion boards of newspaper online sites?
- Does circulation size of the papers influence the availability of structure?
- What kinds of structural strategies, if any, do these sites have to connect discussion boards with the news?

METHOD

This study involves a descriptive, quantitative content analysis of 47 newspaper online news sites. Because this was one of the first attempts to explore structural implications for news-site interactivity, the attempt was to create a list of variables derived from discussions in the available literature, including suggestions for structural features from Rheingold (2000), Outing (2000), Preece (2000), and Kim (2000). Their works described features intended to promote usability and, by extension, a healthy and useful interaction among site users. A total of 19 variables were coded, each aimed at identifying the existence of certain features such as direct links from a home page to a discussion board or requirements for site registration. Conducting a content analysis of online data involves special considerations (McMillan, 2000; Stempel & Stewart, 2000). All of the coding for structural variables took place on one day (February 7, 2003) to control for the possibility that online site templates can change, even over a matter of days. Each variable was coded in a binary mode, with two possible choices. In other words, the individual coding was something akin to a check-off for the existence of a structural feature.

The intent was to gather descriptive data that would offer baseline information on the use—or lack of use—of structural features. Because this area of study is so new, the researchers extracted variables from discussions in the academic and trade literature of online community building and from a study identifying interactive components of 10 online nonnews sites. The variables derived from those searches provided the basis for this study. Later, the 19 variables were collapsed into three scaled variables meant to capture categories of architecture, function, and rules as they relate to Web site structure promoting interactivity.

Architectural variables comprised the largest category. They included evaluations of whether a newspaper's home page included a direct link to its discussion board and whether the discussion board provided an archive of previous posts. The function category included variables such as whether the newspaper included a purpose statement or objective about the discussion board and whether the newspaper included a privacy policy about how information collected during the registration process would be used by the newspaper. Variables analyzed under the rules category included whether there were consequences for users who did not follow the discussion board's rules and whether users could register complaints about other discussion board users. These three scaled variables—architecture, function, and rules—were used in analyses of variance with variables representing different circulation sizes of newspapers that sponsor online news sites.

The strategy for this study was to ensure that the sample of online sites would reflect equitable proportions of sites from different sizes of newspapers. This was based on a presupposition that a newspaper's print circulation remains an important influence on the production of its online site. Because the population distribution of daily U.S. newspapers is skewed toward papers of relatively small circulation size, a random sampling of sites would produce a preponderance of data reflecting the practices of such small-daily sites. To ensure that the study more equitably captured data from the sites of variously sized papers, we sought a stratified sample. Working from the Audit Bureau of Circulation's (ABC) daily circulation figures for 2000, we divided all newspapers into four strata, each representing one fourth of the ABC's total daily circulation of 52.1 million. Thus, each stratum comprised papers with combined circulation that made up slightly more than 13 million paid subscribers. The top stratum of the largest circulation papers contained just 23 members. The bottom stratum, in turn, held 838 members. Twelve newspapers were chosen randomly within each stratum. Table 8.1 provides the list of the newspapers for which sites were sampled.

TABLE 8.1
Sampled Newspaper Online Sites, by Stratum

A	B	C	D
Miami Herald	Oregonian (Portland)	Knoxville News-Sentinel[a]	St. Joseph News-Press
Detroit News	New Orleans Times Pica-yune	Times Union (Albany, NY)	Port Huron Times Herald[a]
USA Today	Orlando Sentinel	Union-News (Springfield, MA)	Valley Morning Star (Harlingen, TX)
New York Times	St. Paul Pioneer Press	Tribune-Review (Greensburg, PA)	Ottumwa Courier[a]
Cleveland Plain Dealer	Rochester Democrat & Chronicle	Augusta Chronicle	Big Spring Herald[a]
New York Daily News	Des Moines Register	Staten Island Advance	Waynesboro Record Herald[a]
Newark Star Ledger	Charlotte Observer	Courier (Houma, LA)	Free Press (Kinston, NC)
Arizona Republic	Daily Oklahoman (Oklahoma City)	Amarillo Globe Times	West Side Sun News
Houston Chronicle	Florida Times-Union (Jacksonville)	Gainesville Sun	Fairfield Daily Republic[a]
San Diego Union	Press-Enterprise (Riverside, CA)	Star-Banner (Ocala, FL)	Marshall News Messenger
Washington Post	Louisville Courier Journal Journal News (White Plains, NY)	Muskegon Chronicle News-Gazette (Champaign, IL)[a]	Homer News Today's Sunbeam (Salem, NJ)

[a]Links to e-the-People.

The coding protocol called for coders to first identify whether the chosen newspapers indeed had online sites that included discussion forums. If no forums were found after a step-by-step search, coders moved down the circulation list to the following newspaper and continued with the same protocol. In the case of the top stratum (largest papers), researchers doubled back to the top of the list and eventually exhausted the population of 23 newspapers, finding only 11 sites with discussion boards. All had Web sites, but less than half contained discussion boards. In the other three strata—where there were proportionally more newspapers to pick through—12 sites were successfully found and coded.

Online sites were most commonly found in the second stratum, which was represented primarily by regional newspapers such as *The Oregonian* and *The San Diego Union-Tribune*, two organizations with busy online discussion boards. However, boards became far less common at the sites of smaller papers. The largest gap that researchers encountered while working down the circulation list was a range of 12 papers before finding a site with a discussion board. That occurred in the stratum of the smallest papers. Some of those papers had no online news sites at all. We carried out the coding, each doing half of the newspaper sites from each stratum. To test reliability, each coded five of the same sites, representing slightly more than 10% of the total. Reflecting the ease of explicitly identifying the dichotomous variables (i.e., was there or was there not a link?), coders recorded matching scores and thus earned a value of 1 in a reliability test of Scott's Pi.

FINDINGS

This research project sought to answer questions about the type and frequency of structural features promoting discussion boards on newspaper Web sites, variance in those features by circulation size of host newspapers, and indications of links between discussion boards and the news. The descriptive data offer a snapshot of how newspaper online sites were structured in February 2003. Table 8.2 provides frequencies for all 19 variables. Of the 19 variables surveyed, two key features were found on every site: (a) users were allowed to post messages anonymously or pseudonymously, and (b) all discussion boards were accessible at no cost. Interactivity on such discussion boards was fundamentally impersonal and free.

There were some constraints. It is worth noting that users were required to go through an online registration process at most (87%) sites, although they were required to register to read posts at just a few (4%). Thus, users who might have begun by scanning news on the site easily could have shifted to a discussion board to continue in a "lurking" mode, reading the postings of more active participants.

TABLE 8.2
Frequencies of Structural Features in Newspaper Web Sites

Structural Features	%
Direct link on home page to discussion board	76
Included purpose statement or objective of discussion board	38
Required users to register to read discussion board postings	4
Required users to register to post on the discussion boards	87
Allowed users to post anonymously or pseudonymously	100
Included a link or information about rules for participating on boards	75
Discussion board posted explicit consequences for users who didn't follow rules	55
Users could register a complaint about another user on the discussion board	45
Users could evaluate other users' posts on the discussion board	23
Newspapers included a link or information about users' privacy with respect to using the discussion boards	32
Newspaper would notify users by e-mail if someone had responded to their post	6
Discussion boards included instructions on how to participate	55
Discussion boards included an FAQ section	45
Users could create a public profile	81
Discussion boards included parameters for joining the discussion	51
Of the discussion boards that had parameters for joining, age identification was a requirement	96
Discussion board threads were archived	85
Free discussion boards	100
Users could post new threads on the discussion boards	87

To join in posting messages would have required a relatively simple extra step. The registration process typically required online users to create a user name and password and to provide an e-mail address. Most of the sites required online users to disclose their age. The Children's Online Privacy Protection Act prohibits Web sites from collecting information from children under age 13. Further, four out of every five sites, such as *The Charlotte Observer* and *Staten Island Advance,* allowed users to create public profiles for review by other users. These profiles gave users the option of including personal information such as their home pages, likes and dislikes, mottos, political affiliation, race, and religion. This sharing of personal information through pseudonymous identities offers a way of sharing—or inventing—to facilitate a sense of online community. It must be noted that the newspaper sites did not verify the accuracy of the information online users provided during registration. Users could easily post false or misleading information and still engage in the discussion forums.

Sites showed mixed results in providing structural constraints aimed at maintaining orderliness. Explicit rules of conduct and consequences for breaking those rules were available on roughly half of the sites. Participants could register complaints about other posters almost half the time (45%) but had the ability to publicly rate or evaluate other posters less often, at about a quarter of the sites (23%). In other words, most sites were more willing to maintain administrative control over postings than to allow participants to get involved in judging the merits of each others' messages. Overall, those structural features that allowed for unconstrained discourse tended to outweigh the features aimed at managing it. Table 8.3 provides a summary of the five features found most often at online sites and the five least used.

To seek evidence about relationships between structural features and the circulation sizes of newspapers operating online sites, researchers carried out an analysis of variance to search for differences among the four print-circulation

TABLE 8.3
Most Common Characteristics of Newspapers' Online Sites

Online discussion boards
1. Users are allowed to post anonymously or pseudonymously.
2. Discussion boards are free to use.
3. Users can post new threads on the discussion boards.
4. Users are required to register before posting to the discussion board.
5. Discussion board threads were archived.

Least common characteristics of newspapers' online discussion boards
1. Newspapers required users to register to read the discussion boards.
2. Newspapers would notify users by e-mail if someone had responded to their post.
3. Users could evaluate other users' posts on the discussion board.
4. Newspapers included a link or information about users' privacy with respect to using the discussion boards.
5. Newspapers included a purpose statement or objective of the discussion board.

strata for the three structural variables. The three coded variables were further collapsed into a single variable that served to measure the overall amount of structural features associated with a site's discussion boards. No significant differences were found at the 95% confidence interval. Among the four circulation strata, the group with the largest mean score, 10.17, was for the sites associated with the smallest papers. In other words, those sites, on average, contained more features promoting interactivity via discussion boards than did the larger papers. Although not significantly higher, this difference prompted a closer inspection.

A closer inspection of the data offers the suggestion of one influence. Seven of the 47 online sites linked their readers to the same discussion board, a national site called e-the-People. All seven were in the lower two strata, and five were in the quarter of the sample representing the sites of the newspapers with the smallest circulation sizes. This one site, then, accounted for almost half of Stratum D's sites and thus had a large influence on its coding. In this study, by the way, researchers encountered no other outside boards similar to e-the-People, where links carried users away from the news site and into a public forum that served a geographically indistinct audience. In all other cases, discussion boards were embedded within a paper's Web site.

Rather than serving as a forum unique to a news site, e-the-People operates as a nonprofit, participant-centered sphere of discourse on issues of national and global importance.[1] The e-the-People site did not have the highest number of coded structural features in the study. That distinction went to the *San Diego Union-Tribune's* site, which had 16 out of the possible 19 features. However, the e-the-People's site inventory was sufficient in comparison with other sites to raise the mean score for the seven e-the-People sites significantly higher than the mean for the other 40 sites (see Table 8.4).

One noteworthy aspect of e-the-People is that newspapers may link to it at no cost. This free use allows news executives with smaller news operations an alternative to paying a licensing fee to vendors for interactive software for their own sites. They can simply enlist with e-the-People. None of the seven sites using e-the-People in this study also provided its own discussion forums.[2] Some of the sites did aim to retain a degree of local identification by framing the e-the-People site with the news organization's own logo or by including its own online advertising, but most did not.

The e-the-People site thus offered a structural dilemma. At the same time that it provided some of the most pervasive features promoting interactivity—such as

---

[1]Most of the links to e-the-People were listed on the news sites' home pages as Town Hall. Thus, users clicking on the link for the first time likely did not realize that they would be connected to a national site. The e-the-People site can be accessed at http://www.e-thepeople.org/ as well as through the previously mentioned links on various online news sites.

[2]Although not sampled in this study, *The Arizona Daily Star* newspaper of Tucson offers an example of an affiliated online news site that provides links both to its own discussion boards and to e-the-People. It can be accessed at http://www.azstarnet.com. The newspaper, with a 2000 daily circulation of 101,000, was larger than any of the seven newspapers that linked to e-the-People in this study.

TABLE 8.4
Difference in Mean Scores on Structural Variables

	Mean	SD	N
e-the-People	11.57	.53	7
All other sites	10.20	3.71	40

Note. $t(45) = -2.21$, $p = .032$.

a sophisticated means for readers to evaluate and comment on the postings of others—it also effectively removed any opportunity for users to identify with or offer feedback to the news site providing the initial link. Users who went to their local news sites to stay connected and to take part in a digital democracy found themselves removed from the place where the news was presented. They ended up in an encouraging forum where discussions tended toward theoretical treatments of national concerns. One thread on the e-the-People board during the time of the coding focused on the ideas of Noam Chomsky; another carried a debate on the essays of classicist commentator Victor Davis Hanson. This represents a wide variation from the local flavor of the *Marshall News Messenger's* discussion boards, where the site prompted users to "sound off on local issues" and included a category for give-and-take on the prospects for high school sports teams in East Texas.

This willingness to link to e-the-People certainly does rank as a strategy in connecting discussion boards to the news, but it would seem to be ultimately a negative strategy because it carries readers away from the news site. The online community fostered within the e-the-People site would seem to be removed by geography and by digital space from the host newspaper's site. In almost all cases, in fact, researchers found little evidence that hosts had built strategic features into their discussion boards to give users the sense that their posts on the boards might somehow be tied to the site's more pervasive journalistic functions. The most obvious strategic connection was simply in the formatting of a site's home page. Many included a link to "forums" right alongside other links to "news," "opinion," and other listings. Once inside a discussion board, however, users generally found few promptings. A few sites invited comments specifically about columnists' recent works, and the rare sites that were overtly monitored—such as that at *The New York Times*—offered occasional queries based on recent news events for participants to address. Primarily, though, the discussion boards appeared to function as publicly accessible pastures outside the news sites' journalistic limits.

CONCLUSIONS

This study found a range of practices among newspaper sites on the use of structural elements promoting interactive discussions and, eventually, community building. This range suggests that the news organizations clearly have not arrived at a consensual standard for operating discussion boards. Indeed, there is some evidence here leading to preliminary conclusions that many papers have adopted a less-than-ambitious plan to integrate such open discussions with their public functions in delivering news. Although three fourths of online newspapers included links to their discussion boards on their home pages encouraging users to participate in the online forum, two thirds failed to include a purpose or mission statement about the discussion board. Thus, the role of discussion boards on most online news sites has yet to be clearly articulated and defined.

Structural elements that allow users to evaluate each post might serve to refine discussions and allow users to share slightly in some of the gatekeeping or monitorial functions. However, less than one quarter of the sites provided that function. One notable exception was e-the-People, where participants' cumulative judgments for and against a posting were carried above the message itself. It might be said that, to borrow from another genre of popular media culture, the e-the-People site was the one place where user response was so powerful that participants could effectively vote one another "off the island."

Such relatively advanced functioning of e-the-People emerged as one of the more intriguing issues. The more popular a post, the higher the post appeared on the discussion board. The site's rating system also supported its mission to "rewrite the code of conduct in the democracy conversation, [and] reject politics-as-usual. We can demand that people start listening, really listening, to each other. We can demand that people engage each other on terms of mutual respect." The rating system not only made users accountable for the content of their posts but also served to nurture reputations for online discussion participants. Like traditional offline community forums, such as actual town hall meetings, e-the-People participants create identities for themselves through their words and actions and can be held accountable for their conduct. All this has the potential for encouraging community building in a virtual context. This structure, however, was an anomaly in this study's evaluation of discussion boards, and the practice of sending users to a detached site has its serious limitations as well. News sites more ideally might find ways to adopt some of e-the-People's features into their own, identifiable boards.

Gatekeeping and Editorial Control

Missing from most discussion boards was direct discourse between journalists and online users. Discussion boards offer newspapers opportunities to engage in two-way conversations with users and practice the democratic ideals newspapers embrace. However, the only interaction found between journalists and users was actually outside the scope of this analysis; it was through e-mail (one-to-one and private) or guided and selectively edited "live" chats with columnists and pundits. Such edited chats represented a stronger and more unidirectional method of gatekeeping. For the largest of the host newspapers, such as *The New York Times*,

The Washington Post, and USA Today, these methods provided for more control and, at times, for the packaging of posted opinion in a format that approached a shaping of interactive comment into news, much as a call-in radio show filters and selects queries from the public. Additionally, Times editors sometimes selected favorite posts and packaged them as an online collection. Such selective editing represents a safer strategy. Indeed, it does create a connection between interactivity and news.

Given the convenience and control built into this firmer model of gate-keeping, it should also be said that neither of these features—e-mail or chat—encourages the wide-open and robust debate that might become a benefit of discussion boards. More editorial control can mean less vitality and, potentially, less diversity of voice and opinion. When journalists retain the last call, their news organization's view of the world is less apt to be challenged. There is a strong indication here that the largest of the newspapers are not comfortable with discussion boards. After all, only 11 of the 23 papers in the top stratum even provided such wide-open interactivity. The second stratum of newspaper sites revealed the most action, both in numbers of sites; virtually every site sampled had boards. It tended to be at the regional newspaper sites, then, where discussion boards flourished, though the existence of structural features fluctuated.

The general lack of gatekeeper involvement found in this study also provided benefits. For example, almost all of the news sites allowed users to post new threads or topics to the discussion boards. Instead of centralizing control, most newspapers allowed users to create their own discourse. At the same time, most newspapers used the limited vehicle of registration to hold users somewhat accountable for their posts. Sites with strong user-evaluation tools thus encouraged other participants to take part in the accountability system as well. In such systems, the use of pseudonyms allows for both freedom and constraint—a license for free expression but a social sanctioning that evolves as posters begin to build their reputations and become part of an online community.

Connections to the News

Although many online newspapers provided the requisite software enabling discussion boards and laying the foundation for the creation of communities, the sites often failed to include the features that would tailor boards to their readers. Again the example of e-the-People is a prime illustration. Those sites providing links to it missed the chance to nurture communities of participants who might begin to perceive the newspaper's site as a kind of public sphere where people naturally congregate to engage with ideas and events of the day. Among the features that build community are those that provide archival searches, which serve to build history, and those that invite users to register complaints about others. The latter allows for self-policing. Only a minority of newspapers included features that encouraged community-centered dialogue. For example, less than 10%

of the online news sites provided users with the structural feature that would no-tify them that someone responded to their post. Less than a quarter of the sites al-lowed other users to rate posts by other users.

Certainly, one reason that newspapers have resisted this sort of community-building is an understandable reliance on routine. Information flows from news-papers to community have been asymmetrical. Traditionally, letters to the editor and op-ed columns are about as far as most papers have gone in terms of every-day interactivity of content. In an era of instant communication and inter-connectivity, the digital delivery of mass-mediated news through the Internet has changed this relationship. However, this study's findings suggest that online news sites have yet to fully embrace the implications of this evolution. Studies of non-news Web sites have shown that Americans use discussion boards as a way to create community. Discussion boards connected to the daily flow of news would seem to be fertile places for community building, notably among those who value free expression and the willingness to expand the range of available ideas. There are limitations, as Palser (2002) and others suggest. However, this study offers evidence that some of these limitations have not been fully ad-dressed.

There may also be new twists and developments in the forms and functions of online news that promote more harmonious integration between news and free speech. As online news delivery continues to win interest for its potential bene-fits, such as a means of reversing the circulation declines in print news delivery, interactive features such as discussion boards deserve to attract more interest as a structure of things to come. For online sites to create space as valuable resources for reader communities, they will need to emulate the functions that are clearly winning over American consumers in other corners of cyberspace. Certainly, the functioning of online communities located within news sites will vary from other types of virtual communities. Participants will be driven more by the impulsive charms of free speech than by the more cautious needs of those seeking emo-tional support or lifelong friendships. Such news-driven communities will need to serve as gathering places where citizens mingle, argue, and share and, perhaps, where journalists occasionally join in the fray. As a form, discussion boards on newspaper Web sites should be considered still under construction.

A prime limitation in a study such as this is the rapid rate of change occurring by week and by day on newspaper sites. Data is difficult to capture and inferences are difficult to maintain when structural features, along with postings them-selves, appear and disappear so quickly on the Internet. We are aware that some sites have dropped their boards since coding occurred, and others have made structural changes to reflect the fluid nature of digital technology and marketing. Any study about interactivity with the news is likely to suffer the same conse-quences in this period of almost constant renovation of Web sites. Further re-search needs to incorporate designs that promise to record as much data as possi-ble at a single time, not an easy task when studying the transient and seemingly endless supply of interactive postings. A worthwhile and ambitious next step would be to seek measures of content and vitality of discussion boards to investigate how the structures of news sites promote variations in participation.

REFERENCES

Althaus, S. L., & Tewksbury, D. (2002). Agenda setting and the "new" news—Patterns of issue importance among readers of the paper and online versions of the New York Times. *Communication Research, 29*(2), 180–207.

Center for Media Research. (2003, January 15). *At-workers prefer Internet news and information.* Retrieved January 15, 2003, from http://www.centerformediaresearch.com/cfmr_briefArchive.cfm?s=0

Chyi, H. I., & Sylvie, G. (2000). The medium is global, the content is not: The role of geography in online newspaper markets. *The Journal of Media Economics, 14*, 231–248.

Depew, D., & Peters, J. D. (2001). Community and communication: The conceptual background. In G. J. Shepherd & E. W. Rothenbuhler (Eds.), *Communication and community* (pp. 3–22). Mahwah, NJ: Lawrence Erlbaum Associates.

Dibean, W., & Garrison, B. (2001). How six online newspapers use Web technologies. *Newspaper Research Journal, 22*(2), 79–93.

Flanagin, A. J., & Metzger, M. J. (2000). Perceptions of Internet information credibility. *Journalism & Mass Communication Quarterly, 77*, 515–540.

Garrison, B. (2003, March). *The perceived credibility of electronic mail in newspaper newsgathering.* Paper presented at the Association for Education in Journalism and Mass Communication Midwinter Conference, Boulder, CO.

Greenspan, R. (2002). *Newspapers look online for revenue.* Retrieved May 23, 2002, from http://cyberatlas.internet.com/big_picture/traffic_patterns/

Gubman, J., & Greer, J. (1997, August). *An analysis of online sites produced by U.S. newspapers: Are the critics right?* Paper presented at the Association for Education in Journalism and Mass Communication, Chicago.

Harris, E. P., & Hooke, F. H. (1923). *The community newspaper.* New York: Appleton.

Horrigan, J. P. (2001, October 31). *Online communities: Networks that nurture long-distance relationships and local ties.* Retrieved February 20, 2003, from http://www.pewinternet.org

Kim, A. J. (2000). *Community building on the Web.* Berkeley, CA: Peachpit Press.

Lesser, E. L., Fontaine, M. A., & Slusher, J. A. (2000). *Knowledge and communities.* Boston: Butterworth-Heinemann.

Lin, C. A., & Jeffres, L. W. (2001). Comparing distinctions and similarities across websites of newspapers, radio stations, and television stations. *Journalism & Mass Communication Quarterly, 78*, 555–574.

Lin, N. (2001). *Social capital: A theory of social structure and action.* Cambridge, England: Cambridge University Press.

Massey, B. L., & Levy, M. R. (1999). Interactivity, online journalism and English-language web newspapers in Asia. *Journalism & Mass Communication Quarterly, 76*, 138–151.

McMillan, S. J. (2000). The microscope and the moving target: The challenge of applying content analysis to the World Wide Web. *Journalism & Mass Communication Quarterly, 77*, 80–98.

A nation online: How Americans are expanding their use of the Internet. (2002, February). Retrieved March 15, 2003, from http://www.NTIA.doc.gov/ntiahome/dn/index.html

Oldenburg, R. (1999). *The great good place: Cafes, coffee shops, community centers, beauty parlors, general stores, bars, hangouts, and how they get you through the day* (3rd ed.). New York: Marlowe.

Outing, S. (2000, September 6). *What's wrong with newspaper discussion boards?* Retrieved October 13, 2002, from http://www.mediainfo.com/editorandpublisher/index.jsp

Palser, B. (2002, January–February). Not for everyone: Online forums are not the best aspect of the Web. *American Journalism Review, 24,* 58.

Preece, J. (2000). *Online communities: Designing usability, supporting sociability.* Chichester, England: Wiley.

Rheingold, H. (1998). *The art of hosting good conversations online.* Retrieved May 12, 2003, from http://www.rheingold.com/texts/artonlinehost.html

Rheingold, H. (2000). *The virtual community: Homesteading on the electronic frontier* (Rev. ed.). Cambridge, MA: MIT Press.

Roberts, M., Wanta, W., & Dzwo, T. H. (2002). Agenda setting and issue salience online. *Communication Research, 29,* 452–465.

Schultz, T. (2002). Mass media and the concept of interactivity: An exploratory study of online forums and reader email. *Media, Culture & Society, 22*(2), 205–221.

Singer, J. B. (1998). Online journalists: Foundations for research into their changing roles. *Journal of Computer-Mediated Communication, 4*(1). http://www.ascusc.org/jcmc/vol4/issue1/singer.html

Singer, J. B. (2001). The metro wide Web: Changes in newspapers' gatekeeping role online. *Journalism & Mass Communication Quarterly, 78,* 65–80.

Stempel, G. H. I., & Stewart, R. K. (2000). The Internet provides both opportunities and challenges for mass communications researchers. *Journalism & Mass Communication Quarterly, 77,* 541–548.

Sundar, S. S. (1999). Exploring receivers' criteria for perception of print and online news. *Journalism & Mass Communication Quarterly, 76,* 373–386.

Sundar, S. S. (2000). Multimedia effects on processing and perception of online news: A study of picture, audio, and video downloads. *Journalism & Mass Communication Quarterly, 77,* 480–499.

Surman, M., & Wershler-Henry, D. (2001). *Commonspace: Beyond virtual community.* London: FT.com.

Wellman, B. (2001). Computer networks as social networks. *Science, 293,* 2031–2034.

Wellman, B., & Gulia, M. (1999). Net surfers don't ride alone: Virtual communities as communities. In P. Kollock & M. Smith (Eds.), *Communities and Cyberspace* (pp. 167–194). New York: Routledge.

Zeng, Q., & Li, X. (2003, May). *Factors influencing interactivity of Internet newspapers.* Paper presented at the International Communication Association annual conference, San Diego.

CHAPTER NINE

Uses and Gratifications of Online and Offline News: New Wine in an Old Bottle?

Carolyn Lin
Michael B. Salwen
Rasha A. Abdulla

The newspaper once reigned as the dominant news medium in America. Faded black-and-white movies attest to how family members at breakfast tables read sections of the newspaper, which was as much a part of the meal as coffee and orange juice. There was the evening newspaper, too. In succeeding years, newspapers faced competition from radio and, later, television. Now online news threatens the venerable medium. Newspapers have responded by going online,[1] reproducing their print media products on the Web with little regard for the different ways audiences may read and process offline and online news (Thalhimer, 1994). This study explores audience members' motives and uses of online news and offline newspapers. The study aims to facilitate our understanding of the cognitive and affective responses to offline and online news consumption behavior.

INTERNET AUDIENCE USE

A recent review of the empirical literature on audience use of the Internet astutely noted, "In spite of the appropriateness and timeliness of the Internet as a topic of study, we know remarkably little about its selection and use" (Flanagin & Metzger, 2001, p. 155). Some evidence suggests that Internet users are avid online

---

[1]At least 1,300 daily newspapers have launched online services since May of 2002. Moreover, newspaper Web sites have attracted more unique visitors than their news media counterparts of magazines, network television, and radio (Newspaper Association of America, 2002).

news consumers (e.g., Aikat, 2000; Pew Research Center for the People and the Press, 2001). For example, a recent UCLA Center for Communication Policy (2001) study revealed that 53.6% of the respondents considered the Internet an important source for news information.

Uses of News

Research conducted by the Pew Research Center for the People and the Press (2001) shows steady increases in the use of online news sources and that 63% of online users go online for news. Some studies indicate that the Web may cultivate an informed electorate. A number of studies indicate that Web users are politically sophisticated and active, and that those "who already harbor an interest in political affairs are surfing the Internet, rather than television, for political information" (Johnson & Kaye, 2000, p. 873). An experimental study of American college students' knowledge of international news reported that even short-term exposure to Web sources about foreign countries increased students' knowledge about the countries (Griffin et al., 1997).

Stempel, Hargrove, and Bernt (2000) found a symbiotic relationship between Internet news use and traditional news consumption that suggests how an online news user may also be an avid information seeker with offline news media. Hence, they contended, online news patronage was not responsible for the general decline in news consumption in the television (both network and local), newspaper, and magazine industries. Comparing these findings with a study on audience preferences across Internet, television, newspaper, radio, and magazine news outlets, the audience still prefers traditional media for general information such as weather, entertainment, sports, and general news (New Media Federation, 2002). Specifically, newspapers were cited as the most preferred source for entertainment news.

Other studies, however, bode ill for the Web as a source of news. In an experimental study, Tewksbury and Althuss (2000) found that online readers of *The New York Times* read fewer major national, international, and political news stories than offline *The New York Times* readers. The online readers also recalled fewer stories than the newspaper readers. Online readers also used online options to go directly to news that interested them, whereas newspaper readers were more likely to follow the newspapers' cues of story importance, peruse the headlines, and acquire at least a passing knowledge of different news stories. Tewksbury and Althuss warned: "With this increased opportunity to personalize the flow of news, fewer people may be exposed to politically important stories. As a consequence, online news providers may inadvertently develop a readership that is more poorly informed than traditional newspaper readers about the core events that shape public life" (p. 459).

Gratifications of News Use

Traditionally, uses and gratifications researchers have been interested in why the audience seeks and consumes media content, including news content. This perspective sees audiences as motivated individuals who actively seek media content to fulfill cognitive and affective needs (e.g., Blumler, 1979; Katz, Blumler, & Gurevitch, 1974; Rayburn, 1996). It is this gratifying media use experience that motivates repeat media gratification seeking through media usage (e.g., Palmgreen, Wenner, & Rayburn, 1981).

A number of studies have identified the gratifications associated with news use. For instance, Katz, Guvrevitch, and Hass (1973) identified newspapers as a useful source for learning about society. Newspapers, by contrast, were seen as meeting a wider and less specialized set of needs. Similarly, Elliot and Quattlebaum (1979) found that newspapers provide surveillance of the environment needs but not entertainment. By the same token, Kippax and Murray (1980) tested the perceived importance of 30 media-related needs. They discovered that newspapers were judged as providing eight specific needs associated with an informational function—including understanding, knowledge, and credibility—instead of any emotional needs.

Lichtenstein and Rosenfeld's (1983) study yielded some additional insights. Their findings suggested that radio, television, magazines, and newspapers were regarded as sources of entertainment and information about everyday life. Magazines and newspapers were judged as useful sources of information about the government, but not as outlets for resolving loneliness (or emotional needs). Weaver (1980) suggested yet another news gratification. His findings established that when interest and uncertainty in political information was high, newspaper use was more strongly related with interpersonal discussion of political information than was television viewing.

Interestingly, dimensions of television news gratifications generally appear similar to those of print news. For instance, Palmgreen, Wenner, and Rayburn (1980) proposed four dimensions of gratifications sought in relation to television news viewing: interpersonal utility, surveillance, entertainment, and parasocial interaction. Levy and Windahl (1984) clustered three gratification factors—entertainment/parasocial interaction, surveillance, and interpersonal utility—that were nearly identical to Palmgreen et al.'s four dimensions. Rubin and Perse (1987) generated three slightly different news-viewing motives—entertainment, passing time, and information—emphasizing the diversion aspect of news consumption.

Currently, online news gratifications studies do not yet exist, except for a small-scale pilot study that used a nonrandom college student sample. Mings (1997) pooled eight dimensions of news and media gratifications from past studies and correlated them with offline and online newspaper use. Her results showed that some students' gratifications sought and obtained associated with offline newspapers were related to certain online newspaper navigation patterns. However, these relationships could not be easily summarized or generalized because results based on 15 respondents are not considered reliable. Nonetheless, the contention that there could be a correlation between offline and online media use gratifications has generally been supported by other online use gratifications studies, either conceptually or empirically.

For example, Lin (1999) found three perceived gratifications of Internet use—entertainment, surveillance, and escape/companionship/identity. Although television viewing and online use motives were generally correlated and parallel with each other, television viewing motives were not significant predictors of likely online use. Ferguson and Perse (2000) also explored the relationship between Internet use and television viewing motives. They concluded that more similarities than differences exist between these media. These findings were further confirmed by additional theoretical explications that indicate a lack of displacement between online service adoption and offline media use (e.g., Lin, 2001). Together, these two bodies of literature validate Stempel et al.'s (2000) assessment that online news use is not significantly relevant to the readership or viewership decline in traditional news media outlets.

The literature reviewed suggests that audience motivations or gratifications for online and offline media use activity are similar and correlated with each other. By implication, online and offline news (including print and electronic news) may follow this intermedia dynamic. Because the gratification dimensions for online news need to be ascertained, the following research questions are posited:

1. What are the gratification dimensions for online news use?
2. Are gratification dimensions for online and offline news different?

To test the theoretical assumptions that (a) there should be a parallel between online and offline news gratifications, and (b) offline news gratifications (e.g., Lin, 1999) should not be significant predictors for online news access (e.g., Ferguson & Perse, 2000; Stempel et al., 2000), the following research hypotheses are advanced:

1. Audience gratifications for online news use will be positively related to gratifications for offline news use.
2. Audience gratifications for offline news use will be insignificant predictors of online news use.
3. Audience gratifications for online news use will be insignificant predictors of offline news use.

RESEARCH METHODS

Overview

A representative U.S. sample of 387 adults (age 18 and older) who read a printed newspaper and online news was drawn using a stratified design. Each of the 50 states and the District of Columbia were represented proportionate to the national population in the 2000 U.S. Census.[2] Respondents were surveyed during the evenings of November 11 to 15, 2001. Residential telephone numbers were drawn from the fall 2001 edition of the national Select Phone telephone software package on compact disc and database published by InfoUSA (Select Phone, 2001). Random residential telephone numbers were generated on a state-by-state basis from the database of more than 100 million telephone numbers using a table of random numbers and the random number selection function built into the Select Phone software. Each resulting state roster of chosen numbers was adjusted using the one up and one down last digit method to include unlisted numbers. If there was no answer, a busy signal, or an answering machine, up to two more attempts were made later that evening or during another evening to reach the number. The response rate, excluding invalid contacts, was 56%.

Other variables included a series of demographics and self-reported political orientations: gender, age in years, race collapsed as White and Black, Hispanic ethnicity (yes or no), a 5-point scale of income categories, a 7-point scale of education level categories, and a 5-point self-reported political orientation scale ranging from *very conservative* to *very liberal* with *middle of the road* as a midpoint.

News Use

Offline Newspaper Use. This was measured by a single item: How many days a week, if any, do you read a printed newspaper? Only those respondents who read a newspaper 1 day a week or more were examined so long as they also qualified as an online news user.

Online News Use. Respondents were asked whether they used the Internet or the World Wide Web. If they were Web users, they were then asked how many days a week, if any, they read an online news media outlet and then how many days a week they accessed news through their Internet service provider (ISP).[3] If they read online news at least 1 day per week on either a news media outlet site or through their ISP, they were coded as Web news users.

---

[2]A total of 619 respondents completed the survey, but the analyses in this study concern only those respondents who read a printed newspaper and online news at least 1 day per week.

[3]The questions were:

- *Many newspapers, news magazines, television stations, and cable television network stations have online news sites. How many days a week, if any, do you read Web sites offered by one or more of these news media outlets?*

- *Internet service providers, such as America Online, Netscape, or Microsoft Network, also have news sites. How many days a week, if any, do you read the news from any of these or other Internet service providers?*

Gratifications

Offline News Gratifications. Respondents answered 15 items that reflect 4 gratification dimensions—entertainment, interpersonal communication, information learning, and surveillance (see items in Table 9.1). They responded using a Likert-type scale ranging from 5 (*strongly agree*) to 1 (*strongly disagree*). To generate gratification groupings, the items were analyzed through a factor analysis principal component extraction and Varimax rotation. The results yielded four gratification dimensions: entertainment ($\alpha = .81$), interpersonal communication ($\alpha = .81$), information skimming (or surveillance; $\alpha = .74$), and information scanning (or information learning) ($\alpha = .72$). One measurement item (i.e., getting quickly to important news) was eliminated from the factor clustering due to loading on two factors.

Online News Gratifications. The same 15 gratification measures were used to gauge this construct. The factor analysis procedure yielded an identical set of gratification dimensions, with one dimension garnering a lower than ideal scale reliability level (see items in Table 9.2).[4] Again, the identical item was deleted from the scale construction process, due to double loading. The four online news gratification dimensions were entertainment ($\alpha = .85$), interpersonal communication ($\alpha = .75$), information skimming (or surveillance; $\alpha = .74$), and information scanning (or information learning; $\alpha = .68$).

FINDINGS

The respondents were typical of a relatively well-educated, middle-class segment of the population that is online. Specifically, the average respondent was 47 years old, completed some college, and had an annual household income in the range of $50,001 to $75,000. Men comprised 47.5% of the sample. The racial composition of the sample underrepresented both the Hispanic and African American populations. Overall, 76.7% of the sample was White, 8.8% African American, 2.5% Asian American, 2.8% Hispanic, and 9.2% others.

Research Question Testing

Research Question 1. The gratification dimensions for both online and offline news users (see Tables 9.1 and 9.2), based on the a priori measurement items, were entertainment, interpersonal communication (or discussion), information skimming (or general surveillance), and information scanning (or infor-

---

[4]By less than ideal, we mean below 0.70.

TABLE 9.1
Factor Analysis Results for Audience Offline (Newspapers) News Gratifications

Variables	Factor				M	SD
	1	2	3	4		
Entertainment						
Finding stories that are fun to read	.77				4.40	.80
Coming across amusing news	.80				4.25	.84
Finding stories that are enjoyable	.76				4.49	.78
Finding entertaining news	.76				3.94	1.08
Information scanning						
Keeping up with what is going on in the news		.80			4.07	1.07
Getting a good overall picture of events in the world		.63			3.92	1.20
Learning what are the major news events of the day		.63			4.34	.96
Following the major news stories of the day		.72			4.30	.93
Interpersonal communication						
Learning about things to discuss with other people			.70		3.68	1.10
Finding topics to use in conversations with other people			.87		4.50	.79
Getting stories to share with other people			.79		3.94	1.04
Information skimming						
Going directly to important news stories				.64	4.42	.88
Coming across amusing news				.86	4.06	.98
Seeking out important news				.74	3.83	1.10
% of variance explained	33	15	10	7		

mation learning). The two sets of gratification dimensions matched perfectly, lending construct validity to the measures. More important, this study adopted an alternative means of conceptualizing the information learning and surveillance gratifications by treating them as action-oriented gratifications. Specifically, the information learning gratification dimension was seen as reflective of the motive associated with scanning essential information for learning purposes. By comparison, the surveillance gratification dimension was regarded as related to the motive of skimming a selected set of information (e.g., important stories of the day) for general surveillance purposes.

Research Question 2. Paired-sample t tests were conducted to explore whether there was a significant difference between the offline and online gratifications. There was no significant difference between the offline and online entertainment (Offline $M = 3.87$, $SD = .84$; Online $M = 3.86$, $SD = .89$), $t = -.16$, $p \leq .88$, and interpersonal communication (Offline $M = 4.08$, $SD = .79$; Online $M = 4.04$, $SD = .81$), $t = -.65$, $p \leq .52$, gratification dimensions. However, both the information scanning (Offline $M = 4.18$, $SD = .78$; Online $M = 4.32$; $SD = .69$), $t = 2.18$, $p \leq .036$, and information skimming (Offline $M = 4.50$, $SD = .55$; Online $M = 4.02$; $SD = .95$), $t = -5.97$, $p \leq .001$, gratification dimensions were significantly different.

TABLE 9.2
Factor Analysis Results for Audience Online News Gratifications

Variables	Factor				M	SD
	1	2	3	4		
Entertainment						
Finding stories that are fun to read	.84				4.40	.81
Coming across amusing news	.78				4.30	.84
Finding stories that are enjoyable	.81				4.10	1.06
Finding entertaining news	.77				3.73	1.20
Information scanning						
Keeping up with what is going on in the news		.78			4.00	1.12
Getting a good overall picture of events in the world		.62			4.12	.95
Learning what are the major news events of the day		.70			4.28	.93
Following the major news stories of the day		.73			3.38	1.17
Interpersonal communication						
Learning about things to discuss with other people			.50		3.70	1.15
Finding topics to use in conversations with other people			.85		4.15	1.05
Getting stories to share with other people			.86		3.86	1.07
Information skimming						
Going directly to important news stories				.84	4.23	1.00
Coming across amusing news				.84	4.03	.99
Seeking out important news				.59	3.79	1.07
% of variance explained	20	17	15	14		

Hypothesis Testing

Hypothesis 1. Table 9.3 reports the correlations between offline and online gratification dimensions. Offline entertainment and interpersonal communication gratifications were significantly correlated with three of the four parallel online gratification dimensions—entertainment ($r = .32$, $p \le .001$), interpersonal communication ($r = .20$, $p \le .01$), and information skimming ($r = .34$, $p \le .001$), with the exception of information scanning gratification ($r = -.06$, $p \le .19$). Whereas the offline information scanning gratification was correlated with both online information skimming ($r = .41$, $p \le .001$) and online information scanning ($r = .17$, $p \le .02$), offline information skimming was only correlated with online information scanning ($r = .51$, $p \le .001$). Based on these results, Hypothesis 1 was partially supported.

Hypothesis 2. The multiple regression results in Table 9.4 demonstrated that, as the equation explained 13% of the total variance, none of the offline news gratifications were significant predictors of online news access level—supporting Hypothesis 2. Instead, online gratification information scanning ($\beta = .27$, $p \le .009$) and annual household income ($\beta = .20$, $p \le .013$) were significant predictors.

TABLE 9.3
Pearson Product–Moment Correlations for Offline
News and Online News Gratifications

Variable	1	2	3	4	5	6	7	8
Offline news gratifications								
1. Entertainment	1.00							
2. Interpersonal communication	.44**	1.00						
3. Informational scanning	.46**	.40**	1.00					
4. Informational skimming	.03	.02	.20**	1.00				
Online news gratifications								
5. Entertainment	.32**	.15*	.09	.19**	1.00			
6. Interpersonal communication	.20**	.47**	.07	.26**	.39**	1.00		
7. Information scanning	−.06	.10	.17*	.51**	.29**	.42**	1.00	
8. Informational skimming	.34**	.29**	.41**	−.06	.18*.	.15*	.10	1.00

*$p \leq .05$. **$p \leq .01$.

Hypothesis 3. Table 9.4 again illustrates that online news gratifications were insignificant predictors of offline news use level. The equation explained 20% of total variance in offline news use. The significant predictors include age ($\beta = .22$, $p \leq .005$) and annual household income level ($\beta = .24$, $p \leq .003$). Interpersonal communication gratification ($\beta = .19$, $p \leq .056$) just failed to attain significance at the .05 level. As the sole significant gratification measure for the equation that barely failed to attain statistical significance, Hypothesis 3 is thus weakly supported.

DISCUSSION

This study tested the reliability of the 15 gratification measures for news consumption. It found identical sets of factor compositions for offline and online news use. The only disappointment was the lower than expected alpha value achieved by the information skimming gratification associated with online news access. As this study picked up where the print news gratification literature left off in the early 1980s, it did so by reviving as well as revising the existing gratification factors. It is satisfying to discover that the four gratification dimensions generated here—entertainment, interpersonal communication, information scanning (or learning), and information skimming (or surveillance)—were similar to dimensions reported in past research (e.g., Kippax & Murray, 1980; Lichtenstein & Rosenfeld, 1983; Weaver, 1980). More important, these sets of offline and online news gratifications suggest that the motives for accessing news do not change from medium to medium, as has been demonstrated between print and television news use (e.g., Levy & Windahl, 1984; Palmgreen et al., 1980) in the past and between print and online news in this study.

TABLE 9.4
Multiple Regression Results for Offline News and Online News Use

Criterion Variable: Online News Use						
Predictor Variable	β	R^2	R^2	R^2 Change	P	VIF
Step 1: Offline news gratifications		.12	.01	.01	ns	
1. Entertainment	−.01				ns	1.61
2. Interpersonal communication	.04				ns	1.96
3. Informational scanning	−.04				ns	2.06
4. Informational skimming	−.12				ns	2.17
Step 2: Online news gratifications		.28	.08	.07	.029	
5. Entertainment	−.40				ns	.88
6. Interpersonal communication	.02				ns	2.06
7. Information scanning	.27				.009	1.78
8. Informational skimming	−.05				ns	1.44
Step 3: Demographics		.36	.13	.05	.056	
9. Gender	.00				ns	1.10
10. Age	−.02				ns	1.16
11. Education	.09				ns	1.22
12. Household income	.20				.013	1.17
Criterion Variable: Offline News Use						
Predictor Variable	β	R^2	R^2	R^2 Change	P	VIF
Step 1: Offline news gratifications		.15	.02	.02	ns	
1. Entertainment	.05				ns	1.61
2. Interpersonal communication	.19				ns	1.96
3. Informational scanning	.10				ns	2.06
4. Informational skimming	−.11				ns	2.17
Step 2: Online news gratifications		.33	.11	.08	.006	
5. Entertainment	−.17				ns	1.88
6. Interpersonal communication	−.13				ns	2.06
7. Information scanning	.06				ns	1.78
8. Informational skimming	.02				ns	1.44
Step 3: Demographics		.45	.20	.09	.002	
9. Gender	.04				ns	1.10
10. Age	.22				.005	1.16
11. Education	−.01				ns	1.22
12. Household income	.24				.003	1.17

This study reconceptualizes information learning and surveillance gratifications to reflect a more behavior-centric approach that will accommodate both offline and online news use activity. In doing so, information learning gratification was branded as the satisfaction an individual receives from information scanning, an activity that prompts the individual to examine and preview the news stories in view before selecting stories of interest. The surveillance gratification has traditionally been treated as a catch-all for all things that audience members may wish to keep up with in their environment (e.g., weather, sports, and headlines). In this study, however, this gratification was conceived as the satisfaction the audience may derive from information skimming, a process that engages the audience in glancing over preselected or familiar repertoires of news items that will keep them in the know. The utility of this reconceptualization effort is particularly evident when one considers the "short-burst" manner in which the audience accesses online news or online content in general, with the exception of certain time-consuming online activities such as playing interactive games or searching for literature on various subjects.

It was most interesting to find that, whereas offline and online news gratifications pertaining to entertainment and interpersonal communication utilities were not differentiated, the information scanning and skimming gratifications were differentiated. Contrary to Tewksbury and Althuss's (2000) findings, the information scanning gratification was more strongly identified with online than offline news use. Moreover, the information skimming gratification was more strongly associated with offline than online news use.

This contradiction could be due to the different sampling and research techniques. Tewksbury and Althuss (2000) used a college student sample that was assigned to either an offline or online version of *The New York Times*. The present study was a telephone survey of a nationally representative sample; the data analyzed were based on those individuals who were actual newspaper and online news readers.

At any rate, it is easy to see how accessing online and offline news involves a different set of procedures. In many ways, it is generally easier to read online news than an offline newspaper. This is because the content of an online newspaper or news site is usually presented in an organized fashion, where a number of news categories typically provides an intuitive lead for the reader to seek news content spanning different interests (e.g., Lin & Jeffres, 2001). When a reader visits the site, he or she need not skim the content to find items of interest and can simply scan the news content that is prepared in a prepackaged fashion.

By contrast, the offline newspaper stories are often presented in a meandering cluster characterized by a layout structure that is both physically and conceptually random, aside from the obvious divisions of sports, business, and other broad segments. If one considers the number of pages contained in Section A of any major metropolitan newspaper, it becomes immediately clear why the audience may skim more than scan the content to make sense out of the jumbled display of news stories throughout the sections. Hence, as a reader will both skim and scan the news content online or offline, the alphabetically organized online news content is much easier to scan and the disarrayed newspaper content is much more suitable for skimming.

This divergent pattern of audience gratification in relation to audience content usage activity is further reflected in the correlation results produced for testing Hypothesis 1. Audience gratifications involving entertainment, interpersonal

communication, and information scanning dimensions were significantly correlated between offline and online news use. The same was not true for the relationship between information skimming gratifications offline and online. It is possible that the skimming activities offline and online differ dramatically in their
process and thus diverge greatly in audience cognitive response toward such a
process. Imagine skimming over a well-classified online Web page menu that
presents news stories based on their content characteristics (e.g., international
politics, national politics, domestic economics, arts and culture, etc.). Then
imagine skimming over numerous headlines of different typefaces scattering
across newspaper pages that are neither organized by whether they are domestic
economic or international politics stories, nor indicative of whether the headlines
represent secondary headlines associated with stories continued from previous
pages. Although these findings revealed a lack of one-on-one correlation between
each dimension in each gratification pair, they generally validate the work of Lin
(1999) as well as Mings's (1997) contention that offline and online media use
gratifications are similar and parallel in respect to both audience cognitive and
affective responses.

When dualistic parallel news gratifications were translated into a predictive relationship between offline or online news access frequency, as hypothesized in Hypothesis 2 and Hypothesis 3, the findings explained the outcomes associated with
the hypothesized relationships between variables and were instrumental in forging
additional theoretical implications. It is worth noting that the intercorrelated nature of the gratifications had a negative effect on the total variance explained in
each of the two multiple regression equations, judging from the VIF (or variance
inflation factors) statistics. This helps explain the lack of predictive strength from
offline news gratification measures in accounting for generating significant predictors and a greater amount of variance in offline news use frequency.

Multicollinearity notwithstanding, offline news gratifications were insignificant
predictors of online news use frequency. This finding, then, substantiates Lin's
(1999) proposition that offline media use gratifications are not predictive of online
service adoption attributable to the distinct content of each media outlet and the
different access patterns associated with the use of each. The present study then
took this proposition a step further. It also tested the predictive relationship between online news gratifications and offline news use. As indicated by the second
multiple regression results, online news gratifications were also insignificant predictors of offline news use. The outcomes of these two predictive equations further
validate the thesis that, although offline and online media use gratifications are
similar and parallel, they are not cross-predictive of the access frequency or adoption likelihood for either the offline or online media service in question.

By implication, in their totality, these findings speak to several important theoretical issues. If we consider the online newspapers provided by the newspaper industry a companion service, it is worth noting that offline news consumption does
not necessarily predict online news use, and vice versa. From a uses and gratifica-

tions perspective, the audience can obtain the same set of media use gratifications from a diverse set of different media outlets associated with print, electronic, and online modalities (Ferguson & Perse, 2000). Hence, the findings that online and offline news gratifications are similar and parallel are theoretically sound.

Yet, the fact that perceived gratifications obtained from one news media type do not translate into adoption likelihood of another news media type poses questions regarding the nature of news media use gratifications. This outcome is also theoretically valid, as it is reasonable to assume that media use gratifications are either media-specific or content-specific; audiences experience gratifications due to the distinct characteristics of each medium's ability to provide content. Although all media types can provide similar gratifications to the same audience, each medium offers a certain unique flavor to the gratifications received by the audience. Thus, although online news media offer the audience an interactive experience that other news media are unable to match, television remains the most important "storyteller" of our time and newspapers retain their status as the ultimate information source.

The distinction between information scanning and skimming gratifications and their relations with offline and online news uses is symptomatic of how each medium type can edge out other media in furnishing audience gratifications. As online news pages become easier to navigate for headlines of interest and skimming effort is thus greatly reduced, online newspapers are perceived as a more gratifying source for scanning the news. In a similar vein, although offline news pages are relatively complex in their content and layout, and thus require more skimming to reach the news stories of interest before news scanning is possible, offline newspapers are perceived as a more satisfactory source for news skimming.

Furthermore, the finding that both offline and online news sources are comparable in their ability to contribute to audience gratifications in the areas of entertainment and interpersonal communication is another testament to the near-identical ability of different media types to provide similar media gratifications. The present study then expands the newspaper gratification research literature by confirming that newspaper reading—either offline or online—can be a source for entertainment. This entertainment utility, however, is enjoyed to a lesser extent than the interpersonal communication utility, as suggested in this study as well as past studies.

There are certain limitations to the findings of this study, including the limitation of only 15 items to prevent an overly lengthy telephone survey. Although these 15 items closely emulated past news gratification studies—both in terms of the number and types of measurement items used—additional insights and stronger content validity could have been possible if extra exploratory gratification measures had been utilized. Another limitation is that generalizations about offline media gratifications were limited to newspapers. Because the study did not examine television news, we can only speculate about television news gratifications based on past research.

CONCLUSION

This study attempted to gather comparative data for audience gratifications associated with online and offline news consumption at a national level. As study results further extended the staying power of the uses and gratifications paradigm, they also helped clarify the specificity of how audience gratifications extracted from different types of media use may converge or diverge while staying on parallel paths. From the mostly comparable levels of perceived news gratifications obtained between offline and online news consumption, it is clear that these two news outlets are supplementary, if not symbiotic, in their ability to serve the audience.

Given the theoretical premises suggested here, the question remains about what else contributes to audience adoption of online news, aside from the obvious perceived gratifications obtained that could motivate adoption. There are a number of additional reasons that could help explain online news adoption. These reasons may include the audience's online use experience and skills; interest in using online media and online news in general; time, opportunity, and technology availability to access online news; online use habits; credibility and quality of delivery of online news; ease of online news navigation; and audience affinity with online media and news.

An online companion news service, whether it is a stand-alone or ancillary service, is perhaps the most effective tool for the newspaper industry to compete against the 24-hour news cycle in the cable news industry. If newspapers are able to attract more users to their Web sites, they may be able to help stabilize existing users and readers as well as cultivate new users and readers for their offline brethren (Boynton, 2000). To successfully accomplish this task, future research will need to better explore multifaceted audience motivations, activity, and affinity surrounding the uses of both offline and online news content, in addition to the extramedia factors discussed here.

REFERENCES

Aikat, D. (2000). Of online news and "rogue" Web sites. In A. B. Albarran & D. H. Goff (Eds.), *Understanding the Web: Social, political, and economic dimensions of the Internet* (pp. 49–71). Ames: Iowa State University Press.

Blumler, J. G. (1979). The role of theory in uses and gratifications studies. *Communication Research, 6*, 9–36.

Boynton, R. S. (2000, July–August). New media may be old media's savior. *Columbia Journalism Review, 39*, 29.

Elliot, W., & Quattlebaum, C. P. (1979). Similarities in patterns of media use: A cluster analysis of media gratifications. *The Western Journal of Speech Communication, 43*, 61–72.

Ferguson, D. A., & Perse, E. M. (2000). The World Wide Web as a functional alternative to television. *Journal of Broadcasting & Electronic Media, 44*, 155–174.

Flanagin, A. J., & Metzger, M. J. (2001, January). Internet use in the contemporary media environment. *Human Communication Research, 27,* 153–181.

Griffin, J. L., Bartz, M. O., Dumrongsiri, N., Johnson, H. R., Leong, E. M., Mehalic, L. L., et al. (1997). The impact of World Wide Web use on foreign country knowledge. *Mass Comm Review, 24*(1–2), 125–131.

Johnson, T. J., & Kaye, B. K. (2000). Using is believing: The influence of reliance on the credibility of online political information among politically interested Internet users. *Journalism & Mass Communication Quarterly, 77,* 865–879.

Katz, E., Blumler, J. G., & Gurevitch, M. (1974). Utilization of mass communication by the individual. In J. G. Blumler & E. Katz (Eds.), *The uses of mass communications: Current perspectives on gratifications research* (pp. 19–32). Beverly Hills, CA: Sage.

Katz, E., Gurevitch, M., & Hass, H. (1973). On the uses of mass media for important things. *American Sociology Review, 38,* 164–181.

Kippax, S., & Murray, J. P. (1980). Using the mass media: Need gratification and "perceived utility." *Communication Research, 7,* 335–360.

Levy, M. R., & Windahl, S. (1984). Audience activity and gratifications: A conceptual clarification and exploration. *Communication Research, 11,* 51–78.

Lichtenstein, A., & Rosenfeld, L. B. (1983). Uses and misuses of gratifications research: An explication of media functions, *Communication Research, 10,* 97–109.

Lin, C. A. (1999). Online service adoption likelihood. *Journal of Advertising Research, 39*(2), 79–89.

Lin, C. A. (2001). Audience attributes, media supplementation, and likely online service adoption. *Mass Communication & Society, 4,* 19–38.

Lin, C. A., & Jeffres, L. W. (2001). Comparing distinctions and similarities across Websites of newspapers, radio stations and television stations. *Journalism & Mass Communication Quarterly, 78,* 555–574.

Mings, S. M. (1997). Uses and gratifications of online newspapers: A preliminary study. *Electronic Journal of Communication, 7*(3). Retrieved December 2, 2002, from http://www.cios.org/getfile/MINGS_V7N397.

New Media Federation. (2002). *The digital age.* Retrieved December 21, 2003, from http://www.naa.org

Newspaper Association of America. (2001). Newspaper links: A gateway to your local newspaper. Retrieved November 17, 2001, from http://www.naa.org

Newspaper Association of America. (2002). Facts about newspapers 2002. Retrieved January 29, 2003, from http://www.naa.org/info/facts02/20_facts2002.html

Palmgreen, P., Wenner, L. A., & Rayburn, J. D., II. (1980). Relations between gratifications sought and obtained: A study of TV news. *Communication Research, 7,* 161–192.

Palmgreen, P., Wenner, L. A., & Rayburn, J. D., II. (1981). Gratification discrepancies and news program choice. *Communication Research, 8,* 451–478.

Pew Research Center for the People and the Press. (2001). More online, doing more, The Pew Internet & American Life Project. Retrieved January 15, 2002, from http://www.pewinternet.org

Rayburn, J. D., II. (1996). Uses and gratifications. In M. B. Salwen & D. W. Stacks (Eds.), *An integrated approach to communication theory and research* (pp. 145–163). Mahwah, NJ: Lawrence Erlbaum Associates.

Rubin, A. M., & Perse, E. M. (1987). Audience activity and television news gratifications. *Communication Research, 14,* 58–84.

Stempel, G. H., III, Hargrove, T., & Bernt, J. P. (2000). Relation of growth of use of the Internet to changes in media use from 1995 to 1999. *Journalism & Mass Communication Quarterly, 77,* 71–79.

Tewksbury, D., & Althuss, S. L. (2000). Differences in reader knowledge acquisition among readers of the paper and online versions of a national newspaper. *Journalism & Mass Communication Quarterly, 77,* 457–479.

Thalhimer, M. (1994). High–tech news or just "shovelware?" *Media Studies Journal, 8,* 41–51.

UCLA Center for Communication Policy. (2001, November). *The UCLA Internet report 2001: Surveying the digital future.* Los Angeles: UCLA Regents.

Weaver, D. H. (1980). Audience need for orientation and media effects. *Communication Research, 7,* 361–376.

CHAPTER TEN

Online News as a Functional Substitute for Offline News

Carolyn Lin
Michael B. Salwen
Bruce Garrison
Paul D. Driscoll

The growth of the Internet since the mid-1990s has been nothing less than phenomenal, considering the inherent complexity involved in accessing the Internet universe via a personal computer. According to recent Nielsen research statistics, at least 72% of Americans have accessed the Internet (Nielsen/NetRatings, 2003b). This adoption rate, even though reflective of general adoption instead of at-home access of Internet services, remains impressive compared to the adoption of television sets and VCRs—the two most quickly diffused media technologies in history (Rogers, 2002).

What this Internet-use diffusion means to society, especially American society, is an emergent topic for research. Of special interest is the phenomenon of accessing news online. The most intriguing question associated with the phenomenon of online news access at this stage of development is whether and how online news use may displace offline news use. Such displacement outcomes point to several important implications for both the news media industry and our society alike. Among them are these: Will the displacement of offline news access by online news use spell the eventual demise of certain types of offline news outlets, assuming that the tidal waves heading toward a paperless society roar forcefully and loudly?

This study explores this evolving news displacement phenomenon between online and offline news outlet usage. Specifically, the relationships between this displacement phenomenon and the amount of offline news consumption—as well as online use activity in general—are investigated. In addition, the potential factors that may help explain such displacement activity are also explicated to help explain the "why" factor for this particular social trend.

ONLINE NEWS USE

About 57% of Americans (or 109 million people) were online users and 56% of them (or 61 million) went online on a daily basis in December 2002. Of these Internet users, 71% reported having accessed news online and about 26% did so on a daily basis (Horrigan & Rainie, 2002). These results contrast interestingly with a study reported by the Newspaper Association of America (New Media Federation, 2002). In this study, the Internet was considered the preferred source for weather, entertainment, sports, and general news by 19%, 13%, 9%, and 11% of those surveyed, compared to 73%, 31%, 36%, and 65% of those who chose television and 13%, 41%, 21%, and 37% of those who mentioned newspapers, respectively.

What these statistics imply is that, as Internet penetration increased 1000% during the 1990s, the phenomenon of media substitution between online and offline modalities topped academic and industry research agendas. This is particularly evident in the realm of news, which was listed as the most popular online activity, selected by most Internet users (Veronis, Suhler, & Associates, 1998). Based on that same survey, time spent with the Internet increased nearly threefold from the mid-1990s through the late 1990s, to more than 45 min per day. Dizard (2000) concluded that "(t)he significance of this figure for the old-line media organizations is that it represents time spent not looking at television, reading a newspaper or going to the movies" (p. 8).

This myriad of both offline and online media outlets for the audience to receive their entertainment and information is symptomatic of what is to come—continuing media substitution among different media outlets that provide either similar or dissimilar content. The media substitution hypothesis suggests that when a new media channel is capable of providing "superior content, technical benefits and cost efficiency" (Lin, 1999, p. 24), then this substitution mechanism may take place, as the new media channel is considered more functionally desirable than the old medium or media.

The media substitution concept can be further divided into three separate dimensions. First, media displacement reflects the scenarios where the adoption of a new medium facilitates the demise of an old medium. For instance, the rise of digital videodisc players helped push analog videodisc players into extinction. Second, media complementarity illustrates how a new medium complements an old medium to enhance the functional value of the old medium. For example, the digital video recorder (e.g., TiVo) complements the existing television set use by allowing commercial zipping, program recording, and playback, as well as nonlinear access to program content during viewing and playback. Third, media supplementation refers to situations when a new medium provides additional desirable content that supplements the use of an old medium. As a case in point, the Internet helps supplement the traditional news media outlets by providing additional access to news and information.

SUBSTITUTION BETWEEN MEDIA

Work on substitution dates to Lasswell's (1948) classic study on media use, in which he accurately foretold television's emergence in competition with radio for audience programming, advertising dollars, and audience leisure time. This substitution outcome has also been observed by subsequent studies that, for instance, linked the easy access to audiovisual entertainment content through television to the substitution of the film media (e.g., Frank & Greenberg, 1980). The technical capabilities of the VCR have also been found to facilitate the substitution of television viewing (e.g., Henke & Donohue, 1989; Lin, 1994) and moviegoing (e.g., Childers & Krugman, 1987; LaRose & Atkin, 1991; Lin, 1993) via time-shifting activity, prerecorded tape viewing, and video library playbacks. Primary reasons cited for this substitution activity included convenience and efficiency in saving time and money. Similarly, early work investigating the influence of cable news on network television viewing found evidence of a displacement effect (Bae, 2000; Baldwin, Barrett, & Bates, 1992).

Extending this analysis to online environments, early Internet use studies reported that a minority of Internet users had slightly reduced their television viewing time (e.g., Berniker, 1995; Crispell, 1997). Another study, however, found the percentages of Americans who preferred to go to a movie, watch a video or cable television, or read a book or magazine—instead of getting online—ranged from 70% to 77% (Snider, 1997). This was supported by yet another national study reporting that, even as Internet use was taking away time spent with television, heavier Internet users still watched more television than lighter Internet users (Shapiro, 1998).

Recent studies have shown continued but slight erosion of offline audiences at the hands of online uses. In particular, a UCLA study suggested that Internet users watched less television but read more books and newspapers than nonusers (Butler, 2000). By contrast, a later UCLA study indicated that Internet users generally read books, newspapers, and magazines as well as listening to the radio and watching television less than nonusers while they were offline (Berman, 2001; UCLA Center for Communication Policy, 2001). Similarly, Kayany and Yelsma (2000) found that usage of online media displaces time spent with television viewing, newspaper reading, telephone usage, and family conversations. The authors concluded that "(a) process of functional displacement may be occurring in which television is being gradually displaced by online media as the primary source of information" (p. 215).

These seemingly conflicting research findings regarding whether Internet use is displacing offline media use and to what extent seem to indicate that the media substitution phenomenon in question remains preliminary in its development. Lin (1999) contended that content offerings on an online service emulate the characteristics of offline print and electronic media. She further posited that the audience may seek to satisfy media-use needs with online service use. Studies assessing Web use motivations (e.g., Ferguson & Perse, 2000; Papacharissi & Rubin, 2000) discovered that uses of the Internet are more goal-directed than those of traditional media. In that regard, the Internet does not provide a functional alternative to traditional media so much as it functions to satisfy such needs as information seeking. In other words, online content is perhaps perceived as a desirable functional supplement for meeting the audience's gratification expectations associated with traditional media use, but it is not yet a functional displacement for them.

SUBSTITUTION BETWEEN OFFLINE AND ONLINE NEWS

Meta-analyses of cross-media competition suggest that the Internet displaces newspapers and broadcast outlets as news sources (Waldfogel, 2002). However, other studies fail to discover any consistent relationship between interest in using Internet services and local news consumption (Busselle, Reagan, Pinkleton, & Jackson, 1999) or use of most other traditional mass media (Coffee & Stipp, 1997; Jeffres & Atkin, 1996; Kang & Atkin, 1999; Perse & Dunn, 1998).

Likewise, Stempel, Hargrove, and Bernt (2000) found mixed results on the issue of Internet displacement of traditional media news sources. Surveying national media consumption patterns from 1995 through 1997—a period of widespread Internet diffusion—the authors found that television news and newspaper use decreased, whereas radio news and talk listenership increased. In particular, the authors uncovered a symbiotic relationship between Internet news use and traditional news consumption, one that casts the online news user as a media junkie who also seeks information from offline news media. Stempel et al. (2000) concluded that online news patronage was not responsible for the decline in news consumption in television (both network and local), newspapers, and magazines.

Focusing on content-specific media functions across the Internet and traditional print and broadcast media, the audience still prefers offline media for information such as general news, weather, entertainment, and sports (New Media Federation, 2002). As Lin (2001) concluded, online media content access might have been perceived as a "functional supplement" to traditional media use. For instance, Aikat (2000) reviewed several marketing reports indicating that Internet users are heavy users of online news. Even so, the audience still prefers traditional media for general information (e.g., weather, sports, entertainment, and general news; New Media Federation, 2002). Other work suggests that Internet users are heavier media users in general, although the Internet has not yet supplanted more traditional media sources.

Eveland and Dunwoody (2002) noted that a simple Web document is similar to traditional print media because it can convey both text and images, but they differ in their content layout and structure. Whereas print media are organized

more in a linear format on separate pages to allow a continuous reading sequence, Web media are formulated more in a nonlinear (or menu-based) format
on the same "home page" to permit an out-of-order reading sequence. This suggests that news users who prefer to scan the headlines quickly and read only those
stories of interest may choose to displace offline news with online news use.

However, this displacement function may also be contingent on yet another
factor—the credibility of the Internet as a news source. Johnson and Kaye (1998)
recounted an anecdote where a campaign analyst "fretted about whether the
public would trust information on the Internet when 'Joe from Dubuque' can
create a Web page that appears as credible as one posted by the news media" (p.
325). Such considerations have ramifications for media displacement, as
"(c)redibility is a crucial issue for the Internet because past research suggests that
people are less likely to pay attention to media they do not perceive as credible"
(Johnson & Kaye, 1998, p. 334). Johnson and Kaye's own findings suggest that
online reading is viewed as more credible than contents delivered by traditional
media.

Similarly, Brady (1996) found that college students regarded the Web as more
in-depth than television. The Pew Research Center (Rainie & Packel, 2001) also
found that online users regarded the Web as a more credible source than traditional media. By contrast, Flanagan and Metzger (2000) found that newspapers
were regarded as more credible than the Internet. Kim, Weaver, and Willnat
(2002) found that the Internet is less credible than online media in reporting online polls. Factors undermining Web credibility include the fact that it is regarded
as "a freewheeling, unregulated outpost for anyone to express his or her opinions" (Johnson & Kaye, 1998, p. 326). By contrast, Reagan, Pinkleton, and
Busselle (2001) found the Internet as credible as television or newspapers in all
cases, although those with access found the Internet more credible than those
without access.

MAJOR ONLINE AND OFFLINE THEMES

The preceding review of media substitution literature seems to illustrate several
major themes in the relationships between different offline and online media. In
essence, the picture of media displacement remains an emergent phenomenon
between online and offline media as well as between online and offline news media use. A more prevalent media substitution function appears to be media
supplementation, where the online news media provide supplemental content to
the users to make their offline news media use experience more complete. Online
news media have not yet shown complementary relations with offline news media, as these two media modalities will not be converged before the widespread
arrival of two-way interactive digital cable television.

Based on the preceding literature review, the following research hypotheses
are proposed to test the relationships between offline news displacement and on-

line news use as well as the differences in online use activity and demographic characteristics between online news users and nonusers. A research question was also posited to address the potential differences between online and offline news access levels among online news users:

H1:   Greater perceived displacement of newspaper, radio, broadcast network, cable network, and local television news by online news is correlated with greater level of online access activity.

H2:   Greater perceived displacement of newspaper, radio, broadcast network, cable network, and local television news by online news is correlated with greater level of online news access.

H3:   Greater perceived displacement of newspaper, radio, broadcast television network, cable network, and local television news by online news is correlated with lower levels of newspaper reading, radio news listening, broadcast television network news viewing, cable news viewing, and local television news viewing, respectively.

H4:   Perceived displacement of audience uses of newspaper, radio, broadcast network, cable network, and local television news will be positively correlated.

H5:   Online news users will have a heavier level of online access activity, and a stronger news interest, than nonnews users.

H6:   Online news users will be younger, better educated, and wealthier than nonnews users.

RQ1: Will online news users access news via an online news source more often than a newspaper, radio, broadcast television network, cable, or local television news source?

METHODOLOGY

A representative U.S. telephone survey gathered data from 792 respondents during the evenings between November 11 and 13, 2002. The sample was drawn using a stratified design to represent the 50 states and the District of Columbia roughly proportionate to their populations in the 2000 U.S. Census. Residential telephone numbers were drawn from the latest available edition of the national Select Phone telephone software package on compact disc and database published by InfoUSA (Select Phone, 2002). Random residential telephone numbers were generated on a state-by-state basis from the database of more than 100 million telephone numbers using a table of random numbers and the random number selection function built into the Select Phone software. Each resulting state roster of random numbers was then adjusted using the one-up and one-down last digit method to include unlisted numbers not included in the database. If there was no answer, a busy signal, or an answering machine, up to two more attempts were made later that evening or during another evening to reach the number. The response rate, excluding invalid contacts, was 50%.[1]

Variables analyzed in this chapter are conceptually and operationally defined as follows:

- *Perceived displacement of offline news by online news.* This concept was measured for the displacement between online news use and consumption of (a) newspapers, (b) radio news, (c) broadcast network evening news, (d) cable network news, and (e) local television news. Respondents were asked to report the extent to which their online news access replaced their offline news consumption on a 5-point scale, ranging from 1 (*does not replace at all*) to 5 (*fully replaces*).

- *Online-access activity level.* Two items were used to assess this concept. The first item asked the respondents the number of days per week, if any, they went online. The response categories ranged from 0 to 7 days a week. The second item assessed the amount of time in minutes or hours per day (open ended) Internet users spent online.

- *Online news access level.* Respondents were instructed to provide answers for the number of days per week they went online to seek out news; the response categories ranged from 0 to 7 days a week. They were also questioned about the amount of time in hours or minutes per day (open-ended) they spent consuming news online.

- *Online news accessed.* The frequency of audience consumption of 11 online news categories was gauged by a 5-point scale, ranging from *all the time* to *never*. Topics included science/technology, business/finance, health/fitness, sports, domestic politics, international news, opinions/commentaries, local news, celebrities/personalities, weather, and crime.

- *Offline news access level.* The frequency of consumption for five different offline news media outlets was measured. Respondents were probed about the number of days per week they spent reading a printed newspaper, listening to radio news (at any location), watching a broadcast television network evening news program (i.e., ABC, CBS, or NBC), viewing an all-news cable television network (i.e., CNN, CNBC, MSNBC, or Fox), and tuning to a local television newscast. The number of days ranged from 0 to 7 days per week.

- *News interest.* A single item was used to reflect the level of interest the respondent had in keeping up with the news. The measurement involved a 5-point scale, ranging from *very uninterested* to *very interested*.

- *Demographic characteristics.* Respondent education level was reflected by seven categories, ranging from "8th grade or less" to "graduate degree"—coded

---

[1]Completion rate used in this study was computed by completions divided by completions + refusals.

on a 7-point scale. The concept of racial or ethnic origin was measured by two items. The first item indicated whether the respondent was of Hispanic or Latino ancestry and the second item recorded whether the respondent was White, Black, Asian, or other. Both items were dummy coded. Respondent age was gathered via an open ended question. Finally, the respondent's annual household income level was classified by 5 categories, ranging from under $25,000 to more than 100,000.

FINDINGS

Out of 792 valid responses, 475 or 60.3% were Internet users (excluding 4 missing cases). Among the Internet users, 210 or 45% were online news users (excluding 7 missing cases). The mean age for the Internet users was 43 years. A typical Internet user had an annual household income between $50,001 and $75,000, although nearly 40% of the Internet user sample's annual income level exceeded $75,000. This upscale profile was also evident with this Internet user sample's education level, as the mean amount of formal education received was some college and 49.6% of the sample had at least a college education. With regard to ethnic and racial composition, 9% of the Internet user sample identified themselves as of Hispanic or Latino ethnic origin, and the racial breakdowns reflected 81.4% Whites, 7.4% Blacks, 3.1% Asians, and 8.1% other. The Blacks and Hispanics or Latinos were underrepresented compared to their respective proportions in the census (i.e., 12.6% and 12.3%).

In terms of news exposure, nearly 73% of non-Internet users, 59% of the Internet users, and 53% of the online news users chose television as their primary news source. Newspapers were a distant second choice, selected by nearly 17% of non-Internet users, 17% of Internet users, and 16% of online news users. Radio was the third choice for news exposure, preferred by nearly 9% of non-Internet users, 12% of Internet users, and 11% of online news users. Magazines were only selected as the primary news source by around 1% across the three categories of news consumers. Although 19% of online news users reported online news as their primary news source, only 1.4% of all Internet users reported online news as their primary news source.

Results from testing the first three hypotheses are reported in Table 10.1. Hypothesis 1 received mixed support. It appears that only perceived displacement of newspaper reading was significantly correlated with both greater number of days spent online per week ($r = .142$, $p \leq .05$) and greater amount of time spent online per day ($r = .139$, $p \leq .05$). Although perceived displacement of broadcast network television ($r = .211$, $p \leq .01$) and cable network news viewing ($r = .25$, $p \leq .001$) was significantly correlated with greater amount of time spent online per day, perceived displacement of radio news listening and local television news viewing was not correlated with either the number of days or amount of time spent online.

TABLE 10.1
Correlations Between Offline News Displacement and Media Use Factors

	Newspaper	Radio News	Network TV News	Cable TV News	Local TV News		
	r	r	r	r	r	M	SD
Online access activity							
Days per week	.142*	.027	.054	.073	−.020	5.81	1.83
Minutes per day	.139*	.054	.211**	.250***	.086	148.1	200.7
Online news access							
Days per week	.248***	.236***	.237***	.133	.201**	4.04	2.27
Minutes per day	.179**	.162*	.228***	.085	.178**	30.88	34.36
Offline news access							
Newspaper reading level	−.487***	−.149*	−.192**	−.131	−.188**	3.97	2.73
Radio news listening level	−.036	−.294***	−.080	−.127	−.103	4.03	2.63
Network TV news viewing	−.091	.058	−.178*	−.051	−.156*	3.26	2.59
Cable TV news viewing	−.064	.103	.034	−.137*	−.002	3.41	2.61
Local TV news viewing	−.212***	−.101	−.263***	−.150*	−.309***	4.27	2.47
Online news accessed							
Science/technology	.029	.142*	.099	.231***	.107	2.61	1.19
Business/finance	.073	.009	.180**	.098	.136*	3.04	1.17
Health/fitness news	.152*	.013	.031	.009	.050	2.80	1.05
Sports news	.040	.027	.143*	.113	.162*	2.84	1.38
Domestic politics	−.061	.044	.139*	.066	.067	3.25	1.16
International news	.011	.042	.080	.042	.016	3.44	1.13
Opinions/commentaries	.039	.263***	.067	.075	.113	2.41	1.13
Local news	.020	.202**	.092	.086	.109	3.36	1.37
Celebrities/personalities	.081	.179**	.112	.108	.068	2.20	1.07
Weather news	.116	.138*	.076	.022	.064	3.67	.22
Crime news	.094	.207**	.043	−.028	.053	3.00	1.23

*p = .05. **p = .01. ***p < .001. All are two-tailed.

Hypothesis 2 also yielded strong but partial empirical support. The results showed that only perceived displacement of cable network news viewing, perceived displacement of newspaper reading ($r = .248$, $p \leq .001$; $r = .179$, $p \leq .01$), radio news listening ($r = .236$, $p \leq .001$; $r = .162$, $p \leq .05$), broadcast network television ($r = .237$, $p \leq .001$; $r = .228$, $p \leq .001$), and local television news viewing ($r = .201$, $p \leq .01$; $r = .178$, $p \leq .01$) were found to be positively correlated with the number of days per week spent accessing online news and the amount of time per day spent accessing online news, respectively.

Significant statistical support was obtained for Hypothesis 3. Perceived displacement of newspaper reading, radio listening, broadcast network news viewing, cable network news viewing, and local television news viewing was found to be significantly correlated with lower newspaper reading frequency ($r = −.487$, $p \leq .001$), radio listening ($r = −.294$, $p \leq .001$), broadcast network news viewing ($r = −.178$, $p \leq .05$), cable network news viewing ($r = −.137$, $p \leq .05$), and local television news viewing ($r = −.309$, $p \leq .001$), in that order.

TABLE 10.2
Correlations Between Different Types of Offline News Displacement

	Newspaper Displacement	Radio News Displacement	Network TV News Displacement	Cable Network News Displacement	Local TV News Displacement
	r	r	r	r	r
Radio news displacement	.236*	1			
Network TV news displacement	.406*	.262*	1		
Cable TV news displacement	.283*	.301*	.463*	1	
Local TV news displacement	.332*	.366*	.663*	.488*	1
M	2.33	1.73	1.80	1.73	1.60
SD	1.2	1.12	1.18	1.13	1.08

$p = .001$ (two-tailed).

Hypothesis 4 was also supported. According to Table 10.2, perceived displacement of newspaper reading, radio listening, broadcast network news viewing, cable network news viewing, and local television news viewing were both significantly and positively intercorrelated with each other. In particular, newspaper displacement was correlated with radio, broadcast network, cable network, and local television news displacement at .236 ($p \leq .001$), .406 ($p \leq .001$), .283 ($p \leq .001$), and .332 ($p \leq .001$), respectively. The correlation coefficients between radio news displacement and broadcast network, cable news, and local television news displacement were .262 ($p \leq .001$), .301 ($p \leq .001$), and .366 ($p \leq .001$), in that order. Broadcast network news displacement was in turn correlated with cable network news and local television news displacement at .462 ($p \leq .001$) and .663 ($p \leq .001$) each. Finally, cable network news displacement was correlated with local television news displacement at .488 ($p \leq .001$).

Table 10.3 contains the test results for Hypotheses 5 and 6. The mean comparisons showed that Hypothesis 5 received strong support. Online news users spent a greater number of days online per week ($t = 7.24$, $p \leq .001$) and a greater amount of time online per day than nonnews users ($t = 3.72$, $p \leq .001$), in addition to showing a stronger interest in news ($t = 3.01$, $p \leq .01$). By contrast, the mean comparison results only provided partial support for Hypothesis 6. Online news users were found to be better educated ($t = 2.18$, $p \leq .05$) and had higher income ($t = -2.2$, $p \leq .05$) than nonnews users but were not younger in years.

The single research question proposed was tested using paired t tests. It was found that the number of days per week spent accessing online news ($M = 4.04$) was significantly greater than the number of days watching broadcast ($M = 3.26$, $p \leq .001$) and cable ($M = 3.41$, $p \leq .01$) network television newscasts. The number

TABLE 10.3
Mean Comparisons for the Characteristics Between
Online News Users and Nonusers

		N	M	SD	t	p
Number of days online per week	Nonusers	210	4.43	2.29	7.24	.000
	Users	257	5.81	1.83		
Amount of time spent online per day	Nonusers	206	84.47	158.16	3.72	.000
	Users	257	148.05	200.74		
Interest in keeping up with the news	Nonusers	207	3.82	1.205	3.01	.003
	Users	256	4.12	.973		
Respondent age	Nonusers	209	42.81	15.55	.88	.381
	Users	250	44.01	13.85		
Respondent education level	Nonusers	209	4.45	1.39	2.18	.030
	Users	250	4.74	1.41		
Respondent income level	Nonusers	172	3.06	1.25	2.20	.033
	Users	218	3.34	1.25		

of days per week spent accessing online news ($M = 4.04$), however, was not statistically differentiated from the number of days spent accessing radio news ($M = 4.03$), local television news ($M = 4.27$), and newspapers ($M = 3.97$).

Additional analyses were executed to explore the potential factors that could explain the displacement of offline news by online news use. A hierarchical multiple regression procedure was executed by regressing significant correlates of perceived displacement of newspaper, radio, broadcast television network, cable network, and local television news—as presented in Table 10.1—as predictors in each of the five separate equations. Table 10.4 illustrates only the standardized beta weights for the final model of the regression procedures for each equation, along with the amount of variance explained for each model of each equation.

For the newspaper displacement equation, the significant predictors included greater number of days per week spent accessing news online ($\beta = .293$, $p \leq .001$), more frequent access of health and fitness news online ($\beta = .149$, $p \leq .01$), and much lower level of offline newspaper reading ($\beta = -.504$, $p \leq .001$)—with the offline newspaper reading variable contributing nearly 27% of the total 37% variance explained for the entire model.

As for the radio displacement equation, the significant predictors were greater amount of time per day spent accessing news online ($\beta = .138$, $p \leq .05$), more frequent access of online opinions/commentaries ($\beta = .165$, $p \leq .05$), as well as lower level of offline newspaper reading ($\beta = -.154$, $p \leq .05$) and radio listening ($\beta = -.306$, $p \leq .001$). Access to opinions/commentaries online was able to contribute 7% of the total 24% of the variance explained in this model.

The total variance explained for the broadcast network evening news displacement equation was 24%. There were three significant predictors for this model: greater amount of time per day spent online ($\beta = .179$, $p \leq .05$), greater number of

TABLE 10.4
Multiple Regression Results for Predicting Offline News Displacement

Variable Entry Steps	Newspaper Displacement β	Radio News Displacement β	Network News Displacement β	Cable News Displacement β	Local TV News Displacement β
Online access activity					
Days per week	−.029				
Minutes per day	.069		.179**	.224***	
R^2	.033*		.062***	.062***	.056**
Online news access					
Days per week	.293***	.071	.190**		.176**
Minutes per day	.058	.138*	.074		.104
R^2	.079**	.055**	.117**		.076
Online news access					
Science/technology		.070		.224**	
Business/finance			.104		.084
Health/fitness news	.149**				
Sports news			.124		.114
Domestic politics			.058		
Opinions/commentaries		.165*			
Local news		.115			
Celebrities/personalities		.081			
Weather news		.043			
Crime news		−.007			
R^2	.100*	.121*	.142	.101**	.192***
Offline news access					
Newspaper reading level	−.504***	−.154*	−.116		−.115
Radio news listening level		−.306***			
Network news viewing			−.113		−.055
Cable news viewing				−.171**	
Local TV news viewing	−.086		−.202**	−.146*	−.264***
R^2	.371***	.238***	.244***	.156**	

*$p \le .05$. **$p \le .01$. ***$p \le .001$.

days per week spent accessing news online ($\beta = .190$, $p \le .01$), and lower level of local television news viewing ($\beta = -.202$, $p \le .01$). Surprisingly, broadcast network evening news viewing offline was not a significant predictor for its displacement by online news access; the same was true for online access of business news, sports news, or domestic political news.

At 16%, the cable network news viewing displacement model garnered the lowest amount of variance explained for its equation, as all three predictor variable blocks contributed approximately equally to the total variance explained. All predictor variables entered into the equations at three different steps turned out to be significant predictors—greater amount of time per day spent online ($\beta = .224$, $p \le .001$), greater access of science/technology news online ($\beta = .224$, $p \le$

.01), and lower level of cable network news ($\beta = -.171$, $p \leq .01$) and local television news ($\beta = -.146$, $p \leq .05$) viewing.

Finally, local television news viewing displacement was significantly predicted by the following variables: greater number of days per week online ($\beta = .176$, $p \leq .01$) and lower level of local television news viewing ($\beta = -.246$, $p \leq .001$). The total amount of variance explained for the equation was 15%; of this, nearly 12% was contributed by the decreased amount of offline viewing.

DISCUSSION

The findings help identify the important predictors for the news displacement phenomenon by online news access. It appears that the number of days per week spent online accessing news was the best predictor for offline news displacement, compared to the amount of time spent accessing news online per day and the amount of days per week and time per day spent on online use. This suggests that, for every day when the Internet user accesses news online, it was done at the expense of consumption of certain types of offline news outlets. In this case, it occurred at the greatest expense of offline newspaper reading, broadcast network evening news viewing, and local television news viewing.

By comparison, the amount of time spent online seeking news had the greatest impact on lowering offline radio news listening. This indicates that if users were able to listen to the same radio news programs (e.g., popular talk shows) or news content online, they would opt for the convenience of online outlets that were not subject to the rigid offline broadcast schedules.

Interestingly, cable network news viewing displacement was not affected by online news access at all; instead, it was a result of time spent with online activity as a whole. This implies that cable news viewing was not vacated by online news access per se; rather, it was simply a casualty of more time spent online, causing less time for watching offline cable news. Given the nature of 24-hour news reporting, avid news consumers have been the loyal core viewers for these cable news networks. As these cable news networks tend to bring up-to-the-minute breaking news as well as a more comprehensive range of news reporting to the viewers, it is possible that online news content is not seen as having a practical advantage when it comes to news delivery schedule flexibility. Where online news access edges out cable network news viewing is with the Internet's capability to allow for instant exchanges of information, discussion, and chats on the breaking news.

In essence, the popularity of the Web sites operated by newspapers, broadcast television networks, cable television networks, radio networks and stations, and local television stations have ironically helped contribute to this displacement phenomenon. To succeed in today's highly competitive media environment, where there are literally hundreds of electronic media channels vying for the audience's eyes and ears, in addition to the numerous nonelectronic media vehicles, news media have adopted a "blanket marketing" strategy. This strategy calls for the embracing of all potential outlets to deliver the news media's content, by establishing any and every possible ancillary channel, including a cable television and World Wide Web presence. The purpose of this strategy is to generate synergy across different content delivery channels and prevent the loss of any audience members to any competitors. Although the benefits of synergy might not have evidenced a strong financial payback for most news media companies, the greatest gain of this multichannel approach has been the flourishing online news establishment and increased online news access by a larger number of online users.

This particular growth phenomenon for online news media is further enhanced by news events that attract a larger amount of public attention, whether they are war, disaster, celebrity news, or anything else. According to Nielsen/ NetRatings (2003a), due to the *Columbia* Space Shuttle tragedy, *Time* magazine's online version experienced 112% growth between January and February 2003— averaging 863,000 unique visitors during the week ending February 2. Of the top 20 news Web sites accessed during January 2003, 8 of them were affiliated with a newspaper establishment (*Editor & Publisher*, 2003). Rounding out the top 10 news Web sites are: MSN Slate, *Newsday*, Netscape, CBS, CNN, MSNBC, Fox, Hearst Newspaper Digital, and *The Washington Post*.

The size of the offline news media audience, according to these findings, was least affected for cable news networks by online news access, followed by broadcast network evening news, radio news, local television news, and newspapers. It would appear that the offline medium that provides the greatest immediacy, requires the least amount of mental effort for consumption, offers the richest presentation of the sights and sounds associated with the news stories—cable network news—was least displaced by online news access. By comparison, the more technologically muted newspapers—a medium that tends to offer a delayed delivery, provides a sightless and soundless news presentation, and demands the greatest amount of mental energy and time from the audience—was the most displaced by online news access.

To further explicate the relationship between online news and offline news access, one may contrast the access level for both based on the number of days per week the audience spent with each (see Table 10.1). With a minimal displacement effect in place, as the number of days per week spent accessing online news was significantly greater than the number of days per week spent watching broadcast and cable network television newscasts, these results suggest primarily the illustration of a media supplementation phenomenon. By contrast, with a greater displacement effect at play, although the number of days spent accessing online news, radio news, and local television news was similar, these findings imply primarily the existence of a media displacement outcome.

Audience displacement notwithstanding, the news media companies thus far have not concerned themselves much with the potential erosions of offline audience ratings or readership to online news access for a good reason. As evidenced by this study, only 1.4% of the Internet users reported online news outlets as their primary source for news and 19% of the online news users agreed as much. Hence, the average level of offline news displacement remains relatively low. Although the mean values for offline newspaper displacement stood at 2.33, the mean values for the displacement of the remaining news media outlets fell below 2 on a 5-point scale, ranging from 1 (*no displacement at all*) to 5 (*full displacement*; see Table 10.2).

With regard to the types of online news accessed that were predictive of offline news displacement, the access of health/fitness news, opinions/commentaries, and science/technology news online was linked to newspaper, radio news, and cable news displacement, respectively (see Table 10.4). It is common knowledge that Internet users have considered online sources a quick way to receive information about health and fitness. According to a recent Pew research report (Horrigan & Rainie, 2002), 81% of Internet users said that they could receive reliable information about health online, in comparison to 45% of non-Internet users. Therefore, it is not surprising that online news users preferred accessing health/fitness news via the quick and rich sources online instead of the slow and difficult-to-gather newspaper articles offline.

As opinions and commentaries on the radio have been considered a big draw for offline news and talk stations, radio talk show enthusiasts inevitably may navigate the vast radio talk landscape online—a universe that is not limited by airing schedules and the temporal nature of offline listening. This means that online users could listen to a variety of radio talk shows from different radio networks or stations via either a live simulcast or a download stream, in addition to listening to shows retrieved from archives.

The 24-hour nonstop format of the cable network news channels stands out as the primary, if not the only, offline electronic news medium that provides a steady slate of science and technology news to fill the time in their news programs. For instance, CNN's Headline News contains a technology segment for every newscast delivered within every 30-min period. These types of science and technology news reports tend to be rather short and jazzy, as compared to the similar reports made available in their online version. It is thus logical for the displacement of science and technology news, as provided by cable networks, by their online counterparts.

On the whole, considering how some other media use and lifestyle variables that could also influence the news displacement phenomenon were not examined in this study, the multiple regression models explained a relatively respectable amount of variance in each of the displacement equations. Specifically, as the displacement level for offline newspaper consumption was the highest, so was the amount of variance explained (37%). This outcome is consistent with the reality of online news consumption, where Internet users "read" more than listen to or watch the news online. As the lowest amount of variance explained (16%) was associated with the cable news displacement equation, this result is also in step with the small size of loyal cable news viewers as compared to that of newspapers, broadcast television networks, radio, and local television news. It is expected that as cable network news attracts a lot fewer audiences to their offerings, the displacement phenomenon is also less pronounced.

Lastly, the comparisons of online use activity strongly indicate that online news users spent a lot more time online than nonusers. Similarly, online news users were also more interested in news than nonusers, aside from being heavier users of newspapers, radio news, cable news, and local television news. Accessing news online and offline on a regular basis is both a cognitively challenging and time-consuming activity. It is thus not surprising to find online news users falling into the category of news enthusiasts. The presumption that online news users will be more upscale in both education and income level was proven true. However, the hypothesis that predicted online news users to be younger than nonusers did not find support from the data. In fact, both groups of online users appeared to be in the middle-age range of 44 to 43 years old—approximating the average age (43) of the Internet user sample for the study (see Table 10.3).

CONCLUSION

Even as this study found empirical evidence supporting the media substitution phenomenon at varying degrees, the larger issues concerning this evolving transformation in audience behavior and media industry structure have yet to be addressed. That is, this potential paradigm shift in news media access—via displacing offline media with online media as the primary source for news and information—carries with it a number of potential social and economic impacts on both the audience and news media alike.

A potential resulting social caveat, for instance, may be that the fluid and immediate nature of the online news gathering and offerings will draw serious concerns regarding the truthfulness, accuracy, and objectivity of such news content. As newspapers were found to be the most displaced news medium in this study, it is also likely that an entire future generation may not ever develop a desirable appreciation for the printed newspaper—the most valuable staple knowledge tool for a literate and informed society.

On another front, a likely economic consequence for the news media industry, for example, may be that the intense competition over audiences will further encourage continuing consolidation of news media ownership between offline and online news media companies via both horizontal and vertical integration. These types of mergers then will help lessen the competition in the news media industry as well as curtail the diversity in news media content. When media ownership and diversity decreases as a result of pseudo-competition—a characteristic reflective of an oligopoly industry structure—then a slew of anticonsumer conducts could follow. These could include pricing inflexibility and poor product quality—subscription fees and content diversity, in this case. As speed and convenience are the essence of online news consumption for most audiences, it is also worrisome that the effect of the "headlining" of all things media may sprout as an inadvertent consequence of offline media displacement. If this effect does take root, then the journalism tradition of reporting, recording, and retelling events and happenings may also be shortchanged. These dynamics then could help redefine the relationship between the audience and the news media as well as reconfigure the role of journalism in society. This media substitution phenomenon then carries implications that reach far beyond the pages of this text. Future studies should endeavor to explore, investigate, describe, analyze, and explain the vast social as well as economic meanings of this emergent media use paradigm.

REFERENCES

Aikat, D. (2000). Of online news and "rogue" Web sites. In A. B. Albarran & D. H. Goff (Eds.), *Understanding the Web: Social, political, and economic dimensions of the Internet* (pp. 49–71). Ames: Iowa State University Press.

Bae, H. S. (2000). Product differentiation in national TV newscasts: A comparison of the cable all-news networks and the broadcast networks. *Journal of Broadcasting & Electronic Media, 44,* 62–77.

Baldwin, T. F., Barrett, M., & Bates, B. (1992). Influence of cable on television news audiences. *Journalism Quarterly, 69,* 651–658.

Berman, D. K. (2001, November 29). Survey suggests Internet use affects TV-viewing habits. *The Wall Street Journal,* p. B11.

Berniker, M. (1995, November 6). Internet begins to cut into TV viewing. *Broadcasting & Cable,* p. 113.

Brady, D. J. (1996, November). *Cyberdemocracy and perceptions of politics: An experimental analysis of political communication on the World Wide Web.* Paper presented at the annual meeting of the Midwest Association for Public Opinion Research, Chicago.

Busselle, R., Reagan, J., Pinkleton, B., & Jackson, K. (1999). Factors affecting Internet use in a saturated access population. *Telematics and Informatics, 16,* 45–58.

Butler, K. (2000, October 30). Study shakes up notions about web use. *Investor's Business Daily,* p. A8.

Childers, T., & Krugman, D. (1987). The competitive environment of pay-per-view. *Journal of Broadcasting & Electronic Media, 31,* 335–342.

Coffee, S., & Stipp, H. (1997, March–April). The interactions between computer and television usage. *Journal of Advertising Research, 37,* 61–68.

Crispell, D. (1997, May). The Internet of TV. *American Demographics,* 14–15.

Dizard, W. (2000). *Old media, new media* (3rd ed.) Reading, MA: Addison-Wesley Longman.

Editor & Publisher. (2003, February 20). Newspapers run 8 of top 20 news sites: Gannett leads newspaper chains in audience. *Editor & Publisher.* Retrieved February 24, 2003, from http://www.editorandpublisher.com/editorandpublisher/headlines/

Eveland, W. P., & Dunwoody, S. (2002). An investigation of elaboration and selective scanning as methods of learning from the web versus print. *Journal of Broadcasting & Electronic Media, 46,* 34–44.

Ferguson, D. A., & Perse, E. M. (2000). The World Wide Web as a functional alternative to television. *Journal of Broadcasting & Electronic Media, 44,* 155–174.

Flanagin, A. J., & Metzger, M. J. (2001, January). Internet use in the contemporary media environment. *Human Communication Research, 27,* 153–181.

Frank, R. E., & Greenberg, M. G. (1980). *The public's use of television.* Newbury Park, CA: Sage.

Henke, L., & Donohue, T. R. (1989). Functional displacement of traditional TV viewing by VCR owners. *Journal of Advertising Research, 29,* 18–23.

Horrigan, J. B., & Rainie, L. (2002, December 29). Counting on the Internet. *Pew Internet & American Life Project.* Retrieved January 2, 2003, from http://www.pewinternet.org

Jeffres, L., & Atkin, D. (1996). Predicting the use of technologies for communication and consumer needs. *Journal of Broadcasting & Electronic Media, 40,* 318–330.

Johnson, T. J., & Kaye, B. K. (1998). Cruising is believing? Comparing Internet and traditional sources on media credibility measures. *Journalism & Mass Communication Quarterly, 75,* 325–340.

Kang, M., & Atkin, D. (1999). Exploring the role of audience uses and gratifications in multimedia cable adoption. *Telematics & Informatics, 16,* 59–74.

Kayany, J. M., & Yelsma, P. (2000). Displacement effects of online media in the socio-technical contexts of households. *Journal of Broadcasting & Electronic Media, 44,* 215.

Kim, S. T., Weaver, D., & Willnat, L. (2002). Media reporting and perceived credibility of online polls. *Journalism & Mass Communication Quarterly, 77,* 846–864.

LaRose, R., & Atkin, D. (1991). Movie distribution modalities and consumer choice. *Journal of Media Economics, 4,* 3–17.

Lasswell, H. D. (1948). The structure and function of communication in society. In L. Bryson (Ed.), *The communication of ideas* (pp. 37–51). New York: Harper.

Lin, C. A. (1993). Exploring the role of VCR use in the emerging home entertainment culture. *Journalism & Mass Communication, 70,* 833–842.

Lin, C. A. (1994). Audience fragmentation in a competitive video marketplace. *Journal of Advertising Research, 34*(6), 1–17.

Lin, C. A. (1999). Online service adoption likelihood. *Journal of Advertising Research, 39*(2), 79–89.

Lin, C. A. (2001). Audience attributes, media supplementation, and likely online service adoption. *Mass Communication & Society, 4,* 19–38.

New Media Federation. (2002). *The digital age.* Retrieved December 21, 2003, from http://www.naa.org.

Nielsen/NetRatings. (2003a, March 13). *Current news events boost traffic to online newspapers.* Retrieved March 14, 2003, from http://www.nielsen-netratings.com/pr/pr_030207.pdf

Nielsen/NetRatings. (2003b, January 14). *More than 72% of the U.S. online population uses Internet applications.* Retrieved March 14, 2003, from http://www.nielsen-netratings.com.

Papacharissi, Z., & Rubin, A. (2000). Predictors of Internet use. *Journal of Broadcasting & Electronic Media, 44,* 175–196.

Perse, E., & Dunn, D. (1998). The utility of home commuters and media use: Implications of multimedia and connectivity. *Journal of Broadcasting & Electronic Media, 42,* 435–456.

Rainie, L., & Packel, D. (2001, February 18). *More online, doing more.* Retrieved February 27, 2001, from http://www.pewinternet.org

Reagan, J., Pinkleton, B., & Busselle, R. (2001, November). *Use and believability of the Internet versus traditional media for nine topics.* Paper presented at the annual meeting of the Midwest Association for Public Opinion Research, Chicago.

Rogers, E. (2002). Information in the next millennium: Captain's log 2001. In C. A. Lin & D. J. Atkin (Eds.), *Communication technology and society: Audience adoption and uses of the new media* (pp. 43–64). Cresskill, NJ: Hampton.

Select Phone Pro CD database, version 2.1. (2002). Omaha, NE: InfoUSA.

Shapiro, E. (1998, June 12). Web lovers love TV, often it's not coming out of the same box. *The Wall Street Journal,* p. B9.

Snider, M. (1997, July 31). As an entertainer, net is still behind TV, reading. *USA Today*, p. 1D.

Stempel, G. H., Hargrove, T., & Bernt, J. P. (2000). Relation of growth of use of the Internet to changes in media use from 1995–1999. *Journalism & Mass Communication Quarterly, 77*, 71–79.

UCLA Center for Communication Policy. (2001, November). *The UCLA Internet report 2001: Surveying the digital future.* Los Angeles: UCLA Regents.

Veronis, Suhler, & Associates. (1998). *Communications industry forecast.* New York: Allyn & Bacon.

Waldfogel, J. (2002, September). *Consumer substitution among media.* Philadelphia: Federal Communications Commission Media Ownership Working Group.

CHAPTER ELEVEN

Online Newspaper Market Size and the Use of World Wide Web Technologies*

Wendy Dibean
Bruce Garrison

Observers have proclaimed the Internet to be the future of communication. Katz (1999), for example, believed that the future of journalism is found on the Internet and that online news would one day become mainstream journalism: "The [World Wide] Web is transforming culture, it is transforming language, transforming information, and we're seeing this in very dramatic and measurable ways, which some liken to the invention of movable type" (pp. 14–15). He noted that the old model of a few people providing information to many is "breaking down" in favor of many providing to many. Rules are being rewritten and the news media are being transformed. The way in which news organizations relate and interact with their audiences is also in transition (Pavlik, 1999).

What does this fundamental shift in communication mean to journalism? How are journalists using these new network tools to reach audiences? In recent years, news media have flocked to the Web. The number of newspapers in the United States offering online editions has grown rapidly. One study reported on-line editions had increased from 745 in July 1996 to 2,059 a year later (Li, 1998). The amount of change that has occurred in online newspapers has been significant. One observable shift has been toward increasing original news reporting by

---

*An earlier version of this chapter was published in the *Newspaper Research Journal* in Spring 2001. The original paper was presented at the Media in Transition Conference at the Massachusetts Institute of Technology, Cambridge, MA, October 8–10, 1999.

online news site staffs. Journalists are less likely to serve as traditional information gatekeepers. Users have larger amounts of information and a wider range of
sources on which to draw (PR Newswire, 1997).

The role of many online newspapers has yet to be defined. In some cases, online editions are little more than electronic versions of the parent newspaper.
Some others are a hybrid of printed newspaper and original content. Some online
news sites contain large amounts of original content created by separate staffs.
Sources of news and information are being widened to meet the needs. At least
one journalist at the Evansville, Indiana, *Courier & Press* argued that online newspapers should think of themselves as full-service independent Web sites. He argued that sites should work with 24-hour deadlines and update content on a frequent and regular basis (Derk, 1999). At the extreme, original content can be an
exclusive investigative report or other reporting not published in the printed editions of the newspaper or anywhere else. Original content may also be a first report of breaking news not yet printed in the traditional newspaper. Of course,
supplementary material that adds to stories in the printed newspaper may also be
considered original content.

A key content issue has been whether newspaper Web sites are considered part
of the print edition or a separate and competing medium (Stone, 1999a, 1999b).
Similar questions about the role of the print news medium arose when newspapers competed against and developed their own radio stations in the 1920s and
again with television stations in the 1950s (Emery & Emery, 1988). Although the
heart of the competition is advertising dollars, news content is also a concern in
the face of any new developing medium (Shaw, 1998). Commercial media influences, such as those by online newspapers, point to a colonization metaphor describing the Internet instead of the commonly described community (Riley,
Keough, Christensen, Meilich, & Pierson, 1998). The ideals of democratic community building on the Internet, they offered, are resisted by online newspapers
as they "stake out" territories by discouraging access to other sites. Peng, Tham,
and Xiaoming (1999) found differing online objectives in online newspapers, but
online newspapers were similar in the goals of seeking additional readers, increasing revenue, and promotion of the print edition (Peng et al., 1999). South
(1999) recently observed that online newspaper staffs often must urge their print
colleagues to think about the needs of online sites. For example, print reporters
and editors do not usually gather audio or video for the print editions, but will assist their online counterparts.

Many newspapers with Web sites have not found the right online model (for
more discussion of online newspaper models, see Chapter 1). Some, including
large publications such as *The Buffalo News, Jackson Clarion-Ledger,* and *Honolulu Advertiser,* did not have Web sites with daily news content as recently as summer 1999 (Dotinga, 1999). The rapidly evolving state of online newspapers can be
characterized by considerable experimentation with content, technologies, and

distribution. Furthermore, the result is frequent changes and often-radical site redesigns. Online newspapers are at an important stage of media convergence. Online newspapers still have many ties to traditional print newspapers, but they also have the potential to utilize many new features from the world of mixed-media digital communication. These included audio, video, animation, and increased user control. The Internet2, when available to the general public and commercial news companies, is expected to have a significant content- and process-changing influence (Phipps, 1999b). Experts have already speculated that gathering and distributing news as well as public consumption will be quite different (Phipps, 1999b).

How do these evolving technologies change news? That question remains unanswered in the literature. This study explores one aspect of the problem by focusing on use of available Web technologies in online news. This study compares use on the basis of newspaper market type and explores whether there are differences between the market types of online newspapers.

The transition to news on the Internet has not been simple. Critics have pointed out that newspapers are not using new technologies to full potential (Outing, 1998). They argue that daily newspapers have not made necessary changes in the way they collect and distribute news (Lasica, 1997b). Some authorities have said that newspapers are following the old model of presenting news every 24 hours instead of providing continuous updates and that they are just creating "shovelware"—the process of taking the content of a print edition and reproducing it on a Web site (Barnhurst, 2002; Cochran, 1995; Marlatt, 1999). Experts have also argued that newspapers are not taking advantage of interactivity, hypertext, and multimedia (Cochran, 1995; Marlatt, 1999). At least one recent study has concluded that U.S. newspapers that publish online editions do not "reinvent themselves" on the Web:

> Instead, the web versions reproduce the substance of their print editions in a way that relates similarly to readers. . . . The results suggest that print publishers use their internet presence as a low-cost place holder that guards their US market position and erects a barrier to the entry of geographical competitors and ideological alternatives in the US news arena. (Barnhurst, 2002, p. 477)

Singer (1998, 1999) suggested four theoretical foundations for the study of online journalism and online journalists. She pointed to gatekeeping theory, diffusion of innovation theory, sociology of news work, and the role of journalism as a cohesive force in a fragmenting society. Other recent new technologies research has focused on uses and gratifications theory as the foundation for study (Leung & Wei, 2000). Analysis of technological devices used for online news delivery is, however, best seen within the diffusion of innovation context (Garrison, 2001; Maier, 2000; Rogers, 1995).

TECHNOLOGIES USED FOR ONLINE NEWS

Research shows increased use of newspaper Web sites. Many users are seeking local news at the sites (Strupp, 1999). Increasing numbers of women are reading
online news (Flagg, 1999). Although audiences that use the Web are growing, a
technology gap has evolved. A recent federal study determined that, although the
Internet has become a major communication force, it has done so at the expense
of some elements of American society. The study concluded that there was a "digital divide" between technology haves and have-nots. Some of the gap is based on
economic levels, but race and geography are also factors (Irving, 1999). Another
study concluded that Internet news audiences were becoming more "ordinary"
in addition to becoming larger. Among its findings were that weather was the
most popular online news attraction in 1999, replacing technology news and information, which had been the top subject 2 years earlier. The report noted that
users were less well educated than 2 years earlier, included more females, and
more users with modest incomes. These demographics indicate changing news
interests. Weather and entertainment news are growing in popularity much
faster than politics and international news (Pew Research Center for the People &
the Press, 1999). Despite the growing interest in online news, many news organizations do not emphasize it nor satisfy demand for it. Web editors admitted that
they are still learning how to use the Web (Strupp, 1999). Because of their nature,
usability of Web sites is a focal point of some research. van Oostendorp and van
Nimwegen (1998) studied scrolling and use of hypertext links for reading and
finding information contained in an online newspaper and concluded that site
designers should "avoid presenting information on deeper hypertextual levels for
which scrolling is necessary."

User Interactivity

Web designers use a handful of interactive tools to enhance their products. These
options include links to other stories, electronic mail contact with journalists,
chat rooms, forums, animations, photographs and biographical information
about reporters and columnists, related coverage, and searchable databases. The
tools also include, of course, multimedia capability, such as providing archived
or live audio and video. Archived news and other information are also available.

According to Outing (1998), "It's a no-brainer that newspapers' archives are
of interest to readers, and a potential revenue stream." Yet, he found that the majority of sites had yet to make their archives available online. He determined that
a number of sites either included no names of staff members or included staff listings but no electronic mail addresses, offering no way for readers to interact with
the staff. He also found a frequent absence of obituaries, birth notices, and other
matters of interest to local readers, especially for small town newspaper Web
sites. Few sites operated online discussion forums (Outing, 1998).

Cochran (1995) noted that the San Jose Mercury Center is one of the best examples of sites using interactivity. It incorporates ways to send electronic mail to groups related to the topic of the article, links to related sites, and connections to sites that offer more information. Cochran (1995) said these features were used so, "if the reader were so inclined, she could have (a) learned about an important issue, (b) gathered additional information not provided by the newspapers, (c) seen what other folks were saying about the proposal, and (d) taken steps to register her position on the issue with lawmakers" (p. 36). Cochran said *The Wall Street Journal*'s personalized version of the newspaper that contained news on just the topics the reader selected was another positive use of available technologies. Massey and Levy (1999) used a five-dimensional conceptualization of interactivity. They looked at complexity of content choice, responsiveness, ease of adding information, facilitation of interpersonal communication, and immediacy. The analysis found a relatively complex choice of content, but the sites did not rate highly on the remaining four dimensions.

Content, Design, Deadlines, and Distribution

Production of an online news site requires more than the effort of one individual, just as traditional newspapers require numerous teams of specialists with a wide range of newsgathering, editing, production, and distribution talents (Stone, 1999a, 1999b). A major characteristic of online news that differentiates it from traditional newspaper news, however, is the nonlinear nature of writing and reporting. Analysis of online news sites has shown that nonlinear storytelling is increasing. Newspaper Web sites use fewer links than broadcast news station Web links but, in general, both types of news sites were increasing in their use of hypertext links. With links and other writing devices, sites can offer users additional depth, background information, graphics, and references to previous coverage (Tremayne, 1999).

Some online authorities feel newspapers should offer more breaking news. Companies like Marimba, PointCast, and Starwave made push news software popular. Multiple deadlines are necessary for newspapers to keep up with other news Web sites. "If you look at newspaper deadlines, that's an artificial deadline based on distribution needs," observed Scott Woelfel, editor-in-chief of CNN Interactive (Lasica, 1997a). "In a way, it's a throwback to the old days when newspapers had three or four editions a day. It will require newsrooms to recruit staff members with an entirely different set of skills," added Valerie Hyman, a professor at the Poynter Institute (Lasica 1997a).

Other critics feel that online news sites often depend too much on wire service content, such as that from Associated Press or Reuters, even though there is no substantial limit to the volume of information that can be provided (Welch, 1999). This is attributed to small budgets, few staff members, and other resource limits. Another criticism of online news is that it often is too fast in passing along information to readers. Some observers feel Web publications are often careless in posting unconfirmed information during breaking stories as well as during other less deadline-intensive circumstances (Lasica, 1997a). When the *Los Angeles Times* first launched its Web site, its goal was to offer the most comprehensive guide to California. It offered calendar events, archived reviews, community databases, and minimal discussion forums and live chat sessions (Outing, 1996a). Users of news Web sites seek local news from local news sites (Phipps, 1999a). Local news content (72%) was more valued than weather information (40%), national news (39%), and classified advertising (38%), among other types of content. Even users (58%) of newspaper Web sites with circulation over 250,000 sought local news. For newspapers with less than 250,000 circulation, the figure jumped (83%).

Individuals who direct or manage newspaper Web sites feel content should drive the site's design, not technology or appearance (Lowrey, 1999). Traditional print design concerns and principles apply to the Web, but there are differences. Many of these involve use of technologies, such as links or multimedia features, available to Web designers but not to print designers. One recent study focused on online newspapers' errors and corrections policies, noting that news organizations did not use the technologies of the Web, such as archiving and hyperlinking, to do a more effective job to influence the flow of accurate information to the public (Nadarajan & Ang, 1999).

Skills and High-Tech Resources

The nature of the Web demands technical skills to maximize its communication potential. Neuberger, Tonnemacher, Biebl, and Duck (1998) found that about half of the newspapers' staff members they studied had journalistic duties, but the authors stated that technical responsibilities were "growing" and that editorial decisions were often left to print editors. Stepp (1996) observed that distribution of online news requires different, additional skills to those of traditional journalists. Most of those skills involved using computers and associated software, but Stepp observed that there must also be an ability to look at the profession in an innovative manner. Expertise and versatility were characteristic of these journalists who are able to work in a wide spectrum of news media and use a broad base of technologies.

Newspapers are learning to "don't go it alone" on the Internet (Outing, 1996b). Outing (1996b) stated, "Newspaper companies generally do not have all the skills and resources necessary to succeed in new media." Some examples of online newspapers that have teamed with other groups include *The Washington Post*, which teamed with *Newsweek* and ABC News to operate the ElectionLine site. Boston.com is an effort of all competing New England media, including *The Boston Globe* (Outing, 1996b). Many of the resources available for online news distribution involve interactivity. For many years prior to widespread development and use of the Web, bulletin boards provided a virtual space for community discussion and distribution of information. One popular form, used for a number of years through commercial online services such as America Online (AOL), is the chat room. Perlman (1999) observed that online newspapers do not use chat rooms or bulletin boards. The potential is there, Perlman noted, citing the increased volume of chat room use that occurred on AOL immediately after the Columbine school shootings in Spring 1999.

Electronic Commerce

Online news sites are moving into the realm of electronic commerce (Noack, 1999). One study found that 65% of online newspaper users were involved in some type of electronic commerce. Although it was not as popular in 1999–2000 as electronic mail, reading newspapers online, and searching for information, online newspaper users are also involved in online shopping and making purchases (Noack, 1999). BarnesandNoble.com started an "affiliate network" that created cobranded marketing and book-selling opportunities. Newspapers involved in the affiliate program included the *Chicago Tribune,* USA Today Online, and LATimes.com. Other newspapers, such as the Hartford Courant Online, have launched online auctions. The SunOne Web site of the *Gainesville Sun* launched a sports boutique. Tampa Bay Online offers CD-ROMs. The Star Tribune Online has developed a project called Gift Generator to connect buyers and sellers (PR Newswire, 1997).

Astor (1996) discussed the quantity and revenues of using syndicated materials on newspaper sites. Newspapers have had difficulty publishing their syndicated and supplemental news service material on their Web sites for legal and other reasons. The *Minneapolis Star Tribune's* online service was one of the first online newspapers to offer syndicated general-interest columns. However, because newspapers have started to generate more revenue, the extra cost of using syndicated materials has become less of a problem.

ONLINE NEWSPAPER MARKET MODELS

Traditional newspaper markets have been divided into categories based on circulation size—such as small, medium, and large—as shown in Table 11.1. Outing (1998) looked at small and medium-size newspaper Web sites, although he did not directly define these classifications. Garrison (1998) defined large newspapers as those with a circulation larger than 50,000 and small newspapers as those with a circulation smaller than 50,000. Chyi and Sylvie (1999) noted differences in the print newspaper's traditional local focus and the boundary transcending capacity of the Internet. They offered an "umbrella" model of online newspaper economic markets that focused on the ability of online news to seek markets at a variety of different levels. Their model included a five-layer approach that was

TABLE 11.1
Online Markets

Model	Description	Examples
National or international	Coverage focuses on national and international news and serves an international audience	*USA Today* *Washington Post* *New York Times*
Regional	Coverage centers on a large geographic region, such as a metropolitan area, with emphasis on local and regional news. Coverage includes substantial national and international news.	*Chicago Tribune* *Miami Herald*/Miami.com *Boston Globe*/Boston.com *Atlanta Journal-Constitution*/ Access Atlanta *Houston Chronicle* *Arizona Republic* *Indianapolis Star/News* *Minneapolis Star Tribune* *Newark Star-Ledger*/ New Jersey Online
Local or community	Serves small towns, communities, or counties usually defined by smallest geographic area. Content is centered on local area news, but other levels also.	Charlotte (FL) *Herald-Sun* Fort Myers (FL) *News-Press* Key West (FL) *Citizen* Weekly newspapers Regional city magazines
Specialized or niche	Coverage devoted to highly specialized or unique subjects and their audiences.	*Wall Street Journal* (business) *Florida Today* (space program) *Financial Times* (finance) Salon.com Subscription newsletters

Note. Data from Chyi & Sylvie (1999), Shaw (1998), "Missed What the Top Analysts," (2000), Lasica (2001), Grimes (2002).

described as community, metro, regional, national, and international. This differs, they noted, from the conventional community, metro, and national levels most often used to describe print newspapers. Chyi and Sylvie (1999) concluded that geography is not relevant for online newspapers, but that online news media do have market boundaries. They also concluded that newspapers must cease "thinking 'local' when it comes to online markets," especially for advertising. They concluded that "the larger the print market, the larger the online product's long distance market" (p. 31).

The goal of this study was to determine how different types of United States daily newspapers use the Web. More specifically, this study compared the approaches of three different market types of online newspapers:

1. Are United States daily newspapers using technologies available for development of World Wide Web sites? If so, to what extent?
2. How do local, regional, and national online newspapers vary in their use of the technological features commonly found in the design of a Web site?

3. How much change in these technology use patterns has occurred within the past year?

METHODS

Three major market types were studied, a modification of the Chyi and Sylvie (1999) approach. Market types were chosen in relation to the audience they cater to, which, in some ways, is based on circulation and market served. *USA Today* and *The New York Times* were selected as the national publications. *The Boston Globe* and *The Orlando Sentinel* were the regional newspapers chosen. *The Naples Daily News*, in Naples, Florida, and *The Macon Telegraph*, in Macon, Georgia, were the local publications used. These six newspapers were chosen because they fit the market types analyzed and because of their journalistic reputations for quality. Each had maintained Web sites for several years. Many other newspapers fit into the three market types and could have been used, but for the needs of this study, only two newspapers for each category were selected.

A longitudinal design was used to determine change in technology use. Eleven consecutive days (November 5–15, 1998) of home pages and top news story pages of the six electronic newspapers were content analyzed for the Time 1 content analysis. A second set of 11 days (July 12–22, 1999) was also studied for the Time 2 content analysis. Li (1998) used the 11-day time frame of analysis, which permitted a complete weekly cycle of news to be covered. These dates were selected because it was believed that there were no significant scheduled news events that could skew routine coverage practices.

The home page was defined as the initial page of the newspaper's Web site. Top news story page was defined as the story link on the home page that is given the most prominence on the page, either by position, size of type, or use of art. The top news story link was found on the home page as the first news story link that also had a large type size (point size of 14 or higher as an image or font size of 4 or higher in HTML), was accompanied by art (photograph or graph), or both. For analysis purposes, the data collected from each of these pages were combined for a total number of use occurrences per day, per site. The units of analysis were the pages of the Web site.

The 15 technology variables included forums, chat rooms, related information for stories, video, audio, Flash, other plug-in-based technologies, Java applets, other language use outside of the basic HTML 4.0 standard, electronic mail, polls with instantaneous results, search tools, consumer services (electronic commerce functions including searchable classifieds, home finders, job finders, and merchandise sales), sign-up for electronic delivery of a personalized newspaper and instantaneous updates of information (including stocks, sports scores, and weather) that are located on the home page and top news article page (see Appendix), and links to these uses of the new technology. Each instance of these features, as well as links to one of the features, was counted on both the home page and the top news article page by two trained coders. Two coders independently coded the same sample of content to establish reliability. The intercoder reliability coefficient was 0.96 for the first analysis and 0.99 for the second analysis, using $R = (2(C_{12}))/(C_1 + C_2)$ (Budd, Thorp, & Donohew, 1967; Riffe, Lacy, & Fico, 1998).

FINDINGS

To what extent are United States daily newspapers using technologies available for development of Web sites? Data in Table 11.2 show that a majority of pages had forums by summer 1999 (31.9% in 1998 and 53.0% in 1999), related information (53% in 1998 and 65.9% in 1999), electronic mail (59.8% in 1998 and 69.7% in 1999), site searches (79.5% in 1998 and 88.6% in 1999), and consumer services (95.5% in 1998 and broken up in 1999 with 100% use of consumer services and 96.9% of electronic commerce). Very little use of chat rooms (2.3% in 1998 and 7.6% in 1999), other languages (6.1% in 1998 and 10.63% in 1999), polls with instantaneous updates (9.1% in 1998 and 25% in 1999), and sign-up for personal delivery (2.3% in 1998 and 25% in 1999) was found. No instances of other plug-in-based technologies were found on any of the sites studied. Flash was not found in 1998, but appeared on a small percentage of pages (0.8%) in 1999. Java applets saw little use in 1998 (15.2%), but dropped to no use in 1999. This was the only decline found among the 15 technology variables. Instantaneous updates (25.8% in 1998 and 37.9% in 1999), audio (12.1% in 1998 and 27.3% in 1999), and video (10.6% in 1998 and 30.3% in 1999) were used on certain sites, but had not taken hold on the majority of newspaper sites.

A breakdown of the technologies used by each newspaper in November 1998 shows dominance by the two regional newspapers. *The Orlando Sentinel* had more occurrences per day in links to related information, audio, video and polls with instantaneous results. *The Boston Globe* had the most occurrences of search engines, consumer services, sign-up for personal delivery, and instantaneous updates. *The Naples Daily News* had the most occurrences of chat rooms and electronic mail, *The Macon Telegraph* had the most occurrences of Java applets, and *The New York Times* had the most occurrences of forums, but none led by a very large margin, as shown in Table 11.3.

Nearly a year later, the regional dominance still held. *The Orlando Sentinel* had more occurrences per day in forums, audio, video, other language use, and polls with instantaneous results. *The Boston Globe* had the most occurrences of links to related information, chat rooms, and electronic mail. Local newspapers' domination disappeared in July. National newspapers grew in dominance in some areas. *USA Today* had the most occurrences of Flash, search engines, and consumer services. *The New York Times* had more occurrences per day of sign-up for personal delivery and instantaneous updates.

TABLE 11.2
Site Pages With at Least One Instance of Technology

Technology	November 1998	July 1999
Forums	31.9%	53.0%
Chat rooms	2.3	7.6
Related information	53.0	65.9
Video	10.6	30.3
Audio	12.1	27.3
Flash	0.0	0.8
Plug-in	0.0	0.0
Java applets	15.2	0.0
Other languages	6.1	10.6
Electronic mail	59.8	69.7
Polls with instantaneous results	9.1	13.6
Search	79.5	88.6
Consumer services	95.5	100.0
Electronic commerce	—	96.9
Sign-up for personal delivery	2.3	25.0
Instantaneous updates	25.8	37.9

Note. $n = 132$ pages.

How do the three market types vary in their use of the technological features commonly found in the design of a Web site? Data show that the market types vary greatly in the technologies they offer readers. National online newspapers showed a considerably higher adaptation of forums in 1998. Local online newspapers showed a notably higher adaptation of Java applets and electronic mail use in 1998. Regional online newspapers showed a remarkably higher adaptation of polls with instantaneous updates, related information, video, audio, polls, search, consumer services, and instantaneous updates in 1998, as shown in Table 11.4. Scheffé post hoc analyses for 1998 showed most significant differences were between regional–local (10) and national–regional (7) market newspapers, but not as often for national–local (4) newspapers.

Use evened out less than a year later. National online newspapers showed the highest adoption of search engines, sign-up for personal delivery, and instantaneous updates. Regional online newspapers showed the highest adoption of forums, chat rooms, other language use, and polls with instantaneous updates. Local online newspapers showed the highest adoption of links to related information, audio, video, and electronic mail. However, none of these were overwhelming. Scheffé post hoc analyses for 1998 showed many of the differences the most significant differences between regional and local market newspapers (nine) and national–regional (six), but not as many for national–local markets (four).

In less than a year, there was growth in almost all areas. July 1999 data show significantly higher occurrences per day in forums, chat rooms, links to related

TABLE 11.3
Occurrences of Web Technologies

	Macon		Naples		Boston		Orlando		NYT		USAT	
	T1	T2	T1	T2	T1	T2	T1	T2	T1	T2	T1	T2
Forum	1.82	.91	.00	.00	.00	.32	.09	**3.45**	**3.73**	1.82	.00	.27
Chat rooms	.00	.00	**.18**	.00	.00	**.45**	.00	.14	.09	.00	.00	.00
Related information	7.18	2.14	3.27	6.64	8.82	**10.09**	**15.36**	6.55	1.91	6.77	3.82	2.18
Audio	.00	.00	.00	.00	.00	2.50	**8.64**	**2.55**	.55	.23	.00	.45
Video	.27	.00	.00	.45	.73	.09	**3.55**	**2.23**	.09	.45	.00	.50
Flash	.00	.00	.00	.00	.00	.00	.00	.00	.00	.00	.00	**.05**
Plug-in	.00	.00	.00	.00	.00	.00	.00	.00	.00	.00	.00	.00
Java applet	**1.82**	.00	.00	.00	.00	.00	.00	.00	.00	.00	.00	.00
Other language	.00	.09	.27	.00	.18	.09	.09	**.41**	.00	.00	.27	.05
E-mail	3.45	1.77	**4.64**	3.18	.64	**4.55**	1.55	1.18	.55	.50	1.09	1.05
Instant poll	.00	.09	.00	.00	.00	.00	**1.00**	**.50**	.00	.00	.09	.23
Search	.73	1.00	1.64	2.05	**9.27**	1.68	2.73	1.05	2.91	1.64	5.27	**4.50**
Consumer services	26.27	21.41	5.55	7.86	**43.82**	21.27	10.09	20.41	14.00	6.77	16.27	**35.86**
Sign-up delivery	.00	.00	.00	.00	**.18**	.05	.00	.23	.09	**1.00**	.00	.32
Instant updates	.00	.00	.55	.23	**5.27**	1.18	.00	.73	1.91	**1.41**	.91	.77

Note. $n = 11$ days. T1 (Time 1) was November 1998; T2 (Time 2) was July 1999. Boldface indicates significant means at $p \leq 0.05$.

TABLE 11.4
Occurrences of Technologies Used by Market Type

Technology	November 1998					July 1999				
	Natl.	*Regl.*	*Local*	*F*	*Sig.*	*Natl.*	*Regl.*	*Local*	*F*	*Sig.*
Forums	**.93**	.02	.48	16.12	.00[abc]	1.05	**1.89**	.45	8.98	.00[ac]
Chat rooms	.02	.00	.05	1.02	.37	.00	**.30**	.00	9.51	.00[ac]
Related information	1.48	6.16	2.66	6.18	.00[ac]	4.48	8.32	**9.03**	4.09	.02[c]
Video	.02	**1.07**	.07	8.38	.00[ac]	.34	**2.52**	.00	25.15	.00[ac]
Audio	.14	**2.16**	.00	5.80	.00[ac]	.48	**1.16**	.23	5.10	.01[c]
Flash	.00	.00	.00	—	—	.02	.00	.00	1.00	.37
Plug-in	.00	.00	.00	—	—	.00	.00	.00	—	—
Java applet	.00	.00	.45	32.68	.00[bc]	.00	.00	.00	—	—
Other language	.07	.07	.07	0.00	1.00	.02	**.25**	.05	6.77	.00[ac]
Electronic mail	.43	.57	**2.02**	64.37	.00[bc]	.77	.61	**2.48**	85.16	.00[bc]
Instant polls	.02	**.25**	0.00	11.76	.00[ac]	.11	**.25**	.05	4.22	.02[c]
Search	2.05	**3.00**	.59	30.21	.00[abc]	**3.07**	1.36	1.52	21.69	.00[ab]
Consumer services	7.34	**13.48**	8.05	7.08	.00[ac]	21.32	20.84	14.64	2.31	.10
Sign-up delivery	.02	.05	.00	1.02	.37	**.66**	.14	.00	36.03	.00[ab]
Instant updates	.70	**1.32**	.14	5.90	.00[c]	**1.09**	.95	.11	13.04	.00[bc]

Note. $n = 11$ days. Boldface indicates significant means at $p \leq 0.05$.
[a]National–regional difference significant at 0.05 level. [b]National–local difference significant at 0.05 level. [c]Regional–local difference significant at 0.05 level.

information, video, electronic mail, polls with instantaneous updates, consumer services, and sign-up for personal delivery. The use of Java applets dropped to nothing in July 1999, as shown in Table 11.5. National online newspapers showed significant growth from November to July in most areas, including forums, links to related information, video, audio, electronic mail, search engines, consumer services, sign-up for personal delivery, and instantaneous updates, as indicated in Table 11.6. Regional online newspapers showed a decline in the use of search engines and a growth in forums, video, other language use, and consumer services. Local online newspapers showed a decline in the use of Java applets and a growth in audio, electronic mail, search engines, and consumer services.

CONCLUSION

Technological innovations change routines and processes. Development of the technology of the Internet and World Wide Web in itself may become the most significant change in world communication in a half-century or longer. It continues to create change in all aspects of life. When technology is so rapidly evolving as the devices and processes of communicating on the Internet have been during this decade, businesses and institutions are required to redefine old rules and create new ones (Ebo, 1998).

TABLE 11.5

Occurrences of Technologies Used

Technology	November 1998	July 1999	t-value	p (Two-Tailed)
Forums	.48	**1.13**	−4.372	.00
Chat rooms	.02	**.09**	−2.067	.04
Related information	3.42	**5.73**	−2.727	.01
Video	.39	**.95**	−2.819	.01
Audio	.77	.62	.531	.60
Flash	.00	**.08**	−1.000	.32
Plug-in	.00	.00	—	—
Java applet	**.14**	.00	4.693	.00
Other language	.07	.11	−.962	.34
Electronic mail	1.01	**1.29**	−3.570	.00
Instant polls	.09	**.14**	−2.150	.03
Search	1.88	**1.98**	−.636	.53
Consumer services	9.62	**18.93**	−7.200	.00
Sign-up delivery	.02	**.27**	−5.614	.00
Instant updates	.72	.72	0.00	1.00

Note. n = 11 days. Boldface indicates significant means at p ≤ 0.05.

TABLE 11.6

Occurrences of Technologies Used by Market Type

Technology	November 1998 National	July 1999 National	t	df	p
Forums	.93	1.05	−1.949	43	.058
Chat rooms	**.02**	.00	1.000	42	.323
Related information	1.48	**4.48**	−3.281	43	.002
Video	.02	**.34**	−2.097	43	.042
Audio	.14	**.48**	−2.189	43	.034
Flash	.00	**.02**	−1.000	43	.323
Plug-in	.00	.00	—	—	—
Java applet	.00	.00	—	—	—
Other language	**.07**	.02	0.813	43	.420
Electronic mail	.43	**.77**	−4.716	43	.000
Instant polls	.02	.11	−1.666	43	.103
Search	2.05	**3.07**	−6.000	43	.000
Consumer services	7.34	**21.32**	−4.279	43	.000
Sign-up delivery	.02	**.66**	−7.931	43	.000
Instant updates	.70	**1.09**	−4.766	43	.000

(Continued)

TABLE 11.6
(Continued)

Technology	Regional	Regional	t	df	p
Forums	.02	**1.89**	−4.905	43	.000
Chat rooms	.00	**.30**	−3.102	43	.003
Related information	6.16	**8.32**	−1.043	43	.303
Video	1.07	**2.52**	−2.594	43	.013
Audio	**2.16**	1.16	1.273	43	.210
Flash	.00	.00	—	—	—
Plug-in	.00	.00	—	—	—
Java applet	.00	.00	—	—	—
Other language	.07	**.25**	−2.074	43	.044
Electronic mail	.57	.61	−0.340	43	.736
Instant polls	.25	.25	—	—	—
Search	**3.00**	1.36	5.808	43	.000
Consumer services	13.48	**20.84**	−3.868	43	.000
Sign-up delivery	.05	.14	−1.274	43	.210
Instant updates	1.32	.95	1.266	43	.212

Technology	Local	Local	t	df	p
Forums	.48	.45	0.374	43	.710
Chat rooms	.05	.00	1.431	43	.160
Related information	2.66	**9.03**	−1.490	43	.143
Video	.07	**2.98**	1.000	43	.323
Audio	.00	**2.16**	−3.556	43	.001
Flash	.00	.00	—	—	—
Plug-in	.00	.00	—	—	—
Java applet	.45	.00	5.717	43	.000
Other language	.07	.05	0.443	43	.660
Electronic mail	2.02	**2.48**	−2.576	43	.014
Instant polls	.00	.05	−1.431	43	.160
Search	.59	**1.52**	−4.687	43	.000
Consumer services	8.05	**14.64**	−14.097	43	.000
Sign-up delivery	.00	.00	—	—	—
Instant updates	.14	.11	0.227	43	.822

Note. $n = 44$ (11 days, two newspapers, two pages). Boldface indicates significant means at $p \leq 0.05$.

The Internet has been considered by some social scientists to be an equalizer. It has the potential to bring communication to equal terms for social and economic groups as well as for businesses and industries. In one way, this study analyzed whether the Internet was a technology equalizer for newspapers that have used the World Wide Web to extend their news distribution reach and contact with audiences. Should small newspapers be different from large ones? Their financial, human, and other resources certainly vary, but this difference has not been found to be the case in terms of social classes using the Internet (Wolf,

1998). There are differences in how newspapers are using the Web and their use of technologies to distribute information to audiences. This study has determined some of the differences.

The most prominent technology used by all three categories of online newspaper was consumer services. This is a potentially interactive component that any person with browser software and online service can utilize. Consumer services usually allow a person to insert a value of something that is desired and it returns what is available in the database. It can be used for automobile sales, home rentals and sales, dating services, and many other classified-related services. The area for the greatest growth, perhaps one of the most significant findings, is electronic commerce. Newspapers are using this tool to increase interaction with site visitors for a variety of purposes and growth of use is occurring at all three levels of service.

The two technologies that were not used or had very limited use were both plug-in-based technologies. These technologies require readers to have extra software on their computers to utilize the technologies. The disappearance of the use of the Java applet can possibly be explained by the inability of the computer industry to standardize this technology in browsers. Java applets cause some readers problems (including computer crashes), so newspapers likely discontinued use as to not upset readers.

Since their creation, online newspapers have experienced change. For example, The Orlando Sentinel has added new services that offer readers e-mail. Some of the newer services were still in testing mode on some sites in late 1998, and so, although they are offered, they may not have shown up very prominently. With time, it is expected that more of the technologies will appear with more prominence on the sites. Because this is still a very new medium and the technology is still being developed, changes occur every day. With this growth, it will be interesting to see how the popularity of online newspapers will grow along with it. The regional newspapers, with a large base of technological use, will steadily grow in popularity. Unless national and local online newspapers catch up in the use of technologies, regional newspapers will take their readership.

It is not probable that any online newspapers will take up use of plug-in-based technologies, such as Flash and Shockwave, unless they are made easier for the consumer. To do this, browser software must be standardized. Integration of these technologies into browsers in the future, for instance, would be one way to increase use. Further study should be conducted to measure this change. Also, other online newspapers should be studied to extend the test of differences in the market types.

National sites may have been slow to get into the technologies of the Web, but they seem to be making up for it. The most change occurred within the national sites. Of the 15 categories of technology, more than half (8) increased in a statistically significant manner. In comparison, regional sites experienced 5 statistically significant technology category increases and 1 statistically significant decrease (search tools). For local sites, there was less change. Local sites experienced only 4 statistically significant increases in technology use categories and one significant decline (Java applets). There are numerous reasons for this—such as increased talent on staff for production, budget increases, shifts in management priorities, changing perceptions of audiences and their needs—but the data do not point to any specific one.

The study revealed that the most widely used technology categories must be studied beyond the limits of this project. It appears one approach would be to further divide categories such as consumer services, electronic mail, and related information into subdivisions. This was done, in part, when electronic commerce was split from consumer services for the second stage of this study and suggests considerable growth in use of electronic commerce. There are also different applications of electronic mail and use of related information devices such as pop-up boxes, for example, that require further investigation. As new technologies are developed, these will also require study for understanding of their contributions to the uses and effects of online news.

REFERENCES

Astor, D. (1996). Syndicated features on the Web: Quantity and revenues? *Editor & Publisher*. Retrieved December 14, 1998, from http://www.mediainfo.com/@@WvKWuhQA0QgdEwAA/plweb-cgi/fastweb?getdoc+archives+Interactive+1174+57++electronic%20newspapers

Barnhurst, K. G. (2002). News geography & monopoly: The form of reports on US newspaper Internet sites. *Journalism Studies, 3*, 477–489.

Budd, R. W., Thorp, R. K., & Donohew, L. (1967). *Content analysis of communications*. New York: Macmillan.

Chyi, H. I., & Sylvie, G. (1999, August). *Opening the umbrella: An economic analysis of online newspaper geography*. Paper presented to the Media Management and Economics Division, Association for Education in Journalism and Mass Communication, New Orleans, LA.

Cochran, W. (1995, May). Searching for right mixture: On-line newspapers seek own identities to compete with ink-stained brethren. *Quill*, p. 36.

Derk, J. (1999, July 3). A plea for new thinking: Let's think of ourselves as Web sites, not online newspapers. *Editor & Publisher, 132*(27), p. 46.

Dotinga, R. (1999, July 3). The great pretenders. *Editor & Publisher, 132*(27), pp. 18–22.

Ebo, B. (1998). Internet or outernet? In B. Ebo (Ed.), *Cyberghetto or cybertopia? Race, class, and gender on the Internet* (pp. 1–12). Westport, CT: Praeger.

Emery, M., & Emery, E. (1988). *The press in America* (6th ed.). Englewood Cliffs, NJ: Prentice-Hall.

Flagg, J. L. (1999, July 3). Women joining men in droves on the Web. *Editor & Publisher, 132*(27), pp. 27–28.

Garrison, B. (1998, August). *Newspaper size as a factor in use of computer-assisted reporting*. Paper presented to the Communication Technology and Policy Division of the Association for Education in Journalism and Mass Communication, Baltimore.

Garrison, B. (2001). Computer-assisted reporting near complete adoption. *Newspaper Research Journal, 22*(1), 65–79.

Grimes, C. (2002, February 6). Premium payments may boost Web revenues. *Financial Times* (London), p. 3.

Irving, L. (1999). *Falling through the Net: Defining the digital divide: Report on the telecommunications and information technology gap in America.* Washington, DC: National Telecommunications and Information Administration, U.S. Department of Commerce.

Katz, J. (1999, Spring–Summer). The future is the Net. *Media Studies Journal, 13*(2), 14–15.

Lasica, J. D. (1997a, October). Get it fast, but get it right. *American Journalism Review NewsLink, 19*(8) [Online]. Retrieved December 14, 1998, from http://www.newslink.org/ajrjd22.html

Lasica, J. D. (1997b, June). Time to freshen up online newspapers. *American Journalism Review NewsLink, 19*(5) [Online]. Retrieved December 12, 1998, from http://www.newslink.org/ajrlasica697.html

Lasica, J. D. (2001, September 20). A scorecard for Net news ethics: Despite a lapse related to the terrorist attack, online media deserve high marks. *Online Journalism Review.* Retrieved January 7, 2002, from http://ojr.usc.edu/content/story.cfm?request=643

Leung, L., & Wei, R. (2000). More than just talk on the move: Uses and gratifications of the cellular phone. *Journalism & Mass Communication Quarterly, 77,* 308–320.

Li, X. (1998). Web page design and graphic use of three U.S. newspapers. *Journalism & Mass Communication Quarterly, 75,* 353–365.

Lowrey, W. (1999, March). *Visual journalism online: Exploring the current wisdom on Internet news design.* Paper presented to the Southeast Colloquium, Association for Education in Journalism and Mass Communication, Lexington, KY.

Maier, S. R. (2000). Digital diffusion in newsrooms: The uneven advance of computer-assisted reporting. *Newspaper Research Journal, 21*(2), 95–110.

Marlatt, A. (1999). Advice to newspapers: Stop the shoveling: Publishing on the Web is no simple cut-and-paste affair. *Internet World Online.* Retrieved July 15, 1999, from http://www.iw.com/print/ current/content/19990715-shoveling.html

Massey, B. L., & Levy, M. R. (1999). Interactivity, online journalism, and English-language Web newspapers in Asia. *Journalism & Mass Communication Quarterly, 20,* 138–151.

"Missed what the top analysts are saying about our digital future? Catch up here." (2000, February 21). *The Guardian* (London), p. 62.

Nadarajan, B., & Ang, P. (1999, August). *Credibility and journalism on the Internet: How online newspapers handle errors and corrections.* Paper presented to the Communication Technology and Policy Division, Association for Education in Journalism and Mass Communication, New Orleans, LA.

Neuberger, C., Tonnemacher, J., Biebl, M., & Duck, A. (1998). Online—The future of newspapers? Germany's dailies on the World Wide Web. *Journal of Computer-Mediated Communication, 4*(1). Retrieved November 17, 2003, from http://www.ascusc.org/jcmc/vol4/issue1/-neuberger.html

Noack, D. (1999, July 10). eBuy: Users of newspaper Web sites open their cyberwallets. *Editor & Publisher, 132*(28), pp. 18–21.

Outing, S. (1996a). L.A. Times launches online . . . again. *E&P Interactive.* Retrieved April 8, 1999, from http://www.mediainfo.com/@@47ILYBQA0ggdEwAA/plweb-cgi/fastweb?getdoc+archives+ Interactive+254+153++electronic%20newspapers

Outing, S. (1996b). Newspapers on the Internet: Lessons they are learning. *E&P Interactive.* Retrieved March 26, 1999, from http://www.mediainfo.com/@@8wj1KxUATxsdEwAA/plweb-cgi/fastweb? getdoc+archives+Interactive+245+155++electronic%20newspapers

Outing, S. (1998). Too many newspaper Web sites get poor grades. *E&P Interactive.* Retrieved February 2, 1999, from http://www.mediainfo.com/@@CD08TBUAThsdEwAA/plweb-cgi/fastweb? getdoc+archives+Interactive+417+96++electronic%20newspapers

Pavlik, J. (1999). New media and the news: Implications for the future of journalism. *New Media & Society, 1*(1), 54–59.

Peng, F. Y., Tham, N. I., & Xiaoming, H. (1999). Trends in online newspapers: A look at the US Web. *Newspaper Research Journal, 20*(2), 52–63.

Perlman, J. A. (1999). Print sites still wary of chatting it up. *Online Journalism Review.* Retrieved May 6, 1999, from http://ojr.usc.edu/sections/features/99_stories/stories_discussion_050699.htm

Pew Research Center for the People & the Press. (1999). The Internet news audience goes ordinary: Online newcomers more middle-brow, less work-oriented. Retrieved January 14, 1999, from http://www.people-press.org/tech98sum.htm

Phipps, J. L. (1999a, July 3). Location is everything on newspaper Web sites. *Editor & Publisher, 132*(27), pp. 23–26.

Phipps, J. L. (1999b, July 3). Online journalism: Superfast Internet access will change reporting and broadcasting. *Editor & Publisher, 132*(27), pp. 28–34.

PR Newswire. (1997, July 11). New Java-powered crossword gives online newspapers a truly interactive puzzle.

Riffe, D., Lacy, S., & Fico, F. G. (1998). *Analyzing media messages: Using quantitative content analysis in research.* Mahwah, NJ: Lawrence Erlbaum Associates.

Riley, P., Keough, C. M., Christensen, T., Meilich, O., & Pierson, J. (1998). Community or colony: The case of online newspapers and the Web. *Journal of Computer-Mediated Communication, 4*(1). Retrieved May 24, 2003, from http://www.ascusc.org/jcmc/vol4/issue1/keough.html

Rogers, E. M. (1995). *Diffusion of innovations* (4th ed.). New York: The Free Press.

Shaw, D. (1998). Can newspapers find their niche in the Internet age? In K. Wickham (Ed.), *Perspectives: Online journalism* (pp. 35–41). Boulder, CO: CourseWise.

Singer, J. B. (1998). Online journalists: Foundations for research into their changing roles. *Journal of Computer-Mediated Communication, 4*(1). Retrieved May 24, 2003, from http://www.ascusc.org/jcmc/vol4/issue1/singer.html

Singer, J. B. (1999, August). *The metro wide Web: How newspapers' gatekeeping role is changing online.* Paper presented to the Newspaper Division, Association for Education in Journalism and Mass Communication, New Orleans, LA.

South, J. (1999). Web staffs urge the print side to think ahead. *Online Journalism Review.* Retrieved June 11, 1999, from http://ojr.usc.edu/sections/features/99_stories/-stories_extras_061199.htm

Stepp, C. S. (1996). The new journalist: The on-line era demands added skills and innovative ways of looking at the profession. *American Journalism Review, 18*(3). Retrieved June 12, 1999, from http://ajr.newslink.org/ajrstep1.html

Stone, M. L. (1999a, July 3). Look who's talking. *Editor & Publisher, 132*(27), p. 16.

Stone, M. L. (1999b, July). Print to Web: It takes teamwork. *mediainfo.com*, pp. 8–14.

Strupp, J. (1999, July 3). Welcomed visitors. *Editor & Publisher, 132*(27), pp. 22–27.

Tremayne, M. (1999, May). *Use of nonlinear storytelling on news Web sites.* Paper presented to the Communication and Technology Division, International Communication Association, San Francisco.

van Oostendorp, H., & van Nimwegen, C. (1998). Locating information in an online newspaper. *Journal of Computer-Mediated Communication, 4*(1). Retrieved May 24, 2003, from http://www.ascusc.org/jcmc/vol4/issue1/oostendorp.html

Welch, M. (1999). Is reliance on the AP draining the life from online news. *Online Journalism Review.* Retrieved May 20, 1999, from http://ojr.usc.edu/sections/features/99_stories/-stories_ap 052099.htm

Wolf, A. (1998). Exposing the great equalizer: Demythologizing Internet equity. In B. Ebo (Ed.), *Cyberghetto or cybertopia? Race, class, and gender on the Internet* (pp. 15–32). Westport, CT: Praeger.

APPENDIX

1. *Forums* are areas on Web pages that allow posting of continuous discussions by readers about any topic.

2. *Chat rooms* are areas on Web pages that allow real-time discussions by readers.

3. *Related information for stories* is links or pullouts of information from other Web sources.

4. *Video* on a Web page is a moving image in the movie format. This does not include animated gifs. Video is usually found in the RealVideo or QuickTime format.

5. *Audio* is any sound that loads on from a Web page. This includes RealAudio.

6. *Flash* is a plug-in-based product that allows for moving graphics and interactivity. Flash can be recognized because it loads the Flash plug-in before the images load.

7. *Other plug-in-based technologies* include Shockwave, QuickTime, IPIX, or any other technology that loads a plug-in before loading the image or information.

8. *Java applets* are scripts added to a Web page to add extra functionality and interactivity. It is usually spotted when the browser prompts "Loading Java" on the status bar. Java applets can be image or text based.

9. *Other language use outside of the basic HTML 4.0 standard* includes the use of such languages as JavaScript, Perl, and C. The most common uses of other languages are the image mouse-overs and scrolling text on the status bar. These are not easily spotted due to the variety of functions. The best way to pick out another language is by viewing the source of the page and searching for the .pl or .c file extensions.

10. *Electronic mail* is any link that allows users to send electronic mail to anyone, including the reporters, editors, and people included in a story.

11. *Polls with instantaneous results* are a spot on a Web page that allows the reader to answer a question and pushes on the next page the results, including all participants up to and including the user.

12. *Search tool* is the ability to enter keywords to find articles or other information on the Web site.

13. *Consumer services* include searchable classifieds, home finders, job finders, merchandise sales, and any other service that makes it easier for the reader to find things apart from news stories and information. This category also included electronic commerce, which allows users to purchase goods or services on the newspaper's Web pages.

14. *Sign-up for electronic delivery of a personalized newspaper* is a spot that allows the reader to enter her or his e-mail address to receive a version of the day's news in his or her e-mail inbox.

15. *Instantaneous updates of information* are information found on a page that is loaded current with each reload. This usually includes stocks, sports scores, and weather updates.

PART THREE

ONLINE NEWS POSTERS

CHAPTER TWELVE

What They Post: Arabic-Language Message Boards After the September 11 Attacks

Rasha A. Abdulla

In the aftermath of the attacks of September 11, 2001 on the United States, the American media tried to convey Arab and Muslim governments' and peoples' re-actions. Although all Arab[1] governments, with the exception of Iraq, condemned the attacks and offered their condolences to the United States, some stories in the news media portrayed a sense of satisfaction, even justice, in some Arab (particu-larly Palestinian) streets. While CNN aired footage of West Bank Palestinians cel-ebrating the attacks, Chomsky (2001) suggested that lack of context and informa-tion in Western media about the Arab world could cause misunderstanding among individuals who do not have a sense of the bigger picture. What is the big-ger picture? How accurate were the media portrayals? To what extent were those pictures a reflection of Arab sentiment?

These questions emphasize the need to know the arguments that were taking place in the Arab world regarding the September 11 attacks. A recent poll by Zogby International surveyed 3,800 Arabs in eight Arab countries.[2] The poll showed that Arabs are discontent with United States politics in the Arab world. The main problem areas were America's attitudes toward Palestinians and policy toward Iraq. On the other hand, the poll showed that Arabs have favorable atti-

---

[1]Most Arabs (90%) are Muslim. However, the majority of Muslims come from Asian countries, including India, Pakistan, Afghanistan, Malaysia, and Indonesia. This study focuses on the Arab world.

[2]The eight Arab countries were Egypt, Jordan, Lebanon, Kuwait, Morocco, United Arab Emirates, Saudi Arabia, and the Palestinian territories.

tudes toward American values of freedom and democracy, education, movies and television productions, and advances in science and technology (Zogby, 2002).

In an attempt to assess the Arab stance, and even more importantly, the logic and the reasons behind it, this chapter offers a content analysis of the major Arabic-language online message boards[3] in the days following September 11. Internet message boards, although not necessarily representative of public opinion, provide an opportunity for people in the Arab world to freely speak their minds. The study combined quantitative and qualitative techniques to examine the messages on the major Arab portals following the attacks. It examines Internet users' attitudes toward the attacks and offers an in-depth explanation of the rationale behind these attitudes, and the reasons and arguments that message posters presented to support their positions.

INTERNET CONTENT ANALYSIS

Some studies have focused on examining online message boards and discussion forums. James, Wotring, and Forrest (1995) conducted an exploratory study of users' perceived benefits of electronic bulletin board use and their impact on other communication activities. They found that users primarily seek (or seek to give) information or education. They also derive a sense of "talking" to other users by virtue of reading and posting messages, in a manner that secures their anonymity if need be. The researchers suggested that this was because of the potential of message postings to reach a large audience with a variety of interests through a fast, cheap, and largely unregulated method of communication.

Bulletin boards provide a sense of community and sharing for people in crisis. Fleitas (1998) analyzed the social effects of chronic illness on children through narratives posted on the Web by the children on a topic-specific Web site that she had designed. She reported that the anonymity of message posters (which are usually considered problematic in Internet research) encouraged the site users to express their opinions. The researcher believed that the lack of barriers of time, space, age, and physical conditions associated with posting a message on the Internet allowed for a broader range of "connected" children to participate in her project.

Rosson (1999) designed a bulletin board site and called it the Web Storybase. She analyzed 133 stories posted by Internet users on the site. Visitors to the site could browse the existing postings, contribute a story, or post an annotation to a story. The site also provided a communication outlet for people about their personal crises or hard times. Having broken down all stories into six themes,

---

[3]The terms *online message boards, discussion boards,* and *discussion forums* all refer to a Web site where participants can read or write comments about a particular topic. *Chat rooms,* on the other hand, refer to an online forum where discussions are conducted synchronously in real time.

"cyber-relationships" was the theme with the biggest share of stories and annotations, with story titles such as "I'll get by with a little help from my cyber-friends" (p. 9).

Miller and Gergen (1998) also looked at Web message postings by people in crisis. Specifically, they examined an online bulletin board dedicated to suicide. They reported that "participants offered each other valuable resources in terms of validation of experience, sympathy, acceptance, and encouragement. They also asked provocative questions and furnished broad-ranging advice" (p. 189). The researchers concluded that online conversations help sustain participants in times of crisis.

A few studies have analyzed political communication on online discussion boards. In an early study, Garramone, Harris, and Anderson (1986) looked at the uses of political computer bulletin board systems (BBSs), an earlier form of Internet discussion boards. They found surveillance and curiosity to be the most salient motivations for political BBS use. BBS use was reported by users to be most efficient in satisfying surveillance needs.

In a later study, Rafaeli and LaRose (1993) also looked at BBSs as examples of what they called "collaborative mass media," media in which "the audience acts both as the source and the receiver of the message" (p. 277). They found that the 126 boards they researched had an average user community of about 900 users per board. Boards that had more diversified content generally had higher contribution levels than boards that were topic-specific.

Online message boards become particularly popular when an incident or event of significance takes place. After the assassination of Israeli Prime Minister Yitzhak Rabin, many people took to cyberspace to discuss the late leader's peace policies. Wittekind (1995) reported that participants on America Online's (AOL's) discussion board condemned the killing, but mostly spoke out against Rabin's policies: "When one group member said he opposed Israel being forced into peace with the PLO, he was answered with a chorus of agreement." On CompuServe, although some participants wondered how a Jew could kill their Jewish leader, most postings focused on Arabs. One participant said, "As long as we have Arabs in Israel, peace will never come. That's what the Torah ACTUALLY says." Another replied, "Because of people like you, peace has no chance. Thank you for killing our hope. A reasonable person would look at this act and realize that the man's wishes for PEACE are predominant, but no . . . you have God on your side" (p. 14A).

Tanner (2001) looked at a Chilean message board affiliated with a Chilean publication. The online discussion board offered the Chilean people a chance to discuss the arrest of ex-dictator president and senator-for-life Augusto Pinochet in October 1998 at the London Clinic. Tanner analyzed 1,670 letters to the editor published on the discussion site. She argued that online discussion boards are part of the public sphere. In this particular case, the site provided a voice for the Chilean people, and helped them generate public opinion and collective memories of their past. In doing so, Tanner argued, the discussion board helped people find a sense of reconciliation.

Tanner (2001) reported that more than 1,000 Chilean people participated in the online discussion. Over a period of 2 years,

> Chileans used the forum to argue over the meanings of justice, reconciliation, for-giveness, truth, democracy, liberty, sovereignty, and human rights. They debated events since the 1960s, examined the more recent transition to democracy, re-viewed 19th-century history, and decried forms of colonialism. They criticized governments, public officials, and political parties; attacked opponents; shared personal experiences; proposed solutions to current social problems; and con-structed visions of their country's future. (p. 383)

Tanner (2001) reported that the online forum users often expressed their ap-preciation and gratitude at the opportunity to express their opinions on the Internet. One participant said, "Long live technology! For the first time, we Chil-eans have the opportunity to attend and participate in a true debate over the his-toric events that occurred in the country during the last 25 years. YES, THIS IS CATHARSIS" (p. 383).

THE INTERNET IN THE ARAB WORLD

The latest figures for Internet users worldwide were estimated at about 680 mil-lion in May 2003. Out of that, the estimated number of users in the Arab world in 2002 was about 6 million (Global Reach, 2003; NUA, 2003). However, with some recent developments in the information technology sectors of Arab countries, the Internet growth rate in the Arab world is exploding. The number of users was ex-pected to multiply by a factor of four in some Arab countries in 2002. However, even then, it would still be under 8 million, less than 3% of the Arab population of 280 million (Abdulla, 2001).

Out of the 6 million Internet users in the Arab world, those who subscribe to an Internet service provider (ISP) are estimated at less than 1 million. This is about a 300% increase from 340,000 in May 1999. It is estimated that, on average, every Internet account in the Arab world is shared by more than 3 people, with the exception of Egypt, where it is estimated that every Internet account is shared by 8 people. Estimates for other individual Arab countries include 5 users per ac-count for Syria, Tunisia, Libya, and Sudan; followed by 4 users for Yemen; 3.5 us-ers for Lebanon, Jordan, and Morocco; 3 users for Saudi Arabia; and 2.5 users for the rest of the Gulf states (Abdulla, 2001; Jarrah, 2000).

The highest growth rate in the Arab world for the year 2000 was in Egypt, where Internet users jumped from 150,000 to about 600,000 (Abdulla, 2001). Following Egypt was Saudi Arabia, a newcomer to the Internet world. The

Internet was introduced to Saudi Arabia only in 1999. Its growth rate was 160%, jumping its Internet population to 300,000 users (Jarrah, 2000).

INTERNET BULLETIN BOARDS AND SEPTEMBER 11

Following September 11, a large number of online bulletin boards were dedicated to discussions of the tragedy. A vast number of memorial Web sites were hastily established to allow people to share their feelings and opinions online.[4] Such boards offered opportunities for users to share messages, poems, pictures, and artistic drawings and illustrations. Almost all online news outlets had some form of a discussion board dedicated to September 11 as well. For example, *The New York Times* set up a Web page entitled "Remembering the Victims."[5] CNN also set up a popular discussion board at its Web site.[6]

Similarly, Arab portals and media outlets created discussion boards for Arab Internet users to voice their opinions about the events of September 11. Although Internet penetration is still marginal in the Arab world, it is worth noting that on-line discussion forums have a huge advantage for the Arab user: They are uncensored. In a part of the world where the media are state-owned and controlled, having a free forum for discussion provides for a relatively rare opportunity. This is particularly true for Arab citizens whose opinions might differ from those of their governments. In the case of September 11, because most Arab states' official stance was to condemn the attacks, the media outlets followed suit. But how real was this sentiment and to what extent was it shared by the Arab people? Unlike most traditional media, where editors and gatekeepers have the ability to frame the news, online discussion boards provide for a better chance to answer this question, because they allow an opportunity for everybody to freely post their opinions on the Web site.

Based on the preceding arguments, the following research questions were formulated for this study:

RQ1: How did Internet users in the Arab world react to the September 11 attacks on the United States through the Masrawy and Arabia bulletin boards?

---

[4]For example, The World Trade Center Memorial Web site (http://thewtcmemorial.com) offers a discussion board where Internet users can post their messages, poems, or artistic drawings and illustrations. The New York City World Trade Center Memorial Web site (http://www.newyorkworld tradecentermemorial.com) offers message postings for the victims' families and for the rescue workers. American Disaster (http://americandisaster.com) is another site that offers an extensive message board for poems, messages, and art. The World Trade Center Memorial Tribute is another outlet for such discussions (http://worldtradecentertribute.org).

[5]Available at http://www.legacy.com/nytimes/Sept11.asp?Memorial=UA93.

[6]Available at http://www.cnn.com/community.

RQ2: What were the main arguments/reasons/themes behind the viewpoints
expressed on the Masrawy and Arabia bulletin boards?

ISLAM AND THE SEPTEMBER 11 ATTACKS

Following September 11, Islam jumped to the forefront of many American
minds. This was perhaps due, first and foremost, to the terrorists' claim that the
horrible crime they committed was against the enemies of God and in the name
of Islam. Most media reports referred to the terrorists simply as "Muslims,"
which helped spread a sense of stereotyping of Muslims as terrorists, as the two
words seemed to be used interchangeably. Fairness and Accuracy in Reporting
(FAIR) reported that following the attacks, the media made "gross generalizations about Arabs and Islam in general." For example, on September 11, former
Secretary of State Lawrence Eagleburger said on CNN, "There is only one way to
begin to deal with people like this, and that is you have to kill some of them even
if they are not immediately directly involved in this thing" ("Media Advisory,"
2001).

Muslims and Arabs in the United States were victims of many hate crimes in
the weeks and months following September 11. Many mosques had to deal with
demonstrations of anti-Islamic sentiments. CNN reported that 250 anti-Muslim
incidents were reported at universities in the following week. "Women students
have been spat at and had their traditional hijab scarves pulled off. Male students
have had turbans plucked from their heads or been targeted because of their
beards. [They have been yelled at,] 'You people are going to die.' " Graffiti on
university building walls read, "Go home, sand niggers" (Jones, 2001; "Racial
Backlash Flares," 2001).

Attacks against Islam as a religion went on in the media. Following the attacks,
evangelist and broadcaster Pat Robertson, founder of the Christian Broadcasting
Network (CBN), said, "Islam is not a peaceful religion that wants to coexist" (Pat
Robertson Official Web site, 2002). Evangelist Reverend Franklin Graham said,
"Islam is a very evil and wicked religion." Almost a year later, Graham appeared
on Fox News Channel, saying that terrorism is part of "mainstream Islam" and
that Islam preaches violence through the teachings of its holy book, the Quran
(Dobras, 2002; "Franklin Graham Smears," 2002).

Perhaps the comment that hurt Muslims' feelings the most worldwide was
Reverend Jerry Falwell's branding of Prophet Mohammad as a "terrorist." In an
interview on *60 Minutes,* Falwell said, "I think Mohammed was a terrorist. I read
enough . . . by both Muslims and non-Muslims, [to decide] that he was a violent
man, a man of war" ("Falwell Brands," 2002).

Princeton University's Bernard Lewis writes about "the roots of Muslim rage."
Over the years, Lewis (1990, 1993, 2002) has claimed that the Muslim world is en-
raged at Western modernity. In his latest book, Lewis (2002) contended that rage

and hatred against the West are basically "what went wrong" with the Muslim world, and are main factors that "produced" the September 11 attacks.

Orientalist Edward Said (1997) argued that Lewis's ideas "have become more strident and reductionist over time" (p. xxx). He pointed to Lewis's "total inability to grant that the Islamic peoples are entitled to their own cultural, political, and historical practices, free from Lewis's calculated attempt to show that because they are not Western (a notion of which he has an extremely tenuous grasp) they can't be good" (p. xxx).

In the wake of the September 11 attacks, Said (2001) wrote that "the carefully planned and horrendous, pathologically motivated suicide attack and mass slaughter by a small group of deranged militants" has been tactfully abused and turned into proof of theses such as Lewis's.

Chomsky (2001) noted that the mainstream media were mistaken in portraying the sentiment of the American people as wanting to kill as many Arabs and Muslims as possible. However, he called this "hysterical intensity" on the part of the media "entirely typical" (p. 30).

With these arguments in mind, this study featured a research question aiming to find out how Arab Muslims viewed Islam in relation to the attacks:

RQ3: How was Islam portrayed and discussed on the Masrawy and Arabia bulletin boards in relation to the September 11 attacks (terrorism or jihad)?

POTENTIAL PROBLEMS WITH INTERNET RESEARCH

Some problems with Internet research that are relevant to this study are worth mentioning at this point. Although anonymity on message boards might encourage honesty, it poses a problem of lack of identity verification. Message posters sign in with a name, but almost nobody signs in with his or her real name[7] (Lindlof & Shatzer, 1998). In this study, I had no way of telling the geographic location where a message originated. Although most messages were written in colloquial Egyptian Arabic,[8] this is a dialect so widely spoken in the Arab world that any Arab (or any non-Arab who is Arabic-literate) could have posted the messages. A few messages were even posted in English. Those could have been written by Arabs whose Web browsers do not support Arabic characters (as some have stated) or by non-Arabs. A few messages were clearly self-marked as posted by Americans.

Multiple submissions constitute another problem frequently encountered in content analysis of discussion boards (Miller & Gergen, 1998; Perlman, 1999).

---

[7]In this study, sometimes participants signed the actual message with a name, supposedly their real name, which was different than their sign-in name.

[8]I am Egyptian. Arabic is my mother tongue.

Several sign-in names were regularly featured on the Web sites examined in this study.

Finally, external validity and representativeness are problems with Internet research (Miller & Gergen, 1998; Stempel & Stewart, 2000). However, although this study is limited to Internet users, who constitute a small percentage of the Arab population, it still provides an understanding of the basic sentiments in the Arab world regarding the events of September 11, and the rationale behind those sentiments, as expressed in one of the few uncensored and uncontrolled forums for discussion in that part of the world.

METHOD

Denzin (1999) explained the structure of online conversations on message boards: "One person makes a statement, another person comments, and then another person comments, perhaps on the comments of the second person, and so on" (p. 109). Thus are formed *threads* of online discussion. The discussion might then grow into different directions or threads that might overlap on occasions, posing another problem or opportunity to the researcher trying to analyze a message board. The researcher is then faced with the choice of either following the main (original) thread, ignoring whatever relevant messages are posted to another thread, or following multiple interrelated threads and dealing with a much more complex sampling procedure.

This study presents a content analysis of message boards on two of the most popular Arabic-language portals: Masrawy (http://www.masrawy.com) and Arabia (http://www.arabia.com). Masrawy, which is colloquial Arabic for "Egyptian," is one of the first and most popular Arabic-language portals on the Internet. The site was originally designed and run by an Egyptian private, small business. It offers a wide variety of services, including free Internet connectivity (for residents of Egypt), free e-mail, and domain name registration. In addition, it also offers a search engine, as well as news, directories, classifieds, health, sports, stock market, entertainment, shopping, auctions, instant chat, and message boards. In April 2002, Masrawy merged with LINKdotNET, Egypt's biggest commercial ISP and the company that has been managing Microsoft's Middle East Web sites since 1997 (Rossant, 2002).

Arabia is another major portal that offers its users the option to access it in Arabic or in English. It is owned and operated by Arabia Online, which is based in Dubai's Internet City in the United Arab Emirates (UAE). With branch offices in UAE and in Jordan, the company has investors from all over the Arab world, including Saudi Prince Al Waleed Bin Talal. Like Masrawy, Arabia offers its users a wide array of services, including a search engine, free Internet access (for residents of Egypt), free e-mail, free greeting cards, news, games, entertainment, business, sports, Arab and international media outlets, horoscopes, an instant messenger service, cartoons, travel, shopping, and chat and discussion boards. Arabia Online estimates that it receives 1.5 million visitors a month, making it the most frequented portal in the Arab world (Rossant, 2002). The messages on both sites are not censored or edited in any way by their moderators or by any Arab government.[9] Both sites offer legal disclaimers for the messages posted.

Due to the nature of this study and the numerous problems associated with selecting a random sample on the Internet (December, 1996; Dominick, 1999; McMillan, 2000; Stempel & Stewart, 2000), I analyzed all messages posted on these two portals regarding the events of September 11. This would help provide a better understanding of the sentiments and rationale behind the messages posted, and therefore would provide a better understanding of what was on the minds of Arab Internet users in the aftermath of September 11.

Still, the sampling process was not without problems. Discussion boards vary in the way they are organized. Some are more structured (and therefore easier to follow and analyze) than others. In this study, the Masrawy discussion board was much more organized than the Arabia board. Masrawy offers fewer overall topics for discussion, and the topics are posted by the message board moderator. Participants can send a message (to the board or to the moderator) suggesting a new topic, after which the moderator posts the suggested topic under a new topic title. Although participants can reply to a particular message by entering that message number, their reply is not posted as a thread, but rather as a new message. Consequently, the postings to a particular topic are easier to access, scan (by title), and quantify.

On the other hand, the Arabia message board allows its users to post new topics as they please. The board also allows for threading of messages. The resulting structure is more problematic for a content analysis researcher (or even for a keen user). For one thing, there is no easy way of knowing how many messages are posted on a particular topic, because the topic could be fragmented under many messages or threads. Each message could be posted as a separate topic, and each message could have a large number of replies in its thread. Although the number of replies is posted, the only way of knowing how many messages relate to a particular topic is to scan every single message title on the board, figure out which ones relate to the topic of interest, and add up the replies to these messages, hoping that all replies actually relate to the topic. For a researcher or a user who wants to get a grasp of "the bigger picture," the process could be time consuming and frustrating, as the site hosts an average of about 50 pages of messages

---

[9]Most Arab governments do not impose any type of censorship on Internet content, if only because of the practical difficulties of doing so given questions of geographical jurisdiction in cyberspace. The few governments that wish to do so resort to restraining access to a site (e.g., pornographic sites) rather than editing or censoring the content. The Egyptian government (which would have geographical jurisdiction over Masrawy.com) does not impose any type of censorship or access restraint on any Internet site. No other Arab governments have restricted access to Masrawy or Arabia.

(or topics) at any given time. The inconvenience becomes much worse if the researcher or user is accessing the Internet through a dial-up connection.

Choosing a unit of analysis carries its problems in Internet research (December, 1996; Dominick, 1999; McMillan, 2000). The unit of analysis for this study is the *message*, defined as a body of text submitted by a user at one point in time, and designated by a single message identification number. There were a few incidents when users had very long messages to submit, and therefore broke them down into two or three messages and submitted them immediately following each other. Those had separate message identification numbers, and were counted as separate messages. Each message that appeared on the Web sites had a user name, a date and time of submission, and a message identification number. Date and time of submission as well as the message identification number were automatically designated by the Web site at the time of submission.

I originally looked at a total of 591 messages on the two portals. Messages on the Masrawy site totaled 517 messages on 104 Web pages, posted between September 11 and September 20.[10] They were all answering the message posted in Arabic by the moderator, "Do you agree with the recent attacks on the United States?" From the Arabia site, I analyzed a total of 73 messages posted under numerous threads. Those messages were posted from September 11 to October 5. A portion of the messages on both sites was eliminated because they were deemed irrelevant (although posted under a relevant title or message heading). For example, some participants would start sending personal messages to each other. Others would try to solicit interest in a different discussion topic by posting their views about the other topic under September 11, because this seemed to be the topic drawing the largest Internet crowds. One thread on the Arabia site was posted in English by a self-identified American, and had 18 replies. It was not, however, included in this analysis because it did not deal with valid discussion points similar to those raised in other messages. Instead, it was mostly a name-calling game between a few Americans and a few Arabs (from September 15–November 5). The total number of relevant messages analyzed for quantification in this study was 265 messages on Masrawy and 47 messages on Arabia, for a total of 312 messages.

Each message was coded for: (a) message identification number (for ease of tracking), (b) source message board (Masrawy, Arabia), (c) date of message submission, (d) user member type (only provided for Masrawy users, categories defined later), (e) gender (male, female, unidentified), (f) attitude toward the September 11 attacks (agree, neither agree nor disagree, disagree, or attitude not mentioned; categories defined later), (g) reasons mentioned (yes, no), (h) Palestinian–Israeli conflict (mentioned, not mentioned), (I) Iraq (mentioned, not mentioned), (j) other political conflicts (mentioned, not mentioned), (k) sympa-

---

[10]However, some messages were posted twice, apparently due to a technical difficulty on the Web site. Those pairs of duplicate messages were counted and analyzed as one message.

thy toward victims (mentioned, not mentioned), (l) reference to the U.S. as government rather than people (mentioned, not mentioned), and (m) Islam (mentioned as probable reason, mentioned as not a probable reason, not mentioned). Naturally, some messages had more than one variable discussed. For example, several messages spoke of the Palestinian–Israeli conflict and Iraq. Therefore, although the categories within each variable are mutually exclusive, the variables themselves are not.

Message posters on Masrawy were classified on the site by member type. If a user registers as under 21 years of age, he or she is classified as a junior member. Those 21 and over are classified as senior members. It has to be noted, however, that users can enter a fake age (and they often do). Following Tanner (2001), I tried to identify gender of message posters if possible, first based on the name or signature if provided, and by the text of the message, because a lot of Arabic words and pronouns require different masculine or feminine endings.

Attitude toward the September 11 attacks was coded as either "agree" for messages showing support for any possible justification, rationalization, or excuses for the attacks (even if the message poster felt sorry for the victims); "disagree" for messages showing disagreement with the attacks in terms of denouncing them, condemning them, disapproving of the act, classifying the attacks as a crime or an act of terrorism, offering condolences for the victims and/or their families (without showing any signs of support or justification for the attacks); or "neither agree nor disagree" if the message posters admitted to not being able to make up their minds or adopt a viewpoint regarding the attacks. Messages that only raised questions or offered comments or possible answers to issues raised in other messages without taking sides were coded as "attitude not mentioned."

Intercoder reliability was determined by having another Arabic speaker, who is fluent in English and has a masters degree in communication, recode a random sample of 10% of valid messages ($n = 32$; 27 messages from Masrawy and 5 messages from Arabia). Agreement rate was calculated after excluding the variables of message identification number, source message board, date of message submission, and user member type to avoid inflating reliability. Using the Holsti (1969) formula, intercoder reliability was determined as .927. I had the final say in cases of disagreement. I recoded the selected random sample. Intracoder reliability was .955.

I translated all Arabic entries to English for the purposes of this study. In doing so, I tried to remain faithful to the tone, structure, and punctuation of the original entry as much as possible.

FINDINGS

Of the 265 valid message posted on Masrawy, 63.4% ($n = 168$) were posted by junior members, and 21.9% ($n = 58$) were posted by senior members. The remaining messages (14.7%, $n = 39$) were listed as "member." Of the 312 valid messages on both discussion boards, 47.8% (n = 149) appeared to be posted by males, 12.5% (n = 39) appeared to be posted by females, and 39.7% (n = 124) had no indication of their sex in their messages. No messages featured an inconsistency of gender portrayal through user name or signature on one hand and the language used in the posting on the other, which suggests that even those who had self-assigned nicknames chose names consistent with their sex.

I now address the findings of each research question.

RQ1: How Did Internet Users in the Arab World React to the September 11 Attacks on the United States Through the Masrawy and Arabia Bulletin Boards?

Of the messages on both sites, 41.0% (n = 128) condemned the attacks of September 11 on the United States as an act of terrorism with no justification, political or otherwise. They were quick to condemn the attacks and offer condolences and prayers for the victims and their families. For example, a male senior member wrote on Masrawy on September 11, "I strongly condemn these attacks. Whoever did this deserves to be burned alive."

On the same discussion board, a male junior member wrote also on September 11:

> Any human being with a heart rejects the killing of children, men, women, elderly people, and all innocent people. There will be victims from all nationalities. We are against killing Palestinians, and also killing Jews. Any religion forbids killing. What did the men and women and children who were killed do? It could've been your brother or your son or your father or your mother or your wife. This is not permissible under any religion.

A male participant wrote on Arabia, "Of course I don't support those attacks. There's nothing heroic about killing innocent civilians. There isn't any difference between an Israeli terrorist and an Arab terrorist."

Some used quite strong language to condemn and denounce the attacks. For example, a member wrote on Masrawy on September 12:

> I or any Arab or Muslim cannot support barbaric, vengeful revenge such as that which I saw yesterday. No, a thousand no to such naïve, idiotic, barbarian operations. If it were in my hands, I would kill every terrorist that had to do with this. My hearty condolences goes out to the victims' families.

This male wrote on Arabia on September 13 (in English), "I too feel bad for all our Middle Eastern families being killed, but two wrongs don't make a right here. All innocent people have a right to live a happy life, both Middle Eastern and Americans."

However, 32.4% ($n = 101$) of the messages posted offered some justification for the attacks, even if they acknowledged feeling sorry for the victims and their families. A female junior member posted one of the very first messages on Masrawy on September 11: "This is a result of American political arrogance. Americans must feel the terror, destruction and devastation that innocent civilians in Palestine feel everyday. They have to know that their racist policies and blind support for Israel will hurt their interests in the Middle East." A male junior member said on Masrawy, "I support these attacks. America has to be forced to realize that there is a nation that deserves to live peacefully on its own land, and they have the right to defend themselves any way they can. If force is the only way, then so be it. I hope the next step is in Israel."

Messages coded as "neither agree nor disagree" accounted for 5.8% ($n = 18$). Those were admittedly undecided, mostly out of pure shock. They could not adopt a viewpoint regarding the attacks. A typical example of these messages is provided by this male participant, who wrote on Arabia on September 11: "I really don't know what to think. My God, who could have thought? I can't believe what happened. Who could have done this?"

The remaining 20.8% ($n = 65$) of messages participated by either raising further issues or questions to the discussion, or by offering comments or possible answers to issues raised in other messages without taking sides. Those were coded as "attitude not mentioned." For example, several messages discussed the identity of the terrorists. A male senior member wrote on Masrawy, "Believe me, the Arabs are not that organized, they could not have done this. I'm telling you, if Arabs were involved in this operation, it would have definitely failed!"

A female senior member wrote on Masrawy:

I have a deep conviction that whoever did this is an American extremist organization, America is full of them. It is very difficult, actually it is impossible, for an outside organization to have carried out these attacks with such precision. Of course no one knows who really did this, but I think it's an inside operation (and we'll pay for it). Other possible suspects include Bin Laden, Iraq, the Red Army, or even Israel, but in cooperation with an inside extremist organization. No outside party could have done this on its own.

RQ2: What Were the Main Arguments/Reasons/Themes Behind the Viewpoints Expressed on the Masrawy and Arabia Bulletin Boards?

Although 68.3% ($n = 213$) of messages mentioned some reasons or rationale behind the viewpoint expressed, the remaining 31.7% ($n = 99$) just expressed their feelings or posed or answered questions without providing any explanation. Among the factors that were prominent in determining bulletin board participants' viewpoints were the killing of innocent civilians, and U.S. foreign policy in the Middle East, particularly with regards to the Palestinian–Israeli conflict, Iraq, and other political conflicts. Other main themes that emerged from the discussion included a perception of the United States as a government rather than a people, as well as a conviction that the September 11 attacks actually hurt Arab interests rather than served them.

Innocent Civilians

Messages condemning the attacks of September 11 on the United States, and even some messages justifying the attacks, felt that the massive killing of innocent civilians in that matter was simply barbaric and inhumane. Overall, 44.9% ($n =$ 140) messages specifically objected to the killing of innocent civilians. Message posters expressed their thoughts in terms of feeling sorry for the victims and extending condolences and prayers to the victims and their families. One male junior member on Masrawy said on September 12:

> I do not agree at all to what happened in the United States, it is pitiful that any educated person would. I'm an Egyptian Muslim, but before anything else I'm a human being, and what happened is not permissible under any religion. I pray for mercy for those who died innocently for no reason, whether they were Muslims, Christians, or Jews. They have their religion and I have mine.[11]

Another male junior member said on Masrawy on September 11, "We cannot be against Palestinian and Iraqi children dying everyday, then approve of American children dying. They're both children, and they're both innocent. If we approve of killing American civilians, we'd be adopting the same double standards that we're so frustrated at the United States for applying in Palestine."
One female senior member wrote on Masrawy on September 14:

> If a building was destroyed without innocent people dying, maybe I'd have been happy, but those who died had nothing to do with anything. It is totally against our Islamic religion to terrorize innocent people. Besides, we have to differentiate between governments and people. Most of the American people do not hurt the Palestinian problem because they don't care about anything outside their borders to begin with. Terrorizing innocent people is not acceptable in Islam, it is totally against the religion.

This member wrote on Arabia (in English), "(I would) agree 100%, if they had done it at night, not at 8:30 am!! It would have been a bit smarter! maaan [sic] so many people died! this is a shame!"

---

[11]"You have your religion, and I have mine" is a literal translation of a verse from the Quran, the Muslim holy book, which dictates tolerance to people different from one's own. Another translation that captures the spirit of the verse is provided on IslamiCity.com: "To you be your way, and to me mine." (The Holy Quran 109:6).

American Government Versus American People

Differentiating between governments and peoples seems to have been an important point to make. A good deal of messages (17.6%, $n = 55$) debated whether the United States should be perceived as a government or as a people. Most messages justifying or supporting the attacks tended to view them as against the U.S. government rather than American individuals.

One of the very first messages posted on Masrawy was by a male senior member, who wrote, "These attacks were intended against symbols of American imperialism. Whoever did this aimed at hitting American economic symbols, not civilians."

Replying to him, another male senior member offered a different perspective: "The problem is these attacks do not only kill activist Americans. They kill innocent people. There could've been Egyptians on those planes, and also the Trade Center has lots of tourists and innocent people. I am of course against the US always siding with Israel, but there are other considerations here."

Another male member posted a message on Masrawy analyzing the political and economic functions of the targets that were hit in the attacks. He said:

Look at the targets of this operation. Civilians were not the targets. The targets were:
The World Trade Center, which houses the major financial analysts and stock brokers who control the balance of power and influence American politics to their favor and increase the gap between the rich and the poor.
The Pentagon, where decisions were made that killed millions of innocent people. Remember bombing civilian shelters in Iraq? Remember the apartment complexes that fell in Beirut from American missiles?

Disagreeing, a male junior member said:

Supporting the killing of innocent civilians is out of the question. Who ever said that innocent civilians are responsible for what happens in Palestine or Iraq or Libya or anywhere else? The American government is the one that shares the responsibility, not the individual American citizen. Americans are known for their complete ignorance of world politics outside of what the American media provide, that is if they watch international news to begin with. But to use planes filled with civilians to bomb a civilian target, those people had nothing to do with anything. This is against all religions. God did not say to kill innocent people.

Another male wrote on Masrawy on September 14 (in English), "Civilians are not responsible for the act(s) of their government. Are the Iraqis responsible for the attack on Kuwait? (No, rather) we blame Saddam."

This message was posted on Arabia on September 11, surprisingly by a member who called himself "iraqiking." He wrote in English, "I agree. In Islam it is *haram* [Arabic for "forbidden in Islam"] to kill anyone who does not pose a direct threat to you. The war against the government is fine, but against the people is wrong. No matter how we feel about the oppression towards the Arabs, we must keep our faith."

Two days later, a male junior member put the issue in layman terms on Masrawy, "If someone tied you up to a pole and kept beating you up everyday, then somebody came along and hit the person who was beating you up, would you be happy or sad?"

To his message, a female senior member replied, "You know what, if someone hits the guy beating me up, I'd be very happy. But if somebody beats up this guy's children, I'd feel terrible for them. They, like me, are innocent."

Similar sentiments were expressed in this message by a male junior member on Masrawy:

> What did those innocent people do? They have nothing to do with American politics. We are human. I cannot imagine anyone could be happy for what happened. I am definitely against American policies, but what do kids have to do with it? Those (killed) were innocent people, maybe even Egyptians and Arabs. I'll give you an example: If we have a murderer, would it be right to take his little son and slaughter him? Thank you. God have mercy on all of us.

U.S. Politics

Of all the messages posted, 78.2% ($n = 244$) mentioned some aspect of dissatisfaction with American politics. Those messages discussed U.S. foreign policy, particularly with regards to the Palestinian–Israeli conflict, Iraq, and other political issues.

The Palestinian–Israeli Conflict. The most prominent political problem that came up in the messages was the Palestinian–Israeli conflict, with 55.4% ($n = 173$). Pro-Israeli American policies in the Middle East seem to be the biggest cause of frustration with the United States, at least as shown by these messages.[12]

A female junior member wrote on September 11 on Masrawy, "I'm against all forms of violence, but in some instances we have to use it so that Americans would see what Palestinians see everyday. Maybe then they'll stop their blind support for Israel, who makes an art out of torturing Palestinians."

One male junior member strongly felt that these attacks brought a sense of missing justice to the situation in the Middle East. These were his words on Masrawy:

---

[12]Although most of the messages quoted here blame the United States, at least in part, for their support for Israel in the Palestinian–Israeli conflict, other messages were posted that argued that the Arabs should blame only themselves. Those messages, however, were not quoted here because they did not deal with the September 11 attacks in any way. Rather, the discussion shifted at this point to a matter of internal Arab politics.

Before we talk about this heroic operation, we have to remind the world, and especially Americans . . . of the martyrs in Palestine, and remind them of Mohamad Al Dorra,[13] [the Palestinian child] whose father had to watch him die as Israelis shot him without listening to his father begging for them to stop, and remind them of the cries of pain and anguish of the Palestinian people.

Al Dorra stimulated a lot of discussion on both Masrawy and Arabia, as the incident has triggered much Arab anger. One male junior member took to Masrawy to answer those who condemned killing innocent civilians in the September 11 attacks, saying "What about Mohamad el Dorra, the Palestinian child who died in his father's arms by Israeli bullets. Wasn't he a child too? Wasn't he innocent too?" A male Egyptian engineer said:

In my opinion I don't think anybody ever supports hitting civilian targets or bombing civilians. But the United States has to think hard and deeply about why such attacks might have occurred. I think that if they look at it objectively, they will realize that the American foreign policy in the Middle East and their double standards in favor of the Israeli allies are what lead to these revengeful attacks.

The Palestinian issue and pro-Israeli American politics in the Middle East appeared to be a common feature in most messages. This message by a male junior member is typical: "I'm against attacking civilians under any circumstances, but this might get the Americans to feel what Palestinians feel and stop their clear bias towards Israel."

Iraq. Iraq was the second major cause of frustration with American politics in the Middle East. Of all the messages posted, 31.1% ($n = 97$) mentioned Iraq. Those who did mention it clearly felt that the United States was to blame, at least in part, for the hunger and devastation that the Iraqi people were suffering. Messages focusing on Iraq were not too different from each other and from the following examples.

A male junior member said on Masrawy, "Iraqi children die by the hundreds everyday because of the lack of milk, food, and medical supplies as a result of the economic embargo. I wonder if Americans know this or even care."

Another male senior member said:

Children in Iraq are dying before their parents' eyes, the elderly and diabetics too, because of the (economic) embargo. There is no food or medicine. Where is the heart of the world public opinion? America itself is terrorizing anybody in the

---

[13]Mohamad Al Dorra is a Palestinian 12-year-old boy, who was captured on film clutching to his father to protect him from "Israeli gunfire showering them from all directions." The boy was killed moments later, and the pictures "fuelled the Intifada in its early days and triggered demonstrations in almost every Arab capital, rendering it iconic of the Palestinian cause and the Israeli army's brutality" (Howeidy, 2001).

world who dares to say they feel for Iraq. . . . Is this acceptable under the tolerant rules of Christianity? I'm telling you, we're not happy about this disaster, but the US has to let go of its arrogance to understand.

This participant wrote on Arabia on September 12 (in English):

What about the many thousands of Iraqi children that are being starved, maimed and terrorized? Are these the actions of a civilized nation? When innocent women and children (and men) were killed by American "heroes" who dropped bombs from 3 thousand miles up in the stratosphere, we were told that it was merely "collateral damage," unfortunate but necessary in order to punish evil. . . . Just as Americans value their lives, they must learn that those of other countries value the lives of their own countrymen equally.

Another participant wrote, "Every person in the Pentagon has blood over their hands. Just yesterday, eight civilians died in an American raid over Iraq. No one did anything about it."

Other Political Conflicts.   Other political conflicts that message posters mentioned as causes of frustration with American politics accounted for 25% ($n = 78$) of messages. The political conflicts included Japan, Vietnam, Libya, Sudan, Somalia, Bosnia, Chechnya, Iran, Lebanon, and Pakistan.

One participant wrote on Arabia on September 12 (in English):

So many nations on this Earth have suffered from American aggression that there must be many millions of people with reason enough to carry out the sort of revenge that has just taken place. It is unfortunate that there had to be collateral damage, albeit trivial compared with what has been meted out by America on weaker nations that posed no threat of retaliation.

A male junior member said on Masrawy, "What happened is not 1/1000 of what happens in Palestine. They really deserved it. I hope that this will remind them of what they did in Iraq, Palestine, Japan, and Vietnam. But I really feel sorry for the victims."
Another male member said:

Did people forget the killings in Iraq??? And in Palestine and Lebanon??? Did people forget Hiroshima and Nagasaki??? Did you forget 2 million victims in Vietnam?? Fueling wars in Afghanistan??? In Korea??? Supporting dictatorships all over the Third World countries???? Robbing the treasures of Africa and Latin America? And finally, supporting Zionism with all their might.

Another male senior member said on Masrawy, "America hit *El Shifa*, the main medical plant in Sudan, and said, 'Oops, sorry, we thought it was a nuclear plant.' "

This participant wrote on Arabia on September 12 (in English), "My heart goes out to the hundreds of thousands of innocent lives that were lost in Hiroshima and Nagasaki."

One of the longer messages on Masrawy was written on September 11 by a male senior member, who provided a list of incidents from the recent history of the Arab–Israeli conflict in the Middle East:

> The Qana massacre[14]
> The martyrs of Al Aqsa mosque who were killed while performing the morning prayers
> Sabra and Shatila[15]
> Those in Deir Yaseen[16] were civilians
> The Egyptian prisoners of war in (the 1956 war) were civilians
> The Intifada martyrs
> Mohamad Al Dorra, he was a child too
> The two-month-old baby who was killed by Israeli settlers while he was on his way to a wedding with his mother; the children whose bones they broke
> Yesterday there were eight killed in Iraq, are those worthless dogs?
> Those who die in Palestine everyday
> All those were innocent, and the world did not do a thing. Bush gave the green light for more killings.
> We are against killing innocent people on any side. And by the way, whoever did this is not an Arab or Palestinian. We are not happy that people died, God have mercy on everybody. But maybe they'll get to feel what it's like.

A female senior member answered:

> Let's not weigh matters with two scales. We are against American policies in Iraq and Palestine. We are against what happened in Bosnia and Herzegovina, in Kosovo, in Chechnya, and in many other parts of the world. How then can we sup-

---

[14]On Thursday April 18, 1996, at least 105 civilians were massacred in the village of Qana, Lebanon, after Israeli artillery pounded a United Nations warehouse packed with refugees. Israel carried on with the bombing ("What Happened," 2002).

[15]On September 16, 1982, as Israel invaded Lebanon, about 150 of the Israeli-allied Lebanese Christian militia of the *Phalange* entered the Palestinian civilian refugee camps of Sabra and Shatila near Beirut. For 40 hours, they raped, killed, and injured a large number of unarmed civilians, mostly children, women, and elderly people inside camps, encircled and sealed by Israeli troops. The estimate of victims varies between 700 (the official Israeli figure) to 3,500. A court case is currently on in Belgium against Ariel Sharon, then Israeli Minister of Defense, charging him and others with war crimes, crimes against humanity, and genocide in relation to the massacres (International Campaign, 2002; Sabra–Shatila, 2002).

[16]On April 9, 1948, 250 Palestinian men, women, and children were massacred in the village of Deir Yaseen, many while asleep. The killings were committed by the Stern and Irgun, two Jewish groups who were active before the establishment of the State of Israel. The attackers went on to mutilate the bodies and cut open the bellies of pregnant dead women. The act horrified the Arab world and led thousands of Palestinians to flee their homes, fearing a similar fate awaited them if they stayed (Farah, 1996).

port killing peaceful, innocent civilians just because we don't agree with their government's foreign policy?

Attacks Hurt Arab Interests

Some message posters seemed aware that these attacks would, in fact, hurt rather than serve any Arab or Muslim interests. For example, one male junior member wrote, "These attacks will not solve any problems and will not make the United States change its pro-Israel policies. And why do Muslims always have to look like terrorists in the eyes of the West? . . . Killing civilians won't serve anyone and will not stop Israel from killing Palestinians, Muslims, and Arabs." A male wrote on Arabia:

> This is pure terrorism. If America's foreign policy is bad, there must be people out there who disagree with it. But after these attacks, we definitely lost any world public opinion. Now [Israeli Prime Minister Ariel] Sharon can do whatever he pleases with America's blessings. The Arabs will now be America's official enemy.

A female junior member wrote:

> Muslims abroad are already facing hassles as a result of these horrible attacks. They just said on the news that veiled Muslim women in the United States and the United Kingdom were advised to take off their veils if they wanted to go out. My brother lives in Chicago, his wife is an American Muslim, she was told to take off the veil.

On September 14, a female junior member took to Masrawy to point out that Arabs and Muslims would be blamed for the attacks. She strongly rejected any accusations:

> The Americans have already fired out their accusations against Arabs and Muslims all over despite all the condemnations issued by Arab and Muslim countries. Of course they're backed by their magic media systems, which can convince the world that the sun will shine tomorrow from the West. They said on American TV that they found a car in the airport that had Arabic-language handbooks for teaching flying. How convenient!!!!! So whoever did this is so idiotic that he left behind him such obvious trail. Oh and he was learning from Arabic handbooks, as in "Flying for Dummies." And why did he leave them in the car? Oh, he was reviewing his notes before he gets on the plane. Anyway, whoever did this knew very well that fingers will be pointed so quickly at Arabs and Muslims.

RQ3: How Was Islam Discussed/Portrayed on the Bulletin Boards in Relation to the Attacks (Terrorism or Jihad)?

Although Islam was portrayed by the terrorists as the reason for their attacks on the United States, this was not supported by the participants in this study. Only 2.2% ($n = 7$) of all messages posted on the two sites mentioned Islam as a probable justification for the attacks. In comparison, 21.2% ($n = 66$) made it a point to stress that such attacks are against the core teachings of Islam. The remaining 76.6% ($n = 239$) did not mention Islam at all in their discussions of why the attacks could have happened.

Those who spoke of Islam as an antiterrorism religion felt very strongly about it. One male junior member wrote on Masrawy (in English), "What happened is *haram* [forbidden in Islam], *haram, haram*. This is NOT Islam. Islam is PEACE."

Another male wrote on Masrawy on September 14 (in English), "I don't see how people can use our wonderful religion to justify such horrible acts. . . . What I know about my religion is that it is about peace, mercy, and compassion. Anything else is not Islamic."

Another male junior member wrote, "This is not *jihad*, this is nonsense. According to our Prophet Mohamad (peace and prayers be upon him), *jihad* is struggle 1) against oneself to achieve a higher level of purity, and 2) against enemies in times of war. This is not *jihad*."

One junior member who signed his message "Muslim till the end" wrote on Masrawy on September 13 (in English):

Killing innocent people does NOT solve anything. Also there is nowhere in Quran where it is said that it is ok to kill someone who did not fight you personally or kill you personally. Allah in Quran says that "killing of one soul, without just (cause), is like killing of the whole people" what does that mean? God did not say killing of a "Muslim soul," He generalized it to say a "soul", which makes it more general.

An Egyptian male wrote on Arabia on September 12 (in English):

This act of terrorism is totally *haram* [forbidden in Islam]. And those idiots who have done this are so stupid. All the majority of sane people with brains want in this lifetime is PEACE. . . . *Wallahi* [By God] it's *haram* [forbidden in Islam] and those responsible will be punished hopefully twice, once on Earth and then again when they get to hell.

Another male said on Arabia, "Islam is a peaceful religion. My heart and prayers go out to all those affected by this tragedy. I feel that my religion is being raped by these terrorists. I wish they would just leave Islam out of it."

DISCUSSION AND CONCLUSIONS

This study has tried to analyze the contents of two popular Arabic-language online message boards regarding the attacks of September 11 on the United States. The results show that more than 41% of the messages condemned the attacks as pure terrorism. However, more than 32% saw some justification behind these attacks even if they felt sorry for the victims and their families.

Messages condemning the September 11 attacks expressed that the massive killing of innocent civilians in that manner was simply barbaric, inhumane, and a contradiction of the core teachings of Islam. On the other hand, those justifying or supporting the attacks viewed them as against the United States government rather than the American people.

More than 78% of the messages mentioned some aspect of frustration or dissatisfaction with American politics in the Middle East. This is an interesting finding, given that those justifying the attacks were some 32%. This means that 46% of those who posted messages felt dissatisfied with American foreign policy in the Middle East, even if they condemned the attacks and supported the victims.

The main reason behind Arabs' frustration with American politics is the Palestinian–Israeli conflict. More than 55% specifically mentioned the Palestinian problem and pro-Israeli American policies to be their major cause of frustration with the United States.

Iraq was the second major reason for Arabs' frustration with American politics, as mentioned by more than 31% of the messages. Message posters felt that the United States is to blame, at least in part, for the hunger and devastation that the Iraqi people are suffering as a result of the economic embargo. Other political conflicts were mentioned in about a quarter of the messages on both sites. Those included Japan, Vietnam, Libya, Sudan, Somalia, Bosnia, Chechnya, Iran, Lebanon, and Pakistan.

Although terrorists claim they carry out their crimes in the name of Islam, those who posted messages on both Masrawy and Arabia rejected this claim as false and unjust. Only 2% of all messages posted on the two sites mentioned Islam as a probable justification for the attacks. In comparison, more than 21% stressed that the attacks are against the core teachings of Islam. The remaining three quarters of the messages did not mention Islam at all in their discussions, which means religion was not on the posters' minds as a possible reason for why the attacks could have happened. They saw the attacks as a political, rather than a religious, issue. In fact, some message posters took to defending their religion, saying they felt it was being raped by the terrorists, who were taking advantage of it to advance their own political agendas. They explained in their messages the basic principles on which Islam was based as a religion of tolerance, mercy, peace, and compassion. A large number of message posters believed that these attacks would in fact hurt, rather than serve, Arab and Muslim interests, and would harm and exacerbate the image of Islam in the West.

ACKNOWLEDGMENTS

I would like to thank the editors, especially Dr. Michael Salwen, for their valuable remarks on an earlier draft of this chapter.

REFERENCES

Abdulla, R. (2001, November). *The Internet in the Middle East: An overview of developments and current status.* Paper presented at the annual meeting of the National Communication Association, Atlanta, GA.

Chomsky, N. (2001). *9-11.* New York: Seven Stories.

December, J. (1996). Units of analysis for Internet communication. *Journal of Communication, 46*(1), 14–38.

Denzin, M. (1999). Cybertalk and the method of instances. In S. Jones (Ed.), *Doing Internet research: Critical issues and methods for examining the Net* (pp. 107–125). Thousand Oaks, CA: Sage.

Dobras, A. (2002, August 14). Rev. Franklin Graham chastises Muslim leaders for their silence. *C & F Report.* Retrieved August 16, 2002, from http://cultureandfamily.org/report/2002–2008-14/r_graham.shtml

Dominick, J. (1999). Who do you think you are? Personal home pages and self-presentation on the World Wide Web. *Journalism & Mass Communication Quarterly, 76,* 646–658.

Falwell brands Mohammed a "terrorist." (2002, October 4). CBS News. Retrieved October 6, 2002, from http://www.cbsnews.com/stories/2002/10/03/60minutes/main524268.shtml

Farah, N. (1996). *A continent called Palestine.* Retrieved April 2, 2002, from http://www.middleeastbooks.com/html/books/farah.html

Fleitas, J. (1998). Spinning tales from the World Wide Web: Qualitative research in an academic environment [Electronic version]. *Qualitative Health Research, 8,* 283–292.

Franklin Graham smears Islam again. (2002, August 6). Council on American Islamic Relations (CAIR). Retrieved August 9, 2002, from http://www.cairnet.org/asp/article.asp?articleid=887&articletype=3

Garramone, G., Harris, A., & Anderson, R. (1986). Uses of political computer bulletin boards. *Journal of Broadcasting & Electronic Media, 30,* 325–339.

Global Reach. (2003). *Global Internet statistics.* Retrieved November 2, 2003, from http://www.glreach.com/globstats/index.php3

Holsti, O. (1969). *Content analysis for the social sciences and humanities.* Reading, MA: Addison-Wesley.

Howeidy, A. (2001, March 29). They killed Al-Dorra again. *Al-Ahram Weekly.* Retrieved April 2, 2002, from http://www.ahram.org.eg/weekly/2001/527/re4.htm

International campaign for justice for the victims of Sabra & Shatila. (2002). Retrieved April 2, 2002, from http://www.indictsharon.net

James, M., Wotring, C. E., & Forrest, E. (1995). An exploratory study of the perceived benefits of electronic bulletin board use and their impact on other communication activities. *Journal of Broadcasting & Electronic Media, 39,* 30–50.

Jarrah, F. (2000). *Number of Internet users in Arab countries edges towards two million.* Dabbagh Information Technology. Retrieved October 28, 2001, from http://www.dit.net/itnews/me_internet/users.html

Jones, G. (2001, September 19). Muslims targets in terror backlash. Retrieved June 22, 2002, from http://www.cnn.com/2001/WORLD/europe/09/19/gen.muslim.attacks/index.html

Lewis, B. (1990, September). The roots of Muslim rage [Electronic version]. *The Atlantic.* Retrieved June 22, 2002, from http://www.theatlantic.com/issues/90sep/rage.htm

Lewis, B. (1993). *Islam and the West.* New York: Oxford University Press.

Lewis, B. (2002). *What went wrong: Western impact and Middle Eastern response.* New York: Oxford University Press.

Lindlof, T., & Shatzer, M. (1998). Media ethnography in virtual space: Strategies, limits, and possibilities. *Journal of Broadcasting & Electronic Media, 42,* 170–189.

McMillan, S. (2000). The microscope and the moving target: The challenge of applying content analysis to the World Wide Web. *Journalism & Mass Communication Quarterly, 77,* 80–98.

Media advisory: Media march to war. (2001, September 17). Fairness and Accuracy in Reporting (FAIR). Retrieved June 20, 2002, from http://www.fair.org/press-releases/wtc-war-punditry.html

Miller, J., & Gergen, K. (1998). Life on the line: The therapeutic potentials of computer-mediated conversation [Electronic version]. *Journal of Marital & Family Therapy, 24,* 189–202.

NUA. (2003). *How many online?* Retrieved November 2, 2003, from http://www.nua.com/surveys/how_many_online/index.html.

Pat Robertson Official Web site. (2002). Retrieved November 1, 2002, from www.patrobertson.com

Perlman, J. (1999, May 6). Print sites still wary of chatting it up. *Online Journalism Review.* Retrieved March 30, 2002, from http://ojr.usc.edu/sections/features/99_stories/stories_discussion_050699.htm

Racial backlash flares at colleges. (2001, September 21). Retrieved June 22, 2002, from http://www.cnn.com/2001/fyi/teachers.ednews/09/21/ec.campus.backlash/index.html

Rafaeli, S., & LaRose, R. (1993). Electronic bulletin boards and "public goods" explanations of collaborative mass media. *Communication Research, 20,* 277–297.

Rossant, J. (2002). Gates eyes the Middle East. *Forbes.* Retrieved May 29, 2002, from http://www.forbes.com/global/2002/0401/027.html

Rosson, M. (1999). I get by with a little help from my cyber-friends: Sharing stories of good and bad times on the Web. *Journal of Computer-Mediated Communication, 4*(4). Retrieved February 9, 2000, from http://www.ascusc.org/jcmc/vol4/issue4/rosson.html.

Sabra–Shatila. (2002). Retrieved April 2, 2002, from http://www.sabra-shatila.be/english/

Said, E. (1997). *Covering Islam: How the media and the experts determine how we see the rest of the world* (rev. ed.). New York: Vintage Books.

Said, E. (2001, September 16). Islam and the West are inadequate banners. *The Observer.* Retrieved June 22, 2002, from http://sf.indymedia.org/news/2001/09/104480.php

Stempel, G. H., III, & Stewart, R. (2000). The Internet provides both opportunities and challenges for mass communication researchers. *Journalism & Mass Communication Quarterly, 77,* 541–548.

Tanner, E. (2001). Chilean conversations: Internet forum participants debate Augusto Pinochet's detention. *Journal of Communication, 51,* 383–403.

What happened. (2002). Retrieved April 2, 2002, from http://www.leb.net/qana/webdoc0.htm

Wittekind, D. (1995, November 5). The Rabin assassination: Cyberspace opinions fly after killing [Electronic version]. *The Atlanta Journal and Constitution,* p. 14A.

Zogby, J. (2002). *What Arabs think.* Retrieved November 14, 2002, from http://www.zogby.com

CHAPTER THIRTEEN

Why They Chat: Predicting Adoption and Use of Chat Rooms

David J. Atkin
Leo W. Jeffres
Kimberly Neuendorf
Ryan Lange
Paul Skalski

Emerging online channels are transforming the American media landscape. The Federal Communications Commission (FCC) even cited the rise of online modalities, and the competition they provide, as a justification for jettisoning restrictions on local TV–newspaper cross-ownership (e.g., Labaton, 2003). Are the glory days of traditional news media numbered? Will emerging online news delivery and discussion modalities replace the Big 3 networks and other "prestige" media outlets?

As other chapters in this volume detail, the Internet is transforming broadcast and print news operations. Major news organizations are moving to integrate Internet services into their operations (e.g., network Web sites). However those less sanguine about FCC deregulation are quick to point out that, although the Web is a distributed network, the most popular competing online services are those operated by traditional media outlets (e.g., Atkin & Lau, 2003).

Given the controversy about whether online news services represent a meaningful alternative to traditional media and the implications of that debate for our larger democracy, we explore the relative appeal and uses of emerging online channels. In particular, we profile the users of newsgroup and related chat room services, focusing on social locators, media use behaviors, and communication needs associated with these online applications.

This chapter was presented as a paper to the Communication Technology and Policy Division, Association for Education in Journalism & Mass Communication, Kansas City, MO, July 30–August 2, 2003.

The growing popularity of the Internet stems, to a large degree, from its ability to provide a mixture of interpersonal and mass media applications. In the realm of online news, an Internet database of people interested in a particular topic—or newsgroup—can allow messages to be stored on the local sites of subscribers. This mass media function can then be supplemented through real-time interpersonal exchanges facilitated via online chat rooms (e.g., Albright, Purohit, & Walsh, 2002; Ibanez, 2002).

Nearly 60% of Americans use the Internet on a daily basis, and they tend to be younger and better educated than the general population, although African Americans and Hispanics are underrepresented in the online universe (Pew, 2001). The average America Online (AOL) household user more than doubled his or her time spent online from the mid- to late 1990s (Dizard, 2000), and the 72.3% of Americans who went online in 2001 lingered about 9.8 hr per week in 2001 (UCLA Center for Communication Policy, 2001). The UCLA survey also found that nearly half (47.9%) of users read news online. More strikingly, a market survey (Veronis, Suhler, & Associates, 2000) identified news reading as the most popular online activity, selected by 87.8% of the audience. Dizard (2000) concluded that "(t)he significance of this figure for the old-line media organizations is that it represents time spent *not* looking at TV, reading a newspaper or going to the movies" (p. 8).

Yet, even as online applications subsume a growing portion of our media diet, relatively little is known about audience uses and interests in Web applications addressing the news. Internet service providers such as AOL are emerging as formidable competitors to traditional media. Of particular interest in the present context, the UCLA Center for Communication Policy (2001) study revealed that only 6.5% of new users and 1.6% of very experienced users (5 years or more) used chat rooms. Some 3.4% of new users and 6.1% of very experienced users indicated visiting newsgroups. Most studies addressing chat rooms lump that application together with such others as Web surfing and e-mail use, which we review in the context of general Web use here.

COMMUNICATION NEEDS

In their review of the research on new media adoption, Jeffres and Atkin (1996) noted that Internet adopters could be distinguished from those of other media by characteristic attitudinal variables. These extend beyond the communication needs linked to traditional media (e.g., escapism)—focused on audience roles as message receivers—to include the need to send messages. This need to communicate with others is a key predictor of interest in using online media.

More recently, Charney and Greenberg (2002) crafted a peer identity motivation, which incorporates the practice of going online to gain peer acceptance of one's ideas. In the context of newsgroups, users can access a Web page, post a message—which may generate feedback from others—and even contact story authors. In that regard, the practice of formulating one's personal identity online involves a social dimension (Lin, 2001). Similarly, Walther and Boyd (2002) maintained that social support provided online by weak-tie networks may, over a wide range of psychological issues, provide emotional support and personal validation.

Focusing on audience Web sites, Eighmay (1997) found that their entertainment value—in tandem with audience perception about their use experience—was involving and relevant. Other work has addressed potential abuses associated with Internet use, including Web addictions that can intrude on work or home and change personal, family, and business relationships (e.g., Ebersole, 2000; Parks & Floyd, 1996).

Newsgroups represent another, related Internet service, one that is perhaps better known under the rubric of bulletin board services (BBSs; e.g., Ogan, 1993). Scholars (e.g., Atkin, Jeffres, & Neuendorf, 1998; Lin, 1999; Morris & Ogan, 1996; Papachrissi & Rubin, 2000) advocate the application of uses and gratifications theory to explore audience adoption of Internet applications, given the similarity of general audience needs and motivations for media content across the television and online media (see Lin, Salwen, & Abdulla, Chapter 9, this volume). James, Wotring, and Forrest's (1995) study of electronic bulletin board use identified informational learning and socialization as the two primary use motives. Industry research (e.g., T. E. Miller, 1996) underscores the importance of such user motives as entertainment, surveillance, escape, entertainment, and, of particular importance for chat rooms, social interaction. To the extent that BBSs can be regarded as an audiovisual extension of existing Web service features, a user's perceived needs (or gratifications) concerning his or her adoption may also be parallel to those of regular Web content uses. Figure 13.1 represents the relative location of newsgroup and chat services on a continuum underscoring the hybrid nature of these emerging "intermass" (Lin, 2002) services.

As Figure 13.1 outlines, the Web offers media programmers as well as audiences distinctive new avenues for news programming. In merging mass as well as interpersonal functions, emerging online technologies blur the neat theoretical domains that scholars had built around those traditionally disparate domains. The question remains, though, as to whether online channels—with their advan-

	Interpersonal	Mass
Computer Mediated	Chat rooms	Newsgroups
Nonmediated	Conversation	Public Address

FIG. 13.1.   A typology of interpersonal and mediated communication applications.

tages in immediacy, capacity, and interactivity—displace or encourage attendance to conventional news media.

MEDIA SUBSTITUTION VERSUS COMPLEMENTARITY

Although media substitution theory posits that new media like the Internet will compete with established media for audience leisure time, scholars have found few displacement effects attributable to the Internet (e.g., Lin, 2002). Merging this perspective with uses and gratifications theory, the dimension of media uses deemed most important here is that involving functional equivalence, which states that media modalities may be functionally equivalent in fulfilling audience needs (e.g., Ferguson & Perse, 2000; LaRose & Atkin, 1991; Reagan, Pinkleton, Aaronson, & Chen, 1995). Researchers (Kang & Atkin, 1999; Lin, 1999; Reagan et al., 1995) suggest that the audience makes distinct selections across a multitude of media channels and content choices. Stempel, Hargrove, and Bernt (2000), for instance, found a positive relationship between Internet news use and traditional news consumption. Because audiences seek to maximize viewing choices in the multichannel environment, including news channels (Heeter & Greenberg, 1985; Lin, 1994a; Neuendorf, Atkin, & Jeffres, 2001), we posit that news junkies would make greater use of similarly focused online as well as mass media channels (i.e., newspapers and news magazines). More formally:

H1:   Newsgroup use frequency will be positively related to use of other news media.

Relationships between media could also be negative or orthogonal, as has been the case with traditional interpersonal and mass media (e.g., Neuendorf, Atkin, & Jeffres, 2002). Focusing on such interpersonal communication channels as the telephone (Dimmick, Patterson, & Sikand, 1996), research suggests that instrumental (information-oriented) gratifications are the strongest predictors of telecommunication media uses. Here, as with computer use, gratifications associated with media adoption are not clustered along gratifications connected with traditional mass media use (Atkin et al., 1998; Lin, 1999, 2001; Perse & Dunn, 1998). Based on that work, we posit that chat room use would be related to use of interpersonal channels (e.g., e-mail). More formally:

H2:   Chat room use will be positively related to use of interpersonal communication channels.

Other studies of new media adoption (e.g., Flanagin & Metzger, 2001; LaRose & Atkin, 1991) find that adoption of emerging entertainment media modalities is linked with negative attitudes toward competing modalities. Johnson and Kaye

(2000) found that those with in interest in political affairs make greater use of the Internet, rather than television, for such information. Lin (1994b) discovered that the level of media use activity—including magazines, newspapers, radio, compact discs, television, VCRs, and video cameras—appeared to be largely irrelevant to the potential adoption of pioneer online services. Others (Jeffres & Atkin, 1996; Perse & Dunn, 1998) also failed to discover any consistent relationship between interest in using Internet services and use of most other traditional mass media. Owing to countervailing findings in the literature on media displacement effects when media contents or functions differ, we posit the following research question:

RQ1: How is use of chat rooms related to use of other media?

INNOVATIVE ATTRIBUTES

Pioneer studies of computer bulletin board use suggest that adopters approximate the demographic profile of general "innovators," whose personal attributes included younger age and more education (Dutton, Rogers, & Jun, 1987; Garramone, Harris, & Anderson, 1986). More recent work confirms this upscale adopter profile (e.g., Atkin et al., 1998). Such findings are consistent with diffusion theory (Rogers, 1995, 2002), which posits that adoption of innovations is resource driven. Scholars (Atkin et al., 1998; Lin, 1998) have also noted that Internet adoption is spurred by such personality traits as novelty seeking and innovativeness needs. Based on these various findings, it is hypothesized that demographics will be related to Internet use; in particular:

H3: Social locators will be related to newsgroup use frequency.
H3a: Respondent age will be inversely related to newsgroup use frequency.
H3b: Respondent education level will be positively related to newsgroup frequency.
H3c: Respondent income level will be positively related to newsgroup use frequency.
H4: Social locators will be related to chat room use frequency.
H4a: Respondent age will be inversely related to chat room use frequency.
H4b: Respondent education level will be positively related to chat room use frequency.
H4c: Respondent income level will be positively related to chat room use frequency.

Innovators and early adopters thus play a decisive role in shaping the critical mass of users for a technology such as BBSs. This represents a critical element in the diffusion process that can help draw additional adopters to expand the diffusion rate to eventually encompass a majority of the potential user population (Markus, 1987). As that process unfolds, we examine the extent to which attitudes supplement demographics as predictors of online technology adoption.

ATTITUDINAL VARIABLES

As Lin (1999) noted, the diffusion of the Internet and the popularity of the World Wide Web quickly turned them into a place where the audience can expect to seek information, entertainment, companionship (e.g., via chat rooms) and personal identity (e.g., via joining newsgroups). Her work suggests that audience online use activities seem to resemble those activities in which the audience regularly engages via the traditional mass media.

Working from a diffusion of innovations perspective, we might expect that those most active in visiting chat rooms or other services would be the more technically capable users. Past work on general Internet adoption (e.g., Atkin et al., 1998) suggests that these individuals would likely fit the innovator profile and are most likely early adopters of interactive Web technologies generally. Such Web enthusiasts would also be more prone to derive gratifications from using the Web (e.g., Charney & Greenberg, 2002). To wit, the enhanced audience control and choice afforded by the new media encourage a relatively active as opposed to passive audience, in general (Lin, 1994a; Papachrissi & Rubin, 2000).

Jeffres and Atkin (1996) found that attitudinal variables, particularly those addressing the needs for communication (e.g., home shopping) served by computer technology, were predictive of Internet adoption intentions. This is consistent with other work on home shopping (Donthu, 1996; Grant et al., 1991). These findings parallel those of an industry study, which established that Internet enthusiasts sought escape, entertainment, interaction, and surveillance gratifications when they went online (T. E. Miller, 1996).

Past studies of Internet adoption (e.g., Lin, 2001) found that gratifications-expectation items (e.g., social interaction) are powerful predictors of online behaviors. Lin used the term *quasisocial interaction* to describe the social interaction activity taking place in these online chat groups (i.e., a two-way communication under an artificial and pseudo-social setting). Thus, where parasocial interaction could satisfy TV viewers' quest to make friends with media characters and thrust themselves into the imaginary social world on screen, "quasisocial interaction could help gratify on-line users' need to establish a relationship with their on-line counterparts and vicariously experience a pseudo-social atmosphere" (Lin, 2001, p. 14). Based on that work, we would anticipate that chat room use would be related to a need to communicate with a diverse set of online others. In the context of this study, then, it is hypothesized that:

H5: Communication needs and interests will be positively related to news-group use frequency.

H6: Communication needs and interests will be positively related to chat room use frequency.

Focusing on innovative attributes, Atkin et al. (1998) found that audiences with more technology use experience—technology junkies—expressed higher levels of interest in adopting newer, different media technology applications. Easton and LaRose (2002) found that online interaction has a positive impact on overall levels of social support by allowing users to increase their social networks via online discussion groups. Given the interrelationships between Internet use applications, we assume that more experienced Web users will be more avid consumers of the applications and utilities offered on the Internet. Our model thus posits that frequency of newsgroup and chat use will be predicted by years spent online. More formally:

H7: Level of online use will be positively related to newsgroup use frequency.

H8: Level of online use will be positively related to chat room use frequency.

The research reviewed previously shows support for relationships among media use, interpersonal communication (networks, relationships, and topics), community ties and attachments, and involvement in communities and organizations (e.g., Jeffres, Neuendorf, Atkin, & Lin, 2002).

Taken together, past work suggests that the influence of Internet utilities on audience behaviors has been measured, rather than revolutionary. Observers (Margolis & Resnick, 2000) thus suggest that we are experiencing a "normalization" of the medium, whereby audiences are using the Web to do old things in slightly different ways (as opposed to wholesale reallocations of communication and leisure patterns). For emerging Internet services, it remains to be seen whether audiences are fundamentally altering their communication behaviors or normalizing the Internet to do old things in new ways.

Given these various adopter attributes and Internet user profiles, we pose the following queries:

RQ2: What is the relative influence of social locators, technology adoption, media use, and user interest variables related to newsgroup use?

RQ3: What is the relative influence of social locators, technology adoption, media use, and user interest variables related to chat room use?

METHODS

Research data were collected from two telephone surveys using a computer-aided telephone interview system; the first ($n = 351$) was conducted from June 20 to July 8, 2001 and the second ($n = 484$) was conducted from October 20 to Novem-

ber 11, 2001. Both samples were generated through random-digit dialing procedures. The geographic region covered by the telephone surveys was an ethnically
diverse metropolitan area of the Midwestern United States, with a population
base close to 2 million. The surveys were presented as a general poll with an em-
phasis on values and what people think is important in life. The response rates
ranged from 45% to 50%. Variables used in this study were operationalized as
follows.

Study 1

Social Networks and Values

Respondents were asked to rate the importance of "being involved in the community" and "having good neighbors" using a scale ranging from 0 to 10. The
two values are correlated at .37 ($p < .001$). The values on which we focus were embedded in a large list of values rated in terms of their importance, and included
the variables that follow.

Civic Culture and Social Values.   Respondents were asked to rate the importance of "participating in the political system," using a scale ranging from 0 to 10.
They were also asked to rate the importance of "tolerance of other people," using a
scale ranging from 0 to 10.

Community Variables

Several measures were constructed for community attachment, community
activities, organizational ties, and community assessment. The operationalizations were based on items used in other studies (see Jeffres et al., 2002) and can be
summarized as follows.

Community Activities.   Respondents were asked to use a scale ranging from 0
to 10 to tell how often they did each of several things, including going to sporting
events, going to cultural events such as plays or the orchestra, going to local muse-
ums, and attending concerts of current musical groups or artists. Responses to
each item were standardized and the scores summed up for a scale ($\alpha = .68$).

Community Ties.   For this measure, respondents were asked, "Do you belong
to any neighborhood or community organization, including block clubs, social
groups, religious groups, business groups, or ethnic clubs?" If they said "yes," they
were asked, "What are they?" The number cited was coded. This item as been used
in various studies cited earlier (e.g., Jeffres et al., 2002).

Media Use

Media use and diversity of sources was measured using the standard set of items as well as several measures for the new technologies; constituent measures include the following.

TV Viewing. Respondents were asked for the number of hours of television they watched yesterday. The scale ranged from 0 for none to 11 for more than 10 hr.

TV News Viewing. Respondents were asked how often they usually watch the news on television: several times a day, about once a day, 5 or 6 days a week, 3 or 4 days a week, 1 or 2 days a week, or less often than that.

Radio Listening. Respondents were asked how many hours they listened to the radio yesterday. Coding was done using the same scale used for television.

Newspaper Reading. Respondents were asked how many days last week they read a newspaper and responses were coded from 0 to 7.

Magazine Reading. Respondents were asked how many different magazines they read regularly. Responses were coded into nine categories: 0, 1, 2, 3, 4, 5, 6 to 10, 11 to 20, and 21 or more.

Book Reading. Respondents were asked how many books they read in the past 6 months. Responses were coded into the same nine categories used for magazines.

Video Viewing. Respondents were asked how many borrowed or rented videos they watched in the past month. Responses were coded into the same nine categories used for magazines.

Film Viewing. Respondents were asked how many times they went out to see a movie in a theater in the past month. Responses were coded into the same nine categories used for magazines.

Media Use Index. Responses to the use of traditional media were standardized and the scores summed up to create an index.

Computer Access. Respondents were asked if they had a personal or laptop computer in their household and responses were coded yes or no.

Internet Access. Respondents were asked if they had access to the Internet at home, at work, or both. Access was coded two ways, as a dummy variable where access anywhere = 1 and no access = 0; and as a continuum where access at both home and work = 2, access at either alone = 1, and no access = 0.

Internet Use. Respondents were asked if they had ever gone on the Internet. Those who said "yes" were asked how often they go on the Internet at work, using a scale ranging from 7 (*several times a day*) to 0 (*almost never*). They also were asked how often they go on the Internet at home using the same scale. Several variables were constructed: (a) a simple usage measure where 1 = has gone on the Internet before, 0 = has never gone on the Internet; (b) Internet access (access = 1); (c) frequency use Internet at work (those without access = –1); (d) frequency use Internet at home (those without access = –1); (e) overall Internet use, combining the scores for usage at home and work. A separate measure gauged the number of years spent on the Internet (see Jeffres et al., 2002).

Media Web Site Use. Respondents were asked how often they visited media Web sites such as one of the TV networks, a newspaper, or radio site, using a 7-point scale ranging from 1 (*almost never*) to 7 (*several times a day*). Those not using the Internet were assigned a value of 0.

E-Mail Use. Respondents were asked "How often do you send or receive messages by e-mail? They responded on a 5-point scale from 1 (*several times each day*) to 5 (*never*).

Chat Room Use. For the dependent variable, respondents were asked if they had ever visited a chat room on the Internet to talk with people about something. Those who said "yes" were asked how often, using the following categories: every day (6), a couple times a week, about once a week, a couple times a month, or less often than that (2). Those who had never visited a chat room before were assigned a 1 and those who had never gone on the Internet were assigned a 0.

Social Categories

The standard social categories were measured, including marital status, the number of people in one's household, age, level of formal education completed, ethnic or racial background, household income, and gender. Dummy variables were constructed for being married, being White, being Black, and being other race or ethnicity (see Jeffres et al., 2002).

Interpersonal Communication Relationships

Two measures of interpersonal communication relationships were used. Respondents were asked how much they agreed with each of the following statements, using a scale ranging from 0 (*strongly disagree*) to 5 (*neutral*) to 10 (*strongly agree*). "Talking about current events with friends or coworkers" and "I prefer talking with people who have the same background as me."

Study 2

A follow-up study conducted the following quarter utilized many of the measures of social locators and media use employed in the first survey. In addition, Study 2 operationalized a key dependent measure, newsgroup use, with the following item: "How often do you visit Web sites in other languages (1 = *almost never* through 7 = *several times a day*).

Because newsgroups revolve around informational channels, we employed an expanded set of content interest/knowledge measures that include the following, arrayed across an 11-point scale ranging from 0 (*strongly disagree*) to 10 (*strongly agree*):

- **Interest in other cultures.** Respondents were asked about the extent to which "I enjoy learning about different cultures."
- **International news.** Respondents were asked "How much attention do you pay to the international news in the newspaper?"
- **Awareness of world events.** This measure was tapped with the item "I'm more aware of what's going on around the world than most of my friends."
- **Tolerance of differences.** Respondent agreement was assessed for an item stating "I tend to value similarities over differences when I meet someone."
- **Communicate with culturally diverse others.** Respondents were asked about their agreement with the statement "In any given month, I communicate with people from a wide variety of backgrounds and cultures."

As in Study 1, we created a series of indexes reflecting respondent knowledge about current events and popular culture (see procedures outlined in the previous section). Data were then subjected to correlational analysis. Selected background variables were then entered into multiple regression analysis. Variance inflation factor inspections revealed no significant multicollinearity problems. Hair, Anderson, Tatham, and Black (1992) defined the variance inflation matrix as "(A)n indicator of the effects the other predictor variables have on the variance of a regression coefficient" (p. 24), noting that it is directly related to the tolerance values. A stepwise regression model was tested in which significant correlates of the dependent variable were submitted simultaneously.

FINDINGS

We first analyzed relationships between Internet use measure and social locators, media use, and content interest dimensions. Overall, nearly a quarter (24.2%) of respondents indicated using newsgroups, and 35.3% had used chat rooms. Correlational analyses of newsgroup use are outlined in Table 13.1.

There was a dearth of relationships between use of newsgroups and social locators, media and content interest, or knowledge variables. Newsgroup use was inversely related to agreement with the sentiment that one "values similarities among people over their differences" ($r = -.123$). Aside from that, the relationship involving marital status approached ($p < .06$) significance, as married individuals made greater use of the new medium ($r = .09$). On balance, though, the number of relationships between newsgroup use and our independent variables is no greater than that which we would expect to see from chance alone. This leaves Hypotheses 1, 3, 5, and 7 without support. Regarding our Research Question 3 on the relative influence of background variables on newsgroups, the re-

TABLE 13.1
Correlations Between Newsgroup and Communication
Technology, Attitudinal Measures

Variable	Newsgroup Visits
Media use	
Hours spent on Web sites	.052
Hours spent shopping online	−.008
Time with radio	.006
Newspaper readership	.023
International news reading	.049
Magazine readership	−.048
Book readership	.002
DVD rentals	−.052
Movie attendance	−.002
Social locators	
Age	−.004
Non-White	.043
Married	.085 ($p \leq .067$)
Female gender	.029
Interests and values	
Communicate with culturally diverse others	.021
Interest in other cultures	.030
Feel aware of world events	−.019
Value similarities among people over differences	−.123*
Interest in other cultures	.030
Interest in new civic ideas	.039
Knowledge of popular culture	.045
Current events knowledge	.049

*$p < .01$.

lationships were not sufficiently robust to warrant any further multivariate analysis.

Correlational analyses of chat room use are outlined in Table 13.2. Per Research Question 1, the data reveal a pattern of relationships to other media that are generally weak and positive in nature. In particular, chat room use is positively related to our media use index (r = .15), computer ownership (r = .25), Internet use frequency (r = .38) and Internet access (r = .27). Separate measures indicate that the more important access is from the home (r = .41), because Internet access at work is not significantly related to chat room use (r = .13). Other Internet use dimensions related to chat use include frequency of Web site use (r = .42), and a combined measure of World Wide Web use at home and at work (r = .45). Use of another interpersonal channel, e-mail, is also related to chat room use (r = .26); this provides modest support for Hypothesis 2. These Internet-based correlates of chat use, combined with that involving years on the

TABLE 13.2
Correlations Between Chat Room Use and Communication
Technology, Attitudinal Measures

Variable	Chat Room Visits
Media use variables	
Years on Internet	.24**
Computer ownership	.25**
Internet access (home or work)	.27**
Internet use frequency	.38**
Internet use frequency (work)	.13
Internet use frequency (home)	.41**
E-mail use	.26**
Media Web site use	.42**
World Wide Web use	.45**
Mass media use index	.15*
Communication diversity	.43**
Social locators	
Age	.32**
Education	.16*
Male gender	.11*
Interests and values	
Interest in U.S. current events	.37**
Interest in arts	.40**
Knowledge of global cultures	.27**
Knowledge of international news	.23**
Knowledge of popular culture	.24**
Tolerant of others	−.06
Have good neighbors	−.12*
Participating in political system	.07
Community ties index	−.07
Community involvement	.26**

*p < .05. **p < .01.

Internet ($r = .24$), underscore and support the role of Internet experience posited in Hypothesis 8.

Social locators are generally unrelated to chat room use. We do, however, see a weak positive relationship with chat use and education ($r = .16$), consistent with Hypothesis 4b. Contrary to Hypothesis 4a, however, we see a positive relationship between age and chat room use ($r = .31$). The only other social locator related to chat room use is gender, as males are more likely to make use of the technology ($r = .11$). Further marginal breakouts suggest that about half (49.6%) of men use chat groups, compared to only 39% of women (sig. $\chi^2 = .05$). On balance, this provides only modest support for the youthful, high-socioeconomic-status adopter profile posited by Hypothesis 4.

Chat room use is positively related to our indexes of popular culture knowledge ($r = .24$) and community involvement ($r = .26$). Visiting chat rooms is also correlated with knowledge of international news ($r = .23$) and with an index capturing knowledge of different regions and cultures ($r = .27$). Although our measures of tolerance of others and community ties are not related to chat room use, "having good neighbors" is inversely related ($r = -.12$) to chat room visits. On balance, these findings provide only modest support for the needs-driven adoption conception outlined in Hypothesis 6.

Table 13.3 outlines the hierarchical regression model, which explained 18% of the variance in chat room use frequency. Exploring the possible media substitution dynamics posed in Research Question 1, traditional media use is unrelated to chat room use. As for the relative influence of various predictor blocks (Research Question 3), the only social locator significantly related to chat room use was age ($\beta = -.253$), which explained nearly 4% of the variance observed. Interestingly, the positive bivariate relationship between age and chat room use was reversed under the controlling influence of other variables in the multivariate analysis; this partially rehabilitates Hypothesis 3's prediction of a youthful adopter profile.

Consistent with the information-seeker profile posited in Hypothesis 6, interest in current events ($\beta = .222$) and communication diversity ($\beta = .144$) were predictors of chat room use. Support for this hypothesis is mixed, however, as interest in the arts bears an inverse relationship ($\beta = -.198$) to chat room usage. Years

TABLE 13.3
Stepwise Multiple Regression Model Predicting Chat Room Usage

Variable	R	Final β	R^2 Change	F Change	Sig. F Change
Years on the Internet	.244	.254	.059	11.941	.001
Age	.317	−.253	.041	8.579	.004
Interest in current events	.367	.222	.034	7.380	.007
Interest in arts	.402	−.198	.027	6.053	.015
Communication diversity	.426	.440	.019	4.401	.037

Note. Total model: $R^2 = .181$; Adj $R^2 = .159$; $F(5, 185) = 8.198$; $p < .001$.

on the Internet (β = .254) emerged as the most powerful positive predictor, explaining nearly 4% of the variance in chat room use. This result provides further support for Hypothesis 8.

In sum, regression results provide mixed expectations for our proposed framework. Chat room use is positively related to years on the Internet and an interest in current events as well as community activities. Age—the only social locator to emerge in our model—was inversely related to chat room use, as was interest in arts activities.

DISCUSSION

This study identified variables related to use of newsgroups and chat rooms in terms of social locators, communication needs, media use habits, and technology adoption. Findings generally fail to confirm the upscale, heavy-media-use, technology adopter profile posited by diffusion theory. The failure of diffusion variables to explain use of these services may reflect the fact that its Internet platform has now reached the "flat" part of its diffusion curve. Thus, as newsgroups and chat rooms surpass their critical mass, differences between users and nonusers have leveled over time. Similar patterns have been observed for cable since the 1980s (Atkin & LaRose, 1994; Dutton et al., 1987; Sparkes & Kang, 1986). In that regard, our sample of urban respondents provides a profile of a service in its mature stages of diffusion.

To the extent the Internet is becoming "normalized," Jeffres et al. (2002) found that the Internet audience is beginning to look much like the consumer audience in general, but behavioral patterns often are linked to social categories. In this case, the failure of income to discriminate between heavy and light users may suggest that these services, particularly newsgroups, have reached a saturation point within an otherwise upscale Internet universe. Yet such Internet applications are not likely to be regarded as "household necessities," in the tradition of the telephone, available to 94% of American homes. Because only a bare majority of Americans own the necessary gateway for Internet services—a powerful 100+ Mhz computer processor and a $20 monthly subscription to an Internet service provider—it remains to be seen whether chat or newsgroups emerge as a "rich man's" substitute for less expensive telephone service plans.

The dearth of relationships involving newsgroups, in particular, provides little support for the notion that this medium represents an electronic forum spurring a more robust democracy. Rather than bring sweeping democratic changes, Web technology is likely to further such recent media trends as audience fragmentation and the attendant hype needed to break through the clutter of multiple media offerings. Relationships between the Web and use of other media uncovered here suggest that emerging online environments are not displacement mechanisms, but will instead make it easier for news junkies to immerse themselves in media content.

In this regard, our findings on newsgroups confirm Levin's (2002) analysis of the Web's influence on politics. He found that, in the world of journalism, the Internet may not be the sweeping force for democracy and diversity that many had envisaged. However, this multiplicity of similarity does not bear content identical to that of TV and print media. For instance, blogs (or Web logs) take advantage of the large capacity of the Internet to provide "micro" perspectives on news events that may fall outside of the existing media-cultural complex's monopoly on powerful communication media. Further work should investigate the relative appeal of these and other emerging online sources.

With chat, the strong explanatory role played by community variables suggests that the medium may, unlike the telephone, help us to reconnect around various community activities. In this regard, the Internet may help offset social trends toward tribalization introduced by earlier interpersonal telecommunication channels like the telephone:

> Where cities had once been created to facilitate the process of human communication, the telephone (aided and abetted by the automobile) made physical proximity optional. The city of local neighborhoods—where social, work and commercial needs were all within walking distance—became the city of segregated districts (financial, industrial, commercial, residential). The telephone promoted the population shift out of the inner cities while helping to expand business operations within cities. (Bates, Albright, & Washington, 2002, p. 94)

Hopefully the linkages among chat room use, current events, and community interests bode well for a future Internet role in helping to detribalize, and perhaps reverse the process of segregation initiated by telecommunication media during the previous century. Of course, the inverse relationship between having good neighbors and use of chat services suggests that the medium can also provide further avenues for those who feel disconnected in their neighborhoods.

The predominance of traditional media among Web sites suggests that differences in Web transmission may now have more to do with style than substance. The selective patterns of online media use uncovered here, to the extent that they relate to public affairs knowledge, suggest that Web modalities are distinguished mainly in terms of their distinctive facility for exchanging and accessing information.

As mentioned at the onset, emerging intermass channels like the Internet pose questions about the degree to which audiences shift away from conventional media to a wider range of emerging technologies. However, rather than displace traditional channels, per media substitution conceptualizations, our findings suggest that Internet use remains orthogonal to such pursuits. This is particularly true of newsgroups.

By contrast, regression results suggest that chat room devotees typically have more experience with the Internet, are younger, are interested in current events, are not interested in the arts, and have a greater interest in diverse community events. These results thus confirm a raft of findings (e.g., Dutton et al., 1987) that suggest that attitudinal variables are more explanatory of technology adoption than conventional media use and social locator variables. We find little evidence here, then, that online media content access is perceived as a "functional supplement" to traditional media use. One explanation for this nonfinding may be that, although functionally similar to a certain degree, traditional media remain better suited to deliver more attractive content in an accessible and affordable fashion, relative to an online service. Moreover, the online media content has yet to achieve the visual quality of print media, or the audiovisual quality of traditional mass media (Lin, 2001).

Another reason for the lack of any relationships with news or any other media may be, as Lin (2001) suggested, that "traditional media remain better suited to deliver more attractive content in an accessible and affordable fashion, relative to an on-line service" (p. 14). She observed that emerging online channels like newsgroups have yet to achieve the visual quality of print media, or the audiovisual quality of television and film and are thus not yet a functional substitute for them. Perhaps, as video and voice functions are merged with the text dimensions now characteristic of newsgroups and chat rooms, displacement mechanisms with telecommunication or other media channels will emerge.

In sum, this study was only able to statistically discriminate adopters and nonadopters for chat users, and such use is chiefly dependent on five factors: how long someone has been using the Internet, the age of the user, the user's interest in the arts, the user's interest in current events in the United States, and interest in diverse community activities. In that regard, these findings are encouraging in that they suggest that audiences will be able to "program" their own content through forums such as the chat room. Because this Internet-facilitated "quasisocial interaction" is absent any social pressures (Kiesler, 1997; Parks & Floyd, 1996), it may eventually help reduce stress and provide the kind of enjoyment associated with mass media. In this way, the Web can perhaps offset the on-going consolidation of ownership characterizing offline mass media. However, these results suggest that wholesale media substitution of new media channels for community activities and community attachments is not yet a concern. Later work should explore more closely the motivations determining the selection of various online modalities for interpersonal as well as news and other mass media applications. Working from the uses and gratifications perspective, for instance, scholars (Lin, 2001; Papachrissi & Rubin, 2000) found that the Internet attracts an active audience that intently seeks out and consumes media content to gratify such needs as entertainment (for mental stimulation), identity (for social integration), diversion (for temporary escape), and surveillance (for information gathering). These cognitive and affective need expectations may be expanded from the study of uses and gratifications, originated with the study of traditional media, and can help shed conceptual light on the Internet as a two-way interactive medium. Further work in this area should explore the social, economic, and political meanings of these emerging intermass technologies.

REFERENCES

Albright, J., Purohit, K., & Walsh, C. (2002). Louise Rosenblatt seeks QtZznBoi@aol.com for LTR: Using chat rooms in interdisciplinary middle school classrooms. *Journal of Adolescent and Adult Literacy, 45,* 692–706.

Andrews, F. M. (Ed.). (1986). *Research on the quality of life.* Ann Arbor: University of Michigan, Institute for Social Research.

Atkin, D., Jeffres, L., & Neuendorf, K. (1998). Understanding Internet adoption as telecommunications behavior. *Journal of Broadcasting & Electronic Media, 42,* 475–490.

Atkin, D., & LaRose, R. (1994). A meta analysis of the information services adoption literature. In J. Hanson (Ed.), *Advances in telematics* (Vol. 2, pp. 91–110). Norwood, NJ: Ablex.

Atkin, D., & Lau, T. Y. (2003, May). *Still on hold: Competitive implications of the Telecommunication Act of 1996.* Paper presented at the annual meeting of the International Communication Association, San Diego, CA.

Bates, B., Albright, K., & Washington, K. (2002). Not your plain old telephone: New services and new impacts. In C. A. Lin & D. Atkin (Eds.), *Communication technology and society* (pp. 91–124). Cresskill, NJ: Hampton.

Charney, T., & Greenberg, B. S. (2002). Uses and gratifications of the Internet. In C. A. Lin & D. Atkin (Eds.), *Communication technology and society: Audience adoption and uses* (pp. 379–407). Cresskill, NJ: Hampton.

Dimmick, J. W., Patterson, S., & Sikand, S. J. (1996). Personal telephone networks: A typology and two empirical studies. *Journal of Broadcasting & Electronic Media, 40,* 45–59.

Dizard, W. (2000). *Old media, new media.* New York: Longman.

Donthu, N. (1996). Observations A: The infomercial shopping. *Journal of Advertising Research, 36*(2), 69–76.

Dutton, W., Rogers, E., & Jun, S. H. (1987). The diffusion and impacts of information technology in households. In P. I. Zorkoczy (Ed.), *Oxford surveys in information technology* (Vol. 4, pp. 133–193). New York: Oxford University Press.

Easton, M., & LaRose, R. (2002, August). *Modeling social support in online discussion groups.* Paper presented to the Association for Education in Journalism & Mass Communication, Miami Beach, FL.

Ebersole, S. E. (2000). Uses and gratifications of Web among students. *Journal of Computer Mediated Communication, 6*(1). Retrieved November 11, 2001, from http://www.ascusc.org/jcmc/vol16/issue1/ebersole.html

Eighmay, J. (1997). Profiling user responses to commercial web sites. *Journal of Advertising Research, 37,* 59–66.

Ferguson, D. A., & Perse, E. M. (2000). The World Wide Web as a functional alternative to television. *Journal of Broadcasting & Electronic Media, 44,* 155–174.

Flanagin, A. J., & Metzger, M. J. (2001). Internet use in the contemporary media environment. *Human Communication Research, 27,* 153–181.

Garramone, G., Harris, A., & Anderson, R. (1986). Uses of political bulletin boards. *Journal of Broadcasting & Electronic Media, 30,* 325–339.

Grant, A., Guthrie, K. K., & Ball-Rokeach, S. (1991). Television shopping. *Communication Research, 18*(6), 773–798.

Hair, J., Anderson, R., Tatham, R., & Black, W. (1992). *Multivariate analysis.* New York: Macmillan.

Heeter, C., & Greenberg, B. A. (1985). *Cableviewing.* Norwood, NJ: Ablex.

Ibanez, I. (2002). Online chat rooms: Virtual spaces of interaction for social oriented people. *CyberPsychology and Behavior, 5*(1), 43–52.

James, M. L., Wotring, C. E., & Forrest, E. (1995). An exploratory study of the perceived benefits of electronic bulletin board use and their impact on other communication activities. *Journal of Broadcasting & Electronic Media, 39,* 30–50.

Jeffres, L. W., & Atkin, D. (1996). Predicting use of technologies for communication and consumer needs. *Journal of Broadcasting & Electronic Media, 40,* 318–330.

Jeffres, L., Neuendorf, K., Atkin, D., & Lin, C. A. (2002, July). *The wired nation.* Paper presented at the meeting of the International Communication Association, Seoul, Korea.

Johnson, T., & Kaye, B. T. (2000). Using is believing: The influence of reliance on the credibility of online political information among politically interested internet users. *Journalism & Mass Communication Quarterly, 77,* 865–879.

Kang, M. E., & Atkin, D. (1999). Exploring the role of audience uses and gratifications in the adoption of multimedia cable. *Telematics & Informatics, 16,* 59–74.

Kiesler, S. (1997). *Culture of the Internet.* Mahwah, NJ: Lawrence Erlbaum Associates.

Labaton, S. (2003, May 13). Plan to loosen network rules goes to FCC. *The New York Times,* pp. 1, C10.

LaRose, R., & Atkin, D. (1991). Movie distribution modalities and consumer choice. *Journal of Media Economics, 4,* 3–17.

Levin, Y. (2002). Politics after the Internet. *The Public Interest, 149*(Fall), 80–94.

Lin, C. A. (1994a). Audience fragmentation in a competitive video marketplace. *Journal of Advertising Research, 34*(6), 1–17.

Lin, C. A. (1994b). Exploring potential factors for home videotext adoption. *Advances in Telematics, 2,* 111–121.

Lin, C. A. (1998). Exploring personal computer adoption dynamics. *Journal of Broadcasting & Electronic Media, 42,* 95–112.

Lin, C. A. (1999). Online service adoption likelihood. *Journal of Advertising Research, 39*(2), 79–89.

Lin, C. A. (2001). Perceived gratifications of online media service use among potential users. *Telematics & Informatics, 19,* 3–19.

Lin, C. A. (2002). Paradigm for communication and information technology adoption research. In C. A. Lin & D. Atkin (Eds.), *Communication technology and society: Audience adoption and uses* (pp. 447–476). Cresskill, NJ: Hampton.

Markus, L. (1987). Toward a "critical mass" theory of interactive media: Universal access, interdependence and diffusion. *Communication Research, 14,* 491–511.

Margolis, M., & Resnick, D. (2000). *Politics as usual: The cyberspace "revolution."* Thousand Oaks, CA: Sage.

Miller, T. E. (1996, July). Segmenting the Internet. *American Demographics, 48.*

Morris, M., & Ogan, C. (1996). The Internet as mass medium. *Journal of Communication, 46*(1), 39–50.

Neuendorf, K., Atkin, D., & Jeffres, L. (2001). Reconceptualizing channel repertoire in the urban cable environment. *Journal of Broadcasting & Electronic Media, 45,* 464–482.

Neuendorf, K., Atkin, D., & Jeffres, L. (2002). Adoption of audio information services in the United States: A bridge innovation. In C. A. Lin & D. Atkin (Eds.), *Communication technology and society: Audience adoption and uses* (pp. 125–152). Cresskill, NJ: Hampton.

Ogan, C. (1993). Listserve communication during the Gulf war: What kind of medium is the electronic bulletin board? *Journal of Broadcasting & Electronic Media, 37,* 177–196.

Papachrissi, Z., & Rubin, A. (2000). Predictors of Internet use. *Journal of Broadcasting & Electronic Media, 44,* 175–196.

Parks, M., & Floyd, K. (1996). Making friends in cyberspace. *Journal of Communication, 46*(1), 80–97.

Perse, E., & Dunn, D. (1998). The utility of home computers and media use: Implications of multimedia and connectivity. *Journal of Broadcasting & Electronic Media, 42,* 435–456.

Pew Research Center. (2001). More online, doing more. *The Pew Internet & American Life Project.* http://www.pewinternet.org

Reagan, J., Pinkleton, B., Aaronson, D., & Chen, C. F. (1995). How do technologies relate to the repertoire of information sources? *Telematics and Informatics, 12,* 21–27.

Rogers, E. (1995). *Diffusion of innovations* (4th ed.). New York: The Free Press.

Rogers, E. M. (2002). Information society in the next millennium: Captain's log 2001. In C. A. Lin & D. Atkin (Eds.), *Communication technology and society: Audience adoption and uses of the new media* (pp. 23–42). Cresskill, NJ: Hampton.

Sparkes, N., & Kang, N. (1986). Public reactions to cable television: Time in the diffusion process. *Journal of Broadcasting & Electronic Media, 30,* 213–229.

Stempel, G. H., Hargrove, T., & Bernt, J. P. (2000). Relation of growth of use of the Internet to changes in media use from 1995–1999. *Journalism & Mass Communication Quarterly, 77,* 71–79.

UCLA Center for Communication Policy. (2001, November). *The UCLA Internet report 2001: Surveying the digital future.* Los Angeles: UCLA Regents.

Veronis, Suhler, & Associates. (2000). *The Internet opportunity.* New York: Author.

Walther, J., & Boyd, S. (2002). Attraction to computer-mediated social support. In C. A. Lin & D. Atkin (Eds.), *Communication technology and social change: Audience adoption and uses* (pp. 153–188). Cresskill, NJ: Hampton.

National Telephone Survey Questionnaires, 2001–2002

SCHOOL OF COMMUNICATION

BASELINE WEB PROJECT 1
February 25–28, 2002

Hello. My name is (**use your first name**). I am a student calling from the University of Miami in Coral Gables, Florida. We are conducting a national opinion survey to find out what people think of the news media. This study is for educational purposes and we are not selling anything. [**NO PAUSE**]

→STATEMENTS YOU MAY USE IF NEEDED←

NOTE: IF PERSON ASKS WHAT THIS SURVEY IS FOR: "This study will be used as a research project for students. The statistical findings will be presented at academic conferences to learn more about what the public thinks of the news media."

NOTE: IF PERSON ASKS "HOW LONG?" THIS WILL TAKE: "It depends on how you answer some questions and how quickly we move through this. It may be as short as two minutes and as long as 6 or 7 minutes. I'll try to move through it quickly."

NOTE: IF PERSON ASKS HOW HIS/HER PHONE NUMBER WAS OBTAINED: "Your phone number was randomly generated by a computer, so your identity is anonymous and only the statistical results will be used for educational purposes"

First . . . (DO NOT PAUSE OR ASK IF IT IS OK. JUMP RIGHT INTO THE SURVEY)

Are you age 18 or older? (CIRCLE ONE)

YES (CONTINUE)   NO (ASK IF THERE IS ANYONE 18;
                      IF NO, POLITELY TERMINATE)

1. →RECORD GENDER NOW!   MALE   FEMALE

I am going to mention some news activities. After I mention each one, please tell me **how many days a week, if any**, you engage in each news activity. First. . .

2. How many days a week, if any, do you discuss **issues or events in the news** with other people, such as family, friends, co-workers and others? [**NOTE: IF LESS THAN 1 DAY PER WEEK, CIRCLE "ZERO"**]

0   1   2   3   4   5   6   7   DK   REF

3. How many days a week, if any, do you read a **printed newspaper?** For this, do not count World Wide Web-based online newspapers [**NOTE: IF LESS THAN 1 DAY PER WEEK, CIRCLE "ZERO"**]

0   1   2   3   4   5   6   7   DK   REF

4. How many days a week, if any, do you listen **to news programs** on the radio while at home, at work, in the car or elsewhere? [**NOTE: IF LESS THAN 1 DAY PER WEEK, CIRCLE "ZERO"**]

0   1   2   3   4   5   6   7   DK   REF

5. How many days a week, if any, do you watch **newscasts** on television that have a news anchor or anchors and news reporters? [**NOTE: IF LESS THAN 1 DAY PER WEEK, CIRCLE "ZERO"**]

0   1   2   3   4   5   6   7   DK   REF

6. How many days a week, if any, do you watch an all-news cable television network, such as CNN, Fox News Network, CNBC, and-or MSNBC? [**NOTE: IF LESS THAN 1 DAY PER WEEK, CIRCLE "ZERO"**]

0   1   2   3   4   5   6   7   DK   REF

7. How many days a week, if any, do you read a major **newsmagazine**, such as *Time, Newsweek,* or *U.S. News and World Report*? [**NOTE: IF LESS THAN 1 DAY PER WEEK, CIRCLE "ZERO"**]

0   1   2   3   4   5   6   7   DK   REF

8. How many days a week, if any, do you go online to use the Internet or World Wide Web? [IF ZERO OR "DK" OR "REF," GO TO #40]

0 (GO TO #40)   DK (GO TO #40)   REF (GO TO #40)

0   1   2   3   4   5   6   7   DK   REF

→IF ZERO (OR "DK" OR "REF") TO Q. 8, GO TO QUESTION # 40

9. And during a typical day, about how much time in—minutes or hours—do you actively spend online? By this I mean time you actively spend online.

FILL IN _____ DK   REF
(INDICATE HOURS OR MINUTES)

→10. Many newspapers, newsmagazines, television stations, and cable television network stations have news sites on the World Wide Web. How many days a week, if any, do you read online Web sites offered by one or more of these conventional news media outlets? [NOTE: IF LESS THAN 1 DAY PER WEEK, CIRCLE "ZERO"]

→0   1   2   3   4   5   6   7   DK   REF

→11. Internet service providers, such as America Online, Netscape, or Microsoft Network also have online news. How many days a week, if any, do you read the news from any of these or other Internet service providers? [NOTE: IF LESS THAN 1 DAY PER WEEK, CIRCLE "ZERO"]

→0   1   2   3   4   5   6   7   DK   REF

→12. Search engines, such as Yahoo!, Lycos or Alta Vista also have online news. How many days a week, if any, do you read the news from any of these or other search engines? [NOTE: IF LESS THAN 1 DAY PER WEEK, CIRCLE "ZERO"]

→0   1   2   3   4   5   6   7   DK   REF

→IF "1" OR MORE DAYS TO EITHER #10, #11 OR #12 [NEWS USER], CONTINUE TO Q. # 13. IF ZERO TO ALL THREE, GO TO Q. # 40

13. And during a typical day when you read news online on the Internet or the World Wide Web, about how much time—in minutes and or hours—do you actively spend reading news online?

FILL IN _____ DK   REF
(INDICATE HOURS OR MINUTES)

14. There are many Web sites **for news** on the World Wide Web. In your opinion, which **ONE NEWS Web site** would you say you use most often FOR your news needs? **(FILL IN THE PERSON'S ANSWER)**

FILL IN _____ DK   REF

→ I am going to mention some things that some **online news readers** do. After I mention each one, please tell me whether you do each thing **A Lot, Sometimes, Rarely, or Never.** First . . .

15. Read online news to learn more about a **news story** that you learned about elsewhere

A Lot   Sometimes   Rarely   Never   DK   REF

16. Participate in online polls about issues **in the news**

A Lot   Sometimes   Rarely   Never   DK   REF

17. Post or read messages in message boards or chat rooms that concern events or issues **in the news**

A Lot   Sometimes   Rarely   Never   DK   REF

18. Post or read messages **about issues in the news** that you subscribe to through your e-mail service, commonly known as a "list serve" or "alert list"

A Lot   Sometimes   Rarely   Never   DK   REF

19. Bookmark or set one or more favorite Web sites **that are news sites**

A Lot   Sometimes   Rarely   Never   DK   REF

20. Listen to audio **news stories** online

A Lot   Sometimes   Rarely   Never   DK   REF

21. Watch streaming video of **news stories** online

A Lot   Sometimes   Rarely   Never   DK   REF

***

→ I am going to mention some **reasons** people have given for following news and current events **on the World Wide Web**. After I mention each one, please tell me whether you **STRONGLY AGREE, AGREE, DISAGREE, STRONGLY DIS-AGREE** or whether you **NEITHER AGREE NOR DISAGREE** regarding the statement for following news on the World Wide Web.

FIRST, do you follow news and current events on the Web . . .

22. Because you find interesting **news stories** by chance while you are on the Web doing other things

St.Agree   Agree   Disagree   St.Disagree   NEITHER   DK   REF

23. Because you can get **news** on the Web that is not available elsewhere

St.Agree   Agree   Disagree   St.Disagree   NEITHER   DK   REF

24. Because you can get **more news** on the Web than from conventional news sources

St.Agree   Agree   Disagree   St.Disagree   NEITHER   DK   REF

25. Because getting news on the Web is **easier** than getting it from conventional news sources

St.Agree   Agree   Disagree   St.Disagree   NEITHER   DK   REF

26. Because getting news on the Web is **convenient** for you

St.Agree   Agree   Disagree   St.Disagree   NEITHER   DK   REF

27. Because you can go to the Web to **learn more about breaking news stories**

St.Agree   Agree   Disagree   St.Disagree   NEITHER   DK   REF

28. Because the Web offers news that reflect your **interests**

St.Agree   Agree   Disagree   St.Disagree   NEITHER   DK   REF

29. Because news stories catch your attention when **logging on or logging off** the computer

St.Agree   Agree   Disagree   St.Disagree   NEITHER   DK   REF

30. Because you can **go directly** to the news that interests you

St.Agree   Agree   Disagree   St.Disagree   NEITHER   DK   REF

31. Because news on the Web is **different** from conventional news sources

St.Agree   Agree   Disagree   St.Disagree   NEITHER   DK   REF

32. Because news on the Web is **more in-depth** than news from conventional news sources

St.Agree   Agree   Disagree   St.Disagree   NEITHER   DK   REF

33. Because news on the Web offers the ability to get **different viewpoints on news stories**

St.Agree   Agree   Disagree   St.Disagree   NEITHER   DK   REF

34. Because you can go online to the World Wide Web to get the news **any time you want**

St.Agree   Agree   Disagree   St.Disagree   NEITHER   DK   REF

35. Because news on the Web is a **quick and easy way** to keep up with the news

St.Agree   Agree   Disagree   St.Disagree   NEITHER   DK   REF

36. Because you find **unusual** news stories online

St.Agree   Agree   Disagree   St.Disagree   NEITHER   DK   REF

37. Because news on the Web is more **reliable** than news from conventional news sources

St.Agree   Agree   Disagree   St.Disagree   NEITHER   DK   REF

38. And when you read news on the Web, do you **ever notice** the advertisements that are on the Web pages?

YES   **NO (Go to # 40)**   DK **(Go to # 40)**   REF **(Go to # 40)**

39. Some people find advertisements **to be annoying.** In general, would you say you find the advertisements while you read online news to be MORE AN-NOYING, LESS ANNOYING, or JUST AS ANNOYING as advertisements in conventional news media, **or would you say** you DO NOT FIND THE ONLINE ADVERTISEMENTS TO BE ANNOYING?

MORE   LESS   JUST AS   NOT ANNOYING   DK   REF

#40 STARTS HERE
Just a few final questions for classification purposes . . .

40. How old are you? _____ (FILL IN) DK REF

41. What is the highest level of education that you have completed? (OPEN-ENDED. READ CATEGORIES ONLY IF NEEDED. TRY TO GET AN ANSWER THAT FITS INTO A CATEGORY).

No high school (8th grade or less)

Some high school (including presently in high school)

High school or vocational school degree

Some college (but not a degree, including presently in school)

Undergraduate college degree

Some graduate work (but not a degree, including presently in graduate school)

Graduate degree (Masters, Ph.D. Law, medicine)

DK REF

42. Generally speaking, how would you describe yourself politically? Would you say you are very conservative, somewhat conservative, somewhat liberal, very liberal, or would you say you are politically middle of the road?

V.CON SO.CONS SO.LIB V.LIB MIDDLE DK REF

43. And during a typical day, about how much time—in minutes and or hours—do you **actively spend** watching television? By this I do not mean time the TV set is on, but time you spend watching television.

FILL IN _____ DK REF

44. Would you describe yourself as White, Black, Asian, or other? (**IF PER-SON SAYS "HISPANIC," ASK IF WHITE-HISPANIC, BLACK-HISPANIC, ASIAN-HISPANIC, OR HISPANIC OF SOME OTHER RACE. IF PERSON THEN INSISTS ON "HISPANIC," DON'T PUSH THE MATTER ANY FURTHER AND COUNT AS A "REFUSE").**

WHITE BLACK ASIAN OTHER (What?): _____

DK REF

45. Are you of Hispanic or Latino ancestry?

YES NO DK REF

46. And finally, I will mention some income categories. Please stop me when I mention the category that reflects your family's total annual income (**READ ONE**

AT A TIME, NOT TOO FAST SO THE PERSON CAN STOP YOU AT ANY TIME)

Under $25,000 $25,001–$50,000 $50,001–$75,000
$75,001–$100,000   More than $100,000   DK   REF

Thank you for participating in this survey.
Your help is greatly appreciated.

REMINDER→ Did you record the respondent's GENDER?

SCHOOL OF COMMUNICATION

ONLINE NEWS CREDIBILITY STUDY
February 4–7, 2002

Hello. My name is (use your first name). I am calling from the University of Miami School of Communication in Coral Gables, Florida, where I am a student. We are conducting a national survey as part of a class research project to find out what people think of the news media. This study is for educational-classroom purposes. We are not selling anything.

(DO NOT PAUSE OR ASK IF IT IS OKAY. PROCEED QUICKLY INTO THE QUESTIONS. . . .)

1. First . . . Are you 18 years old, or older?

    YES (CONTINUE)   NO (POLITELY TERMINATE IF NO ONE
                                    AGE 18 OR HIGHER IS HOME)

2. (RECORD GENDER NOW. DO NOT ASK):   MALE   FEMALE

3. (RECORD TELEPHONE NUMBER AREA CODE NOW. DO NOT ASK):

_____

4. How many days a week, if any, do you:

Read a newspaper	0	1	2	3	4	5	6	7

                    DK   REF

(IF ONE OR MORE DAYS, GO TO THE NEXT QUESTION. IF NONE, SKIP TO QUESTION NO. 18)

5. When you read a newspaper, what type of news would you say you read most often . . . local, national, or international news?

(CIRCLE THE CATEGORY CHOSEN. IF THE RESPONDENT CHOOSES MORE THAN ONE CATEGORY, REPEAT . . . ASK THE RESPONDENT TO CHOOSE ONE ONLY. IF UNSUCCESSFUL, THEN CIRCLE TOGETHER THE MULTIPLE CATEGORIES CHOSEN BY THE RESPONDENT.)

    LOCAL   NATIONAL   INTERNATIONAL
    DK   REF

I'd like to know what you think about newspapers as a source of news and information. I'm going to mention some descriptive words ... and, after I read each word, please tell me whether the word describes your feelings. Give me your answer in terms of whether you strongly agree, agree, disagree, strongly disagree, or whether you are neutral. Do you think newspapers are ...

Newspapers

6. Trustworthy	SD	D	N	A	SA	DK	REF
7. Current	SD	D	N	A	SA	DK	REF
8. Biased	SD	D	N	A	SA	DK	REF
9. Fair	SD	D	N	A	SA	DK	REF
10. Report the whole story	SD	D	N	A	SA	DK	REF
11. Objective	SD	D	N	A	SA	DK	REF
12. Dishonest	SD	D	N	A	SA	DK	REF
13. Up-to-date	SD	D	N	A	SA	DK	REF
14. Believable	SD	D	N	A	SA	DK	REF
15. Balanced	SD	D	N	A	SA	DK	REF
16. Accurate	SD	D	N	A	SA	DK	REF
17. Timely	SD	D	N	A	SA	DK	REF

18. How many days a week, if any, do you:

Watch
television news   0   1   2   3   4   5   6   7

DK   REF

(IF ONE OR MORE DAYS, GO TO THE NEXT QUESTION. IF NONE, SKIP TO QUESTION NO. 32)

19. When you watch television news, what type of news would you say you watch most often ... local, national, or international news?

(CIRCLE THE CATEGORY CHOSEN. IF THE RESPONDENT CHOOSES MORE THAN ONE CATEGORY, REPEAT ... ASK THE RESPONDENT TO CHOOSE ONE ONLY. IF UNSUCCESSFUL, THEN CIRCLE TOGETHER THE MULTIPLE CATEGORIES CHOSEN BY THE RESPONDENT.)

LOCAL   NATIONAL   INTERNATIONAL

DK   REF

I'd like to know what you think about television news as a source of news and information. I'm going to mention some descriptive words ... and, after I read each word, please tell me whether the word describes your feelings. Give me your answer in terms of whether you strongly agree, agree, disagree, strongly disagree, or whether you are neutral. Do you think television news is ...

Television news

20. Trustworthy	SD	D	N	A	SA	DK	REF
21. Current	SD	D	N	A	SA	DK	REF
22. Biased	SD	D	N	A	SA	DK	REF
23. Fair	SD	D	N	A	SA	DK	REF
24. Report the whole story	SD	D	N	A	SA	DK	REF
25. Objective	SD	D	N	A	SA	DK	REF
26. Dishonest	SD	D	N	A	SA	DK	REF
27. Up-to-date	SD	D	N	A	SA	DK	REF
28. Believable	SD	D	N	A	SA	DK	REF
29. Balanced	SD	D	N	A	SA	DK	REF
30. Accurate	SD	D	N	A	SA	DK	REF
31. Timely	SD	D	N	A	SA	DK	REF

32. Do you ever use a computer?

_____ YES

_____ NO   (IF NO, SKIP TO QUESTION NO. 63)

_____ DK

_____ REF

33. Is the computer that you use most of the time . . . (CHECK ONLY ONE)

_____ at home

_____ at work or at school

_____ at a library, or

_____ elsewhere (WHERE? _____)

_____ DK

_____ REF

34. Do you access the Internet?

_____ YES

_____ NO   (IF NO, SKIP TO QUESTION NO. 63)

_____ DK   _____ REF

35. Many newspapers, news magazines, television stations, and cable television networks have sites on the World Wide Web. How many days a week, if any, do you read Web sites offered by one or more of these conventional news media outlets? [NOTE: IF LESS THAN 1 DAY PER WEEK, CIRCLE "ZERO"]

0   1   2   3   4   5   6   7   DK   REF

36. Internet service providers, such as America Online and the Microsoft Network, also have online news content. How many days a week, if any **do you read the news** from any of these or other similar Internet service providers? [**NOTE: IF LESS THAN 1 DAY PER WEEK, CIRCLE "ZERO"**]

0   1   2   3   4   5   6   7   DK   REF

37. Internet search engine portals, such as Yahoo!, Lycos, Excite, or Alta Vista, also have online news sites. How many days a week, if any **do you read the news** from any of these or other Internet service providers? [**NOTE: IF LESS THAN 1 DAY PER WEEK, CIRCLE "ZERO"**]

0   1   2   3   4   5   6   7   DK   REF

(IF ONE OR MORE DAYS, GO TO THE NEXT QUESTION. IF NONE, FOR QUESTIONS NO. 35, NO. 36, AND NO. 37, SKIP TO QUESTION NO. 63)

38. When you read online news, what type of news would you say you read most often . . . local, national, or international news?

(CIRCLE THE CATEGORY CHOSEN. IF THE RESPONDENT CHOOSES MORE THAN ONE CATEGORY, REPEAT . . . ASK THE RESPONDENT TO CHOOSE ONE ONLY. IF UNSUCCESSFUL, THEN CIRCLE TOGETHER THE MULTIPLE CATEGORIES CHOSEN BY THE RESPONDENT.)

LOCAL   NATIONAL   INTERNATIONAL
DK   REF

I'd like to know what you think about online news as a source of news and information. I'm going to mention some descriptive words . . . and, after I read each word, please tell me whether the word describes your feelings. Give me your answer in terms of whether you strongly agree, agree, disagree, strongly disagree, or whether you are neutral. Do you think online news is . . .

Online news

39. Trustworthy	SD	D	N	A	SA	DK	REF
40. Current	SD	D	N	A	SA	DK	REF
41. Biased	SD	D	N	A	SA	DK	REF
42. Fair	SD	D	N	A	SA	DK	REF
43. Report the whole story	SD	D	N	A	SA	DK	REF
44. Objective	SD	D	N	A	SA	DK	REF
45. Dishonest	SD	D	N	A	SA	DK	REF
46. Up-to-date	SD	D	N	A	SA	DK	REF
47. Believable	SD	D	N	A	SA	DK	REF
48. Balanced	SD	D	N	A	SA	DK	REF
49. Accurate	SD	D	N	A	SA	DK	REF
50. Timely	SD	D	N	A	SA	DK	REF

51. How many minutes would you say you spend reading an online news site on a typical day? **(BE SURE TO GET RESPONSE IN MINUTES)**

_____ MINUTES _____ DK _____ REF

52. Where would you say you get most of your online news?

_____

53. When viewing an online news site, how important is it to you that the site comes from a news organization that you know?

_____ EXTREMELY IMPORTANT

_____ VERY IMPORTANT

_____ SOMEWHAT IMPORTANT

_____ NOT VERY IMPORTANT

_____ NOT IMPORTANT AT ALL

_____ DK

_____ REF

54. In terms of your computer skills, would you say that you are a beginner, an intermediate user, or an expert? **(CHECK ONLY ONE)**

_____ BEGINNER

_____ INTERMEDIATE

_____ EXPERT

_____ DK

_____ REF

55. About how many days a week do you go online to access the Internet or the World Wide Web? **(BE SURE TO GET RESPONSE IN DAYS)**

0　　1　　2　　3　　4　　5　　6　　7　　DK　　REF

56. . . . And about how many days a week do you go online to send and receive E-mail? **(BE SURE TO GET RESPONSE IN DAYS)**

0　　1　　2　　3　　4　　5　　6　　7　　DK　　REF

57. On a typical day, how many minutes do you spend using the Internet and World Wide Web? **(BE SURE TO GET RESPONSE IN MINUTES)**

_____ MINUTES _____ DK _____ REF

58. Which type of Internet connection do you have on the computer that you use the most? Is it . . . **(READ OPTIONS IF THEY DON'T ANSWER)**

_____ 56 K or other dial-up modem

_____ or "always-on" or broadband connection

_____ DK

_____ REF

59. How safe do you feel regarding your privacy when using the Internet?

_____ Very safe

_____ Somewhat safe

_____ Neither safe nor unsafe

_____ Somewhat safe

_____ Very unsafe

_____ DK

_____ REF

60. How you ever made an online purchase using your credit card?

_____ Yes

_____ No

_____ DK

_____ REF

61. If you have a choice of news media for information about a news story, which would you choose? Would it be television, radio, print, or online news? **(SELECT ONLY ONE)**

_____ TELEVISION NEWS

_____ RADIO NEWS

_____ PRINT NEWS

_____ ONLINE NEWS

_____ DK

_____ REF

62. Which single news medium do you first turn to when you learn about an *important* news story? Is it television, radio, newspapers, or online news? **(SELECT ONLY ONE)**

_____ TELEVISION NEWS

_____ RADIO NEWS

_____ PRINT NEWS

_____ ONLINE NEWS

_____ DK

_____ REF

Now, just a few final questions for classification purposes . . .

63. How old are you? _____ YEARS (FILL IN)

DK   REF

64. What is the highest level of education that you have completed? (ASK RE-
SPONDENT AND FILL IN; READ CATEGORIES ONLY IF NEEDED. TRY TO
GET AN ANSWER THAT FITS INTO A CATEGORY).

_____ NO HIGH SCHOOL DEGREE

_____ HIGH SCHOOL OR VOCATIONAL SCHOOL DEGREE

_____ SOME COLLEGE (NO DEGREE, INCLUDING STILL
PURSUING A DEGREE

_____ UNDERGRADUATE COLLEGE DEGREE

_____ GRADUATE DEGREE (NOTE: THIS INCLUDES A LAW
DEGREE, MD DEGREE OR OTHER PROFESSIONAL DEGREE)

_____ DK

_____ REF

65. How long have you been living in the community where you now live?
(TRY TO GET ANSWER IN MEASURABLE TIME, SUCH AS DAYS, YEARS
OR MONTHS).

_____ (FILL IN)

DK   REF

66. Are you a newspaper subscriber? (READ ALTERNATIVES BELOW):

_____ Yes   _____ NO   _____ DK   _____ REF

67. Are you a cable or satellite television subscriber? (READ ALTERNA-
TIVES BELOW):

_____ Yes   _____ NO   _____ DK   _____ REF

68. Would you describe <u>yourself</u> as White, Black, Asian, or other? (**READ AL-TERNATIVES BELOW**):

_____ WHITE

_____ BLACK

_____ ASIAN

_____ NATIVE AMERICAN

_____ OTHER _____

_____ DK

_____ REF

69. Are <u>you</u> of Hispanic ancestry?

_____ Yes

_____ NO

_____ DK

_____ REF

70. Where would you say you most often read, watch, or listen to news each day? (**READ ALTERNATIVES BELOW**):

_____ AT HOME

_____ AT WORK OR SCHOOL

_____ OTHER (_____)

_____ DK

_____ REF

71. Our last question: I am going to read a series of <u>total household incomes</u>. Please stop me when I get to the level that best represents your household (**READ ALTERNATIVES BELOW**):

_____ UNDER $25,000

_____ FROM $25,001 to $50,000

_____ FROM $50,001 to $75,000

_____ FROM $75,001 to $100,000

_____ MORE THAN $100,000

_____ DK

_____ REF

INTERVIEWERS: BEFORE YOU FINISH THIS INTERVIEW, DID YOU RE-MEMBER TO RECORD:

- THE RESPONDENT'S <u>GENDER</u> ON PAGE 1?
- DID YOU REMEMBER TO RECORD THE TELEPHONE NUMBER <u>AREA CODE</u> ON PAGE 1?

Thank you very much for participating in this study. Your help is greatly appreciated.

SCHOOL OF COMMUNICATION

TRADITIONAL AND ONLINE NEWS USE PROJECT

November 11–15, 2001

Hello. My name is **(use your first name).** I am a student calling from the University of Miami in Coral Gables, Florida. We are conducting a national opinion survey to find out what people think of the news coverage of the current world situation. We are not selling anything. [NO PAUSES]

NOTE: IF PERSON BALKS, USE YOUR STUDENT STATUS AS AN APPEAL: "I am a student doing this as part of a class project.

NOTE: IF PERSON ASKS "HOW LONG?": "If we move through this, we can be done in 8–10 minutes."

NOTE: YOU MAY SAY THE FOLLOWING TO GAIN COOPERATION: "Your phone number was randomly generated by a computer, so your identity is anonymous and only the statistical results will be used for educational purposes"

First . . . (DO NOT PAUSE OR ASK IF IT IS OK. JUMP RIGHT INTO THE SURVEY)

Are you age 18 or older? (CIRCLE ONE)

YES (CONTINUE)   NO (ASK IF ANYONE THERE IS 18, AND
                        IF NO, POLITELY TERMINATE)

1. →(RECORD GENDER NOW!:   MALE   FEMALE
(ASK ONLY IF YOU ABSOLUTELY FEEL YOU MUST)

To fight the war on terrorism, some government officials have proposed laws relating to journalists and Internet use. I'm going to mention some of these proposed laws. After I mention each one, please tell me whether you strongly agree, somewhat agree, somewhat disagree, strongly disagree, or whether you **neither agree nor disagree** with each proposed law. [NOTE: IF THE PERSON BELIEVES THIS IS ALREADY LEGAL, THEN ASK WHETHER HE OR SHE THINKS IT SHOULD BE LEGAL]

First, should the government have the legal right to . . .

2. Stop journalists from interviewing persons that it labels as terrorists.

ST.AGREE   SO.AGREE   SO.DISAGREE   ST.DISAGREE   NEITHER   DK   REF

3. Force journalists to disclose their confidential news sources when the government believes that the information will help it fight the war on terrorism.

ST.AGREE   SO.AGREE   SO.DISAGREE   ST.DISAGREE   NEITHER   DK   REF

4. Stop journalists from broadcasting or publishing news stories that it believes will hinder its fight in the war on terrorism.

ST.AGREE   SO.AGREE   SO.DISAGREE   ST.DISAGREE   NEITHER   DK   REF

5. Require journalists to report official government information in their news stories that the government believes will help it fight the war on terrorism.

ST.AGREE   SO.AGREE   SO.DISAGREE   ST.DISAGREE   NEITHER   DK   REF

6. Close down Web sites on the Internet that the government believes spread enemy propaganda.

ST.AGREE   SO.AGREE   SO.DISAGREE   ST.DISAGREE   NEITHER   DK   REF

7. Monitor the Internet and Web use activities of people that it considers dangerous.

ST.AGREE   SO.AGREE   SO.DISAGREE   ST.DISAGREE   NEITHER   DK   REF

8. Require Internet companies, upon request, to give government agencies information about subscribers.

ST.AGREE   SO.AGREE   SO.DISAGREE   ST.DISAGREE   NEITHER   DK   REF

9. About what percentage of the news **that you watch or read** these days involves the war on terrorism? Give your answer as a percentage, from 0% and 100% and anything in-between.

(FILL IN) _____ %   DK   REF

10. Do you think that, due to the news coverage of the war on terrorism, the public's level of fear has "Increased A Lot," "Increased Somewhat," "Decreased Somewhat," "Decreased A Lot," or would you say it has not changed.

INC.LOT   INC.SOME   DEC.SOM   DEC.LOT   NOT.CHANGED   DK   REF

11. Do you think that, due to the news coverage of the war on terrorism, **your own** level of fear has "Increased A Lot," "Increased Somewhat," "Decreased Somewhat," "Decreased A Lot," or would you say that your own level of fear has not changed.

INC.LOT   INC.SOME   DEC.SOM   DEC.LOT   NOT.CHANGED   DK   REF

12. Regardless of whether you use the Internet, do you think that, due to the Internet coverage of the war on terrorism, that the level of fear among most Internet and World Wide Web users has "Increased A Lot," "Increased Somewhat," "Decreased Somewhat," "Decreased A Lot," or would you say that most Internet users' levels of fear have not changed.

INC.LOT   INC.SOME   DEC.SOM   DEC.LOT   NOT.CHANGED   DK   REF

13. Do you use the Internet or World Wide Web?

YES   NO (GO TO Q. 33)   DK (GO TO Q. 33)   REF (GO TO Q. 33)

14. Many newspapers, newsmagazines, television stations, and cable television network stations have online news sites. How many days a week, if any, do you read Web sites offered by one or more of these news media outlets? [**NOTE: IF LESS THAN 1 DAY PER WEEK, CIRCLE "ZERO"**]

0   1   2   3   4   5   6   7   DK   REF

15. Internet service providers, such as America Online, Netscape, or Microsoft Network also have news sites. How many days a week, if any, **do you read the news** from any of these or other Internet service providers? [**NOTE: IF LESS THAN 1 DAY PER WEEK, CIRCLE "ZERO"**]

0   1   2   3   4   5   6   7   DK   REF

IF ("0" TO BOTH #14 AND #15, BUT NOT EITHER ONE) GO TO QUESTION # 33. ALSO GO TO # 33 IF DK OR REF

16. About what percentage of the news **that you read online** these days involves the war on terrorism?

(FILL IN) _____ %   DK [GO TO #18]   REF [GO TO #18]

[**NOTE: IF ZERO PERCENT, GO TO #18**]

17. Do you think that, due to **your online reading** of the news coverage of the war on terrorism, that **your own** level of fear has "Increased A Lot," "Increased Somewhat," "Decreased Somewhat," "Decreased A Lot," or would you say that **your own level of fear** has not changed.

INC.LOT   INC.SOME   DEC.SOM   DEC.LOT   NOT.CHANGED   DK   REF

#18 STARTS HERE*

Now please tell me whether you strongly agree, somewhat agree, somewhat disagree, strongly disagree, or whether you **neither agree nor disagree** with the following general statements **about your online news reading experiences.**

First, Online news reading is good for . . .

18. Keeping up with what is going on in the news (SC)

ST.AGREE   SO.AGREE   SO.DISAGREE   ST. DISAGREE   NEITHER   DK   REF

19. Learning about things to discuss with other people (IN)

ST.AGREE   SO.AGREE   SO.DISAGREE   ST. DISAGREE   NEITHER   DK   REF

20. Going directly to important news stories (SE)

ST.AGREE   SO.AGREE   SO.DISAGREE   ST. DISAGREE   NEITHER   DK   REF

21. Finding stories that are fun to read (E)

ST.AGREE   SO.AGREE   SO.DISAGREE   ST. DISAGREE   NEITHER   DK   REF

22. Getting a good overall picture of events in the world. (SC)

ST.AGREE   SO.AGREE   SO.DISAGREE   ST. DISAGREE   NEITHER   DK   REF

23. Finding topics to use in conversations with other people (IN)

ST.AGREE   SO.AGREE   SO.DISAGREE   ST. DISAGREE   NEITHER   DK   REF

24. Learning what are the major news events of the day (SC)

ST.AGREE   SO.AGREE   SO.DISAGREE   ST. DISAGREE   NEITHER   DK   REF

25. Skipping the unimportant news and going to important news (SE)

ST.AGREE   SO.AGREE   SO.DISAGREE   ST. DISAGREE   NEITHER   DK   REF

26. Coming across amusing news (E)

ST.AGREE   SO.AGREE   SO.DISAGREE   ST. DISAGREE   NEITHER   DK   REF

27. Seeking out important news (SE)

ST.AGREE   SO.AGREE   SO.DISAGREE   ST. DISAGREE   NEITHER   DK   REF

28. Finding stories that are enjoyable (E)

ST.AGREE   SO.AGREE   SO.DISAGREE   ST. DISAGREE   NEITHER   DK   REF

29. Following the major news stories of the day (SC)

ST.AGREE   SO.AGREE   SO.DISAGREE   ST. DISAGREE   NEITHER   DK   REF

30. Getting stories to share with other people (IN)

ST.AGREE   SO.AGREE   SO.DISAGREE   ST. DISAGREE   NEITHER   DK   REF

31. Getting quickly to important news (SE)

ST.AGREE   SO.AGREE   SO.DISAGREE   ST. DISAGREE   NEITHER   DK   REF

32. Finding entertaining news (E)

ST.AGREE   SO.AGREE   SO.DISAGREE   ST. DISAGREE   NEITHER   DK   REF

#33 STARTS HERE ***

33. About how many days a week, if any, do you read a printed newspaper? For this, do not count Internet or online newspapers. [IF **"LESS THAN ONE,"** CODE AS **"0"**].

0   1   2   3   4   5   6   7   DK   REF

IF ZERO ("0") OR DK OR REF, NON-NEWSPAPER READER, GO TO QUESTION # 49

Now please tell me whether you strongly agree, somewhat agree, somewhat disagree, strongly disagree, or whether you **neither agree nor disagree** with the following general statements **about your newspaper reading experiences.**

First, newspaper reading is good for . . .

34. Keeping up with what is going on in the news (SC)

ST.AGREE   SO.AGREE   SO.DISAGREE   ST. DISAGREE   NEITHER   DK   REF

35. learning about things to discuss with other people (IN)

ST.AGREE   SO.AGREE   SO.DISAGREE   ST. DISAGREE   NEITHER   DK   REF

36. Going directly to important news stories (SE)

ST.AGREE   SO.AGREE   SO.DISAGREE   ST. DISAGREE   NEITHER   DK   REF

37. Finding stories that are fun to read (E)

ST.AGREE   SO.AGREE   SO.DISAGREE   ST. DISAGREE   NEITHER   DK   REF

38. Getting a good overall picture of events in the world. (SC)

ST.AGREE   SO.AGREE   SO.DISAGREE   ST. DISAGREE   NEITHER   DK   REF

39. Finding topics to use in conversations with other people (IN)

ST.AGREE   SO.AGREE   SO.DISAGREE   ST. DISAGREE   NEITHER   DK   REF

40. Learning what are the major news events of the day (SC)

ST.AGREE   SO.AGREE   SO.DISAGREE   ST. DISAGREE   NEITHER   DK   REF

41. Skipping the unimportant news and going to important news (SE)

ST.AGREE   SO.AGREE   SO.DISAGREE   ST. DISAGREE   NEITHER   DK   REF

42. Coming across amusing news (E)

ST.AGREE   SO.AGREE   SO.DISAGREE   ST. DISAGREE   NEITHER   DK   REF

43. Seeking out important news (SE)

ST.AGREE   SO.AGREE   SO.DISAGREE   ST. DISAGREE   NEITHER   DK   REF

44. Finding stories that are enjoyable (E)

ST.AGREE   SO.AGREE   SO.DISAGREE   ST. DISAGREE   NEITHER   DK   REF

45. Following the major news stories of the day (SC)

ST.AGREE   SO.AGREE   SO.DISAGREE   ST. DISAGREE   NEITHER   DK   REF

46. Getting stories to share with other people (IN)

ST.AGREE   SO.AGREE   SO.DISAGREE   ST. DISAGREE   NEITHER   DK   REF

47. Getting quickly to important news (SE)

ST.AGREE   SO.AGREE   SO.DISAGREE   ST. DISAGREE   NEITHER   DK   REF

48. Finding entertaining news (E)

ST.AGREE   SO.AGREE   SO.DISAGREE   ST. DISAGREE   NEITHER   DK   REF

#49 STARTS HERE***
Just a few more questions for classification purposes . . .

49. How old are you? _____ **(FILL IN)**   DK   REF

50. What is the highest level of education that you have completed? (OPEN-ENDED. READ CATEGORIES ONLY IF NEEDED. TRY TO GET AN ANSWER THAT FITS INTO A CATEGORY).

No high school (8th grade or less)

Some high school

High school or vocational school degree

Some college (but not a degree, including presently in school)

Undergraduate college degree

Some graduate work (but not a degree, including presently in graduate school)

Master's level, or other graduate degree (including MBA and law degree)

Some post-master's work (but not a degree, including still pursing a degree)

Doctoral, Ph.D., MD (Physician)

DK   REF

51. Generally speaking, how would you describe yourself politically. Would you say you are very conservative, somewhat conservative, somewhat liberal, very liberal, or would you say you are middle of the road?

V.CON   SO.CONS   SO.LIB   V.LIB   MIDDLE   DK   REF

52. Are you of Hispanic or Latino ancestry?

YES   NO   DK   REF

53. Would you describe yourself as White, Black, Asian, or other? (IF PERSON SAYS "HISPANIC," ASK IF WHITE-HISPANIC, BLACK-HISPANIC, ASIAN-HISPANIC, OR HISPANIC OF SOME OTHER RACE. IF PERSON THEN INSISTS ON "HISPANIC," DON'T PUSH THE MATTER ANY FURTHER AND COUNT AS A "REFUSE").

WHITE   BLACK   ASIAN   OTHER (What?): _____

DK   REF

54. And lastly, I will mention some income categories. Please tell me which one reflects your family's total annual income

Under $25,000 $25,001–$50,000 $50,001–$75,000

$75,001–$100,000   More than $100,000   DK   REF

Thank you for completing this survey. Your help is greatly appreciated.

CALLER: BEFORE YOU FINISH THIS QUESTIONNAIRE, DID YOU REMEM-
BER TO RECORD THE RESPONDENT'S <u>GENDER?</u> QUICKLY SCAN YOUR
QUESTIONNAIRE TO BE SURE YOU CLEARLY MARKED/CIRCLED ALL
ANSWERS. AVOID MESSY CIRCLES OR CHECKS THAT APPEAR TO
TOUCH TWO POSSIBLE ANSWERS.

SCHOOL OF COMMUNICATION

FEAR, NEWS USE AND TERRORISM PROJECT

November 15–16, November 18–20, November 27, 2001

Hello. My name is _____ and I'm calling from the Communica-
tion Research Center at the University of Miami in Coral Gables, Florida. We're
conducting a national opinion survey to find out how people feel about the terrorism events in our country and opinions about news media coverage of the terrorist threat. We're definitely not selling anything.

First . . . are you age 18 or older? (circle one)   YES   NO

                                                      Is there anyone there
                                                      age 18 or over we might
                                                      speak with?

                                                      Yes   No
                                                      (Begin intro (Politely
                                                      again)   Terminate)

1. Record Gender Now!   MALE   FEMALE

I'm going to read some words that some people have used to describe their feelings since the terrorist attacks on the World Trade Center and the Pentagon on
September 11th. After I read each word, please respond by using a 1 to 5 scale to
describe **how you feel today** about the threat of terrorism, where 1 **means the
word does not describe your feelings at all and 5 means the word very accurately describes your feelings.** The first word is . . .

	Doesn't Describe At All				Very Accurately Describes		
2. SCARED	1	2	3	4	5	DK	REF
3. ANXIOUS	1	2	3	4	5	DK	REF
4. CALM	1	2	3	4	5	DK	REF
5. WORRIED	1	2	3	4	5	DK	REF
6. FRIGHTENED	1	2	3	4	5	DK	REF
7. UNCONCERNED	1	2	3	4	5	DK	REF

Some people have done certain things to protect themselves from possible new
terrorist attacks. Please tell me whether, since the September 11th attacks, you
have done any of the following:

8. Have you inquired about obtaining or actually
purchased, or taken antibiotics for possible use
against anthrax infection? Y N dk ref

9. Did you decide to put off or cancel taking
a trip? Y N dk ref

10. Have you avoided going to shopping malls,
sporting events, or other public places? Y N dk ref

11. Have you examined your mail looking for
suspicious letters or packages? Y N dk ref

12. Have you shopped for or purchased a gas
mask or protective suit? Y N dk ref

13. On an average day, about how much time, if any, do you spend reading a
printed newspaper? For this, do not count Internet or online newspapers. [**Note:
do not write in both spaces! If the person says ½ hour, either write ½ in the
hour space or 30 minutes in the minute space. Do not write in both!**]

Hours_____ Minutes _____ (If zero, dk, or ref go to question 21.)

14. About what percentage of the time you spend reading newspapers is used
for reading stories about terrorist attacks and the war on terrorism? Give your answer as a percentage, from 0% to 100% or anything in between.

(FILL IN) _____ % DK REF (If zero, dk, or ref, go to question 21.)

I'm going to read some statements about **printed newspapers'** coverage of ter-
rorism attacks and the war on terrorism. For each statement, please tell me if you
**Strongly Disagree, Disagree, neither Agree nor Disagree, Agree, or Strongly
Agree.** First . . .

15. Newspaper coverage of terrorism has been overly sensationalized.

Strongly Disagree Disagree Neither Agree Strongly Agree DK REF

16. Newspaper coverage helps reassure the public that the real risks of becoming a victim of terrorism are small.

Strongly Disagree Disagree Neither Agree Strongly Agree DK REF

17. Newspaper coverage of terrorism has been believable.

Strongly Disagree Disagree Neither Agree Strongly Agree DK REF

18. Newspaper coverage of terrorism has been accurate.

Strongly Disagree   Disagree   Neither   Agree   Strongly Agree   DK   REF

19. Some people say that the terrorism coverage **in newspapers** has made them more fearful. How fearful would you say **you have** become because of your reading of newspaper coverage about the war on terrorism? Would you say your own level of fear has **"Increased A Lot," "Increased Somewhat," "Decreased Somewhat," "Decreased A Lot," or would you say it has not changed?**

Increased A Lot   Increased Some   Decreased Some   Decrease A Lot   No Change

20. And how afraid would you say coverage of terrorism **in newspapers** has made **the public in general**? Would you say **the public's** level of fear has "Increased A Lot," "Increased Somewhat," "Decreased Somewhat," "Decreased A Lot," or would you say it has not changed?

Increased A Lot   Increased Some   Decreased Some   Decrease A Lot   No Change

21. On an average day, about how much time, if any, do you spend **watching television news?**
[Note: do not write in both spaces! If the person says ½ hour, either write ½ in the hour space or 30 minutes in the minute space. Do not write in both!]

Hours _____   Minutes_____   (If zero, dk, or ref, go to question 29.)

22. About what percentage of the time you spend watching television news is used watching stories about terrorist attacks and the war on terrorism?

(FILL IN) _____ %   DK   REF   (If zero, dk, or ref, go to question 29.)

I'm going to read some statements about **television news coverage** of terrorism. For each statement, please tell me if you **Strongly Disagree, Disagree, neither Agree nor Disagree, Agree, or Strongly Agree.** First . . .

23. TV news coverage of terrorism has been overly sensationalized.

Strongly Disagree   Disagree   Neither   Agree   Strongly Agree   DK   REF

24. TV news coverage helps reassure the public that the real risks of terrorism are small.

Strongly Disagree   Disagree   Neither   Agree   Strongly Agree   DK   REF

25. TV news coverage of terrorism has been believable.

Strongly Disagree   Disagree   Neither   Agree   Strongly Agree   DK   REF

26. TV news coverage of terrorism has been accurate.

Strongly Disagree   Disagree   Neither   Agree   Strongly Agree   DK   REF

27. Some people say that the terrorism coverage on **television** has made **the public in general** more fearful. How fearful would you say **the public has** become because of television coverage of terrorism? Would you say **the public's** level of fear has **"Increased A Lot," "Increased Somewhat," "Decreased Somewhat," "Decreased A Lot," or would you say it has not changed?**

Increased A Lot   Increased Some   Decreased Some   Decrease A Lot   No Change

28. And how afraid would you say coverage of terrorism on **television** has made **you?** Would you say **television** coverage has made **your** own level of fear "Increase A Lot," "Increase Somewhat," "Decrease Somewhat," "Decrease A Lot," or would you say it has not changed?

Increased A Lot   Increased Some   Decreased Some   Decrease A Lot   No Change

29. Do you use the Internet or World Wide Web?

YES   NO   (if NO, dk, or ref, go to question 44.)

30. Do you use the Internet or World Wide Web to read news stories posted at online sites such as America Online, the Microsoft Network, or from online news sites run by newspapers, television stations and other news media outlets?

YES   NO   DK   REF   (if NO, dk, or ref, go to question 44.)

31. On an average day, about how much time, if any, do you spend reading news online? [**Note: do not write in both spaces! If the person says ½ hour, either write ½ in the hour space or 30 minutes in the minute space. Do not write in both!**]

Hours _____ Minutes _____   DK   REF   (If zero, dk, or ref, go to question 44.)

32. About what percentage of the time you spend reading online news is used for reading news about terrorist attacks and the war on terrorism? [**Note: if asked, you should have them include time spent with audio or video news streams.**]

(FILL IN) %   DK   REF   (If zero, dk, or ref, go to question 44.)

I'm going to read some statements about **online news sites'** coverage of terrorism. For each statement, please tell me if you **Strongly Disagree, Disagree, neither Agree nor Disagree, Agree, or Strongly Agree.** First . . .

33. Online news coverage of terrorism has been overly sensationalized

Strongly Disagree   Disagree   Neither   Agree   Strongly Agree   DK   REF

34. Online news coverage helps reassure the public that the real risks of terrorism are small.

Strongly Disagree   Disagree   Neither   Agree   Strongly Agree   DK   REF

35. Online news coverage of terrorism has been believable.

Strongly Disagree   Disagree   Neither   Agree   Strongly Agree   DK   REF

36. Online news coverage of terrorism has been accurate.

Strongly Disagree   Disagree   Neither   Agree   Strongly Agree   DK   REF

37. Some people say that the terrorism coverage in **online news sites** has made them more fearful. How fearful would you say **you have** become because of **online coverage** on terrorism? Would you say your own level of fear has "Increased A Lot," "Increased Somewhat," "Decreased Somewhat," "Decreased A Lot," or would you say it has not changed?

Increased A Lot   Increased Some   Decreased Some   Decrease A Lot   No Change

38. And how afraid would you say coverage of terrorism in **online news sites** has made **the public in general**. Would you say the **public's** level of fear has "Increased A Lot," "Increased Somewhat," "Decreased Somewhat," "Decreased A Lot," or would you say it has not changed?

Increased A Lot   Increased Some   Decreased Some   Decrease A Lot   No Change

I'm going to read a list of things **that people who go online** have said they do to communicate with others about terrorism. For each, please tell me whether you do any of the following **often, sometimes, seldom or never**. First, do you . . .

39. **send** email messages to family, friends or coworkers about terrorism?

Often   Sometimes   Seldom   Never   DK   REF

40. **use** instant messaging to communicate with someone about the terrorism?

Often   Sometimes   Seldom   Never   DK   REF

41. **read** comments about the terrorism issue on a web site bulletin board, chat room or on an e-mail list serv?

Often   Sometimes   Seldom   Never   DK   REF

42. **post** comments on a web site bulletin board, chat room or an e-mail list serv about terrorism?

Often   Sometimes   Seldom   Never   DK   REF

43. **Listen to** online audio news stories or watch online video news stories about the terrorism issue?

Often   Sometimes   Seldom   Never   DK   REF

44. Some people say it is very likely that there will be another terrorist attack inside the United States in the next three months. Do you. . . (read the responses)

Strongly   Disagree   Neither   Agree   Strongly   DK   REF
Disagree   Agree   Agree
                          nor Disagree

45. Some people say you can protect yourself from becoming a victim of terrorism by taking precautions. Do you. . . (read the responses)

Strongly   Disagree   Neither   Agree   Strongly   DK   REF
Disagree   Agree   Agree
                          nor Disagree

I'm going to read some statements about the role of government in investigating terrorism. After each statement, please tell me if you **Strongly Agree, Agree, Neither Agree nor Disagree, Disagree, or Strongly Disagree.** First . . . [**Note: If the person believes an action has already happened, then ask how much he or she agrees with it using the same response set.**]

46. It should be easier for the government to monitor telephone calls in order to investigate terrorism.

Strongly   Disagree   Neither   Agree   Strongly   DK   REF
Disagree   Agree   Agree
                          nor Disagree

47. It should be made easier for the government to read people's e-mail in order to investigate terrorism.

Strongly   Disagree   Neither   Agree   Strongly   DK   REF
Disagree   Agree   Agree
                          nor Disagree

48. It should be made easier for the government to track people's credit card purchases in order to investigate terrorism.

Strongly   Disagree   Neither   Agree   Strongly   DK   REF
Disagree   Agree   Agree
                          nor Disagree

49. The government should be allowed to detain people indefinitely if there is reason to believe they know something about terrorist attacks.

| Strongly Disagree | Disagree | Neither Agree nor Disagree | Agree | Strongly Agree | DK | REF |

50. The government should be allowed to secretly search someone's property without a warrant or a judge's approval in order to investigate terrorism.

| Strongly Disagree | Disagree | Neither Agree nor Disagree | Agree | Strongly Agree | DK | REF |

51. The government should be allowed to issue national identification cards so it can better keep track of people.

| Strongly Disagree | Disagree | Neither Agree nor Disagree | Agree | Strongly Agree | DK | REF |

52. The government should have the legal right to stop the broadcast or publication of a news story if it believes it is necessary to fight terrorism.

| Strongly Disagree | Disagree | Neither Agree nor Disagree | Agree | Strongly Agree | DK | REF |

53. The government should have the legal right to force journalists to reveal their confidential sources of information if it believes it is necessary to fight terrorism.

| Strongly Disagree | Disagree | Neither Agree nor Disagree | Agree | Strongly Agree | DK | REF |

54. The news media should be allowed to broadcast or publish stories about government incompetence in fighting terrorism, even if it hurts the public morale.

| Strongly Disagree | Disagree | Neither Agree nor Disagree | Agree | Strongly Agree | DK | REF |

55. The news media should be allowed to cover stories about people or groups who believe that U.S. policies were to blame for the terrorist attacks.

| Strongly Disagree | Disagree | Neither Agree nor Disagree | Agree | Strongly Agree | DK | REF |

56. The government should have the legal right to ban access to certain World Wide Web sites on the Internet if it believes the Web site contains enemy propaganda.

Strongly Disagree	Disagree	Neither Agree nor Disagree	Agree	Strongly Agree	DK	REF

Just a few more questions.

57. How old are you?   _____ (Fill In)

58. What is the highest level of education that you have completed?

_____ No high school

_____ Some high school

_____ High school or vocational school degree

_____ Some college

_____ College degree

_____ Some graduate work

_____ Graduate degree

59. Generally speaking, how would you describe yourself politically? Would you say you're very conservative, somewhat conservative, somewhat liberal, very liberal, or would you say you are middle of the road?

V. Cons	Somewhat Cons	Somewhat Lib	V. Liberal	Middle of Road	DK	REF

60. Do you live in or near a large urban area?   YES   NO

61. Are you of Hispanic or Latino ancestry?   YES   NO   DK   REF

62. Would you describe yourself as White, Black, Asian, or other? (IF PERSON SAYS "HISPANIC," ASK IF WHITE-HISPANIC, BLACK-HISPANIC, ASIAN-HISPANIC, OR HISPANIC OF SOME OTHER RACE.)

63. I'm going to mention some income categories. Please stop me when I reach your household's total annual income level.

Under $25,000	>	$25,001 to $50,000	$50,001 to $75,000	>	$75,001 to $100,000
More than $100,000	DK	REF			

That's it. Thank you for completing this survey. Your help is greatly appreciated.

SCHOOL OF COMMUNICATION

DISPLACEMENT SURVEY

November 11–13, 2002

Hello. My name is **(first name)** and I'm a student calling from the University of Miami in Coral Gables, Florida. We're conducting a national opinion survey to find out what people think of the news media. This study is for educational purposes and we are not selling anything. [**NO PAUSE—GO RIGHT TO THE FIRST QUESTION**]

STATEMENTS YOU MAY USE IF NEEDED

IF PERSON ASKS WHAT THIS SURVEY IS FOR: This study will be used as a research project for graduate students. The statistical findings will be presented at academic conferences to learn more about what the public thinks of the news media.

IF PERSON ASKS HOW LONG THIS WILL TAKE: If we move through this, we can be done in a few minutes.

IF PERSON ASKS HOW HIS/HER PHONE NUMBER WAS OBTAINED: Your phone number was randomly generated by a computer, so your identity is anonymous and only the statistical results will be used for educational purposes.

First, are you age 18 or older?

YES	NO
(CONTINUE)	**Is there anyone at home age 18 or older we can talk with?**

1. RECORD GENDER NOW ON ANSWER SHEET!   MALE   FEMALE

2. How interested are you in keeping up with the news? Answer using a 1 to 5 scale, where 1 is VERY UNINTERESTED in keeping up with the news and 5 is VERY INTERESTED in keeping up with the news.

1	2	3	4	5		DK	REF
Very Uninterested				Very Interested			

3. Overall, where would you say you tend to get most of your news? Do you get your news primarily from talking to other people, such as family, friends, or co-workers, or do you get your news from the news media, such as television, radio, newspapers, magazines, and the Internet?

PEOPLE   NEWS MEDIA   DK   REF

4. Among the news media, which one news medium do you use the most to get your news? Is it television, radio, newspapers, magazines, the Internet, or do you use none of them?

TV   RADIO   NEWSPAPERS   MAGAZINES   INTERNET   NONE   DK   REF

5. About how many days a week, if any, do you go online to use the Internet or the World Wide Web?

0   1   2   3   4   5   6   7   DK   REF

IF 0 (ZERO) OR DK OR REF, GO TO Q. #39; IF 1 OR MORE DAYS, CONTINUE

6. And during a typical day when you are online, about how much time—in minutes or hours—do you actively spend online connected to the Internet or World Wide Web?

FILL IN _____ (INDICATE MINUTES[M] /HOURS[H])

DK   REF

7. How many days a week, if any, do you go online intending to find out about the **NEWS**?

0   1   2   3   4   5   6   7   DK   REF

IF 0 (ZERO) OR DK OR REF, GO TO Q. #39; IF 1 OR MORE DAYS, CONTINUE

8. During a typical day when you access **news online**, about how much time—in minutes or hours—do you spend reading **news online**?

FILL IN _____ (INDICATE MINUTES[M]/HOURS[H])   DK   REF

I am going to list some different types of news. After I read each one, please tell me how frequently you read each type of news **online**. Respond by answering ALL THE TIME, OFTEN, SOMETIMES, RARELY, or NEVER.

9. Science and technology news	ALL	OFTEN	SOMETIMES	RARELY	NEVER	DK	REF
10. Business and finance news	ALL	OFTEN	SOMETIMES	RARELY	NEVER	DK	REF
11. Health and fitness news	ALL	OFTEN	SOMETIMES	RARELY	NEVER	DK	REF
12. Sports news	ALL	OFTEN	SOMETIMES	RARELY	NEVER	DK	REF
13. Domestic politics	ALL	OFTEN	SOMETIMES	RARELY	NEVER	DK	REF
14. International news	ALL	OFTEN	SOMETIMES	RARELY	NEVER	DK	REF
15. Opinion and commentaries	ALL	OFTEN	SOMETIMES	RARELY	NEVER	DK	REF
16. Local news	ALL	OFTEN	SOMETIMES	RARELY	NEVER	DK	REF
17. Celebrities and personalities	ALL	OFTEN	SOMETIMES	RARELY	NEVER	DK	REF
18. The weather	ALL	OFTEN	SOMETIMES	RARELY	NEVER	DK	REF
19. Crime news	ALL	OFTEN	SOMETIMES	RARELY	NEVER	DK	REF

20. How many days a week, if any, do you read a printed newspaper?

0   1   2   3   4   5   6   7   DK   REF

IF 0 (ZERO) OR DK OR REF, GO TO Q. #22; IF 1 OR MORE DAYS, CONTINUE

21. To what extent, if any, does your online news reading replace your printed newspaper reading? Answer by giving a number from 1 to 5, where 1 means "does not replace at all" and 5 means "fully replaces."

1   2   3   4   5   DK   REF

22. How many days a week, if any, do you discuss issues and events in the news with other people, such as family, friends, or co-workers?

0   1   2   3   4   5   6   7   DK   REF

IF 0 (ZERO) OR DK OR REF, GO TO Q. #24; IF 1 OR MORE DAYS, CONTINUE

23. To what extent, if any, does your online news reading replace your conversations about news with other people? Answer by giving a number from 1 to 5, where 1 means "does not replace at all" and 5 means "fully replaces."

1   2   3   4   5   DK   REF

24. How many days a week, if any, do you listen to news on the radio?

0   1   2   3   4   5   6   7   DK   REF

IF 0 (ZERO) OR DK OR REF, GO TO Q. #26; IF 1 OR MORE DAYS, CONTINUE

25. To what extent, if any, does your online news reading replace your radio news listening? Answer by giving a number from 1 to 5, where 1 means "does not replace at all" and 5 means "fully replaces."

| 1   2   3   4   5   DK   REF

26. How many days a week, if any, do you watch a television network evening news program on ABC with Peter Jennings, on CBS with Dan Rather or on NBC with Tom Brokaw or their substitutes?

| 0   1   2   3   4   5   6   7   DK   REF

IF 0 (ZERO) OR DK OR REF, GO TO Q. #28; IF 1 OR MORE DAYS, CONTINUE

27. To what extent, if any, does your online news reading replace your network TV-evening news viewing? Answer by giving a number from 1 to 5, where 1 means "does not replace at all" and 5 means "fully replaces."

| 1   2   3   4   5   DK   REF

28. How many days a week, if any, do you watch an all-news cable TV network, such as CNN, CNBC, MSNBC, or the Fox News Network?

| 0   1   2   3   4   5   6   7   DK   REF

IF 0 (ZERO) OR DK OR REF, GO TO Q. #30; IF 1 OR MORE DAYS, CONTINUE

29. To what extent, if any, does your online news reading replace your all-news cable TV network viewing? Answer by giving a number from 1 to 5, where 1 means "does not replace at all" and 5 means "fully replaces."

| 1   2   3   4   5   DK   REF

30. How many days a week, if any, do you watch local TV news?

| 0   1   2   3   4   5   6   7   DK   REF

IF 0 (ZERO) OR DK OR REF, GO TO Q. #32; IF 1 OR MORE DAYS, CONTINUE

31. To what extent, if any, does your online news reading replace local TV news viewing? Answer by giving a number from 1 to 5, where 1 means "does not replace at all" and 5 means "fully replaces."

| 1   2   3   4   5   DK   REF

Question 32 Starts Here

I'm going to read statements about how some people think about the news. After I read each statement, please tell me whether you strongly agree, agree, disagree, strongly disagree, or neither agree nor disagree with the statement. First . . .

32. The news reported in the different news media is basically all the same.

SA   A   D   SD   Neither   DK   REF

33. News on the World Wide Web is much like the news available elsewhere in other news media.

SA   A   D   SD   Neither   DK   REF

34. Using local news media is just as good or better for keeping up with the news as using non-local news media

SA   A   D   SD   Neither   DK   REF

35. There are definite differences in the news stories that are reported in different news media

SA   A   D   SD   Neither   DK   REF

36. Some news media are better than other news media for keeping up with the news.

SA   A   D   SD   Neither   DK   REF

37. The World Wide Web often has unique news stories that are not reported elsewhere.

SA   A   D   SD   Neither   DK   REF

38. The major news stories of each day are the same no matter which news media you turn to.

SA   A   D   SD   Neither   DK   REF

SKIP TO QUESTION #44

#39 STARTS HERE

39. How many days a week, if any, do you read a printed newspaper?

0   1   2   3   4   5   6   7   DK   REF

40. How many days a week, if any, do you listen to news on the radio?

0   1   2   3   4   5   6   7   DK   REF

41. How many days a week, if any, do you watch a television network evening news program on ABC, CBS, or NBC anchored by Tom Brokaw, Peter Jennings, Dan Rather or their substitutes?

0   1   2   3   4   5   6   7   DK   REF

42. How many days a week, if any, do you watch an all-news cable TV network, such as CNN, CNBC, MSNBC, or the Fox News Network?

0   1   2   3   4   5   6   7   DK   REF

43. How many days a week, if any, do you watch local TV news?

0   1   2   3   4   5   6   7   DK   REF

Just a few more questions for classification purposes

44. In what year were you born? _____ (FILL IN)   DK   REF

45. What is the highest level of education that you have completed? (OPEN-ENDED. READ CATEGORIES ONLY IF NEEDED. TRY TO GET AN ANSWER THAT FITS INTO A CATEGORY).

No high school (8th grade or less)
Some high school
High school or vocational school degree
Some college (but not a degree, including presently in school)
Undergraduate college degree
Some graduate work (but not a degree, including presently in graduate school)
Graduate degree (Masters, PhD, Law, medicine)
DK   REF

46. Are you of Hispanic or Latino ancestry?

YES   NO   DK   REF

47. Would you describe yourself as White, Black, Asian, or other?

WHITE   BLACK   ASIAN   OTHER (What?): _____

DK   REF

48. And finally, I will mention some income categories. Please stop me when I mention the category that reflects your household's total annual income.

Under $25,000
$25,001–$50,000
$50,001–$75,000
$75,001–$100,000
More than $100,000
DK
REF

Thank you for completing this survey. Your help is greatly appreciated.

Remember to Record Gender

Author Index

A

Aaronson, D., 306, *322*
Abdulla, R., 282, *301*
Adams, M., 69, *77*
Aikat, D., 222, *234*, 240, *253*
Albright, J., 304, *320*
Albright, K., 318, *320*
Allen-Mills, T., 69, *77*
Alter, J., 67, *77*
Althaus, S. L., 207, *219*, 222, 231, *236*
Altheide, D. L., 166–167, *180*
Anderson, J. Q., 148, *161*
Anderson, R., 281, *301*, 307, 313, *320, 321*
Andrews, F. M., *320*
Andsager, J. L., 189, *200*
Ang, P., 262, *274*
Arant, M. D., 148, *161*
Armstrong, D., 66, *77*
Astor, D., 263, *273*
Atkin, D., 239, 240, *254*, 303, 304, 305, 306,
    307, 308, 309, 310, 312, 317, *320, 321*
Atwood, L. E., 188n4, 189, *200*
Aucoin, D., 66, *78*

B

Bae, H. S., 239, *253*

Bahadur Kremmer, J., 72, *77*
Balding, T., 6, *44*
Baldwin, T. F., 239, *253*
Ball-Rokeach, S., 308, *320*
Banning, S. A., 188, *200*
Barnhurst, K. G., 259, *273*
Barrett, M., 239, *253*
Barringer, F., 11*t*, 22, *44*
Bartz, M. O., 222, *235*
Basil, M. D., 169, *183*
Bates, B., 239, *253*, 318, *320*
Becker, L. B., 167, *180*
Begley, S., 165, *180*
Bennahum, D. S., 65, *77*
Berke, R. L., 185, *200*
Berman, D. K., 239, *253*
Berman, J. A., 104n81
Berniker, M., 239, *253*
Bernt, J. P., 222, 224, *235*, 240, *255*, 306, *322*
Bertelsen, D. A., ix, *xiii*
Biebl, M., 262, *274*
Biswas, R., 169, *180*
Black, W., 313, *321*
Blanchard, M. A., 188, *200*
Blasi, V., 166, *180*
Blumler, J. G., 223, *234, 235*
Bogart, L., ix, *xiii*
Boyd, S., 305, *322*
Boynton, R. S., *234*

Brady, D. J., 241, 253
Brashers, D. E., 168–169, 180
Brendan, K. I., 53, 77
Brosius, H. B., 188, 200
Brown, D., 167, 180, 185, 200
Brown, J. D., 188, 200
Bruce, I., 187, 200
Bryant, J., 167, 168, 169, 180, 182, 183
Budd, R. W., 266, 273
Burgess, J., 5, 45
Busselle, R., 240, 241, 253, 254
Butler, K., 239, 253

C

Callahan, C., 68, 77
Cantor, J., 171, 181
Cantril, H., 198n15, 200
Carlson, D., 3, 5, 45
Carpini, M. X. D., ix, xiii
Carveth, R. A., 167, 180
Casey, W., 15, 45
Chapin, J. R., 188, 189, 201
Charney, T., 304–305, 308, 320
Chen, C. F., 306, 322
Childers, T., 239, 253
Chomsky, N., 279, 285, 301
Christensen, T., 258, 275
Christian, N. M., 48–49, 77
Chyi, H. I., 18, 45, 207, 219, 263–264, 265, 273
Cobbey, R. E., 167, 180
Cochran, W., 53, 68, 77, 259, 261, 273
Coffee, S., 240, 253
Cohen, J., 190, 201
Cook, F. L., 168, 182
Coombs, W. T., 187, 201
Couper, M. P., 150, 162
Crispell, D., 239, 253
Crockett, H. J., 167, 181
Cutbirth, C. W., 187, 201

D

Dahlgren, P., 190, 201
Darling, J., 104n82
Davis, J. A., 167, 181
Davison, W. P., 170, 181, 189, 201
December, J., 287, 288, 301
Deggans, E., 64, 77

della Cava, M. R., 62, 78
Denzin, M., 286, 301
Depew, D., 209, 219
Derk, J., 258, 273
Detenber, B. H., 190, 201
Deuze, M., 17, 22, 45
Dibean, W., 6, 18, 45, 207, 219
Dillman, D. A., 150, 163
Dillon, J. F., 189, 203
Dimmick, J. W., 306, 320
Dizard, W., 238, 253, 304, 320
Dobras, A., 284, 301
Dominick, J., 287, 288, 301
Donohew, L., 266, 273
Donohue, T. R., 239, 254
Donthu, N., 308, 320
Doob, A. N., 167, 181
Dotinga, R., 258, 273
Driscoll, P., 170, 182, 188, 189, 201, 203
Drudge, M., 62–66, 71, 78, 96–98
Duck, A., 262, 274
Duck, J. M., 187, 188–189, 201
Dumrongsiri, N., 222, 235
Dunn, D., 240, 254, 306, 307, 322
Dunning, D. A., 189, 203
Dunwoody, S., 240, 253
Dupagne, M., 170, 181, 188, 189, 202, 203
Durkin, K., 190, 201
Dutton, W., 307, 317, 319, 320
Dzwo, T. H., 207, 220

E

Easton, M., 309, 320
Ebersole, S. E., 305, 320
Ebo, B., 269, 273
Edelman, B., 106
Eighmay, J., 305, 320
Elder, J., 185, 200
Elliot, W., 223, 234
Emery, E., 258, 273
Emery, M., 258, 273
Engel, D., 188, 200
Erbring, L., 129, 145
Eveland, W. P., 190, 201, 240, 253
Ewinger, J., 58, 78

F

Faber, R. J., 170, *182*, 188, *202*
Fagin, M., 105n87
Farah, N., 297n16, *301*
Farhi, P., 15, *45*, 62, *78*
Feeney, M. K., 55, *78*
Feldman, J. J., 169, *182*
Ferguson, D. A., 224, 233, *234*, 240, *254*, 306,
      320
Fetzer, B. K., 189, *202*
Fico, F. G., 266, *275*
Finberg, H. I., 149, *162*
Fischoff, B., 168, *182*
Flagg, J. L., 260, *273*
Flanagin, A. J., 148–149, 150, 151, 152, *162*,
      207, *219*, 221, *235*, 241, *254*, 306, *320*
Fleitas, J., 280, *301*
Floyd, K., 305, 319, *321*
Fontaine, M. A., 207, *219*
Forrest, E., 280, *301*, 305, *321*
Fost, D., 57, 58, *78*
Fouhy, E., 41, *45*, 135, *144*
Frank, R. E., 239, *254*
Franklin, B., 179, *181*
Frederick, E., 187, *202*
Friedman, T. L., 116n135
Fitzgerald, M., 190, *201*

G

Garcia, J., 66, *78*
Garramone, G., 281, *301*, 307, *320*
Garrison, B., 6, 18, *45*, 207, 208, *219*, 259, 263,
      273
Gates, D., 12, *45*
Gaziano, C., 151, 152, 153, *162*
Gerbner, G., 167, *181*
Gergen, K., 281, 285, 286, *302*
Gibbon, P., 190, *201*
Gilbert, K., 168, *181*
Gladstone, J., 92n39
Grabowicz, P., 147, *162*
Graham-Yooll, A., 188, *201*
Grant, A., 308, *320*
Grant, D., 105n87
Greenberg, B. A., 306, *321*
Greenberg, B. S., 304–305, 308, *320*
Greenberg, M. G., 239, *254*
Greene, J., 60–61, *78*

Greenspan, R., 206, *219*
Greer, J., 208, *219*
Griffin, J. L., 222, *235*
Grigg, C. W., 167, *182*
Grimes, C., 19, 33, *45*, 264t, *273*
Gross, L., 167, *181*
Grossman, L. K., 63, *78*
Gubman, J., 208, *219*
Gulia, M., 207, *220*
Gunther, A., 170, *181*, 188–189, 190, *201*
Gurevitch, M., 223, *235*
Guthrie, K. K., 308, *320*

H

Hacker, K. L., 186, *201*
Hafner, K., 107n95
Hair, J., 313, *321*
Hansell, S., 136, *144*
Hansen, K. N., 47, *78*
Hardon, A., 68, *78*, 187, *201*
Hargrove, T., 222, 224, *235*, 240, *255*, 306, *322*
Harris, A., 281, *301*, 307, *320*
Harris, E. P., 205, 206, *219*
Hass, H., 223, *235*
Heath, L., 168, *181*
Heeter, C., 306, *321*
Henke, L., 239, *254*
Heyboer, K., 16–17, *45*, 49, *78*
Hilden, J., 100n71
Hirsch, P., 167, *181*
Hogg, M. A., 187, 188–189, *201*
Holsti, O., *301*
Hooke, F. H., 205, 206, *219*
Hoorens, V., 189, *201*
Horrigan, J. B., 238, 251, *254*
Horrigan, J. P., 206, *219*
Houston, F., 53, *78*
Hovland, C. I., 151, *162*
Howeidy, A., 295n13, *301*
Hu, Y., 151, *163*
Huang, L. N., 170, *182*, 188n3, 189, *202*
Hwa, A. P., 188, *201*

I

Ibanez, I., 304, *321*
Infante, D. A., 152, *162*
Innes, J. M., 189, *202*

Irvine, C., 179, *182*
Irving, L., 260, *274*
Isikoff, M., 165, *180*

J

Jackson, K., 240, *253*
James, M., 280, *301*, 305, *321*
Jarrah, F., 282, 283, *301*
Jeffres, L., 207, *219*, 231, *235*, 240, *254*, 304, 305, 306, 307, 308, 309, 310, 312, 317, *320, 321*
Johnson, H. R., 222, *235*
Johnson, T., 148, 149, 150, *162*, 222, *235*, 241, *254*, 306–307, *321*
Jones, G., 284, *301*
Jun, S. H., 307, 317, 319, *320*
Jurkowitz, M., 66, *78*

K

Kahn, J., 106n91
Kang, M., 240, *254*, 306, *321*
Kang, N., 317, *322*
Katz, E., 223, *235*
Katz, J., 257, *274*
Kayany, J. M., 239, *254*
Kaye, B. K., 133, *145*, 148, 149, 150, *162*, 222, *235*, 241, *254*, 306–307, *321*
Keefe, R., 5, *45*
Keeton, W. P., 107n96
Kennemer, J. D., 189, *202*
Kenworthy, T., 4, *45*, 53, *78*
Keough, C. M., 258, *275*
Kiesler, S., 319, *321*
Kim, A. J., xi, *xiii*, 207, 209, *219*
Kim, S. T., 241, *254*
Kinsley, M., 59–61, 71, *78*
Kiousis, S., 149, 150–151, *162*
Kippax, S., 223, 229, *235*
Kirby, K., 104n80
Klein, W. M., 189, *203*
Kohut, A., 150, *163*
Kramer, S. D., 33, *45*
Krugman, D., 239, *253*
Kubey, R. W., 168, *181*
Kuczynski, A., 67, *78*
Kurtz, H., 6, *45*, 56, 60, 61, 64, *78*

L

Labaton, S., 303, *321*
Lacy, S., 266, *275*
Lamias, M. J., 150, *162*
Lang, A., 168, *181*
LaRose, R., 239, *254*, 281, *302*, 306, 309, 317, *320, 321*
Lasica, J. C., 55, *78*, *162*
Lasica, J. D., 18, *45*, 259, 261, 262, 264t, *274*
Lasorsa, D. L., 170, *181*, 187–188, 189, *202*
Lasswell, H. D., 239, *254*
Lau, T. Y., 303, *320*
Lee, C., 188, *202*
Leong, E. M., 222, *235*
Lesser, E. L., 207, *219*
Leung, L., 259, *274*
Leventhal, H., 168, *181*
Levin, Y., 318, *321*
Levins, H., 6, *45*
Levy, M. R., 133, *145*, 207, *219*, 223, 229, *235*, 261, *274*
Lewenstein, M., 168, *181*
Lewis, B., 284–285, *301*
Lewis, M., 133, *145*
Lewis, S., 105n86
Li, X., 207–208, *220*, 257, 265, *274*
Lichtenstein, A., 223, 229, *235*
Lichtenstein, S., 168, *182*
Lin, C. A., 127, *145*, 207, *219*, 224, 231, 232, *235*, 238, 239, 240, *254*, 305, 306, 307, 308, 309, 310, 312, 317, 319, *321*
Lin, N., 207, *219*
Lindlof, T., 285, *301*
Lo, V., 189, *202*
Lowrey, W., 262, *274*
Lowry, B., 61, *78*
Lynch, D., 149, *162*

M

MacDonald, G. E., 167, *181*
Maddox, B. D., 70n19, *79*
Maier, S. R., 259, *274*
Malhotra, S., ix, *xiii*
Marcus, G. E., 167, *182*
Marcus, L., 308, *321*
Margolis, M., 309, *321*
Marlatt, A., 49, *78*, 259, *274*
Martin, S. A., 47, *78*
Massey, B. L., 133, *145*, 207, *219*, 261, *274*

Matera, F., 187, *202*
McClosky, H., 167, *181*
McCombs, M. E., ix, *xiii*
McGrath, K., 151, 152, 153, *162*
McKenna, F. P., 189, *202*
McLean, D., 117n137
McLeod, D. M., 190, *201*
McMillan, S., 210, *219*, 287, 288, *302*
Medoff, N. J., 133, *145*
Mehalic, L. L., 222, *235*
Mellich, O., 258, *275*
Metzger, M. J., 148–149, 150, 151, 152, *162*,
    207, *219*, 221, *235*, 241, *254*, 306, *320*
Meyer, P., 150, 151–152, *162*
Michalowski, R. S., 166–167, *180*
Milban, D., 185, *202*
Miles, S., 12, *45*
Miller, B., 187, *202*
Miller, G., 64, 65, *78*
Miller, J., 281, 285, 286, *302*
Miller, R., 20, *45*
Miller, T. E., 305, 308, *321*
Mings, S. M., 223–224, 232, *235*
Mitchell, A., 65, *78*
Morgan, M., 167, *181*
Morris, M., 133, *145*, 305, *321*
Mueller, J., 179, *181*
Mulder, R., 150, *162*
Mullin, B. A., 189, *201*
Mundy, P., 188–189, *201*
Murray, J. P., 223, 229, *235*
Mutz, D., 190, *201*

N

Nadarajan, B., 262, *274*
Nass, C., 150, 152, 153, 157, *162*
Nathanson, A. I., 190, *201*
Neuberger, C., 262, *274*
Neuendorf, K., 305, 306, 307, 308, 309, 310,
    312, 317, *320, 321*
Neuwirth, K., 187, *202*
Newhagen, J., 133, *145*, 150, 152, 153, 157,
    162, 168, *181*, 188, *202*
Nie, N. H., 129, *145*
Noack, D., 263, *274*
Nunn, C. A., 167, *181*

O

Ogan, C., 133, *145*, 305, *321*
Ognianova, E., 151, *162*
Oldenburg, R., 207, *219*
Outing, S., xi, *xiii*, 208, 209, *220*, 259, 260, 262,
    263, *274*

P

Packel, D., 241, *254*
Palmgreen, P., 152, 153, *163*, 223, 229, *235*
Palser, B., 5, 6, 14, 22, *46*, 69, *78*, 135, *145*,
    186, *202*, 208, 209, 218, *220*
Papacharissi, Z., 240, *254*
Papachrissi, Z., 305, 308, 319, *321*
Parks, M., 305, 319, *321*
Patterson, S., 306, *320*
Paul, B., 170, *181*, 188, *202*
Pavlik, J., 257, *274*
Pellechia, M., 179, *182*
Peluso, T., 168, *181*
Peng, F. Y., 258, *274*
Perlman, J. A., 263, *274*, 285, *302*
Perloff, L. S., 189, *202*
Perloff, R. M., 170, *182*, 188, 190, *202*
Perse, E. M., 223, 224, 233, *234, 235*, 240, *254*,
    306, 307, *320, 322*
Peters, J. D., 219
Peterson, T. B., 42–44, *46*
Phipps, J. L., 259, 262, *275*
Picard, R., 14, *46*
Piereson, J., 167, *182*
Pierson, J., 258, *275*
Piller, C., 55, *78*
Pinkleton, B., 240, 241, 253, *254*, 306, *322*
Poindexter, P. M., ix, *xiii*
Potts, R., 169, *182*
Preece, J., xi, *xiii*, 209, *220*
Price, V., 170, *182*, 188n3, 190, *201, 202*
Prothro, J. W., 167, *182*
Pryor, L., 147, *162*
Purohit, K., 304, *320*

Q

Quattlebaum, C. P., 223, *234*
Quint, B. E., 6, *46*

R

Rafaeli, S., 281, *302*
Rainie, L., 238, 241, 251, *254*
Rayburn, J. D., II, 223, 229, *235*
Reagan, J., 240, 241, *253*, *254*, 306, *322*
Recer, P., 116n134
Reeves, B., 168, *181*
Reid, A., 95n52
Resnick, D., 309, *321*
Rheingold, H., xi, *xiii*, 206, 207, 208, 209, *220*
Rice, D. T., 92n39
Rich, F., 68, *78*
Riffe, D., 169, *180*, 266, *275*
Riley, P., 258, *275*
Rimmer, T., 151, *162*
Roberts, M., 207, *220*
Robinson, M. J., 150, *163*
Rogers, E., ix, *xiii*, 237, *254*, 259, *275*, 307, 317,
    319, *320*, *322*
Rojas, H., 170, *182*, 188, *202*
Rosenfeld, L. B., 223, 229, *235*
Ross, R., 137, *145*
Rossant, J., 286, 287, *302*
Rosson, M., 280, *302*
Rubin, A., 240, *254*, 305, 308, 319, *321*
Rubin, A. M., 223, *235*
Rubin, R., 152, 153, *163*
Rucinski, D., 170, *182*, 188, *203*

S

Said, E., 285, *302*
Salmon, C. T., 170, *182*, 188, *203*
Salwen, M. B., 170, *181*, *182*, 187, 188, 189,
    194n10, *201*, *202*, *203*
Samoriski, J., 6, *46*
Sanchez, D., 169, *182*
Sancton, T., 67, *78*
Schaeffer, D. R., 150, *163*
Schramm, W., 42–44, *46*
Schultz, T., 208, *220*
Schwartz, J., 106n93
Schweiger, W., 148, 149, *163*
Scott, J., 65, *79*
Sefton, D., 187, *203*
Seigenthaler, J., 188, *203*
Shah, H. D., 170, *182*, 188, *202*
Shannon, E., 67, *78*
Shapiro, E., 239, *254*

Shapiro, M. A., 189, *203*
Shatzer, M., 285, *301*
Shaw, D., 258, 264t, *275*
Shaw, D. J., 16, 18, 20, *46*
Sheatsley, P. B., 169, *182*
Sherry, J. L., 179, *182*
Siebert, F. S., 42–44, *46*
Signorielli, N., 167, *181*
Sikand, S. J., 306, *320*
Sinderbrand, R., 92n38
Singer, J. B., 16n4, *46*, 207, 208, *220*, 259, *275*
Slavin, P., 185, *202*
Slovic, P., 168, *182*
Slusher, J. A., 207, *219*
Smith, S., 14–15, 33, *46*
Smith, T., 15, *46*
Snider, M., 239, *255*
Sobowale, I. A., 167, *180*
Sorensen, E., 53, *79*
Sorkin, M. D., 69, *79*
South, J., 258, *275*
Sparkes, N., 317, *322*
Sparks, G. G., 171, 179, *182*
Spirek, M., 179, *182*
Stein, N., 54, 55, 59, *79*
Stempel, G. H., III, 210, *220*, 222, 224, *235*,
    240, *255*, 286, 287, *302*, 306, *322*
Stepp, C. S., 262, *275*
Stewart, R. K., 210, *220*, 286, 287, *302*
Stipp, H., 240, *253*
Stone, M. L., 149, *162*, 258, 261, *275*
Stouffer, S., 167, *182*
Strupp, J., 260, *275*
Sullivan, C., 14, *46*
Sullivan, J. L., 167, *182*
Sundar, S., 149, 150, *163*, 207, *220*
Surman, M., 206, 207, *220*
Sylvie, G., 18, *45*, 207, *219*, 263–264, 265, *273*
Sypher, H., 152, 153, *163*

T

Tamborini, R., 168, *182*
Tanner, E., 281–282, 289, *302*
Tatham, R., 313, *321*
Taylor, S. E., *203*
Terry, D. J., 187, 188–189, *201*
Tewksbury, D., 70n19, *79*, 170, *182*, 188n3,
    202, 207, *219*, 222, 231, *236*
Thalhimer, M., 47, *79*, 221, *236*

Tham, N. I., 258, *274*
Thorp, R. K., 266, *273*
Thorson, E., 189, *201*
Tonnemacher, J., 262, *274*
Traugott, M., 150, *162*
Tremayne, M., 261, *275*
Tyler, T. R., 168, *182*

V

van Dijk, J., 186, 187, *201*, *203*
van Nimwegen, C., 260, *275*
van Oostendorp, H., 260, *275*
Varisco, D. M., 178, *182*
Vincent, R. C., 169, *183*

W

Wakshlag, J., 168, *183*
Waldfogel, J., 129, 130, *145*, 240, *255*
Walsh, C., 304, *320*
Walther, J., 305, *322*
Wanta, W., 151, *163*, 207, *220*
Washington, K., 318, *320*
Weaver, A., 70n19, *79*
Weaver, D., 151, *162*, 241, *254*
Weaver, D. H., 223, 229, *236*
Wei, R., 189, *202*, 259, *274*
Weinstein, N. D., 189, *203*
Weise, E., 3, 4, *46*
Weiss, W., 151, *162*

Welch, M., 261, *275*
Wellman, B., 206, 207, *220*
Wenner, L. A., 223, 229, *235*
Wershler-Henry, D., 206, 207, *220*
White, H. A., 189, 190, *200*, *203*
Wilkins, K. G., ix, *xiii*
Williams, J. A., 167, *181*
Willnat, L., 241, *254*
Wills, T. A., 189, *203*
Wilson, K., 66, *79*
Wimmer, K. A., 104n81
Windahl, S., 223, 229, *235*
Wittekind, D., 281, *302*
Wolf, A., 271–272, *275*
Wotring, C. E., 280, *301*, 305, *321*

X, Y

Xiaoming, H., 258, *274*
Yang, S., 188, *202*
Yaukey, J., 137, *145*
Yelsma, P., 239, *254*

Z

Zagorin, A., 67, *78*
Zeitz, H., 189, *202*
Zeng, Q., 207–208, *220*
Zillmann, D., 168, 169, *180*, *182*, *183*
Zittrain, J., 106
Zogby, J., 280, *302*

Subject Index

A

ABC News, 262
A Beautiful Mind, 63
ACLU v. Ashcroft (2003), 88n25
ACLU v. Reno (1999), 86n18
ACLU v. Reno (2000), 86n19
Advertising, see also Electronic commerce
    economic model, 12, 14–15, 48, 60, 62, 73
    online news usage, 135–137
Afghanistan, 31, 33, 52, 165
    Al Qaeda, 69, 185–186
    Taliban, 51, 69, 185–186, 191–192
African Americans, 170
Agence France Presse, 39, 41, 63
Al-Ahram Weekly Online (Egypt), 43–44
Albuquerque Journal, 14
Al-Jazeera, 69, 187
Alpert, Bill, 103n79
Alta Vista, 51
Amazon.com, 54, 111
American Airlines, 68, 165–166, 191
American Journalism Review, 135
American Library Association v. U.S. (2002),
    89n28
American Network, Inc. v. Access America/Con-
    nect Atlanta, Inc. (1997), 96n58
America Online (AOL)
    chat rooms, 263, 281

electronic newspapers, 3, 5
    "fluff news," 53
    liability immunity, 109–110, 112–113,
        115–116
    news coverage, 53, 64, 71, 97
    online newspapers, 5–6, 14, 22
    online usage, 131, 132, 304
    origins, 5
    Time Warner merger, 39
Ananova (Great Britain), 74
Andreessen, Marc, 5
Anthrax, 29, 51, 165, 185
APB.com (All Points Bulletin), 48, 49, 58
Apple Computer, Inc., 54
Arabia Online, 286–287
Arab-Israeli online newspapers, 42–44
Arab message boards, see Terrorism-response
    message boards
Arab News (Saudi Arabia), 44
Arafat, Yasser, 43
Arizona Daily Star, The, 214n2
Arnett, Peter, 186
Ashcroft v. ACLU (2002), 87n20
Ashcroft v. Free Speech Coalition (2002), 90n34
Asian Americans, 166
Ask Jeeves, 51
Associated Press (AP), 39, 41, 50, 51, 67–68,
        132, 136, 161, 261
Atlanta Journal-Constitution, 19

AT&T, 4–5
Audit Bureau of Circulation (ABC), 210
Australia, 103–104

B

BabyCenter.com, 48
Banamex v. Rodriguez (2002), 104n82
Barker, Gerry, 24
Barnes & Noble, 54, 263
Barron's, 39
Barron's Online, 103
Baseball Weekly, 37
Batzel, Ellen L., 113–114
Batzel v. Smith (2003), 113–114
Bauer, Eric, 20, 22
Bauer, Gary, 61–62
Ben Ezra, Weinstein, and Co., Inc. v. America
    Online, Inc. (2000), 111n109
Bensusan Rest. Corp. v. King (1997), 96n59
Berkman Center for Internet and Society (Har-
    vard Law School), 106
Berners-Lee, Tim, 5
Bierce, Ambrose, 55
Bill of Rights, 82
bin Láden, Osama, 187
Blanket marketing strategy, 249–250
Blogs, 69n18, 318
    warblogs, 69–70
Blumenthal, Sidney, 64, 97, 110, 115
Blumenthal v. Drudge, 97, 110, 115
Borders, 54
Bosnia, 296, 300
Boston Globe
    community board site model, 16
    online emergence, 20
    online news coverage, 20, 22
    online staff, 20
    online usage, 20
    regional market model, 19, 265, 266
    Web site, 20, 21f, 262, 268t
Boston Marathon, 22
Boston Red Sox, 20
Broadcast regulatory model, 82–83
Broder, Jonathon, 56
Buchwalter, Charles, 137
Buffalo News, The, 258
Bulletin boards, 262–263, 280–281, see also
    Message boards; Terrorism-response
    message boards

Burger King Corp. v. Rudzewicz (1985), 93n45
Bush, George W., 57–58

C

Cable Act (1992), 84
Cable television
    economic model, 83–84
    judicial system, 83–85
    legislation, 84
    media substitution, 239, 241, 242, 243,
        244–252
    public, educational, and governmental
        (PEG) programming, 84
    regulatory model, 83–85
    signal bleed, 84–85
Caen, Herb, 55
Calder v. Jones (1984), 94–95, 98, 99, 100
Carafano v. Metrosplash.com, Inc. (2003),
    111–112
CBS, 73, 102, 250
Central Intelligence Agency (CIA), 3, 55, 185
Challenger, 168
Charlotte Observer, The, 213
Chat rooms
    Internet service providers (ISPs), 263, 281
    online newspapers, 263, 276
Chat room usage
    attitudinal variables, 308–309
        hypothesis eight, 309, 315–316, 317
        hypothesis five, 309, 314
        hypothesis seven, 309, 314
        hypothesis six, 309, 316–317
        research question three, 309, 314–315, 316
        research question two, 309
    communication needs
        quasisocial interaction, 308
        research review, 304–306
        social interaction, 308–309, 310, 312–313
    innovative attributes, 307–308, 309
        hypothesis four, 307, 316
        hypothesis three, 307, 314, 316
    media substitution-complementarity,
        306–307
        hypothesis one, 306, 314
        hypothesis two, 306, 315–316
        research question one, 307, 315, 316
    media usage, 311, 314t
    online access, 311–312
    research agenda, 320

research analysis, 317–320
research conclusions, 319–320
research introduction, 303–304
research measures
  newsgroup usage, 313, 317–318
  study one, 310–313
  study two, 313
research methodology, 309–313
research overview, xii, 303
research results, 314–317
research sample, 309–310
uses-gratification theory, 306, 319–320
Chechnya, 296, 300
Chicago Tribune
  electronic commerce, 263
  online emergence, 3, 5, 22
  online news coverage, 22, 24, 65
  online staff, 24
  online usage, 22
  regional market model, 19
  Web site, 22, 23*f*, 24
Child Online Protection Act (COPA) (1998),
  86–88, 91, 213
Children's Internet Protection Act (CIPA)
  (2000), 89–91
Chile, 281–282
China, 106
Chomsky, Noam, 215
Christian Broadcasting Network (CBN), 284
Christian Science Monitor, 65
Clark, Jim, 5
Clinton, Bill
  administration coverage, 55
  Jones, Paula lawsuit, 53
  Lewinsky, Monica scandal, 33, 41, 49, 55–57,
    62–63, 64–66, 71
  Starr, Kenneth investigation, 56, 64–65
Clinton, Roger, 28
CLTV (Chicago), 24
CNET.com, 48
CNN (Cable News Network)
  CNN Interactive, 52–53, 66, 76–77, 261
  connectivity-content models, 17
  Headline News, 251
  media publicity, 55
  online advertising, 136
  online news coverage, 52–53, 54, 63, 64, 66,
    68, 186, 279
  online news credibility, 148, 161
  online usage, 131, 132, 250
  personal jurisdiction, 102
  Web site, 76–77, 261, 283

Columbia, 250
Columbia University School of Journalism
  (New York), 101
Communication research
  overview, x–xii
  research increase, ix
  theoretical frameworks, x
Communications Decency Act (CDA) (1996),
  65, 85, 88, 91, 107, 108–109, 113–115
*Communication Stream of Conspiracy Com-
  merce, The*, 65
Community board site model, 16
Community-building Web sites, *see* Online
  newspaper Web sites
Community market model, *see* Local-
  community market model
Complementary media
  chat room usage, 306–307, 314, 315–316
  media substitution, 238, 240, 241
CompuServe
  electronic newspapers, 3, 5
  liability immunity, 108–109
Connectivity-content models, 17–18
Conseco, Inc. v. Hickerson (1988), 100n72
Continuous news model, 15–16
Contra Costa Times, 35
Core, Richard, 26, 28
Courier & Press (Indiana), 258
Cremers, Tom, 113–114
Cross burning, 91
Crossfire (CNN), 63
Crowe, Russell, 63n11
Cruz v. Ferre (1985), 84n8
Cubby, Inc. v. CompuServe, Inc. (1991), 108
Cybersell, Inc. v. Cybersell, Inc. (1997), 95n54

D

Dallas Morning News
  online emergence, 24
  online news coverage, 3–4, 24, 26, 48, 66
  online staff, 24
  online usage, 24
  Web site, 24, 25*f*, 26
Deadlines, 261–262
Delphi, 66
de Sola Pool, Ithiel, 73
Diallo, Amadou, 49
Diana, Princess of Wales, 52, 54, 55
Digital democracy, ix

Digital Subscriber Line (DSL), 137, 138
Discussion boards, *see also* Message boards;
Terrorism-response message boards
connectivity-content models, 17–18
online newspapers, 17–18, 206, 207, 208,
209–210, 211, 212–219
Discussion forums, 17, 275, 280
Displaced media, *see* Media substitution
Doe v. GTE Corp. (2003), 115
Domestic jurisdiction, *see* Legal jurisdiction
Dow Jones & Co. v. Gutnick (2002), 103–104
Dow Jones & Company, 103–105, 136
Dow Jones & Company, Inc. v. Harrods,
104–105
Drudge, Matt, 56, 62–66, 71, 96–98, 110, 115
Drudge Report, 56, 62–66, 107, 110
Duggan, Paul, 58

E

Eagleburger, Lawrence, 284
EBay, 111
Economic model, *see also* Electronic commerce; Fee-based Web sites
advertising model, 12, 14–15, 48, 60, 62, 73
cable television, 83–84
media substitution, 252–253
online magazines, 59–62
online newspapers, 12, 14–15
online news trends, 47–48, 49, 59–62, 72–73
subscription fee model, 12, 14, 48, 60–61,
62, 73, 83–84
EContent, 14–15
Edelman, Benjamin, 106
Editorial independence
online magazines, 55, 59, 72
online newspaper Web sites, 216–217
online news trends, 49, 55, 59, 72–73
Editor & Publisher
connectivity-content models, 17
discussion boards, 208
national-international market model, 18
online usage, 250
Egypt, 43–44, 282, 286
el Dorra, Mohamad, 295
Electronic commerce, *see also* Advertising; Economic model
online newspapers, 263, 276
search engines, 50–51
El Nuevo Herald (Florida), 29

Enron, 33
Estes, Ben, 22, 24
E-the-People, 214–215, 216, 217–218
European Union, 104
Excite, 51
Exclusive news site model, 17

F

Fairness in Accuracy and Reporting (FAIR),
284
Falwell, Jerry, 284
Falwell v. Cohn (2003), 99n67
FCC v. Pacifica Foundation (1978), 83n6
Federal Bureau of Investigation (FBI), 58, 113,
165, 185
Federal Communications Commission (FCC),
303, *see also specific court case*
Fee-based Web sites, 14*t*, 135–137
micropayments, 136
Feed, 53–54, 60, 61
Fever, Douglas, 39, 41
Financial Times, The (London), 19
First Amendment
online journalism, 81–92, 104–106, 108–109
terrorism fear, 167, 179
Forman, Jay, 67
Form-coloration hypothesis, 42–44
Foster, Vincent W., Jr., 65
Fourteenth Amendment, 92–93
Four Theories of the Press (Siebert et al.), 42–44
Fox News Channel, 250, 284
France, 104
Franken, Bob, 53
Freedom Forum, 17
Freedom of Information Act, 58

G

Gainesville Sun (Florida), 263
Gannett Corporation, 35
Gatekeepers
online newspaper Web sites, 208–209, 213,
215–217
online news trends, 64
Gates, Bill, 59, 60, 61
Gator, 137
General Motors (GM), 52
Gentry v. eBay, Inc. (2002), 111n110

Germany, 149
Gitlow v. New York (1925), 82n2
González, Elián, 31, 33, 41
Google, 50, 106
Google News, 50, 107
Gopher networks, 3
Graham, Franklin, 284
Green v. America Online (2003), 111n109
Grueskin, Bill, 37, 39
Guantanamo Bay (Cuba), 31
Gutnick, Joseph, 103
Gutnick v. Dow Jones & Co. (2001), 103n77
Gwertzman, Bernard, 31, 33

H

Halpern, Deb, 76
Hamling v. U.S. (1974), 86n22
Hanson, Victor Davis, 215
Hartford Courant, The, 98–99, 102, 263
Hearst Newspaper Digital, 250
Heisman Trophy, 51
Helicopteros Nacionales de Colombia, S.A. v. Hall (1984), 93n43
Hernando Today (Florida), 75
Highlands Today (Florida), 75
Honolulu Advertiser, 258
Hope, Bob, 67–68
Hot Wizard, 60
Hussein, Saddam, 69
Hyde, Henry, 55–57, 58, 65, 72
Hyman, Valerie, 261

I

India Today, 72
InfoUSA, 122, 153, 171–172, 191, 225, 242
Ingle, Robert D., 6
International jurisdiction, see Legal jurisdiction
International market model, see National-international market model
International Shoe Co. v. Washington (1945), 93
Internet regulatory model, 85–92
Internet service providers (ISPs), see also specific provider
"fluff news," 53
legal liability immunity, 86, 107–117
message boards, 53
online news trends, 49, 50, 53, 71

original news production, 53
Iran, 296, 300
Iraq, 69, 186, see also Terrorism-response message boards
Isikoff, Michael, 64
Israel, 43, 44, 51, see also Terrorism-response message boards

J

Jackson-Clarion-Ledger, 258
Jane Doe v. America Online (1998), 112n115
Jane Doe v. America Online (2001), 112n113
Japan, 170, 296, 300
Java applets, 272–273, 276
Jerusalem Post (Israel), 43, 44
Jewish Star Times (Florida), 29
Jones, Paula, 53
Jones, Shirley, 94–95
Jones v. Wilkinson (1986), 84n8
Jordan, 282, 286
Judicial system
broadcast regulation, 82–83
cable regulation, 83–85
domestic jurisdiction, 92–96
international jurisdiction, 103–106
Internet regulation, 85–92
filtering requirements, 89–91
Internet service providers (ISPs), 108–117
personal jurisdiction, 92–102
effects test, 94–96, 98–99, 100
sliding scale test, 93–94, 95, 97, 99–101
print media regulation, 82
Jupiter Media Metrix, 137

K

Keeton v. Hustler Magazine, Inc. (1984), 95n51, 102
Keillor, Garrison, 54–55
Kennedy, John F., Jr., 54
Key West Citizen (Florida), 19
Kinsley, Michael, 59–61, 62, 71
Knight-Ridder, Inc., 4–5, 14, 29
Viewtron, 5
Kohut, Andrew, 130
KRXO (Oklahoma City), 116
KTLA-TV (Los Angeles), 26
Kuczynski, Alex, 67n16

L

Laforet, Vincent, 31, 33
Leahy, Patrick, 51
Lebanon, 282, 296, 300
Legal jurisdiction
  domestic
    Fourteenth Amendment, 92–93
    judicial system, 92–96
  international, 102–106
    First Amendment, 104–106
    judicial system, 103–106
  personal
    defined, 92
    effects test, 94–96, 98–99, 100
    First Amendment, 92
    Fourteenth Amendment, 92–93
    judicial system, 92–102
    online news, 96–102
    sliding scale test, 93–94, 95, 97, 99–101
    trademark infringement, 95–96
Legal liability immunity
  "Good Samaritan" blocking/screening,
    108–116
  Internet service providers (ISPs), 86,
    107–117
  judicial system, 108–117
  legislation, 107, 108–117
Legislation, *see also* Media regulation
  cable television, 84
  liability immunity, 107, 108–117
  media regulation, 85–87, 89–91
  online journalism, 84, 86–88, 89–91, 107,
    108–109, 113–115, 213
Legón, Jeordan, 29, 31
Lewinsky, Monica, 33, 41, 49, 55–57, 62–63,
  64–66, 71
Lewiston Tribune (Idaho), 14
Libya, 296, 300
Local-community market model
  online newspapers, 19
  online newspaper technologies, 263–264,
    265, 267, 269, 271*t*, 272–273
  usage changes, 265, 266, 267, 268*t*, 269,
    270–271*t*, 272–273
  usage comparison, 264, 267, 269,
    270–271*t*, 272
Los Angeles Times
  Gateway, 5
  online emergence, 26
  online news coverage, 26, 28
  online staff, 28
  online usage, 26
  regional market model, 19
  Times Link, 26
  Web site, 26, 27*f*, 28, 262
Lycos
  online usage, 130
  search engine, 51

M

Macon Telegraph, The (Georgia), 265, 266, 268*t*
Magazines, *see* Online magazines
Marimba, 261
Market models, *see* Local-community market
  model; National-international market
  model; Regional market model; Special-
  ized market model
Marshall News Messenger (Texas), 215
Masterson, Chase, 111
Matchmaker.com, 111
McCurry, Michael D., 65n12
McGrath, Peter, 64
McLuhan, Marshall, 70
McVeigh, Timothy J., 3–4, 26, 48, 66
Media competition
  media substitution, 252–253
  online news trends, 47–48, 49, 53, 54, 60,
    71–72, 73
  radio, 73
Media convergence, 73–77
Media ethics, 57–58, 63–66
Media General News Center, 75–77
Media regulation
  First Amendment, 81–82, 83, 84, 85, 86, 88,
    89, 91–92
  judicial system, 82, 83, 84–92
  legislation, 85–87, 89–91
  regulatory models, 81–92
    broadcast model, 82–83
    cable model, 83–85
    Internet model, 85–92
    print model, 82
Media substitution
  audiovisual entertainment, 239
  blanket marketing strategy, 249–250
  cable television, 239, 241, 242, 243, 244–252
  chat room usage, 306–307, 314, 315–316
  dimensions of
    complementary media, 238, 240, 241

displaced media, 238, 239, 240–242
  supplemental media, 238, 239–240, 241
  economic model, 252–253
  media competition, 252–253
  media substitution, 239–240, 242, 243, 244–252
  online news credibility, 241
  online news usage, 238, 242, 243, 244, 245t
  online-offline news substitution, 240–241, 242, 243, 246–252
  print media, 239, 240–241, 242, 243, 244–252
  radio, 239, 240, 242, 243, 244–252
  research agenda, 253
  research conclusions, 252–253
  research hypotheses, 241–242, 244–249
  research introduction, 237
  research measures, 243–244
  research methodology, 242–244
  research overview, xii, 237
  research question, 242
  research results, 244–249
  research review, 239–241
  research sample, 242–243
  television, 239, 240, 241, 242, 243, 244–252
  user characteristics, 243–244, 246, 247t
Meet the Press, 66
Message boards, see also Discussion boards;
  Terrorism-response message boards
  Internet service providers (ISPs), 53
  news trends, 53, 59
  search engines, 53
Miami Herald, The
  online emergence, 29
  online news coverage, 29, 31
  online staff, 29
  online usage, 29, 31
  regional market model, 19
  supplemental news site model, 16–17
  Web site, 29, 30f
Micropayments, 136
Microsoft Corporation, 48, 52, 59, 60, 61, 286
Middle East crisis (2002), 42–44
Millennium Enterprises, Inc. v. Millennium Music, LP (1999), 96n59
Milliken v. Meyer (1940), 93n42
Minneapolis Star Tribune, 263
Morocco, 282
Mosaic, 5
MSNBC
  connectivity-content models, 17
  online news coverage, 64, 71
  online usage, 131, 132, 250
Murdoch, Rupert, 66
Museum Security Network Web (Amsterdam), 113–114

N

Naples Daily News (Florida)
  local-community market model, 19, 265, 266
  Web site, 268t
Nashua Telegraph (New Hampshire), 14
National Enquirer, The, 94–95, 99
National-international market model
  online newspapers, 18, 39
  online newspaper technologies, 263–264, 265, 266, 267, 269, 270t, 272
  newspaper usage, 264, 266, 267t
  usage changes, 265, 266, 267, 268t, 269, 270–271t, 272–273
  usage comparison, 264, 267, 269, 270–271t, 272
National Press Club, 66
National Telephone Survey Questionnaires (2001–2002) (University of Miami)
  Baseline Web Project 1, 121–124, 323–330
  Displacement Survey, 356–362
  Fear, News Use and Terrorism Project, 171–172, 348–355
  Online News Credibility Study, 153, 331–339
  Traditional and Online News Use Project, 340–347
NBC, 73
NBC v. U.S. (1943), 83n4
Neill, Rob, 35
Neogen Corp. v. Neo Gen Screening, Inc. (2002), 101n73
Netscape, 5, 250
New Haven Advocate, 98–99, 100, 101
New Republic, 59, 71
News Corp, 66
Newsday, 66, 250
Newsgroups, 313, 317–318
NewsLink, 6, 13t
News links, online newspapers
  community-building, 209, 210, 212, 214–215, 216, 217
  technology, 260, 261, 262, 265–266, 276
Newspaper Association of America, 73
Newspaper Guild, 54

Newsweek
  online news coverage, 62–63, 165
  Web site, 262
New Yorker, 59
New York Times, The
  connectivity-content models, 17
  ethics, 57–58
  media publicity, 55, 58
  national-international market model, 18,
    265, 266
  New York Times On The Web, 31
  online economic model, 12
  online emergence, 3, 31
  online news coverage, 31, 33, 57–58, 59, 65,
    67, 69, 185
  online service model, 16
  online staff, 31
  online usage, 31, 131, 222, 231
  personal jurisdiction, 102
  Pulitzer Prize, 33
  Web site, 31, 32*f*, 208, 215, 216–217, 268*t*,
    283
New York Times Company, 16
Niche market model, *see* Specialized market
  model
Nicosia v. De Rooy (1999), 96n56
Northern Light Search, 51–52

O

O'Donnell, Michael, 55
Oklahoma City bombing, 3–4, 48, 53, 66,
  68n17
Online Journalism Awards (Columbia University), 48, 49, 61
Online Journalism Review, 148
Online magazines, *see also* Print media; *specific*
  magazine
  economic model, 59–62
  editorial independence, 55, 59, 72
  erroneous news stories, 67
  exclusive news stories, 54, 55–58, 70–71, 72
  news trends, 53–66, 67, 69, 70–71, 72
  news usage, 128, 129, 130
  original news production, 69, 70–71
Online news credibility
  credibility defined, 150
  credibility measures, 150–152, 153–154
  media substitution, 241

National Telephone Survey Questionnaires
    (2001–2002) (University of Miami),
    153, 331–339
  news consumption, 154, 155*t*
  news preferences, 154, 156
  print media comparison, 148–149, 150,
    151–152, 156–158, 159–161
  radio comparison, 148–149
  research agenda, 161
  research analysis, 158–161
  research introduction, 147–148
  research methodology, 152–154
  research overview, xi, 148
  research questions, 152
  research results, 154–158, 159*t*, 160*t*
  research review, 148–149
  research sample, 152–153, 154, 155*t*
  television comparison, 148–149, 150, 151,
    152, 156–158, 159–161
Online newspapers, *see also* Print media; *spe-*
    cific newspaper
  Arab-Israeli, 42–44
  connectivity-content models
    discussion boards, 17–18
    index-category sites, 17
    mainstream sites, 17
    meta-comment sites, 17
  economic model, 12, 14–15
  fee-based sites, 14*t*
  form-coloration hypothesis, 42–44
  industry brands, 6, 12*t*
  industry leaders, 6, 11*t*, 20–41
  market models
    local-community model, 19
    national-international model, 18, 39
    regional model, 19
    specialized model, 19
  NewsLink rankings, 6, 13*t*
  news sites, 11*t*
  origins, 4–6, 12
  parent companies, 6, 11*t*
  research conclusions, 41–42
  research introduction, 3–4
  research overview, x, 4
  service models
    community board site model, 16
    continuous news model, 15–16
    exclusive news site model, 17
    supplemental news site model, 16–17
  usage rates, 6, 7*t*, 8*f*, 9*t*, 10*f*, 11*t*, 12, 128,
    129

Online newspaper technologies, *see also specific newspaper*
market models
local-community model, 263–264, 265, 267, 269, 271t, 272–273
national-international model, 263–264, 265, 266, 267, 269, 270t, 272
regional model, 263–264, 265, 266, 267, 268t, 269, 271t, 272
specialized model, 263–264
market-models
online usage, 264, 266, 267t
online-usage changes, 265, 266, 267, 268t, 269, 270–271t, 272–273
online-usage variance, 264, 267, 269, 270–271t, 272
online technology
bulletin boards, 262–263
chat rooms, 263, 276
consumer services, 272, 276
deadlines, 261–262
electronic commerce, 263, 276
forums, 275
Java applets, 272–273, 276
news content, 261–262
news distribution, 261–262, 276
news links, 260, 261, 262, 265–266, 276
news resources, 262–263
plug-in based, 272, 276
staff skills, 262
syndication, 263
user demographics, 260, 271–272
user interactivity, 260–261
Web site design, 260–261, 262
research agenda, 273
research conclusions, 269, 271–273
research introduction, 257–259
research measures, 265–273, 275–276
research methodology, 265–266
research overview, xii, 259
research questions, 264, 265, 266, 267, 268t, 269, 270–271t, 272–273
research results, 266–269, 270–271t
research sample, 265
Online newspaper Web sites, *see also specific newspaper*
circulation size impact, 207–208, 210–211, 212, 213–214
community-building features
archival searches, 217
behavioral rules, 208–209, 210, 213, 216, 217

discussion boards, 206, 207, 208, 209–210, 211, 212–219
gatekeepers, 208–209, 213, 215–217
interactivity promotion, 206, 207–209, 214–216, 217–219
news connections, 209, 217–219
news links, 209, 210, 212, 214–215, 216, 217
no-cost accessibility, 212, 214
privacy policy, 210
site frequency, 212t
site registration, 209–210, 212–213, 217
user anonymity, 212, 213, 217
editorial control, 216–217
intercommunication, 206
online communities, 205–206, 208, 209, 218
online usage, 205–206
research agenda, 218–219
research analysis, 215–219
research introduction, 205–206
research limitations, 218–219
research methodology, 209–212
research overview, xi, 206
research questions, 209
research results, 212–215
research review, 206–209
research sample, 210, 211t
social capital, 207
Online news trends
breaking news stories, 68–70, 71–72
economic model, 47–48, 49, 59–62, 72–73
advertising model, 12, 14–15, 48, 60, 62, 73
subscription fee model, 12, 14, 48, 60–61, 62, 73
editorial independence, 49, 55, 59, 72–73
erroneous news stories, 66–68
ethics, 57–58, 63–66
exclusive news stories, 47, 48, 54, 55–58, 62–66, 70–71, 72–73
gatekeepers, 64
Internet service providers (ISPs), 49, 50, 53, 71
journalism awards, 48
magazines, 53–66, 67, 69, 70–71, 72
media competition, 47–48, 49, 53, 54, 60, 71–72, 73
media convergence, 73–77
message boards, 53, 59
original news production, 47–49, 50, 52, 53, 54, 69, 70–71, 73
radio, 73

Online news trends *(cont.)*
   research conclusions, 70–73
   research introduction, 47–50
   research overview, x, 49–50
   search engines, 50–53, 71
   shovelware, 49
   social impact, 47, 48, 49–50, 62–66, 68–73
   supplemental news, 47, 52–53, 72–73
Online news usage, *see also specific media*
   advertising response, 135–137
   fee-based sites, 135–137
   interactivity behavior, 133–135
   magazine comparison, 128, 129, 130
   media use, 127–130
   National Telephone Survey Questionnaire
      (2001–2002) (University of Miami),
      121–124, 323–330
   news discussion, 127, 128, 129
   news preferences, 141–144
   news sites, 130–132
   print media comparison, 128, 129
   radio comparison, 128–130
   research methodology, 121–124
   research overview, x, 121
   research results, 127–144
   research sample, 124–127
   television comparison, 127, 128, 129, 130
   usage rationale, 139–141, 142*t*
   user access, 137–139
   user categorization
      news user, 122–124
      nonuser, 122–124
      Web user, 122–124
   user computer skills, 137, 138
   user privacy, 144
Oregonian, The, 211
Orlando Sentinel, The, 265, 266, 268*t*

P

Paglia, Camille, 54–55
Pakistan, 296, 300
Palestinian Authority, 43–44
Palo Alto Weekly (California), 3
Pan American, 101
Panavision.com, 95–96
Panavision Intern, L.P. v. Toeppen, 95–96, 99
Patentwizard, Inc. v. Kinko's, Inc. (2001),
   111n110
Pavlovich v. Superior Court (2002), 96n57

Persian Gulf War, 54, 186
Personal jurisdiction, *see* Legal jurisdiction
Pew Research Center (Washington, DC),
   130–131
Pinochet, Augusto, 281–282
PointCast, 261
Powell, Colin, 43
Poynter Institute, 17, 208, 261
Presidential campaign
   1996, 130–131, 188
   2000, 28, 29, 33, 57–58, 61–62, 130–131
Print media
   media substitution, 239, 240–241, 242, 243,
      244–252
   news credibility, 148–149, 150, 151–152,
      156–158, 159–161
   news usage, 128, 129, 130
   regulatory model, 82
   terrorism-fear impact, 176, 177, 178, 180
   uses-gratification theory
      online-offline news gratification, 223–224,
         226, 227*t*
      online-offline news usage, 222, 225
Prodigy
   electronic newspapers, 3, 26
   liability immunity, 108–109
Pulitzer Prize, 33, 41
Purie, Aroon, 72

R

Rabin, Yitzhak, 281
Radio
   media substitution, 239, 240, 242, 243,
      244–252
   news credibility, 148–149
   news usage, 128–130
   online news trends
      economic model, 73
      media competition, 73
      original news production, 73
      regulatory model, 82–83
Red Lion Broadcasting Co. v. FCC (1969), 82n1,
   83n5
Regional market model
   online newspapers, 19
   online newspaper technologies, 263–264,
      265, 266, 267, 268*t*, 269, 271*t*, 272
   usage changes, 265, 266, 267, 268*t*, 269,
      270–271*t*, 272–273

usage comparison, 264, 267, 269, 270–271t, 272
Regulation, see Media regulation
Reno v. ACLU (1997), 85–86, 104
Reno v. Sullivan (1991), 90
Restatement (Second) of Tort (1997), 110n106, 112–113
Reuters (Great Britain), 39, 41, 50, 51, 66, 261
Revell v. Libov (2002), 101
Robertson, Pat, 284
Ross, Andrew, 55
Royko, Mike, 55
Rumorville USA, 108

S

Sable Communications of California, Inc. v. FCC (1989), 87n21
Salinger, Pierre, 67
Salon, 48, 54–62
    economic model, 61–62
    editorial independence, 55, 72
    exclusive news stories, 54, 55–58, 70–71, 72
    online emergence, 54, 61
    original news production, 69, 70–71
San Diego Union-Tribune, 211, 214
San Francisco Examiner, 54
San Francisco Free Press, 54
San Jose Mercury News
    online economic model, 14
    online emergence, 5–6, 33
    online news coverage, 3, 33, 35
    online staff, 35
    regional market model, 19
    San Jose Mercury Center, 5–6, 14, 19, 33, 261
    Web site, 34f, 35, 261
Sarasota Herald-Tribune (Florida), 19
Saudi Arabia, 44, 106, 282–283
Savage, Dan, 61–62
Schnapp v. McBride (1998), 99n67
Schneider v. Amazon.com (2001), 111n110
Scripps Howard News Service, 68
Search engines, see also specific search engine
    algorithmic-based news, 50
    electronic commerce, 50–51
    home-page design, 50–53
    message boards, 53
    news coverage, 50–53
    online news trends, 50–53, 71

original news production, 50, 52
    self-promotion, 47, 50–51
    supplemental news, 52–53
Sedition Act, 166
Select Phone, 122, 153, 171–172, 191, 225, 242
September 11, 2001, see Terrorism coverage; Terrorism fear; Terrorism-response message boards
Service models, 15–17, 272, 276
Sharon, Ariel, 43–44, 298
Sheppard, Sam, 58
Shovelware, 49
Simpson, O. J., 52, 54, 58, 66, 68
60 Minutes, 284
Skuttlebut, 108
Slate, 54, 57
    economic model, 59–61
    editorial independence, 59, 72
    erroneous news stories, 67
    media competition, 60
    online emergence, 59
    original news production, 70
    social impact, 71
Smith, Bob, 113–114
Snodgrass, Cherie, 56
Snodgrass, Fred, 56
Social capital, 207
Somalia, 296, 300
Sommer, Norm, 56
Southeastern Promotions, Ltd. v. Conrad (1975), 84n9
Specialized market model
    online newspapers, 19
    online newspaper technologies, 263–264
Starr, Kenneth, 56, 64–65
Star Tribune (Minnesota)
    electronic commerce, 263
    online service model, 15
Starwave, 261
Staten Island Advance, 213
Strategic Lawsuit Against Public Participation (SLAPP), 114
Stratton Oakmont, Inc. v. Prodigy Services Co. (1995), 108
Street (Miami), 29
    supplemental news site model, 16–17
Subscription fee model, 12, 14, 48, 60–61, 62, 73, 83–84
Suck, 53–54, 57, 61
Sudan, 282, 296, 300
Suicide, 91–92, 281
Sulzberger, Arthur, Jr., 12

Sunday Mirror, 66
Supplemental media, 238, 239–240, 241
Supplemental news
   online news trends, 47, 52–53, 72–73
   search engines, 52–53
   service model, 16–17
Syria, 282

T

Talbot, David, 54, 56, 59, 61, 62, 65
Tampa Bay Online (TBO), 75, 263
Tampa Tribune, 75–76
Technologies of Freedom (de Sola Pool), 73
Technology, *see* Online newspaper technologies; Online newspaper Web sites; *spe-*
   cific technology
Tehelka (India), 72
Telco Communications v. An Apple A Day
   (1997), 98n63
Telecommunications Act (1996), 84
Television, *see also* Cable television
   media substitution, 239, 240, 241, 242, 243,
     244–252
   news credibility, 148–149, 150, 151, 152,
     156–158, 159–161
   news usage, 127, 128, 129, 130
   terrorism-fear impact, 167–168, 176, 177,
     178, 180
   uses-gratification theory
     online-offline news gratification, 223, 224
     online-offline news usage, 222
Terrorism coverage
   anthrax, 29, 51
   September 11, 2001, 28, 33, 41, 49–50,
     68–70, 71–72
Terrorism fear
   anthrax, 165
   civil-liberty restrictions, 166–167
     hypothesis one, 167, 176, 179
     hypothesis six, 171, 177, 179
     research measure, 172–173
   danger-avoiding measures, 168–170
     hypothesis three, 169–170, 176
     research measure, 174
   First Amendment, 167, 179
   National Telephone Survey Questionnaires
     (2001–2002) (University of Miami),
     171–172, 348–355
   news media exposure, 167–170

   hypothesis two, 169, 176, 180
   online news, 176, 177, 178–179, 180
   print media, 176, 177, 178, 180
   research measure, 174
   television, 167–168, 176, 177, 178, 180
   news media restrictions
     hypothesis six, 171, 177, 179
     research measure, 173
     research analysis, 179–180
     research introduction, 165–166
     research measures, 172–175
     research methodology, 171–175
     research overview, xi, 165
     research results, 175–179
     research sample, 171–172, 175–176
   September 11, 2001, 165, 178, 185–186, 187,
     188, 189, 198
   third-person effects
     anthrax, 185
     behavioral outcomes, 170, 171, 175,
       178–179, 191, 196–200
     civil-liberty restrictions, 171, 177
     gender-differences, 169, 171, 177, 179,
       180, 196–197, 198, 199–200
     new media environment, 186–187
     news media restrictions, 171, 177, 191,
       192–193, 194, 196t, 197–198, 199–200
     online news usage, 193–194
     perceptual bias, 170–171, 174–175, 177,
       180, 190, 194, 198–200
     research agenda, 200
     research analysis, 180, 198–200
     research hypotheses, 171, 176–177, 179,
       190, 191, 194–196
     research introduction, 185
     research measures, 174–175, 192–193
     research methodology, 191–193
     research overview, xi, 185–186
     research results, 176–179, 193–198
     research review, 187–189
     research sample, 191, 193
     social distance corollary, 189–191,
       194–196
Terrorism-response message boards
   Arabia bulletin board, 283, 285, 286–289
   Arab online-usage, 282–283
   Islamic portrayal, 284–285, 298–299, 300
   Masrawy bulletin board, 283, 285, 286–289
   message-board research, 280–282
   research analysis, 299–300
   research introduction, 279–280
   research limitations, 285–286, 287–288

research measures, 288–289
research methodology, 286–289
research overview, xii, 280
research questions, 283–284, 285, 290–300
research results, 289–299
research sample, 287
September 11, 2001, 279–280, 283–285, 287, 288, 289–300
terrorism response, 283, 290–291, 299
terrorism-response reasoning
  Arab interests, 298
  innocent civilians, 292, 300
  Iraqian policy, 279, 295–296, 300
  Middle East politics, 279, 294–298, 300
  Palestinian-Israeli conflict, 279, 294–295, 300
  U.S. conflicts, 296–298, 300
  U.S. government versus citizen, 279–280, 293–294, 300
Thelen, Gil, 76
Third-person effects, *see* Terrorism fear
Time Online
  news credibility, 148
  online usage, 250
Times Union (New York), 49
Time Warner
  AOL merger, 39
  Pathfinder, 66
Tunisia, 282
Turner, Ted, 54
Turner Broadcasting System v. FCC (1994), 84n7
TWA, 66–67

online usage, 35, 37
personal jurisdiction, 102
Web site, 35, 36f, 37, 216–217, 268t
USA Weekend, 35
Uses-gratification theory
  chat rooms, 306, 319–320
  offline-news gratification/online-news usage (hypothesis two), 224, 228, 230t, 232–233
  online-news gratification/offline-news usage (hypothesis three), 224, 229, 230t, 232–233
  online-offline news gratification
    hypothesis one, 224, 228, 229t, 231–232
    online news, 223–224, 226, 228t
    print media, 223–224, 226, 227t
    research measures, 226, 227t, 228t
    television, 223, 224
  online-offline news usage
    online news, 221–222, 225
    print media, 222, 225
    research measures, 225
    television, 222
  research analysis, 229–233
  research conclusions, 234
  research introduction, 221
  research limitations, 233
  research methodology, 224–226
  research overview, xi–xii, 221
  research questions, 224, 226–227, 228t
  research results, 226–229
  research review, 221–224
  research sample, 224–225, 226, 231

U

United Arab Emirates (UAE), 286
United Kingdom Press Association, 74
United States Civil War, 166
United States v. American Library Association (2003), 89–91
United States v. Playboy Entertainment Group, 84
University of Illinois, 5
U.S.A. Patriot Act, 166
USA Today
  electronic commerce, 263
  national-international market model, 18, 265, 266
  online news coverage, 37, 59, 66

V

Vietnam, 296, 300
Vietnam War, 54
Virginia V. Black (2003), 91n37

W

Wallen Ridge State Prison (Virginia), 98–99
Wall Street Journal
  international jurisdiction, 103, 105
  Journal Interactive Edition, 19
  online economic model, 14, 48, 136
  online emergence, 37
  online news coverage, 37, 39, 67

Wall Street Journal (cont.)
   online staff, 37, 39
   online usage, 39, 136
   personal jurisdiction, 102
   specialized market model, 19, 48
   Web site, 37, 38*f*, 261
Wal-Mart, 52
Walsh, Joan, 58
Washington Post
   ethics, 57–58
   national-international market model, 18, 39
   online news coverage, 39, 41, 56, 57–58, 185
   online service model, 15
   online staff, 39, 41
   online usage, 39, 250
   Pulitzer Prize, 41
   Web site, 39, 40*f*, 41, 206, 216–217, 262
Watchtower Bible & Tract Soc. of N.Y., Inc. v.
   Village of Stratton (2000), 90n35
Web sites, *see* Fee-based sites; Online newspaper technologies; Online newspaper Web sites; *specific media*
Web Storybase, 280–281
WFLA-TV (Florida), 75, 76
WGN-TV (Chicago), 24
Woelfel, Scott, 261
Word, 61
World Association of Newspapers (WAN), 6
World War I, 166
World War II, 166, 170
World-Wide Volkswagen Corp. v. Woodson (1980), 93n41
Wright, Susan Webber, 53

Y

Yahoo!
   connectivity-content models, 17
   international jurisdiction, 104
   online advertising, 136
   online usage, 130, 132
   search engine, 51, 71
Yahoo v. League Against Racism and Anti-
   Semitism and the Union of Jewish Stu-
   dents (2001), 104n83
Yardley, Jim, 58
Yemen, 282
Young, Stanley, 98–99
Young v. New Haven Advocate (2002), 98–99, 100, 101, 102

Z

Zeran, Kenneth, 109, 110n104, 112–113, 115–116
Zeran v. America Online, Inc. (1997), 110n104, 112–113, 115–116
Zeran v. Diamond Broadcasting, Inc. (1997), 116n136
Zippo Manufacturing Co. v. Zippo Dot Com, Inc., 93–94, 97
Zittrain, Jonathan, 106

Milton Keynes UK
Ingram Content Group UK Ltd.
UKHW031136141024
449569UK00006B/150

9 780805 848229